The Politics of Illusion

A Political History of the IRA

Henry Patterson

Serif
London

This edition first published 1997 by
Serif
47 Strahan Road
London E3 5DA

and

1436 Randolph Street
Chicago IL 60607

First published, in a slightly different form, as *The Politics of Illusion:
Republicanism and Socialism in Modern Ireland*
by Hutchinson Radius in 1989

British Library Cataloguing-in-Publication Data.
A catalogue record for this book is available from the British Library.

ISBN 1 897959 31 1

Designed by Ralph Barnby.
Photoset in North Wales by
Derek Doyle & Associates, Mold, Flintshire.
Printed and bound in Great Britain by
Biddles of Guildford and King's Lynn.

Contents

For Sam and Alex

Preface

This is not a narrative history of the wider republican movement or of the IRA. Many individuals and incidents in that tradition do not figure here and those in search of them should
look to the standard histories of Bowyer-Bell, Coogan, and
Bishop and Mallie. *The Politics of Illusion* is concerned with the
social and political dynamics of the republican movement, and
this means that I pay much more attention to the relations
between republicanism and the transformations of Irish society
since partition in 1921 than is often the case in studies of the
republican tradition.

The book could not have been written without the assistance
of those who agreed to be interviewed – Gerry Adams, Jack
Brady, Anthony Coughlan, Francie Donnelly, Jimmy Drumm,
Sean Garland, Cathal Goulding, Eoghan Harris, Seamus
Harrison, Roy Johnston, Seamus Lynch, Tomás MacGiolla,
Paddy Joe McClean, Dessie O'Hagan, Eamonn Smullen, Kevin
Smyth and Jim Sullivan. I also received assistance from Mary
McMahon. Eric Byrne and Ellen Hazelkorn gave me valuable
criticism of what I had written on Official Republicanism in
Dublin in the mid-1970s. Richard Dunphy gave me access to his
major work on the history of Fianna Fáil up to 1948. Anthony
McIntyre gave a critical perspective on the 'peace process'.
Rogelio Alonso allowed me to see the transcript of his interview
with Bernadette McAliskey. The book as a whole benefited
from many conversations with Paul Bew, particularly on the
nature of Sinn Féin's 'modernisation' since the mid-1970s.
Carmel Roulston's work on the recent history of the
Communist Party of Ireland was of great value, as were her
detailed criticisms of the first draft of the book, which much
improved it. Neil Belton was a source of support to the devel-

opment of my work on Ireland and provided an intelligent and detailed editorial control to the first edition. Stephen Hayward and Serif were invaluable in their support and enthusiasm for a new edition. Sam Patterson provided much needed assistance with the index.

None of the people I have mentioned has any responsibility for the positions and interpretations of the author.

I would like to acknowledge the assistance of the staffs of the National Library of Ireland; the State Paper Office, Dublin Castle; the Linenhall Library, Belfast; the Library, University of Ulster at Jordanstown and the British Library at Colindale. My research benefited from grants and study leave given by the Research Sub-Committee of the Faculty of Humanities of the University of Ulster and from the assistance of Jennifer Irwin and Joan Philipson.

Henry Patterson
Belfast 1997

Introduction

The capacity of the current IRA to wage the longest sustained military campaign in the history of Anglo-Irish relations has been poorly reflected on by those who have written the main accounts of the republican movement. In part this is due to the movement's own pronounced tendency to project a mono-chrome remembrance of itself – as a principled and self-sacrificing minority which has challenged British rule down through the centuries despite and because of the apathy and 'materialism' of the majority of the Irish people. Histories of republicanism which focus primarily on its violent activities to the exclusion of political and social context have done little to challenge such definitions.

More recently the level of reflection on republicanism has suffered from the rise of the academic 'terrorism industry', whose typologies have succeeded only in draining terrorism of any national or historical specificity. As Edward Said has observed:

> The most striking thing about 'terrorism', as a phenomenon of the public sphere of communication and representation in the West, is its isolation from any explanation or mitigating circumstances, and its isolation as well from representations of most other dysfunctions, symptoms and maladies of the contemporary world.[1]

The tendency to decontextualise current Irish terrorism is reinforced by the incongruity of a 'national liberation' struggle which, as its main non-violent nationalist critic pointed out, had, in the first twenty years of 'the Troubles', killed twice as many Irish Catholics as the security forces of the 'occupying power'.[2] Nevertheless, to focus simply on the activities of Irish terrorists, whether their more newsworthy irruptions in Britain or Europe or the banally brutal killings of Irish Protestants in and out of uniform, is to limit ourselves to a moral outrage which is by now paper-thin and, ever more palpably, a diversion from serious thought about contemporary Ireland.

A key characteristic of the unproductive labelling of contemporary republicanism by its critics is that the terms used tend to abstract the movement from those political and ideological tendencies in the mainstream of Irish life which have in 1988, sustained the morale and ambitions of the republican leadership. British government ministers have referred to Sinn Féin as a 'Marxist' organisation, while in a speech to the annual conference of his party in 1988, John Hume referred to them as 'Fascists'.[3] At the same time it was easy for Sinn Féin leaders like Gerry Adams and Danny Morrison to point out that at various times in the previous twenty years they had had talks and negotiations with leading British politicians and members of British governments. The British government would re-open a 'back channel' to the IRA in 1990 and maintain it against a background of rising IRA violence in mainland Britain, until 1993. John Hume would be in public and private discussions with Gerry Adams from 1988 until the time of writing this new edition. Clearly, the very ambiguities in the relations between the state and constitutional nationalism and republicanism revealed the existence of a tendency which, despite the stridency of anti-terrorist rhetoric, treated republicanism as a force not totally beyond recognition.

While we need a more serious understanding of what sustains republican violence, it is an evasion to conclude, with a recent history of the IRA, that, 'The history of republicanism since Wolfe Tone has shown that as long as there is a British presence in Ireland it is an ineradicable tradition.'[4] The real question is not whether a 'republican tradition' exists; rather, it concerns the various transformations the tradition has undergone and the very variable degree of popular support that has existed for it. The present leadership of Sinn Féin admits that, as a result of a divisive and demoralising ceasefire negotiated between the then leadership of the IRA and the Northern Ireland Office in 1975, 'a most critical stage' was reached, and that, 'If changes had not taken place in a short time then the IRA would have been defeated.'[5] These changes, which will be dealt with later, produced a very different relationship between force and politics from that established with the formation of the Provisional IRA in 1969-70. There is a parallel between the post-1975 changes and those following the defeat of the IRA's military campaign against the Northern Ireland state between 1956 and 1962. After 1962 there was a 'rethinking' which contributed to the split in the IRA and Sinn Féin in 1969. The participants in these developments tend to see them from an essentially internal perspective. A central argument of this book, in contrast, is that the ability of physical force republicanism to resuscitate itself after its regular defeats, although partly to be explained by certain moral-existential characteristics of the 'republican personality', derives from the complex relation between the legacy of the 'incomplete' Irish national revolution of 1918-21 and a range of social, economic and communal grievances which republicanism can, more or less successfully, exploit.

Until the Treaty split and Civil War, the revolutionary nationalist movement of Sinn Féin and the IRA, which had emerged in the aftermath of the Easter Rising of 1916, had strongly insisted on the trans-class and generally 'non-sectional' nature of its project. However in the wake of defeat, the opponents of the new order were forced to look to a range of hitherto neglected issues as a means of maintaining and expanding support. The conditions of small farmers and landless labourers; low wages, unemployment and bad housing in Dublin and the larger towns; the fears and resentments of the Catholic minority in the newly established Unionist regime in Northern Ireland: all would represent opportunities for republicans. Yet they would be severely inhibited by the ideological legacy of nationalist purism and by the organisational weight of a secretive militarism which maintained a deep distrust of 'politics'. In the inter-war period and again in the 1960s and 1970s, in reaction to the defeats of what came to be seen as an apolitical and purely militarist republicanism, there emerged what this book will call 'social republicanism': an effort to rally the masses to the 'anti- imperialist struggle' by taking up economic and social issues. This book is a study of social republicanism and its role in a number of crucial periods in modern Irish history. It will demonstrate the extreme difficulty that republicanism has experienced in managing the tensions that involvement in economic and social issues creates. These derive in part from the secretive nature of the tradition but also from the real danger that when such issues are taken seriously the central objective of republican struggle is put in question. From Peadar O'Donnell in the 1930s to Gerry Adams in the 1980s, the attractions of social republicanism are clear, but so are its dangers for those committed to the legitimacy of 'armed struggle'. Once republicanism takes up material issues – land annuities and rural depopulation in the 1920s and 1930s, or unemployment and poverty in the Catholic ghettos of the 1980s and 1990s – it risks marginalisation through state-sponsored reform. Thus another key factor bearing on the ability of the republican movement to maintain popular support is the state's response. The decline of the IRA in the 1930s is largely explicable by the absorptive capacity of de Valera's political and social programme; and by the same token no analysis of the state of the IRA and Sinn Féin in the 1980s could avoid the issue of Thatcherism. There has been too much emphasis by historians on the 'republican tradition', taking us back through nineteenth-century examples of Fenianism and 1848 to Wolfe Tone and the United Irishmen in the 1790s; such an emphasis on an apparently unchanging tradition can blind us to the need to examine the very specific historical circumstances in which republicans operated, and which they were sometimes able to turn to their advantage. We need a more discontinuous, 'conjunctural' analysis that breaks with the fatalism of traditional approaches which, ironically, unconsciously mimic the self-serving certainties of the republican world view.

Notes

1. Edward Said, 'Identity, Negation and Violence', *New Left Review*, No. 171, September/October 1988, p.47.
2. See speech of John Hume to the annual conference of the Social Democratic and Labour Party, *Irish Times*, 28 November 1988.
3. Ibid.
4. Patrick Bishop and Eamon Mallie, *The Provisional IRA*, London 1987, p.359.
5. Ibid. p.26.

1 The Origins of
Social Republicanism

At the core of republican ideology since 1921 has been the idea of the incomplete nature of the Irish national revolution of 1918-21. The pervasiveness and strength of this notion derive from its fusion of two crucial aspirations within Irish nationalism – for a 'sovereign' 32-county state and also for a state that would be socially, economically and culturally different from Britain. It is to the Irish revolutionary of 1848, James Fintan Lalor, that we can look for the origin of the captivating idea that, since the 'Conquest' had been a double process of political and economic expropriation, the 'Reconquest' must necessarily be a dual process too. For Lalor, the core of the reconquest lay in the expropriation of the landlords and the reappropriation of land by the Irish peasantry.[1] For James Connolly and later Irish socialists and social republicans like Peadar O'Donnell, reconquest was a national revolution that was simultaneously a social revolution.

Connolly's influence was immense, given his double significance as a socialist of international stature and an executed leader of the 1916 Rising when he and his Irish Citizens' Army, an organisational embodiment of the fierce battles of the 1913 Dublin lock-out, had participated in the revolutionary nationalist insurrection in Dublin. In one of his earliest articles he had written:

> If you remove the English army tomorrow and hoist the green flag over Dublin Castle, unless you set about the organisation of a Socialist Republic your efforts will be in vain. . . Nationalism

without socialism – without a reorganisation of society – is only national recreancy.[2]

The dominant force in Irish nationalism from the 1880s to 1916 was the Irish Parliamentary Party. For Connolly, this was a bourgeois leadership which endorsed not only existing economic relations between Ireland and Britain but the whole system of 'foreign', i.e. capitalist, property relations that British colonisation had imposed on Ireland. A merely political independence which left capitalist relations of production intact was practically meaningless. Only the Irish working class had an objective interest in Irish independence and he therefore deduced that the only true national revolution would be a socialist one. Connolly had created a powerful paradigm linking the failure of the dominant political forces in nationalist Ireland to their class nature. The nationalist project of a 32-county state independent of British influence was accepted; only the capacity of the Irish middle class to realise it was questioned.

Thus not only did Connolly seriously under-estimate the capacity of the Protestants of Ulster, including the majority of Belfast's working class, to frustrate the aspiration for territorial unity, he also failed to anticipate the space which existed in Catholic Ireland for a nationalism that was not as obesely bourgeois as that of the Irish Parliamentary Party and yet in no sense socialist – a space which the revivified Sinn Féin organisation would fill in the aftermath of 1916. Connolly's lack of foresight is more understandable given the original Sinn Féin ('Ourselves Alone'). Founded by Arthur Griffith in 1905, Sinn Féin began life as a small if energetic alliance of Irish language and cultural revivalists, economic nationalists and a smattering of representatives of the underground physical force tradition (the Irish Republican Brotherhood) which had made little political advance before 1916. It had also been characterised, particularly in Griffith's writings, by a fierce hostility to trade union militancy and socialism. The post-1916 reconstruction of Sinn Féin into a broad nationalist front capable of displacing the Irish Parliamentary Party stemmed, in large part, from a transformation in the attitudes of rural Ireland to separatist nationalism. Connolly's essentially urban focus was unlikely to anticipate this decisive shift.

Connolly's own evaluation of the main social forces that would make the Irish revolution was fundamentally flawed by his failure to come to grips with the nature of rural Ireland and the central role within it of a rural middle class. That the work of Ireland's only socialist of international standing has had so little to say about rural Ireland would have serious debilitating effects on the subsequent history of Irish socialism. As Joe Lee has cogently argued, Connolly lacked a substantial grasp of the land question which so concerned the majority of the Irish population: 'Connolly's fatal tactical error was his reluctance to acknowledge the existence of rural Ireland.'[3] When he did deal with the countryside, it was to depict a peasantry which the British government's land legislation of the late nineteenth century had assisted into the stage of capitalist farming. He believed that this peasantry now faced inevitable impoverishment as Irish farming found itself in competition with the large-scale, mechanised farming of North America. Only social ownership of all the resources of Ireland and a protected economy could save the rural population from impoverishment. This catastrophist view of the future of Irish agriculture ignored, as Marx had done earlier,[4] the economic and social weight of the Irish rural middle class, which was far from doomed to extinction. It led inevitably to the view that the only substantial middle class, in Catholic Ireland at least, was urban and economically tied to the British market, with a limited form of Home Rule as its ultimate political ambition.

Connolly was therefore able to provide an optimistic prognosis for the coming Irish revolution, which would resolve the major contradictions between nationalism and socialism and town and countryside. If the middle class was so integrated in the existing nexus of economic relations with Britain, any 'true' nationalist would see that real independence necessitated a social revolution. Town and countryside would be reconciled in a worker-peasant alliance brought about as impoverishment by international competition forced the peasants to see the limits of individual ownership and the necessity of a system of agricultural and manufacturing co-operatives.[5] The pleasing symmetry of these ideas may help to explain their continuing influence long after the War of Independence had demonstrated their profound inadequacy in grasping central economic and political realities. What actually happened was that a substantial section of the rural middle class showed itself willing to contemplate a much more radical form of settlement with Britain than Home Rule, and to support an armed campaign to obtain it. There would prove to be a space for a revolutionary nationalism with a conservative social content.

Social Forces and the Irish Revolution

The rural order from which nationalists drew their support was divided between a large peasant class involved in small- and medium-scale farming and a growing stratum of rich cattle graziers, with holdings of at least 200 acres, and more usually between 400 and 600 acres. These 'ranchers', as they were popularly termed, were particularly concentrated in three regions – the lowlands of north Leinster, the plains of east Connaught and north Munster and the mountain pastures and boglands of west Connaught.[6] The co-existence in the west of ranches alongside peasants on small overcrowded holdings was a source of often bitter tension and would create problems for Sinn Féin during the War of Independence. It would also cast a long shadow over republican radicalism in the subsequent period.

In 1911 there were 328,743 Irish farmers, of whom over 100,000 farmed fewer than 10 acres. There were, in addition, 450,000 workers in agriculture – farm labourers and the much more substantial group of 'relatives assisting'. At the top of the rural hierarchy were the 32,000 farmers with more than 100 acres.[7] There were thus two possible lines of fissure in the Irish countryside: between rich farmers and labourers or, particularly in the west, between the land-hungry smallholders and the ranchers in their midst. Such tensions were all the more likely to erupt once the British land legislation culminating in the Wyndham Act of 1903 removed the landlord class as a unifying focus of resentment. An estimated two-thirds to three-quarters of Irish farmers had become owners of their land by the outbreak of the First World War. Nevertheless, significant agrarian grievances remained, particularly among small farmers. The war slowed the process of land purchase and also shut off the safety valve of emigration. One historian has suggested of the 1916-21 period that

It may indeed be that the real dynamism which underlay the national movement remained the pressure of population on the land. Land hunger, exacerbated by the cessation of emigration, seems to have remained the only force which generated large-scale popular action.[8]

The War of Independence had coincided with a major upsurge of rural social conflicts and trade union militancy. In the west of Ireland, which had a large concentration of the poorest land and the smallest farms and where the Land Acts had done least to satisfy peasant land hunger, there was an upsurge of peasant activity aimed at forcing a radical redistribution of land. Such activity was described by the Unionist *Irish Times* as 'Agrarian Bolshevism' and was often regarded with little less hostility by Sinn Féin, which established arbitration courts to bring the land war under control. Dan Breen, one of the key guerrilla leaders in the War of Independence and later a militant opponent of the Treaty, subsequently told Peadar O'Donnell that if anyone had talked of dividing up estates in his area he would have had him shot.[9] As Paul Bew has pointed out:

> When, after 1916, Sinn Féin emerged as a new force in nationalist politics – sanctified by the 'blood sacrifice' of the Easter Rising – it was able to outflank the Irish Party both on the left and on the right in agrarian matters according to convenience. In short, by 1918 Irish agrarian radicalism was, from the nationalist point of view, a profoundly ambiguous force.[10]

Sinn Féin's first association with agrarian protest, in 1917 and early 1918, was short-lived and typically instrumental. In the words of one IRA man,

> I hadn't the slightest interest in the land agitation, but I had every interest in using it as a means to an end . . . to get these fellows into the Volunteers . . . Up to that they were just an unorganised mob.[11]

Soon, however, Sinn Féin and the IRA were concerned that social agitation was disrupting 'national' unity and scaring off potential supporters, and in February 1918 the standing committee of Sinn Féin expressed its opposition to unauthorised land-seizures and cattle drives.[12] In his path-breaking provincial study of the Irish revolution, David Fitzpatrick shows how Sinn Féin organisers encouraged members who were small farmers and labourers to take part in agitation for the breaking

up of the large grazing ranches of the west, in the early part of
1918 and again in early 1920 when the struggle was far more
violent and widespread. However although participation may
have consolidated Sinn Féin support amongst the poorest sections of the Irish peasantry, it also fomented hostility among
the larger farmers and the more comfortable members of the
rural community whose support was a real political and material necessity for Sinn Féin:

> Republicanism itself had been tamed by the men of substance
> almost from the start. Like the Home Rule movement, which it
> so closely resembled, Sinn Féin was heavily dependent upon
> shopkeepers, employers and large farmers for income, and the
> Republican county councils for their rates . . . systematic intimi-
> dation might have alienated a substantial and articulate group
> of Irishmen from the Republican cause, thus breaching the
> underlying principle of consensus nationalism.[13]

Sinn Féin's electoral triumph in 1918 – with 73 Sinn Féiners
elected as against 26 Unionists and 6 members of the old Irish
Parliamentary Party – exaggerated both the size and the nature
of its political victory. Irish Labour abstained from the elections
and the Irish Parliamentary Party contested few seats. Also significant in the present context was the economic and social
void at the centre of the Sinn Féin programme. Seán O'Faoláin
drily summed it up: 'The policy of Sinn Féin has always been,
since its foundation, that simple formula: Freedom first; other
things after.' The author of the first scholarly account of the
Civil War expands on this judgment: 'At whatever cost to ideological coherence, unity had to be preserved and divisive issues
avoided.'[14]

The electoral demise of the Irish Parliamentary Party owed
more to its failure to deliver Home Rule due to Ulster Unionist
resistance, and to Lloyd George's botched attempt to impose
conscription on Ireland in 1918, than to positive popular support for the establishing of a republic. The Easter Rising and
the execution by the British of its leaders had unleashed a tide
of emotional nationalism which viewed the failures of the
Parliamentary Party as terminal. The very success of the land
legislation in making owners of a majority of Irish farmers
removed any material interest they had in the continuation of
the Union. It was precisely because the Irish programme on the

land question had been largely met by the British parliament that an Irish constitutional party at Westminster became irrelevant. As a sympathiser of the defunct party noted in 1919: 'Until Irish land purchase was peacefully completed, the man who would suggest the withdrawal of the Irish party from London would make himself the laughing stock of Irish politics.'[15] Those who were most likely not to have been satisfied by the land legislation, who would have liked a much clearer commitment from Sinn Féin to the interests of small farmers and farm labourers, were disappointed as it made clear its overriding commitment to an appeal to all social classes.

The result was a distinct lack of enthusiasm for the 'national struggle' in the province where smallholders had seen their agrarian struggles denounced by Sinn Féin and sometimes repressed by the IRA. Connaught, the most aggressively nationalist province in previous periods of agrarian agitation, was relatively restrained in the War of Independence, the central role passing to the province of Munster with its much more substantial class of medium-sized farmers. In his pioneering analysis of the period, Rumpf relates the land question to participation in the War of Independence:

> The districts where the most violent agrarian unrest occurred during the period were not the centres of the national struggle. The social aspirations of the landless men were not primarily expressed in terms of hostility to the British administration. To a certain extent such aspirations were directly excluded from the national struggle, for the spirit which dominated the IRA leadership at all levels inculcated a deep suspicion of any attempt to mix social aims with the pure cause of the national struggle. The social condition of many areas of the west was not favourable to an active national fight. The main national resistance was concentrated in more prosperous districts, such as de Tocqueville noticed was the case in the French Revolution, and was also true of the German Peasants' Wars.[16]

A nationalism linked positively to the demands of the poorest and most marginal elements in the peasantry would have risked losing the support of the most powerful class in the Irish countryside and would have represented a substantially weaker challenge to the British state. Even if it had prosecuted the struggles of the smallholders against the 'ranchers', it would not have been creating the basis for a worker-peasant alliance:

the aim of the land-hungry peasants was a comfortable holding, not the inauguration of some 'co-operative commonwealth'. It was symptomatic of Connolly's weakness in this area that he was forced onto the terrain of Gaelic revivalism in explaining supposed peasant openness to co-operation and alliance with workers by the invocation of a racial memory of 'the traditions . . . of the common ownership and common control of the land by their ancestors'.[17]

Sinn Féin's essential coolness or hostility to agrarian militancy was mirrored in its relation to the upsurge of trade union activity between 1917 and 1920. Wartime inflation which ate into working-class living standards, an increased demand for labour which, by 1917, had combined with the introduction of compulsory tillage to cause a labour shortage in agriculture, and resentment at the unequal impact of wartime hardships: these were the key factors in a major growth in union membership. Between 1916 and 1920, the numbers represented by the Irish Labour Party and Trade Union Congress (ILPTUC) rose from 100,000 to 225,000 – a quarter of Irish wage-earners.[18] The Irish Transport and General Workers' Union, established as a proto-syndicalist organisation by James Larkin in 1909, grew massively from 5,000 in 1917 to 130,000 at the end of 1920.[19]

Unionisation spread into new areas and hitherto unorganised sectors of the working class. Most explosive was the organisation of the most neglected stratum in the Irish countryside – the farm labourers. Although they constituted only 18 per cent of the agricultural labour force in the 26-country area in the early 1920s, they were a regionally concentrated group: only 6 per cent in Connaught but almost 33 per cent in Leinster. In twelve Leinster and east Munster counties labourers represented about a third of the agricultural labour force.[20] They would contribute significantly to the growing number of strikes, strikers and strike days that Ireland saw between 1917 and the slump which set in at the end of 1920. Such strikes, especially when accompanied, as they often were, by well organised picketing, sympathetic action and even active sabotage, and adopting the iconography of 1917, with red flags and even detachments of 'Red Guards', helped, in Fitzpatrick's words to 'strike fear into the heart of republicans'.[21] In June 1920 the illegal Irish parliament, Dáil Éireann, issued a proclamation clearly depicting such activities as sectional diversions:

'The present time when the Irish people are locked in a life and death struggle with their traditional enemy, is ill chosen for the stirring up of strife among our fellow countrymen.'[22]

In 1919 the Dáil had created arbitration courts and a Central Conciliation Board. Like the Sinn Féin courts of justice and the land courts, these institutions had the dual function of dislodging the British administration and defusing unrest. Emmet O'Connor provides an astringent summary of the role of such institutions and of the Dáil's Department of Labour, headed as it was by Constance Markievicz, the one Sinn Féin leader to proclaim herself a socialist:

> These efforts had the practical effect of asserting Dáil Éireann's legitimacy to employers and employees, reducing strife and settling grievances, usually on the basis of precedents set out by [British] government machinery ... The Department also played a propagandist function being advertised by Sinn Féin as an illustration of its concern for trade unionists. However, nowhere is there any indication of structural reform appearing on the departmental agenda.[23]

When the post-war slump began to push up unemployment in early 1921, the republican government examined ways of dealing with it and put forward recommendations for increased tillage, extension of public works and the promotion of profit-sharing industries. It did not, however, contemplate legislation in any of these areas, contenting itself with appeals to patriotism. It ignored a shrill memorandum from Markievicz, forecasting a violent revolution unless the Dáil moved to deal with 'disaffected workers'. Her proposals were hardly revolutionary: the establishment of food co-operatives, more road works and the gimmicky idea of seizing and re-opening a meat factory 'to show the workers we had their interests at heart'.[24]

The largely integrative approach of Sinn Féin and the Dáil to labour issues, their refusal to take sides with labour against capital, was viewed by many in the labour movement as a poor response to the positive role of the ILPTUC and individual unions in the War of Independence. In 1918 the labour movement, outside the predominantly Unionist parts of Ulster, had joined in the campaign against conscription and on 23 April had organised a 24-hour general strike against it. In December the ILPTUC abstained from the general election to allow Sinn

Féin a straight fight against the Parliamentary Party. In April 1920 the ILPTUC staged a two-day general strike for the release of republican prisoners on hunger strike. Other important examples of labour contributions to the nationalist campaign were the nine-day total stoppage organised by the Limerick Trades Council against British militarism in April 1919, and the seven-month dockers' and railway workers' action against the handling and movement of munitions. For Sinn Féin this was little more than what would have been expected from any patriotic group of Irishmen. At the most it called for some show of listening to the voice of labour. Thus the Labour leader Thomas Johnston was allowed to draw up a statement of social aims which the first Dáil would adopt as its 'Democratic Programme'. Considered too radical in its original form, the statement was amended by Seán T. O'Kelly and reduced to what O'Faoláin described as terms of 'a purely pious and general nature that committed nobody to anything in particular'.[25] It typified the largely verbal and emollient concessions that mainstream republicanism was prepared to make to keep labour within the ambit of a political and military strategy firmly under republican control. Only after the Treaty split and the onset of civil war did some republicans begin to fashion a version of the War of Independence that depicted the source of the ultimate 'betrayal' as the IRA's predominating hostility to popular economic struggles.

The Civil War and the Emergence of Social Republicanism

Charles Townshend sums up the achievement of revolutionary nationalism by the time of the Treaty negotiations in December 1921 as follows:

> Physical force, whether or not as a result of its alliance with politically sophisticated Sinn Féin, had demonstrably worked. It had extracted from the British concessions which they had hitherto refused. It had prised open, in the more dramatic metaphor preferred by its adherents, England's grip on twenty-six out of the thirty-two counties of Ireland.[26]

Yet since physical force was incapable, in the words of the IRA's effective commander, Michael Collins, of 'beating the British out of Ireland militarily',[27] the militant nationalist aspiration

for a republic was to be disappointed. The limit of British con-
cession was to be dominion status within the British Empire
and Commonwealth and, most offensive of all to the purer
republicans, the provision for members of the parliament of
the new Irish Free State to take an oath of allegiance to the
British monarch as head of the Commonwealth.

The debate on the Treaty split Sinn Féin and the IRA and led
to a bitter civil war between the 'Free State' forces, which lost
over 800 dead, and the anti-treaty 'Republican' forces, which
lost many more. Casualties were far in excess of the numbers of
Irish Volunteers killed in the period between 1916 and 1921.[28]
On the republican side in the Dáil the predominant concerns
were issues like the Oath of Allegiance to the Crown, which
symbolised the profound distance separating a 26-county
British dominion from the republic proclaimed in 1916. Many
commentators since have attempted to explain what one Treaty
supporter disparagingly referred to as the 'mystical, hysterical,
neurotic worship of "The Republic" '.[29]

Part of the explanation must be sought in the necessary
amorphousness of the political and social ideologies of the revolutionary elite. Predominantly lower middle-class profession-
als, journalists, and teachers, their origins lay disproportionately in the ascending class in post-Famine Ireland, the rural
middle class. Their thinking about the economic and social
dimensions of 'freedom' tended towards pieties about the
need to avoid the extremes of capitalism and socialism and the
massive industrial conurbations of Britain and other capitalist
states, with their unhealthy polarisation of classes brought
about by excessive disparities of income. Thus even the paper
of Arthur Griffith, the most vigorous advocate of tariff-based
capitalist economic development, denounced the evils of the
English factory system and 'dreamed in Wellsian terms of tech-
nological revolutions that would make such developments
unnecessary in Ireland'.[30] Socialism and trade union militancy
were often seen as twin examples of 'foreign' doctrines likely to
divide the nation. Gaelic revivalism with its references to a 'pre-
conquest' utopia of co-operative *Gemeinschaft* reinforced this
approach, as did the Catholic Church's attitude to social questions, based on Pope Leo XIII's encyclical *Rerum Novarum*, with
its discussion of the twin evils of socialist internationalism and
the doctrine of the class struggle.[31] Rejecting certain features
of industrial capitalism while leaving unquestioned the current

economic realities in Ireland, Sinn Féin was able to represent itself as a more profound challenge to British rule than the 'bourgeois' Parliamentary Party while not disturbing the equilibrium of its wealthier supporters.

But precisely because the substance of Sinn Féin economic and social philosophy was an accommodation with the main lines of development of the post-Famine economic order, its rhetoric of difference with the Parliamentary Party took on a largely moralistic and 'principled' tone. This meant that it would prove difficult, and ultimately impossible, for the Sinn Féin elite to avoid a split when faced with such an impure settlement as the Treaty. For of course the Treaty was a compromise brought about by the realities of relative military and economic power. For many in the Sinn Féin leadership, just as the inspiring memory of a higher Gaelic civilisation would prove sufficient to insulate an independent Ireland from the 'excesses' of capitalism, so another act of revolutionary will would force the British finally to concede the unalloyed Republic. Despite the overwhelmingly political and constitutional focus of the Treaty debates, there was a link between the capacity of revolutionary nationalism to spiritualise real social and economic antagonisms into a language of 'principles' and abstract freedom, and its profound difficulty in adjusting to a situation in which the criteria which had so often been used to marginalise 'sectional' projects like that of labour, could now be turned against those who would settle for something less than complete independence.

The anti-Treaty position was given major social sustenance by the large reservoirs of agrarian dissatisfaction, particularly in Connaught, which would prove much more active in the Civil War than it had in the War of Independence. For many small farmers and farm labourers, republican intransigence was very clearly a function of perceived class interest. The defeat of the republicans would be accompanied by the simultaneous defeat of the remnants of agrarian radicalism: in Meath, Clare and Waterford pro-Treaty forces physically repressed small farmers' and labourers' militancy.[32]

As his cause went down to defeat, a leading anti-Treatyite would produce in prison the few brief notes on which much of the subsequent vocation of social republicanism based itself. Liam Mellows wrote to Austin Stack, who before the Civil War had been successively Minister of Justice and Minister of

Home Affairs and was now a prominent anti-Treatyite. Mellows expressed his dissatisfaction with the republicans' apolitical approach, which 'could only judge of situations in terms of guns and men'.[33] He was influenced by an editorial in a recent edition of the *Workers' Republic*, the newspaper of the tiny Communist Party of Ireland (CPI), which had urged a social and economic programme capable of winning the masses to the support of the Republic. Mellows pressed the republican leadership to set up a government and to translate the Dáil's 1919 Democratic Programme into 'something definite. This is essential if the great body of workers are to be kept on the side of Independence.' A more specific social programme was justified by his interpretation of the Treaty split which showed that,

> the commercial interest, so called, money and gombeen men are on the side of the Treaty. We are back to Tone . . . relying on 'the men of no property'. The 'stake in the country' people were never with the Republic. . . We should recognise that definitely now and base our appeals upon the understanding and needs of those who have always borne Ireland's fight.

As the only radical document to be produced by a republican during the period, Mellows's *Jail Notes* were to become a major inspiration for leftist republicans – especially after his execution at the hands of the Free State government. Charles Townshend refers to him as 'the lone socialist within the leadership'.[34] This judgment at once inflates the socialist component of Mellows's outlook and encourages an underestimation of his longer-term significance. Only 21 when he met Connolly in 1913, he was already well integrated into the physical force underground tradition through his membership first of the republican 'boy scout' movement, Na Fianna Éireann, and subsequently of the IRB. His horizons are well summed up in his declaration to his mother in 1913, 'I'm going to be another Robert Emmet.'[35] Emmet had led a confused and doomed insurrection in Dublin in 1803, gaining entry to the republican tradition largely through his florid speech from the dock and subsequent execution. Roy Foster's judgment on Mellows's hero is acerbic: 'His ideas were those of elite separatism: neither social idealism nor religious equality appear to have figured.'[36] A leader of the 1916 insurrection in Galway, Mellows then spent some time in the United States where he displayed signs of being influenced by Connolly's *Labour in Irish History* – though what took his attention was its assertion that capitalism was a foreign import and that pre-Conquest Ireland was a 'communistic clan' society.[37]

The real significance of Mellows becomes more apparent if certain dissonances in the *Jail Notes* are acknowledged. Thus he suggested that the new social programme should follow the lines of the CPI's strategy which called for state control of industry, transport and the banks as well as the seizure and division of 'the lands of the aristocracy'.[38] At the same time, he claimed that such a programme 'does not require a change of outlook on the part of republicans, or the adoption of a revolutionary programme as such'. Although the IRA Executive had begun to develop a more radical land policy, it was ingenuous at least to suggest that the sort of specifically radical programme that the CPI was demanding would have been welcome to the great majority of the anti-Treaty leaders. Their moralistic republicanism would have bitterly resisted any 'reduction' of their cause to a class movement.

More fundamentally, the apparent radicalisation of Mellows's republicanism simply served to provide another means of avoiding the realities of popular acceptance of the Treaty. The pro-Treaty position was conveniently ascribed to a rump of 'pro-imperialist' moneyed elements who, with the help of the British and the support of the Catholic Church and the 'unprincipled' leadership of the labour movement, were hoodwinking the people. As a radical nationalist, Mellows assumed the fundamental unity of the nation. Apart from the West British bourgeois excrescences, any divisions amongst the people were artificially fostered by 'Imperialism'. This conjured out of existence realities like the Ulster Unionists, and in the 26-county area it reduced the substantial support for the Irish Labour Party and Trade Union Congress (until 1930 the political and trade union wings of the Irish labour movement were organically linked), which had given de facto support to the Treaty, to the question of the supposed corruption of its leadership: 'The official Labour Movement has deserted the people for the fleshpots of the Empire.' In fact in the elections earlier in 1922 the ILPTUC had won almost as much support as the anti-Treatyites and had seventeen of its eighteen candidates elected.[39]

That there was more to the question than a corrupt leadership was at least partly recognised when, in his letter to Stack, Mellows mentioned a visit made by leaders of the ILPTUC to the republicans occupying the Four Courts in Dublin (it would be the shelling of the Four Courts by the pro-Treaty supporters that signalled the beginning of the Civil War): 'They remarked that no effort had been made to put the Democratic Programme into execution.'[40] Mellows concluded, therefore, that the working class was 'naturally' for the Republic, but had been temporarily alienated by the inadequate policies of the republican movement. That for many workers the Treaty was a regrettable but necessary compromise that could be built on, while the anti-Treaty cause threatened only a barren, internecine and destructive conflict, was not a thought which a republican like Mellows, no matter how radical some of his language, could contemplate.

What Mellows really signifies is not a turn to socialist republicanism but the first of a number of attempts to preserve intransigent revolutionary nationalism by tapping into perceived social discontent. Thus in a late communication he takes up the issue of unemployment:

> The unemployment question is acute. Starvation is facing thousands of people ... The Free State government's attitude towards striking postal workers makes clear what its attitude towards workers generally would be. The situation created by all these must be utilised for the Republic. The position must be defined: Free State-Capitalism and Industrialism-Empire; Republic-Workers-Labour.[41]

All the ambiguity of social republicanism is in those lines: the Free State is identified with a mode of production – capitalism – but the Republic has no stated foundation except in solidarity with the vaguely defined cause of Labour. It was symptomatic that Mellows should have referred in his *Jail Notes* to Wolfe Tone and the 'men of no property'. The Dublin Protestant who, with the assistance of Belfast Presbyterian radicals, would found the Society of United Irishmen in 1791 and play a crucial role in the events which culminated in the 1798 Rebellion, was subsequently canonised as the 'Father of Republicanism'.[42] In 1796 Tone had written:

Our freedom must be had at all hazards. If the men of property
will not help us they must fall; we will free ourselves by the aid
of that large and respectable class of the community – the men
of no property.[43]

Rather than an 'embryonic socialist statement',[44] this is a bourgeois revolutionary's acknowledgement that in certain circumstances it may be necessary to make an instrumental and risky
appeal to the 'lower orders'. As Richard Dunphy has noted of
the limits of republican egalitarianism when it used the
rhetoric of Tone,

What was under attack was the notion of aristocracy, not the
existence of socio-economic inequalities. The old, Anglo-Irish
ruling class, together with the large farmers, the ranchers, distinguished by blood, by titles would make way for those who had
worked their way to the top. Hard work, forbearance, meritoc-
racy – these were the corner-stones of the egalitarian faith of the
republicans. Such a man, having worked his way to success,
would not be a bourgeois but a patriot . . .[45]

This ambiguous populist egalitarianism would prove to be a
potent resource for those who, in the next few decades, would
indeed rework republicanism in a constitutional and 'radical'
direction under the leadership of Eamon de Valera and the
new political formation, Fianna Fáil.

The cross-class alliance of the War of Independence did not
split along clear lines of class, but its ending released the
defeated side from some of the restraints that had prevented
Sinn Féin from taking up economic and social issues. Of
course, there were still many in the anti-Treaty Sinn Féin and
IRA who maintained a position of rigid and abstract opposition. The Irish Republic proclaimed in 1916 by a 'Provisional
Government' had based its claim to the allegiance 'of every
Irishman and Irishwoman' on a 'right' established by past
insurrections: a real turn towards the solipsistic and self-referential, and away from those within the physical force tradition
who still accepted the provision of the 1873 Irish Republican
Brotherhood constitution forbidding its 'Supreme Council'
from initiating a war with England until they had the support
of the mass of the people.[46] By the end of the Civil War there
was much evidence of what Townshend describes as:

a Robespierrist vision of the public good . . . A sense of democratic values existed, but it was modified by the belief that Sinn Féin understood what ought to be the will of the people if they were sufficiently nationally aware.[47]

Thus Mary MacSwiney, one of the most prominent of Sinn Féin diehards in the inter-war period, gave a typical response to the popular majority for the Treaty:

The people of a nation may not voluntarily surrender their independence, they may not vote it away in the ballot box even under duress and if some, even a majority be found, who through force or cupidity, would vote for such a surrender, the vote is invalid legally and morally and a minority is justified in upholding the independence of their country.[48]

Increasingly, however, the lack of popular credibility of such purism began to force a degree of rethinking in Sinn Féin and the IRA. This was aided by the increasingly clear conservatism of the governing party, now called Cumann na nGaedheal, which helped to 'socialise' the Civil War fracture. The first post-Mellows attempt to associate the republicans more clearly with social radicalism came in a number of articles written by Constance Markievicz for the Scottish socialist paper *Forward* and republished as a pamphlet, 'What Irish Republicans Stand For'. As a close friend of Connolly's and a member of the Irish Citizens' Army who had received a death sentence (commuted because of her sex) for her role in the 1916 Rising, Markievicz was the Sinn Féin leader most able to put a red gloss on republicanism.

The basic theme represents a Gaelicised version of Connolly. Thus Britain had spent 800 years trying to replace the 'Gaelic State' with the 'Feudal Capitalist State'. The Free State was a further attempt to force 'the English social and economic system' on the Irish people. However there was resistance, as the people 'cling instinctively and with a passionate loyalty to the ideals of a better civilisation, the tradition of which is part of their subconscious, spiritual and mental state'. Connolly's admiration for 'his Celtic forefathers, who foreshadowed in the democratic organisation of the Irish clans, the more perfect organisation of the free society of the future', was quoted and linked to the claim that popular support for republicanism existed because 'the ideals embodied in that Republic touched all that was most vital and most Gaelic in the imagination and race memory of the people.' The Treaty was depicted as a counter-revolution 'for the purpose of breaking up the development of the Co-operative Commonwealth in Ireland'.[49]

This was rewriting history with a dazzling mixture of red and green inks, and Markievicz was obviously strained to provide her readers with examples of revolutionary republicanism in action. Some were pure fabrications: the Democratic Programme was said to have been drawn up by de Valera and, perhaps even more incredibly, to 'emphasise and develop the ideals of the Gaelic state', predictably unspecified. Other instances may not have impressed many Scottish socialists: describing her stint as Minister for Labour, she spoke of how, 'The people, both employers and workers, believed in the justice of their own Republican government, and of our desire to act fairly, and to secure the best for the worker without ruining the employer.' There was an appeal to Irish shopkeepers, 'if they [did] not want their children to be reduced to the condition of starving wage slaves', to join the workers in reorganising businesses on 'true co-operative lines'.[50]

This attempt to inflate republican social radicalism was one of the earliest indications of a move by a section of the anti-Treatyites from purity to politics and a more populist republicanism centring on economic protectionism – 'Why encourage the peaceful penetration of Ireland by English capitalism?' – and a distinctive Irish strategy of balanced economic development:

> We should guard against the conquest of Ireland by foreign capital, and the development of her villages along the lines that have created the 'Black Country' and the this-world Hells to be found in Glasgow, Liverpool and all British industrial cities.[51]

Behind the whimsical mystifications there was a clear attempt to establish the popular credentials of the key republican political leader, Eamon de Valera, whose 'noble simplicity of life' was contrasted with the Free State government: 'the future aristocracy of Ireland . . . who are rolling around in limousines and acquiring fine residences'. Markievicz's articles represent the first substantial attempt by republicans to use class discontents and a populist Gaelic version of Connolly to criticise the new state. The mystificatory and manipulative version of this strategy embodied in these writings would soon be contested by a more substantial version from within the IRA itself.

Notes

1. For a very useful analysis of Lalor's significance, see Mary Daly, 'James Fintan Lalor and Rural Revolution' in Ciaran Brady (ed.), *Worsted in the Game: Losers in Irish History*, Dublin 1989.
2. See 'Socialism and Irish Nationalism' in the edition of Connolly's writings edited by Desmond Ryan, *Socialism and Nationalism*, Dublin 1948, p.25.
3. Joe Lee, *The Modernisation of Irish Society 1848-1918*, Dublin 1973, p.151.
4. On Marx, see P. Bew, P. Gibbon and H. Patterson, *The State in Northern Ireland*, Manchester 1979, Chapter 1.
5. James Connolly, *The Reconquest of Ireland*, Dublin 1968, pp.62-3.
6. Paul Bew, 'Sinn Féin, Agrarian Radicalism and the War of Independence 1919-21' in D. G. Boyce (ed.), *The Revolution in Ireland*, London 1988, p.220.
7. Ibid.
8. Charles Townshend, *Political Violence in Ireland* (Oxford 1983), p.339.
9. Interview with O'Donnell quoted in James McHugh, 'Voices of the Rearguard: A Study of *An Phoblacht*, Irish Republican Thought in the Post-Revolutionary Era 1923-1937', unpublished MA thesis, University College, Dublin, 1983, p.34.
10. Bew, op.cit., pp.221-2.
11. Michael Hopkinson, *Green against Green: A History of the Irish Civil War*, Dublin 1988, p.45.
12. Ibid.
13. David Fitzpatrick, *Politics and Irish Life 1913-21: Provincial Experience of War and Revolution*, Dublin 1977, p.207.
14. Hopkinson, op.cit., p.5.
15. Bew, op.cit., p.224.
16. E. Rumpf and A.C. Hepburn, *Nationalism and Socialism in Twentieth Century Ireland*, Liverpool 1977, p.55.
17. Connolly, op.cit. p.60.
18. Emmet O'Connor, 'Syndicalism in Ireland 1917-1923', unpublished PhD thesis, University of Cambridge, 1984, p.50.
19. Adrian Pimley, 'The Working-Class Movement and the Irish Revolution 1896-1923' in Boyce (ed.), op.cit., p.210.
20. Dan Brady, *Farm Labourers: Irish Struggle 1900-1976*, Belfast 1988, p.10.
21. Fitzpatrick, op.cit., p.252.
22. Brady, op.cit., p.55.
23. O'Connor, op.cit. p.148.
24. Ibid.
25. Hopkinson, op.cit., p.45.
26. Townshend, op.cit., p.360.
27. Hopkinson, op.cit., p.9.
28. Ibid., p.273.

29. P.S. O'Hegarty, *A History of Ireland under the Union*, London 1952, p.781.
30. Tom Garvin, *Nationalist Revolutionaries in Ireland 1858-1928*, Oxford 1987, p.131.
31. O'Connor, op.cit. p.125.
32. Bew, op.cit.
33. All quotes are from C. D. Greaves, *Liam Mellows and the Irish Revolution*, London 1971, pp.363-8.
34. Townshend, op.cit., p.363 note 1.
35. Greaves, op.cit., p.48.
36. R.F. Foster, *Modern Ireland 1600-1972*, London 1988, p.286.
37. Greaves, op.cit., p.155.
38. Quotations from the Irish Communist Organisation, *Notes From Mountjoy Jail by Liam Mellows*, London 1965.
39. Rumpf and Hepburn, op.cit., p.32; the first preference votes were: pro-Treaty 239,193, anti-Treaty 133,864; Labour 132,511; Independents 63,641 and Farmers 51,074.
40. Irish Communist Organisation, op.cit.
41. Ibid.
42. See, for example, Des O'Hagan, *The Republican Tradition*, Dublin 1975, p.2.
43. Quoted in Richard Dunphy, 'Class, Power and the Fianna Fáil Party: A Study of Hegemony in Irish Politics 1923-48', unpublished DPhil thesis, European University Institute, Florence, 1988, p.60.
44. O'Hagan, op.cit.
45. Dunphy, op.cit., p.59.
46. Bulmer Hobson, *Ireland Yesterday, Today and Tomorrow*, Tralee 1968, p.33.
47. Townshend, op.cit., p.329.
48. Charlotte H. Fallon, *Soul of Fire: A Biography of Mary MacSwiney*, Cork and Dublin 1986, p.86.
49. All quotations from C. Markievicz, *What Irish Republicans Stand For*, Glasgow 1923.
50. Ibid. and Dunphy, op.cit., p.54.
51. Markievicz, op.cit.

2 Republicanism in Inter-war Ireland

The Civil War ended in April 1923 with a ceasefire signed by de Valera as president of the 'Government of the Republic of Ireland' and Frank Aiken as Chief of Staff of the IRA.[1] The declaration contained an ambiguous but significant clause:

> That the ultimate Court of Appeal for deciding disputed questions of national expediency and policy is the people of Ireland, the judgment being by majority vote of the adult citizenry, and the decision to be submitted to, and resistance by violence excluded, not because the decision is necessary, right or just or permanent, but because acceptance of this rule makes for peace, order and unity in national action and is the democratic alternative to arbitrament by force.[2]

For many of the defeated republicans, of whom over 12,000 were imprisoned at the time of the ceasefire,[3] democratic criteria would come into play only after the overthrow of the whole Treaty settlement – the 'people of Ireland' could not be truly represented through 'corrupt' institutions like the Free State and the Northern Ireland state. In the IRA were many who regarded physical force as crucial in bringing about change, and who saw 'politicians' above all as an unnecessary evil. The military front in the War of Independence had been opened independently of the Dáil and the government of the Republic, and during the war the military men showed increasing contempt for the politicians.[4] After the Treaty, the tendency to effective IRA autonomy developed to a high degree, and although the IRA had taken an oath of loyalty to the Dáil during the War of Independence, the anti-Treaty IRA was largely independent of control by de Valera as president of the notional republic.

However military defeat gave the politicians an opportunity to reassert themselves. De Valera successfully urged participation in the general election of August 1923, and although the republicans did unexpectedly well, given the imprisonment of many candidates and election workers, the result inevitably stirred up the suspicions of some in the IRA that Sinn Féin was destined for incorporation in the Free State.[5] It certainly became difficult to ignore the fact that, while the Free State government lacked massive popularity and although there was still substantial republican support, it was the support of a minority: a clear majority had voted for candidates who accepted the Treaty. The maintenance of a purist abstentionism held out little prospect of increasing Sinn Féin support against a state which could rely on popular memories and revulsion over the Civil War to isolate republicans so long as it seemed that they were simply preparing for a 'second round'.

By 1925, with more and more evidence that abstentionism was depleting popular support, de Valera and a substantial section of the Sinn Féin leadership had decided that the road to the 'Republic' lay in a long march through the institutions of the Free State and that this meant entering the Dáil. A pivotal role would be played by the Dublin-based Sinn Féin leader, Seán Lemass, soon to emerge as the economic strategist of the new party and the architect of its hegemony over the urban working class. Lemass was an abrasive critic of those in Sinn Féin whose idealist insistence on the 'de jure' republic of 1919 prevented them from acknowledging current realities:

There are some who would have us sit by the roadside and debate abstruse points about 'de jure' this and 'de facto' that, but the reality we want is away in the distance and we cannot get there unless we move.[6]

The split in Sinn Féin came in March 1926 at a special Árd Fheis to consider de Valera's proposal that, once the oath of allegiance was removed, 'It becomes a question not of principle but of policy whether or not republican representatives enter the Dáil'. The proposal was narrowly rejected and de Valera and his lieutenants moved quickly to begin the process of organising a new political formation – Fianna Fáil (Soldiers of Destiny) – which would rapidly consign the idealist intransigents of Sinn Féin to the margins of Irish political life. The relation of the new party with the IRA would be a complex and ambiguous one.

At the General Army Convention of the IRA in November 1925, Frank Aiken – the Chief of Staff and a de Valera supporter – admitted that some members of the 'government of the Republic' were discussing the possibility of entering the Dáil. He provoked substantial and angry support for a resolution from the Tirconail battalion in Donegal, calling on the IRA to sever its connection with the 'shadow' republican government composed of the Sinn Féin members of the second Dáil. The resolution was stridently anti-political:

> That in view of the fact that the Government has developed into a mere political party and has lost sight of the fact that all our energies should be devoted to the all-important work of making the Army efficient so that the renegades who, through a coup d'état, assumed governmental powers in this country, be dealt with at the earliest opportunity, the Army of the Republic sever its connection with the Dáil, and act under an independent Executive, such Executive be given the power to declare war when, in its opinion, a suitable opportunity arises to rid the Republic of its enemies and maintain it in accordance with the proclamation of 1916.[7]

This motion was proposed by Peadar O'Donnell, who would soon personify social republicanism and would play a crucial role in republican political development in the inter-war period. O'Donnell saw himself as the link with the legacy of Mellows and set out self-consciously to politicise the IRA.

Born in 1893 into a small farming family in Meenmore near Dungloe in Donegal, Peadar O'Donnell trained as a teacher before the war. Radicalised in part by an uncle who returned from the United States where he had been a 'Wobbly', a member of the syndicalist Industrial Workers of the World, he was crucially influenced by a trip to Scotland, on which he had been sent by the people of Aranmore island off the Donegal coast, where he was teaching. He was to report on an agricultural strike that was affecting the seasonal earnings so crucial to the economy of the island, as to many other parts of the Donegal seaboard where tiny holdings of poor land could not provide for large families. Emigration to the United States was a structured necessity for such families – five of O'Donnell's eight brothers and sisters emigrated. For those who remained, seasonal work as migrant harvesters in Scotland was commonplace.[8] It was in Scotland that his radicalism was given a distinct socialist inflection: 'Glasgow was my doorway to the world of working-class struggle. There was no turning back for me.'[9]

O'Donnell left school-teaching in 1917 to become a full-time organiser for the Irish Transport and General Workers' Union, now entering a period of rapid expansion, but his own priorities were soon apparent as he became involved in the IRA in 1919 and resigned from the union job in 1920 to devote himself full-time to IRA activities. By the time of the Treaty he was in command of the 2nd brigade of the IRA's Northern Division.[10] He opposed the Treaty, was captured in the battle for the Four Courts in June 1922 and imprisoned until his escape in March 1924.

Like Mellows, whom he got to know in Mountjoy Jail, O'Donnell became convinced that the anti-Treaty leadership would go down to defeat because of its lack of a radical social programme to win the masses to the 'Republic':

> The IRA, apart from himself, George Gilmore, Paddy Ruttledge, perhaps Seán Lemass, Seán Moylan and Tommy Mullins, were just as conservative as the First and Second Dáil governments.[11]

In a subsequent interview, he summed up the central inadequacy of the existing republican leadership:

> Very dedicated men, almost religious men . . . All they stood for was that they would not accept the Treaty, they had no alternative programme. They were the stuff that martyrs are made of, but not revolutionaries . . . We had a pretty barren mind socially, many on the Republican side were against change. Had we won, I would agree that the end results might not have been much different from what one sees today.[12]

However he saw his approach as more developed than that of Mellows, whom he saw not like some on the left as a socialist republican but rather as 'a great Fenian [the Gaelic name for the insurrectionary nationalists of the IRB, associated particularly with their failed rising in 1867] who saw the poor as the freedom force of the nation; as Tone did'.[13] For O'Donnell, social discontent was not something that an existing republican leadership could use for its own purposes; rather it demanded a transformation in republicanism, which would become a broad popular alliance capable of 'completing' the national revolution in a socially and economically radical way.

As a leading member of the IRA after the Civil War – he was on the Army executive of twelve elected by the Army Convention and on the seven-man Army Council – he was in a strong position to attempt to socialise republicanism. He was helped by his own significant literary talents – he wrote four novels between 1925 and 1930 and would produce major works of autobiography and contemporary historical analysis. As editor of *An Phoblacht*, the IRA's weekly newspaper, from 1926 to 1930, he would use his position to help usher in a period of energetic if amorphous and contradictory republican leftism in an attempt to maintain a continuing and vital role for the IRA. This was all the more necessary given the increasing appeal of Fianna Fáil to many IRA members who were disillusioned with the post-1923 impasse of Sinn Féin. Fianna Fáil organisers who toured the country to build the new organisation could often rely on local IRA commanders to bring their membership into the new party – numerous IRA companies were transformed into Fianna Fáil *cumainn* or branches. The skilful ambiguities through which the Fianna Fáil leadership expressed the party's own relationship to the physical force tradition allowed many such republicans to join Fianna Fáil without breaking their link with the IRA. It would be this ambiguous symbiosis that initially encouraged the social republican project and ultimately absorbed it.

Land Annuities and Left Republicanism 1926–1932

There is now a considerable literature on both Irish socialism and republicanism in the twentieth century, yet little has been written about the agitation which attempted very clearly to link republican objectives to a major social and political issue: the movement against the payment of land annuities to England, which was launched in 1926 by Peadar O'Donnell in his native Donegal. A major reason for this neglect is, ironically, the very success of the movement which imposed itself on de Valera and the national leadership of Fianna Fáil. The Fianna Fáil

victory in 1932 and its subsequent domination of Irish politics
has tended to obscure the important role that left republicanism played in creating what Seán O'Faoláin referred to as 'a
distinct social flavour about de Valera-ism'.[14] A related and
important issue is the significance of the agitation for the
understanding of the nature of social republicanism.

The early 1930s were to see one of the two major attempts
since the Treaty to move the republican movement in a socialist direction, the Republican Congress of 1934. The reasons for
the quick collapse of this initiative will be only partly understood if their origins in O'Donnell's project of the 1920s are
not grasped. For in his writings of the period, and particularly
in *An Phoblacht*, O'Donnell articulated perhaps the only serious
attempt since partition to create a project of social and political transformation based on a Gaelicised version of Connolly's
writings. This project of pushing republicanism to the left
would exercise a continuing influence in subsequent decades
and, despite its failure, it would become the unsurpassable
limit of republican radicalism until the 1970s. Its intrinsic subordination to a fundamentally nationalist political project
meant, however, that it would be incapable of undermining
Fianna Fáil's populist appeal.

The land annuities were those due to be paid by Irish farmers under the 1891 and 1909 Land Acts and amounted to £3
million a year.[15] Under the 1920 Government of Ireland Act
the new governments in Belfast and Dublin were to have
retained the annuities, but this provision was held to have been
superseded by the Treaty. The annuities were dealt with under
the Anglo-Irish Financial Agreement of 1923, the terms of
which were never published. The Irish government was to col-
lect the annuities from the tenants and pay them into the
British government's Purchase Annuities Fund. The Irish government's undertaking to pay the annuities was confirmed
under the Ultimate Financial Settlement agreed with the
British in March 1926. The political sensitivity of the issue was
indicated by the fact that the Free State government did not
publish details of the settlement until eight months after it had
been signed.

Although the Labour Party had raised the annuities issue in
the Dáil, the mainstream of anti-Treatyite Sinn Féin and later
Fianna Fáil were notably slow to take up the issue. As
O'Donnell explains in his own history of the agitation, he

became aware of it when small farmers from his native Donegal Gaeltacht (Gaelic-speaking area) told him about the threats of legal action they had received from the Irish Land Commission for non-payment. Non-payment in parts of Donegal went back to 1918 when peasants supported by the local IRA Commander had decided to pay neither rent nor annuities. By the time Free State courts were established, some peasants had accumulated up to eight years of arrears.[16] Similar situations existed in other small-farming areas in the west and south-west. For O'Donnell, the harsh economic reality that made it impossible for the small farmers to pay arrears, even if they had wanted to do so, was the most potent material symbol of the failure of the Sinn Féin revolution of 1919-21. As the manifesto of Saor Éire, which O'Donnell had a hand in drawing up, was to put it in 1931, the first Dáil in 1919,

> set its face against all tendency towards direct action by the masses to recapture their inheritance . . . The small farmers and landless men demanded restoration of the ranches [sic] they demanded the relief of rent and in these vital issues the government betrayed them.[17]

After the Treaty split there was on the anti-Treaty side a slightly more sympathetic audience for the views of agrarian radicals. In May 1922 the IRA Army Council produced an agrarian policy and P.J. Ruttledge, 'Director of Civil Administration', issued an order to local commandants to seize certain lands and properties and hold them in trust for the Irish people. These included all lands in the possession of the Congested Districts Board, created by the British administration in the 1890s to deal with the problem of the most impoverished parts of the west of Ireland, all properties of absentee landlords and those who spent the greater part of their time abroad, and all but 100-200 acres and mansion houses of landlords residing permanently in Ireland. Divisional land courts were to be established.[18] It soon became clear, however, that the leadership of the anti-Treaty side was predominantly unsympathetic to a clear identification with agrarian radicalism. Thus in his *Jail Notes*, Liam Mellows reminded Austin Stack that the IRA already had a land programme which should now be actualised as part of the struggle 'if the great body of workers are to be kept on the side of Independence'.[19] But as

O'Donnell was to say later of de Valera, 'He was numb rather than hostile to the working class struggle. He was as scared as Griffith [the founder of Sinn Féin in 1905] of the gospel of Fintan Lalor.'[20]

For O'Donnell, the anti-Treaty leadership had failed to learn the crucial lesson of the War of Independence. This he stated clearly in a polemic with the purist Mary MacSwiney in the pages of *An Phoblacht*. His attitude to her organisation, Sinn Féin, was the same as it was to the pre-Treaty Sinn Féin:

> It is a compromise with the conquest. To attempt to define Sinn Féin as the undoing of the conquest and restoration of the common ownership of land, among other things, thus coming bang up against the order that has arisen out of the conquest – unthinkable. It would break up the 'national' movement.[21]

It was Connolly who had developed the notion that the substance of the socialist task in Ireland was the country's 'reconquest' from the capitalist structures which English colonisation had imposed. This was an ambiguous notion. It could mean simply that, just as the imposition of foreign rule on Ireland had profound economic and social dimensions as well as political ones, the breaking of that foreign rule would necessarily involve equally radical economic and social transformations. However this facet of the notion was sometimes linked to a more romantic Gaelic revivalism. As David Howell has noted, Connolly's major work, *Labour in Irish History*, must be placed firmly within the broad current of the Gaelic literary and cultural revival which developed from the 1880s. Connolly was particularly influenced by Alice Stopford Green's *The Making of Ireland and its Undoing*, which focused on the destruction of Gaelic culture following the conquest of the sixteenth and seventeenth centuries. This was presented as a rupture which rendered subsequent developments abnormal. The liberation of Ireland required a reconnection with the older traditions.[22]

Such a viewpoint naturally tended to privilege those sections of the Irish population seen to be nearest to Gaelic traditions, and in the conditions of the 1920s this inevitably meant a focus on the peasantry of the western periphery. It was, of course, in these areas that the greatest concentration of small farmers was wresting a living from the poorest soils in Ireland. Agitation against annuities would inevitably have tended to focus on those areas where their burden was hardest to bear. For O'Donnell, however, there was more to the issue than material conditions in these areas. He believed that the annuities issue enabled him to give the crucial material and class dimension to the republican struggle against the 'imperialist' Free State regime:

> to talk of nationhood as something outside the people on which they are to rivet their eyes and struggle towards is wrong . . . organisation will only come from the struggles of the hard-pressed to drive hunger out of their lives. I am convinced that the hard-pressed peasantry and the famishing workless are the point of assembly.[23]

The small farmers of the western periphery were crucial to his project for reasons that went beyond any strategic calculations of their conditions or class interests. O'Donnell in fact gave them a privileged role in the anti-imperialist struggle. As he plainly stated in his introduction to Brian O'Neill's *The War for the Land in Ireland*:

> In my opinion the relationship between the social rights of the toilers and the fight for national independence has been more persistently maintained by the small farmer population, even than by the industrial workers in the south.[24]

This valuation of the peasantry owed more to Gaelic revivalism than to socialist ideology. As Terence Brown has pointed out, the 1920s saw the confirmation of the west and of the Gaeltachts as the main locus of Irish nationalist cultural aspiration. The acutely depressed conditions in rural Ireland in this period, manifested in high levels of unemployment and emigration, weighed particularly heavily on the Gaeltacht areas, and for a central tendency in nationalism this became a critical issue. Brown quotes Douglas Hyde, the Irish Protestant co-founder of the Gaelic League, commenting on a recently published report of the Gaeltacht Commission in 1926:

> Remember that the best of our people were driven by Cromwell to hell or Connacht. Many of our race are living on the seaboard. They are men and women of the toughest fibre. They have been for generations fighting with the sea, fighting with

the weather, fighting with the mountains. They are indeed the
survival of the fittest. Give them but half a chance and they are
the seeds of a great race . . . it will save the historical Irish nation
for it will preserve for all time the fountain source from which
future generations can draw for ever.[25]

O'Donnell made clear his fealty to an ultra-Gaelic version of
Connolly's 'reconquest' when he specified that his objective
was 'not merely to set up a Republic but to restore the old
Gaelic civilisation on the ruins of the capitalist state foisted on
us by Imperialism'.[26] Clearly this meant that the preservation of
the Gaeltacht areas was crucial, for their peasantries were the
least corrupted bearers of Gaelic and anti-capitalist values.
When decrees for non-payment of annuities were issued
against peasants in the Tirconail Gaeltacht in Donegal, where
the agitation had begun, O'Donnell responded in a typically
revivalist way:

> Are the remnants of Gaelic stock to be sought out among the
> rocks and stripped naked under a cruel winter? Are these
> homes stamped unmistakably with the personality of these
> Gaelic folk – and they are as yet a vital, unbroken set of people
> – to be razed because tribute to England is not being paid?[27]

Thus Gaelicised, the annuities were an issue that had significant potential for Fianna Fáil. In April 1927 the desperate state
of some small farmers was tragically revealed in the Gaeltacht
area in west Cork with the death from starvation of a farmer, his
wife and two of their five children. (O'Donnell took the name
of their village, Adrigoole, as the title of a novel published in
1929.) The *Nation*, a weekly newspaper supporting Fianna Fáil,
took up the issue in a way broadly similar to the approach of *An
Phoblacht*:

> The policy of our efficient Minister of Agriculture is having
> unexpected success. He informed the country recently that as
> far as he was concerned, help would be given only to those farm-
> ers who can help themselves . . . The Berehaven man, with his
> uneconomic holding could not help himself, and went to the
> devil . . . If he had been one of the rich farmers he could have
> helped himself out of public funds. But unhappily for him and
> his kind he belonged to the Celtic fringe, he is a remnant of the
> old Irish that were driven by the invaders to the bogs and moun-

tains. . . Last year, 30,000 people, mainly from the Celtic fringe, left Ireland in order to escape the fate that awaits the land-holder along the coast. Yet the grass is growing on the empty plains of Meath.[28]

There was a hint of the traditional agrarian radical demand for the break up of the grazing ranches. But the *Nation*'s main advice to its readers was, if they wanted to 'save the Gael', to vote Fianna Fáil in the forthcoming election. At this time Fianna Fáil had no concrete agrarian policy; although there was some sympathy for O'Donnell's campaign,[29] the position of the national leadership and of de Valera in particular was much more cautious.

It was the potentially divisive nature of the campaign which obviously worried de Valera. Soon after the extraordinary Sinn Féin Árd Fheis in 1926 and the subsequent decision to set up the new party, de Valera wrote to Joseph McGarrity, the leading figure in the Irish-American republican support group, Clan na Gael, explaining the decision:

> You will perhaps wonder why I did not wait any longer. It is vital that the Free State be shaken at the next general election, for if an opportunity be given it to consolidate itself further as an institution – if the present Free State members are replaced by Farmers and Labourers and other class interests, the national interest as a whole will be submerged in the clashing of rival economic groups.[30]

This clear avowal of the need to preserve Ireland from the dangers of class politics helps to explain much of the tortuous legalism which characterised de Valera's position on the annuities. In July 1927 he dealt with the issue in an interview with the *Manchester Guardian*:

> Our farmers ought certainly to pay something for the privilege of using the land. But perhaps what they pay should not be annuities calculated to compensate the landlord for his legal claim to rent, but rather a land tax which could be graduated more justly and scaled down in accordance with the farmers' ability to pay. Still I do not assert that those who advanced the money which the British Treasury used to buy out the landlords should not be repaid. But the question, by whom their money should be repaid, has still to be settled. I am not for a repudiation of debt. A future Republican government could not ignore all the acts of

its predecessor, but the financial settlement which Cosgrave has made with England is absurd and will be reopened.[31]

At the 1927 Fianna Fáil Árd Fheis a resolution proposed by a priest from South Mayo was passed calling on the Land Commission 'in urgent cases where writs have been issued and seizure or sale is imminent' not to take legal action where a farmer was able to pay the current annuity and was prepared to pay arrears by instalment.[32] There was considerable distance between this and O'Donnell's campaign in Donegal where the peasants had been organised to withhold annuities and resist seizures and sales. The decision of the conference to set up a special policy committee on the issue showed a determination that the party should benefit from it, but the report clearly demonstrated that the issue would be presented as a national grievance against England with the minimum possible social content. The basic argument was to be the legal one: that the continued payment of annuities was contrary to the Government of Ireland Act and the Treaty. In power, Fianna Fáil would reopen the question with Britain and uphold the right of the Free State to retain the annuities. The funds so retained would be used 'to help tenant farmers and to facilitate the purchase and distribution of land under the 1923 Act with special reference to the Gaeltachts and the Congested Districts'.[33] Legalistic appeals to British legislation had little attraction for either agrarian radicals or republican purists. Discussing the annuities issue at Sinn Féin's Árd Fheis, the party president, J. J. O'Kelly, 'referred to the means by which the lands of Ireland were confiscated by alien adventurers . . . His advice to Irish farmers was not to pay another penny in way of land annuities.'[34]

As O'Donnell admitted, however, by the end of 1927 there was a great danger of the agitation collapsing in its original areas of support: 'I was desperately in need of some help to widen the area of struggle and to bring new voices onto the land annuities platform.'[35] In a significant article, he implicitly recognised the limits of a strategy too closely tied to the peasant periphery. He spoke of 'a quivering uneasiness in the collective mind of the working masses . . . a tiredness, a distrust, a cynicism', and of the feeling that the peasantry were 'a hard, mean, clutching, self-centred, self-seeking lot who really want to pay out nothing'.[36] It was symptomatic of the large element of idealism that remained in even so 'materialist' a republican as O'Donnell that suspicion of the peasantry is explained by factors like 'tiredness' and 'cynicism'. Urban working-class lack of interest in the annuities issue reflected the failure of even radical republicans to link it to a broader strategy of economic and social change. O'Donnell saw in the annuities issue a symbol of the continuing imperialist burden which the Free State government was prepared to impose upon a large section of the Irish people. This approach assumed that in the struggle against this burden an effective radical alliance could be built between 'peasants' and workers. As we shall see, the social republicans' grasp of the political possibilities in urban Ireland was a tenuous one, but even their rural strategy failed to appreciate the complexity of rural class structure. It was this failure which ensured Fianna Fáil's easy capture of the issue.

The situation of peripheral isolation encouraged a move towards Fianna Fáil and this was facilitated by an approach from Colonel Maurice Moore, a member of the Free State Senate who had been waging a campaign against the legality of the continued payment of annuities to England. Moore had produced a pamphlet, *British Plunder and Irish Blunder,* which he wished O'Donnell to serialise. Until then *An Phoblacht* had taken little notice of his speeches for, as O'Donnell admitted, 'It would not occur to me to link up with a Free State Senator who could invoke no better argument than British Acts of Parliament.'[37] However Moore was now a member of Fianna Fáil and on its executive was able to put his case strongly to de Valera. Association with Moore made it easier to go about the task of getting Fianna Fáil TDs onto annuities platforms: de Valera had banned them from appearing on platforms with O'Donnell. In February 1928 a national anti-annuities campaign was launched at a meeting presided over by Moore in the Rotunda, Dublin. O'Donnell shared the platform with three Fianna Fáil TDs, Gerry Boland, Dr Jim Ryan and Patrick Ruttledge, one of the foremost agrarian radicals in Fianna Fáil, whose frequent speeches on the poverty and unemployment in Mayo were well received in *An Phoblacht.* In his speech, O'Donnell raised the 'Call off the Bailiffs' and 'No Rent' slogans which continued to embarrass de Valera, and Ruttledge made the point that while

the platform held people who did not agree on some points . . . on this matter of ending the payment of an illegal and immoral tax to England, they could agree and work in harmony, maybe opening the way to big things in the future.'[38]

A national 'Anti-Tribute League' was created, with a leadership dominated by western radicals who personified the very close links – both ideological and familial – that still remained between the IRA and Fianna Fáil. Its chairman was Frank Barrett, chairman of Clare County Council. An ex-member of the Army Council whose brother was still in the IRA, he was now a leading member of Fianna Fáil.[39] The vice-chairman was Eamonn Corbett, an IRA comrade of Mellows, who was now chairman of Galway County Council.[40] The campaign attempted to get county councils in areas where annuities agitations existed to pass resolutions against the payment of the annuities to England and also demanding the suspension of legal action for arrears. By the end of the year such resolutions had been passed by Clare, Galway, Kerry and Leitrim county councils and the campaign was getting good publicity and support from the *Mayo News* and other western tribunes of agrarian radicalism.[41] But the radicalism articulated by the *Mayo News* represented only one strand, however, and, for all its importance, a minority strand in Fianna Fáil. As de Valera's semi-official biographers have noted, one of the major problems facing the new party was the fear amongst sections of the public of its supposed radicalism. In drafting an election address in 1927, de Valera protested that,

> The sinister design of aiming at bringing about a sudden revolutionary upheaval, with which our opponents choose to credit us, is altogether foreign to our purpose and programme.[42]

The linking of the annuities issue directly to the conditions and needs of the small farmers, the anti-big farmer ethos of the campaign and its aura and rhetoric of direct action to resist the bailiffs were not the forms in which de Valera wanted the issue to be articulated. The increasing involvement of the Fianna Fáil leadership in the annuities question was associated with a sustained attempt to drain it of any specific class dimension. Thus the *Nation* began to publish articles by lawyers proving the illegality of the payments to England. If they made any appeal to history then it was done in such a way as to include the majority of the agricultural population. In a typical article by a lawyer, the regional and class dimensions of O'Donnell's revivalism is obliterated in a simple identification of 'historic struggles' and 'the farmer':

> As a matter of political economy, the need to help the agricultural industry requires no emphasis. But the farmer has surely other claims that go nearer to the hearts of his countrymen. He, above all, is the Gael of age-long tradition. Far away in the dawn of history, he it was who tilled the land, built up its traditions and fought the battles for the liberty of our country.[43]

The secretary's report to the 1929 Fianna Fáil Árd Fheis could report on the party's

> vigorous pursuit of the campaign for the retention of the land annuities. No question, in recent times, has aroused such widespread interest among the people, as is evidenced by attendance at public meetings and the demand for literature on the subject.[44]

In February of that year, however, the National Executive had already adopted a resolution committing the future Fianna Fáil government to use the retained annuities for the abolition of rates on agricultural land. The conservatism of this proposal was clear to many western radicals. As the *Connaught Telegraph* noted:

> What affiliation have the congests of the west with the Farmers' Union which is composed of the men monopolising the grazing ranches of the country? How will derating affect the thousands of congests in Mayo with the 14/- worth of land as compared with the grazing farmers having hundreds of acres of which he tills not a sod?[45]

Such an approach was clearly radically different from O'Donnell's, although he accepted that after the repudiation of the payments to England the peasants would continue to make some payment. However all arrears were to be cancelled, something against which de Valera had set his face; the payment was to be not in excess of half the present annuity, and the money was to be used for agricultural credit and for the financing of co-operative enterprises.[46] But as the world depression hit Ireland in 1929, O'Donnell began to predict

confidently that a tide of radicalism would force Fianna Fáil to
the left if it wanted to survive.

Fianna Fáil strove, with some difficulty, to adapt and mould
the themes of the annuities campaign to other pre-existing
themes of its discourse on the land question. The object was to
create an agrarian stance sufficiently radical to consolidate its
support amongst the small farmers of the west but not liable to
alienate the more solid members of the farming community.
Thus while the republicans under O'Donnell's influence might
agitate against payment of the annuities, de Valera's approach
was to emphasise that annuities would continue to be paid but
then retained in Dublin. To make this more palatable, he
promised that while some of the money would be used for derating, it would also be used to speed the process of land purchase and redistribution, particularly in the Gaeltachts and
Congested Districts.[47]

From 1929 to the election of 1932, *An Phoblacht* and O'Donnell
formed a bloc with the agrarian radicals in Fianna Fáil in
an intense assault on the 'imperialist' Free State regime and its
main internal class support – the 'ranchers'. The basic assumptions of the agrarian radicals were clear enough. Of 378,000 Irish
agricultural holdings, some 255,000 or 67.5 per cent were valued
at under £15 per year. These were the small men of rural Ireland:
the total valuation of all these holdings did not reach
£2 million, whereas the total valuation of all the holdings
together exceeded £9.5 million. It took 315,000 of the smaller
holdings, or 92 per cent of the whole, to reach a valuation of half
of the Free State, while the remaining half was accounted for
by 33,000 holdings (sometimes non-residential and ranching) or
a little over 8 per cent.[48] For the radicals the political implication
was obvious: the lands valued at £5.5 million should be divided
and peopled by agriculturalists on holdings from £20 to £50
pounds in valuation. Thus the *Mayo News* declared:

> The spoken and written statements of Eamon de Valera our
> great chief, openly and candidly convey to the ranchers that this
> state of things which keeps our people in poverty must end, as
> a consequence they are putting forth every effort to defeat him.
> Those men who lock up God's storehouse have the acres, but
> they have not the votes.[49]

The *Mayo News* was typically blasé about the major obstacles to
such radicalism:

Roughly we have agriculturalists living on land valued at two million pounds. They are our only originating source of wealth, and all other classes in the community are directly or indirectly deriving their income from them. They are a small number of men occupying land of the valuation of £5,500,000 whose sole occupation is, as the late Michael Davitt put it, watching cows' tails growing. They confine the land to growing blades of grass. They are practically worthless as an originating source of wealth to the community. The loss to the community per acre of such land is the difference between the life sustaining capacity of an acre of tilled land and an acre of grass.[50]

A typical rural radical dismissal of any productive role for urban social classes, and displaying the moralistic 'tillage' mentality which blithely dismissed meat, the mainstay of Ireland's exports, as 'practically worthless', this passage ignores important political realities. It was one thing to put the top 8 per cent as 'enemies of the people', but quite another to put the top 32.5 per cent in this category. Yet this article implicitly identified Fianna Fáil with 67.5 per cent of Irish farmers and against the 32.5 per cent at the top. However much some western radicals might like such an approach, the Fianna Fáil leadership attempted to avoid it; their adoption of agricultural derating was a sign of their willingness to compromise with larger farmers.

Nevertheless, the weight of the western small farmer and landless labourer component in the party's support base, together with the undoubted influence of the annuities agitation in giving a national political focus to intensifying agrarian unrest from 1929 on, forced even de Valera to sound a radical note. Thus at a meeting in Irishtown, County Mayo, where the Land League had been launched in 1879, he presented Fianna Fáil in terms of a utopian rural radicalism:

The Ireland his party stood for was the Ireland of Fintan Lalor – an Ireland which still was their own from sod to sky ... with the country's resources fully developed, employment and the means of existence for a population of 20 million could easily be supplied.[51]

In the 1932 election campaign he seemed to be willing to contemplate a much more radical attack on the large farmers:

What about the rich lands? Have they been divided? In Meath, the richest land in Ireland, 5 per cent of farmers own 41 per cent of the land. These are the farmers who own 200 acres each; 631 persons own 234,575 acres: 631 own practically a quarter of a million acres of the best land in Ireland . . . In Tipperary 485 persons own 200,000 acres and in Kildare 6 per cent of farmers own over 172,000. . .[52]

In office Fianna Fáil would disappoint many of its rural supporters, but its first years of power nevertheless witnessed a considerable increase in the pace of land redistribution. The Land Act of 1933 was crucial here: under it, the Land Commission was empowered to expropriate, with compensation, any property that seemed suitable and distribute it among small farmers and the landless. This was coupled with the withholding of the land annuities which precipitated English tariff reprisals on Irish exports and brought the dislocation of the crucial cattle export trade. A brief irruption of Irish fascism in the form of the Blueshirt movement was the intense and fevered reaction of the large farmers who saw the Fianna Fáil victory as a form of agrarian 'Bolshevism'.

The radical element in Fianna Fáil's appeal in 1932 was heavily influenced by the pressure of social republicanism. The annuities campaign had developed in a way that appeared to vindicate O'Donnell's line inside the IRA. He put this forward very clearly in an exchange with Mary MacSwiney who opposed the introduction of class issues into republican discourse:

> My method of influencing an organisation is to raise issues behind it and force it either to adjust itself so as to ride the tidal wave or get swamped . . . If we wake up the country Fianna Fáil would either have to rearrange itself to stand for the people's demand or it would be swept as wreckage around the steps of the Viceregal Lodge.[53]

Implicit in this was the idea that although Fianna Fáil had forsaken the pure ground of the Republic, it was still a party which could be forced in a progressive and anti-imperialist direction. For O'Donnell, the conversion of the IRA to social republicanism was an essential prerequisite for a reconstitution of anti-Treatyism through the transformation of Fianna Fáil or, if that proved impossible, a new united front of 'anti-imperialist' forces. Ironically, he was to have more success in pushing Fianna Fáil in a radical, autarkic nationalist direction than in transforming the IRA.

Saor Éire and the 'Lurch to the Left'

O'Donnell later noted how the international situation helped his campaign to change the IRA:

> By the end of the 1920s the world economic crisis had made itself felt so sharply in Ireland as an agricultural crisis that middle and even bigger farmers found the current annuity an embarrassment, and suddenly our movement became self-propelled.[54]

One of O'Donnell's motives in instigating the IRA's break with Sinn Féin and the Second Dáil in 1925 had been to get the IRA involved in social agitations, but he admits that he was to be relatively unsuccessful. Although a member of both the Executive Council and the Army Council and editor of *An Phoblacht,* he had been unable to involve the IRA as a body in the annuities agitation.[55] His use of *An Phoblacht* to publicise the annuities issue was a source of conflict in republican ranks:

> Quite good-intentioned fellows are sizzling with anger against me for using *An Phoblacht* to push my own set of activities in republican groups in the country. The working-class note will split the compactness of the 'real republic' I am threatened . . . It is my firm conviction that it is by making the working-class ideals active and dominant within the Republican movement that good can come to the revolutionary movement in the country.[56]

In January 1929 a proposal by O'Donnell and a small group of left IRA men to found a radical political organisation tentatively called Saor Éire (Free Ireland) was rejected by the Army Convention. Instead, volunteers were permitted to join a new political organisation, Comhairle na Poblachta, which was designed as a united front of non-Fianna Fáil republicans.[57] The first statement of the new organisation on Irish unity reflected the attitudes of IRA Chief of Staff, Moss Twomey, 'a dedicated right-wing Fenian, scrupulous in his religious observance',[58] rather than those on the left:

> [Irish unity] has become an absolute necessity if Ireland is to remain a Christian entity in a world rapidly becoming pagan . . . to get the clean, Gaelic, Christian mind of Ireland in revolt

against the beastliness of English Imperial paganism should be the task of every right-minded citizen of Ireland.[59]

But as the 1929 slump cut off emigration outlets in the USA (between 1926 and 1930 over 90,000 had emigrated there[60]), there was a major decline in the remittances which had helped many small farmers eke out their living. The deteriorating economic and social conditions gave a new immediacy and attractiveness to O'Donnell's ideas. He was later to claim that it was the inadequate response of the IRA leadership which prevented a revolutionary resolution of the crisis and benefited Fianna Fáil:

There was no political face to this mass unrest . . . it was a great lurch to the left on definite terms . . . As it became clear that the government had in mind to subject the IRA to a mounting system of police thuggery, the possibility of another armed clash forced itself into Republican discussions and with it came talk of the need for a Republican policy. We were back to Mellows. At any time the IRA chose, it could have put itself at the head of the whole Republican movement, pushing past Fianna Fáil, de Valera and all, to reach the 1919 position at one stride, by releasing its members into the land annuities agitation.[61]

However the essential ambiguities of social republicanism are apparent in the fact that a few pages later in his account of this period, O'Donnell gives a very different evaluation of the possibilities. What he now appears to have desired was active IRA involvement in the annuities movement as a means of returning a Fianna Fáil government of a particular type, one forced by popular pressure to adopt agrarian and other economic policies considerably to the left of what they were committed to:

Facing a general election we believed we could add enough push to de Valera's campaign to over-run the government party . . . de Valera and those round him wore no halos for us . . . These men would be incapable of the comprehensive, state-sponsored schemes, which alone could reach out to the small farm countryside, expand industry . . . National leadership was not the challenge facing us. . . Our task was to give coherence to the Fenian radicalism that characterised the crisis. The way to do that would be to put forward a short list of candidates to serve as a rallying point for second tier leadership to impose this militancy on the Fianna Fáil Executive.[62]

This essential lack of clarity as to what was possible in 1931-1932 reflects the fundamental strategic void at the heart of physical force republicanism, whatever its ideological complexion. Its alternative to Fianna Fáil populism was either the ideal 'Republic' to be brought about by another attempt at the forcible overthrow of the Free State or an equally abstract social republicanism. Although the latter was prepared to dirty its hands with material grievances, it would seek to direct them to an objective which, for all its Marxist coloration, was effectively as detached from the possibilities of the situation as the 'Republic' of purist dreams.

The apparent radicalisation of the IRA leadership in the two years after the rejection of the Saor Éire proposal represented a desperate attempt to staunch what Bowyer Bell has described as the 'wholesale desertion' of its members to Fianna Fáil as it moved towards power.[63] A movement which was estimated to have 20-25,000 members in 1926 had declined to a hard core of about 5,000 at the beginning of 1929, although even then its paper *An Phoblacht* sold 8,000 copies while the Fianna Fáil weekly, the *Nation*, sold 6,000.[64] John McHugh has suggested that in the late 1920s there were three main elements in the IRA – the left, led by people like O'Donnell and George Gilmore, which was a definite minority but with disproportionate influence through its effective control of *An Phoblacht*; a strong bloc of apolitical militarists, well represented by the Chief of Staff, Twomey; and another relatively small group which adhered to Catholic social doctrines.[65] The largest group which, like the bulk of the ordinary volunteers was drawn from small farmers, landless labourers and urban workers, was not unsympathetic to the left. Its own conditions and experiences were reflected in a diffuse social-radical variation on traditional republicanism. The further attraction of social republicanism was that it offered volunteers a deeper rationale for refusing incorporation in constitutional politics through the blandishments of Fianna Fáil.

But while the language of publications and meetings would be increasingly affected by borrowings from the Communist International, and a few republicans like O'Donnell would have close and friendly relations with the tiny coterie of Irish Communists, the substance of the relationship was largely instrumental. Here was a declining movement in desperate need of the issues and language to justify its continued existence.

One of the police reports which the Cumann na nGaedheal government was using in an effort to alert the Catholic hierarchy to an approaching 'red' threat that included the IRA, gave an astringent estimate of the actual relationship between the IRA and social radicalism:

> There can be little doubt that there are in the IRA men who dislike Communism and similarly in Communist circles men who regard the IRA as merely sentimental, old-fashioned patriots, but a union has evidently been arranged on the basis that both parties will do their best to destroy the present order of things. The value of this from the IRA point of view is obvious, every unemployed man, every small farmer who has to pay a Land Commission annuity, every struggling small trader, every discontented worker, will now be told that the IRA is his ally . . . The depression in agriculture and the repercussions here of the world-wide industrial slump will thus be turned into motive power for the IRA. It was fairly clear that the IRA could not continue to live on its original base. The number of people who are prepared to imperil their lives and fortunes for the difference between the existing state on the one hand and a Republic such as the USA or France on the other hand is negligible. That a civil war – even a short one – was fought even partly on such a basis was due to purely temporary and personal causes which have already lost much of their force. The men who wished to keep the IRA alive had therefore to look around for support springing from some other motives than the traditions of Irish independence and they found support in the widespread movement against the system of private property and private enterprise. . .[66]

Undoubtedly the predominant tendency in the IRA looked to the annuities movement and to the intensification of problems of unemployment and agricultural depression as the material from which a 'second round' could be engineered. The intense problems of the small farmer in the west, exacerbated by depression and the effective closure of emigration outlets, produced optimum conditions for a recrudescence of a form of republican intransigence which can be identified primarily as a form of traditional rural resistance to an 'oppressor' state. It was in many ways a land war disguised as a national struggle.

O'Donnell, who attended a congress of the Communist International's European Peasant Committee (the Krestintern), was eager to give his annuities agitation an 'internationalist' flavour, and in March 1930 the Anti-Tribute League was transformed into the Irish Working Farmers Congress, which met in Galway. The rhetoric of the meeting did much to convince the police and the government of the reality of a 'red' menace:

> This Congress accepts the platform and programme of the European Peasant Congress . . . by fighting on this platform, in alliance with town workers for the common interest of all toilers against capitalist exploitation, against land annuities . . . the working farmers are at the same time fighting for the complete independence of our country.'[67]

In fact, the alliance with urban workers was as speculative a construction as the link between the farmers' struggles against annuities and the fight for 'complete independence'. The substantial reality was a widespread spirit of lawlessness in many rural areas. At the centre of this was the incapacity of tens of thousands of farmers to pay annuities, the growth of arrears and the resultant action by the Land Commission to recover them, which could take the form of seizure of animals and even of the land itself. O'Donnell had always seen in the occasions of conflict between bailiffs and farmers the opportunity to demonstrate the 'imperialist' nature of the Free State and the possibility of a new republican offensive which, unlike the usual IRA military activities of the period – arms aids, the shooting of policemen and intimidation of jurors – would not leave the masses cold or hostile.

By 1931, as the police complained of a 'growing feeling against payment of debts and against private property',[68] and the government adopted an increasingly repressive demeanour, the IRA's secret paper commented on 'an amazing resurgence of feeling throughout the country during the present year . . . Several companies and battalions have doubled and trebled their strength.'[69] This 'Fenian Radicalism', as O'Donnell termed it, drew its strength predominantly from the areas with a history of participation in the annuities agitation. According to the police, the areas most disturbed by illegal drilling and other forms of 'irregularism' were Tipperary, Kerry, Leitrim and Donegal.[70] These were also often areas with strong traditions of agrarian agitation and anti-Treatyism. There was in many parts of the western periphery a potent

mixture of present economic grievance and an abiding ideological tradition which the Department of Justice characterised
thus: 'For generations there has been in Ireland the tradition
of opposition to the state – a readiness in word and action, to
question the authority of its institutions.'[71]

For the mainstream of the IRA leadership and much of its
membership, the Saor Éire radicalisation was opportunistic. It
held out the prospect of using material grievances to launch a
new campaign. For them, O'Donnell's re-coding of republicanism in the language of class struggle held out the possibility
of enlisting new masses for traditional objectives. The ambiguities of social republicanism were apparent in O'Donnell's
address to a massive republican gathering at Bodenstown in
June 1931:

> What is the state machine? To understand the machine it is nec-
> essary to see that the British ruling class pushed in here, not just
> to place soldiers in Dublin, Cork and Belfast but to enrich them-
> selves by the order of life they would establish here ... Every
> struggle that arises, every strike in the cities, every fight on the
> land must be interpreted in this light so that the mass of the
> people may be led into revolt against the machinery of the state
> ... not merely against the police.[72]

One interpretation of O'Donnell's speech is as a restatement
of Connolly's identification of the conquest with imposed capitalism and of real freedom with socialism. This was probably
O'Donnell's intended meaning. However, articulated at the
grave of Wolfe Tone to a gathering of republicans, most of
whose knowledge of Connolly's writings would have been min-
imal, its actual significance was different.[73] It was an invitation
to republicans to reinterpret concrete economic and social
grievances and struggles as part of the national struggle. While
this may have had the temporary advantage of raising IRA
morale by apparently opening up new opportunities, it also
had the effect of interpreting the 'class struggle' in Ireland in
terms of fundamentally nationalist objectives. For most republican supporters – the small farmers and workers – the most
appropriate mixture of social objectives and nationalism would
be that provided by Fianna Fáil. In 1930 and 1931, for many of
those in the IRA, the growth of social tension, the increasingly
repressive response of the government and the radical noises

of even the Fianna Fáil leadership presaged a massive attack on the whole Treaty settlement, in which the IRA would be able once again to become a popular force. In one sense, therefore, a move to the left also appealed, as holding out the possibility of intensified state repression and, in response, a non-parliamentary break with the institutions of the Free State. For a brief period this appeared to be a possible outcome. But the IRA, too narrowly entrenched in the traditional redoubts of rural resistance, underestimated the urban and rural appeal of Fianna Fáil's mild social reformism and pacific, gradualist dismantling of the Treaty settlement.

The IRA's General Army Convention meeting in Glendalough in April 1931 had adopted the Saor Éire programme. Its goal was now apparently 'to achieve an independent revolutionary leadership of the working class and working farmers towards the overthrow in Ireland of British Imperialism and its ally, Irish Capitalism'.[74] The initial public manifestation of the new programme was its first congress in Dublin attended by over 150 delegates in September. Not surprisingly, *An Phoblacht* hailed it: 'Saor Éire gives a lead which, if acted upon, will achieve the Reconquest.'[75] Claiming continuity with the 1916 Proclamation, the manifesto attacked the First Dáil for opposing 'the direct action of the masses' and denounced Fianna Fáil as

> the party of the Irish middle class . . . [By] retaining much of the phraseology of their more robust days, Fianna Fáil ties up to their party a strong backing among the National population. They promise a higher tariff wall, so they get the small manufacturer and delude a section of workers in Irish industry; they promise to prevent the shipment of land annuities to England and make that, with derating, a gesture towards farmers. But the crisis is exposing them. They fail to campaign for the maintenance of the unemployed; they fail to support workers against wage cuts; they are unable to support the campaign against forced sales; they oppose the slogan 'No Rent', they refuse to support the demand for the overthrow of the land monopoly without compensation and to the consternation of their own youth they condemn rising IRA activity.[76]

This denunciation implicitly recognises the real ideological and material appeal of Fianna Fáil policies to both workers and small farmers, but then blithely denies it, either classifying it as illusory or simply raising more 'leftist' demands for which there was in fact no substantial constituency.

The shallowness of this attempt to overtake Fianna Fáil by windy appeals to 'organised committees of action amongst industrial and agricultural workers' was apparent even at the time, as were some of the more ludicrous aspects of the attacks on de Valera's party. Sean Hayes, who presided at the conference and was a veteran of the annuities campaign, was a Fianna Fáil county councillor and would soon be a TD for the party.[77] The links of personality, ideology and outlook between many in the IRA and Fianna Fáil made the Saor Éire denunciations distinctly unimpressive. Even more demoralising for the minority of serious leftists in the IRA was the shallowness of the new commitments. O'Donnell was later to criticise Saor Éire as 'evasive action', the adoption of a social programme as an alternative to active involvement in popular struggles.[78] And a more forthright dismissal of the whole venture came from Frank Edwards, a member of the IRA in Waterford city and later an International Brigader in Spain:

> It was a most undemocratic way to send out invitations [to the Saor Éire Congress], just the Commandant and the Adjutant. It was IRA through and through. They got a county council member from Clare [Hayes] as chairman ... He startled everybody by commencing with a religious invocation. Then to cap it all Fionan Breathnach stood up later and said we should adjourn the meeting as some wished to attend the All Ireland in Croke Park that afternoon. It showed you how seriously they were taking their socialism.[79]

A convinced socialist who was selling 600 copies of *An Phoblacht* a week at the time, Edwards emphasises that, for all its proclaimed leftism, the IRA effectively functioned not as the scourge but rather as the left wing of Fianna Fáil. Of *An Phoblacht*'s readers he concludes disconsolately: 'I suppose it was the people who voted for Fianna Fáil afterwards who bought them. We republicans had nothing to offer them politically.'[80]

The Republican Congress Minus Workers and Protestants

The Catholic bishops received their copies of the Department of Justice memorandum on 'subversive teachings and activities' and duly responded in a joint pastoral letter on 18 October 1931. Saor Éire was condemned as a 'frankly communistic org-anisation' trying to 'impose upon the Catholic people of Ireland the same materialistic regime, with its fanatical hatred of God, as now dominates Russia and threatens to dominate Spain'.[81] The government introduced new Public Safety legis-lation under which twelve organisations including Saor Éire, the IRA and the Revolutionary Workers' Groups (precursors of the Communist Party of Ireland, whose earlier incarnation had been dissolved) were banned, military tribunals were intro-duced and hundreds were arrested.

Seán Cronin claims that the church-state offensive took the IRA by surprise: 'They had moved out of the shelter of "national rights" into the exposed ground of "social rights" and were bombarded by everyone.'[82] The Catholic Church's offen-sive certainly demonstrated the clear ideological constraints on the agrarian radicalism of which people like O'Donnell had such high hopes. The *Mayo News*, which, as a militant supporter of small farmer agitation, had published one of O'Donnell's pamphlets,[83] made its position on Saor Éire very clear. Reprinting the manifesto in full, it then attacked it at length, particularly for its claim to continuity with 1916:

> Patrick Pearse and his co-signatories of 1916 placed 'the cause of the Irish Republic under the protection of the Most High God'. The engineers of the new Workers' Republic at their first conference sent fraternal greetings to the Russian Soviets whose proclaimed policy is anti-God, who excel in obscene caricatures of the Blessed Virgin. The proclamation on which Saor Éire takes its stand, was drafted not by Patrick Pearse, but by Mr Stalin in Moscow. The whole programme is foreign as well as anti-Christian, it is against every tradition and principle of Irish nationality . . . [If] the mask of Republicanism under which it is masquerading were torn off this face, it would show itself in all its anti-National and anti-Christian ugliness.[84]

The response of the bulk of republicans was to discard the Saor Éire programme and forcibly assert their fidelity to nation and Catholicism. The remnants of Sinn Féin were produced to vouch for the soundness of those who had unfortunately pro-duced a 'misguided' social programme. Mary MacSwiney, while opposing Saor Éire ('It is a bad national policy to divide the people on a class basis') claimed that of those who produced the policy, 'Most . . . are practising Catholics and not one single one of my acquaintance would stand for an anti-Christian state.'[85] A stalwart of the IRA and the annuities movement like Eamonn Corbett would publicly proclaim: 'Many of us are indifferent or hostile to communistic ideas and propaganda but feel very strongly on the national question.'[86]

When the periodical *Irish Rosary* claimed that on a trip to Moscow in 1929 O'Donnell had been trained in 'anti-religious propaganda' he sued (unsuccessfully) for libel, denying the charge and adding, 'On the contrary, I am a Catholic.'[87] Republicans were long used to withstanding attacks from the Church – after all, they had been excommunicated during the Civil War, but such anathemas had concerned their role as an 'armed conspiracy' and had not questioned their Catholicism. The new assault provoked a headlong retreat from a public leftism which had never been securely grounded anyway. The organisation now joined the broad opposition front including Fianna Fáil, Sinn Féin and the Labour Party, which denounced the increased repression and the government's conservative incapacity to deal with the economic crisis, but from a safely Catholic position.

Sinn Féin's Árd Fheis dissociated the 'republican movement' from 'anti-Christian propaganda' and proposed a social order based on 'Christian principles'. For people like MacSwiney and the leading IRA man and later supporter of the left Republican Congress, Michael Price, this meant the principles set out in papal encyclicals. Price quoted Aquinas, Pius V and Leo XIII to back up his ideas for social reform.[88] James Connolly had set the pattern for this dressing up of radicalism in theological garb in his *Labour, Nationality and Religion*. Understandable in some ways in a country where Catholicism had such deep roots, this approach created problems with which, by definition, it could not cope in dealings with Ireland's substantial Protestant population. But the pressure to conform was irresistible, as one organisation after another proclaimed its fidelity to social reform according to Catholic social principles. As a leader of the Labour Party put it: 'They already had the framework of an equitable social system especially suited to the people in the Encyclicals of Pope Leo XIII and his illustrious successor, the present Holy Father.'[89]

For de Valera and Fianna Fáil it would prove relatively easy to ignore the government's allegations that they were party to an

upsurge of 'Bolshevist' agitation and to benefit from the dis-
comfiture of social republicanism. De Valera was in some ways
more robust in his response to the government assault than the
leadership of the IRA. Quick to point to the paltry number of
Communists in the Free State, he went on to establish that any
'extremism' was caused by the country's manifest and major
economic and social problems. These demanded a solution, but,

> a solution having no reference whatever to any other country, a
> solution that comes out of our own circumstances, that springs
> from our own traditional attitude towards life, a solution that is
> Irish and Catholic.[90]

De Valera's own tendency to substitute a spiritual republican
asceticism for economic policy (he informed the *Manchester
Guardian* that he wanted to free Ireland 'from the domination
of her grosser appetites and induce a mood of spiritual exalta-
tion for a return to Spartan standards'[91]) was quite compatible
with electoral promises to provide employment for all who
wanted it and to solve the problems of the congested districts
and the Gaeltachts.[92]

In less than a decade his hopes for an Ireland with a population of 20 million would appear empty, a product, as O
Tuathaigh puts it, of his conventional nationalist belief in the
creative powers of political sovereignty.[93] However in 1931 and
1932 such beliefs inspired the hopes of many small farmers and
unemployed workers, while the IRA could only vacillate
between its desire to re-establish its national credentials and a
residual tendency to criticise the new Fianna Fáil government
from the left. The Church's assault notwithstanding, the rising
political tensions produced by the government's drive against
'anti-state' organisations and the frequent clashes between
republicans and the newly-formed Army Comrades'
Association (a precursor of the fascist Blueshirts) led to a gen-
eralised upsurge of republican sentiment and activity. This benefited both Fianna Fáil and the IRA, whose membership
increased, passing 8,000 by 1934.[94] In the 1932 and 1933 elections, the IRA told its volunteers to campaign for Fianna Fáil,
adding the proviso that such support did not imply acceptance
of the limits of de Valera's objectives.

When it came to specifying the difference between Fianna
Fáil and IRA objectives, the political hollowness of militant

republicanism became evident. The mainstream evinced an uneasy and ambiguous attitude, lending some credibility to the government's gradual dismantling of the Treaty, but rejecting de Valera's requests for the disbanding of the IRA and a 'fusion of forces' against the 'anti-national reactionary forces'.[95] A vestigial radicalism was also maintained: thus an IRA statement of 1933 urging members to vote for Fianna Fáil also registered dismay at the government's 'attempt to stabilise and build up an economic system, which for all that it relieves unemployment at the moment, will perpetuate the evils of social injustice. . .'[96] The IRA Convention in March 1933, however, adopted a new policy statement, 'The Constitution and Governmental Programme of the Republic of Ireland', which formalised the retreat from Saor Éire. It promised social reforms, restrictions on wealth and welfare for the poor, but also stressed the individual right to private property and provided for the safeguarding of private enterprise. There was nothing here with which de Valera could not agree, and at least one thing that must have seemed a boon: the Convention also issued an order prohibiting volunteers from writing or speaking on economic, social and political questions.[97]

For Moss Twomey, Sean MacBride, son of the executed 1916 leader John MacBride and Maud Gonne who became Chief of Staff in 1936-37, and the majority of the IRA leadership, there would have been little dispute with the claim (from a Fianna Fáil negotiation document) that, 'They [Fianna Fáil and the IRA] have at bottom the same national and social outlook.'[98] The recreation of republican unity through fusion was desired by both; at issue were the terms of the fusion. In de Valera's view, Fianna Fáil, which he insisted on characterising as a broad national movement, 'the resurrection of the Irish nation',[99] should absorb the IRA. The latter appeared to envisage a much more equal partnership in a united front to re-establish the Republic. Meanwhile, they would maintain their separate existence and right to take military action. De Valera had offered fusion on the basis of the republican ceasefire proposals of 1923, which among other things claimed that, 'The sovereignty of the Irish Nation and the integrity of its territory is inalienable.'[100] In five meetings with Sean MacBride in the first eighteen months of Fianna Fáil rule, de Valera maintained that, apart from the 'outstanding difficulty' of partition, the spirit of these proposals could be implemented by his government.[101]

As the government withheld the annuities, entered the Economic War with England and was assailed by a strident big-farmer onslaught in the form of the Blueshirts, its republican credentials were validated not only by the republican electorate but also by increasing numbers of IRA volunteers who were absorbed into the army and a new volunteer force. O'Donnell later commented on this period:

> I realised when Fianna Fáil came to power in 1932 that the IRA had no meaning as an armed force. They could offer so many concessions to the Republican viewpoint that it was bound to blur the issues that still divided us. But it would reinforce more than ever my early belief that a government was permitted in Dublin only so long as it remained a bailiff for the conquest.[102]

The development of the Blueshirts in 1933 was to provide O'Donnell and his supporters in the IRA with another issue which they hoped would allow a clear political demarcation to be drawn between 'real' and 'fake' republicanism: the struggle against Irish fascism would displace the anti-annuities movement as the main mobilising issue for social republicanism. The Blueshirt movement originated in the anti-republican Army Comrades' Association founded in 1931 by veterans of the Free State army. After the Fianna Fáil victory in 1932, the ACA opened its membership to the general public. In March 1933 de Valera called a snap election which increased his parliamentary majority, and in the same month he sacked General Eoin O'Duffy, Cumann na nGaedheal's appointee as Chief of Police. O'Duffy made himself the focus of the ACA, which he renamed the National Guard, and gave it a distinctive style when he instituted the fascist salute and the wearing of a blue shirt as a uniform. At its height, it claimed a membership of 100,000, and for a year from the autumn of 1933 it seemed a formidable force. However the challenge would be easily defused; the movement's collapse reflected the leadership's failure to create a broad-based coalition of opposition. The Blueshirts were too dependent on one social group, the big farmers and their sons, particularly the large cattle farmers in Limerick, Cork, Waterford and Kilkenny, who were suffering from the disruption of the cattle trade by the Economic War.

For O'Donnell and his supporters, however, Irish fascism represented the issue that would allow the IRA to take the initiative against de Valera's increasingly successful incorporation of its constituency. Throughout 1934 there were continuous clashes between republicans and Blueshirts and the police and army. The Blueshirts had adopted the tactics of the anti-annuity movement, organising non-payment of rates and land annuities, and resisting attempts to seize animals. Republican attacks on Blueshirt meetings allowed the government to adopt a statesmanlike stance, more or less even-handedly dispensing 'justice'. In 1934, the military tribunal established to deal with such disturbances convicted 349 Blueshirts and 102 IRA men. Naturally enough, the IRA bitterly denounced any action directed against it as a betrayal, but there is no sign that it decreased the government's popular appeal. For the left in the IRA, de Valera could never defeat the Blueshirts because he left the economic and social basis of the movement – the large farmer class – untouched.

An apocalyptic vision of the fascist threat merged with traditional obsessions:

> The British preparations for war are being reflected here in the hectic drive of the Imperialists for power. Britain at war can only be safe when Ireland is gripped in the steel jacket of the Imperialist-Fascist dictatorship.[104]

Precisely because there was so little evidence of the Blueshirts' capacity to mount a real challenge to the state (after all, 'constitutional' republicanism of the Fianna Fáil variety could easily label Irish fascism as an essentially anti-national minority, given its Free State origins), social republicans were driven to portray it mythically, as part of a British assault on the Irish nation. Fianna Fáil would now be portrayed as a government unable to satisfy the demands of its small-farmer and worker supporters and, more critically, unable to prevent a political counter-revolution from the 'imperialist' elements in the country. Social republicanism would be proved correct in its estimate of Fianna Fáil's reformism, but such prescience as it could claim was small compensation for the continuing subordination of its social radicalism to a nationalist political project. So much became apparent in the short-lived Republican Congress.

At the 1934 IRA Army Convention, Michael Price, who had moved considerably from his position of opposition to Saor Éire, proposed that the IRA should adopt as its objective a

Republic as visualised by Connolly. The leadership, no doubt mindful of the recent intense assault from the Church on Saor Éire, opposed the Workers' Republic as a goal, and when his resolution was defeated Price withdrew. O'Donnell and George Gilmore then proposed a resolution that the IRA should mobilise a 'united front' campaign for a Republican Congress, a rallying of republican opinion which 'would wrest the leadership of the National Struggle from Irish Capitalism'.[105] A majority of the delegates supported the resolution, but the vote of the leadership ensured its defeat and O'Donnell and his supporters left the IRA.

The Congress supporters established a newspaper and local groups in preparation for a national conference to launch the united front. The almost immediate collapse of the project when the conference met in Rathmines in September 1934 demonstrated the strict limitations of even the most radical forms of social republicanism. The immediate cause of the split was a division between those who wished for a commitment to the slogan of a Workers' Republic and those, led by O'Donnell and Gilmore, who wished the Congress to mobilise around the struggle for the Republic, which Fianna Fáil was incapable of leading to a successful conclusion.[106] The O'Donnell position, which had a pyrrhic victory, was consistent with the dominant tendency of social republicanism since the annuities campaign. It aimed at a united front of IRA members, rank-and-file Fianna Fáilers, Labour Party members and workers and small farmers, who would be appealed to on an amalgam of national and social issues. Within this combination, the nationalist inflection was quite systematic.

The first issue of the Congress's paper had defined the main task as the struggle against the Blueshirts: 'Above all else, an organ of mass struggle against fascism: that must be the slogan of every committee working towards the Republican Congress'.[107] But fascism was portrayed as a stalking horse for the traditional enemy:

> Once in power, British backing beyond anything given those that played England's game in 1922 would be given. For, Britain seeks to have Ireland in chains before adventuring into the war for which she is feverishly preparing.[108]

Like the annuities campaign, anti-fascism was to provide material for a popular upsurge to 'complete' the national revolution. Fianna Fáil's alleged inability to deal with the Blueshirts was traced to its unwillingness to challenge the 'conquest' in rural Ireland by expropriating the ranchers without compensation and redistributing their land to the small farmers and the landless. In a pamphlet written at the beginning of the Economic War, O'Donnell had argued that the anti-rancher policy was the central task in completing the national revolution:

> The thinning down of the rural life and the organised dependence on Britain was the economic organising of our national enslavement. It is the national issue that is in the forefront in breaking down that dependence and increasing rural employment. This rancher-based cattle trade versus tillage fight is now primarily a fight on the national issue.[109]

Large-farmer and rancher support for fascism appeared greatly to strengthen the social republican case against Fianna Fáil policies. In fact, there was not a lot of evidence that small farmers were as yet dissatisfied with the pace of the government's agrarian reforms, and, more significantly, even the Congress's paper had to record serious rural unease with the radical tone of social republicanism. A supporter from Tipperary reported: 'Very few people in the country districts know anything about James Connolly. There is a prejudice against his policy.'[110] More specifically, another supporter complained that the slogan 'Seize the ranches' was not well received and served to generate much confusion:

> The words 'confiscation' and 'communism' and all sorts of other -isms are thrown at those who use it and unfortunately some small farmers believe that the adoption of such a policy will lead to the seizure of their little farm.[111]

If the fascist threat to the government and its agrarian reforms had been as substantial as the Congress supporters claimed, there would perhaps have been some hope for its strategy of arousing the countryside.

The Congress analysis of Fianna Fáil's supposed weakness in the face of the Blueshirts directly followed Marx's diatribe against the failure of European bourgeoisies to carry through the revolutions of 1848:

Fianna Fáil cannot fight Fascism. Irish Capitalism is caught between two threats – the threat of Imperialist dictatorship on the one hand and the fear of the roused working class and small farmer population on the other. This is the secret of Fianna Fáil's hesitation.[112]

In fact, the 1934 local government elections in Mayo, in which O'Duffy had been predicting a major victory, represented a substantial defeat for his movement – as the *Mayo News* commented: 'The county council and municipal elections in the Irish Free State have pricked and deflated the Blueshirt balloon.'[113] The mainstream IRA, which had consistently refused to accept the Congress analysis of the fascist threat, noted that the election 'proved conclusively that the Imperialist-Fascist organisation commands the support of only a minority of the people'.[114] No doubt the IRA leadership was pleased to see the main mobilising efforts of the Congress so quickly deflected. The Rathmines split would reveal the other strategic weaknesses of social republicanism.

The initial statement of the Congress group had declared that the way to make 'the Republic a main issue dominating the whole political field' was to identify it with the workers and small farmers: 'A Republic of a united Ireland will never be achieved except through a struggle which uproots Capitalism on its way.'[115] But there was no evidence that the discontents of parts of rural Ireland had any affinities with the struggles of urban workers, and even less on which to base the Congress's hopes in urban Ireland. Here the social republicans were fatally handicapped by a broader republican incapacity to relate seriously either to the existing labour movement or to the Protestant workers of Ulster.

Michael Price, addressing the Woodworkers Union for the Congress organising committee, explained that the Irish Labour Party was not being invited to participate. One of the reasons for attacking the Labour Party was that 'they are certainly not leading any struggle for the overthrow of capitalism' – which was certainly true if unsurprising – but the core of his complaint was that it had 'betrayed the Connolly teaching and tradition in 1922 ... The Irish Labour Party is shifty on the Republican issue.'[116] Price and the other social republicans were true to Mellows here in choosing Labour's relation to republican objectives as the fundamental test of its progressive claims. In a communication to Frank Gallagher (later a key member of Fianna Fáil), Mellows defined the left-republican position on the leadership of the Labour Party:

> By their acceptance of the Treaty and all that it connotes . . . they have betrayed not only the Irish Republic but the Labour movement in Ireland and the cause of the workers and peasants throughout the world.[117]

Throughout the period of social-republican dominance *An Phoblacht* was characterised by a lack of serious coverage of the labour movement, especially as compared with its intense concern with the annuities campaign. What it did have to say tended towards denunciations of the 'anti-national' role of the leadership. Particular venom was reserved for the man who had led the Labour group in the Dáil, Thomas Johnston. An Englishman, Johnston brought out the more xenophobic impulses in his republican critics. O'Donnell seems to have been typical of those whose judgement of the labour movement was permanently distorted by the passions of the Civil War. (A biographer relates an incident which reveals the depth of republican resentment at Labour's 'betrayal': when O'Donnell was in jail during the Civil War, his wife went to Johnston's office and 'warned him to his face that if anything happened to Peadar, he himself would not be alive that night'.[118])

As the annuities campaign developed, the lack of interest which it generated in urban Ireland, and particularly in the labour movement, seems to have alienated O'Donnell even more. The labour movement was charged with forsaking the legacy of Connolly, and although this was sometimes argued in the ultra-left language of the Comintern during its highly sectarian 'Third Period', the core charge against Labour was a nationalist one. In a typical blast in an article on Connolly, O'Donnell appeared to dismiss not only the leadership but the rank and file of the Labour Party as well:

> I have not the slightest doubt but that outside the Republican movement . . . there are no right elements. That section of the working class element that follow Johnston will supply the thugs and police to be hired by the Imperialists in the event of any treasonable goings on such as 1916.[119]

At the heart of social-republican alienation from the Labour Party and those workers who supported it was the belief, encouraged by O'Donnell in particular, that the small farmers were the 'oppressed' group most receptive to a nationalist inflection of their grievances. O'Donnell put this clearly in his introduction to Brian O'Neill's 'Marxist' *The War for the Land in Ireland:*

> In my opinion the relationship between the social rights of the toilers and the fight for national independence has been more persistently maintained by the small farmer population, even than by the industrial workers in the south.[120]

The only concrete proposals that social republicanism offered the working class were a mixture of Third Period leftism – to forsake the existing 'reformist' trade unions and set up rival rank-and-file committees – and the nationalistic demand that all unions in the Free State should have their headquarters there.[121] This attack on the role of the British-based 'amalgamated unions' ('English Unions for English interests') was a traditional nationalist one: Arthur Griffith had bitterly attacked James Larkin as an emissary of 'English trade unionism' before the First World War. It would be taken up and encouraged by Fianna Fáil and, together with Catholic anti-communism, was to provoke a long and debilitating split in the trade union movement in 1944.[122]

If social republicanism's lack of rapport with the working class in the Free State was ultimately a product of its subordination of class to nationalism, the intense interest which the Congress displayed in developments in the Protestant working class in the North might appear surprising. The republican position on the Ulster Protestants varied between a hostile view of them as the bigoted descendants of alien Planters and a more sympathetic, if ultimately patronising, view of them as a section of the Irish people who, for a variety of reasons, had been separated from their place in the nation by British machinations. *An Phoblacht* expressed both views. A hostile editorial in 1928 outlined a flippant, but common, nationalist 'solution' for the Ulster Protestants:

> There are in our North-Eastern counties a large number of people who pride themselves on both their Scottish ancestry and

their loyalty to the English crown. Why not swap these worthies for our exiles in Scotland, who will give an undivided allegiance to Ireland?[123]

Here there was much common ground with Fianna Fáil. When de Valera was arrested in Northern Ireland, *An Phoblacht* gave prominent coverage of a large protest meeting in Dublin addressed by Fianna Fáil TDs. The sentiments expressed towards the Ulster Unionists were uniformly hostile and bellicose: 'Buy no Belfast goods ... until they were willing to become part of the Irish nation.' They were referred to as 'the Orangemen and Freemasons of Belfast', and Sean McEntee, soon to be a Cabinet minister, declared that he and his comrades 'would not rest until the Republican flag was floating not alone on Cave Hill but on Stormont'.[124] For the social republicans, the very notion of the 'reconquest', while it could at times be expressed in suitably 'left' anti-capitalist terms, was hard put to incorporate Protestant workers. It was usually presented as an 'uprising' of Gaelic Ireland and of the urban and rural poor to seize back their rightful inheritance, and many who used the notion clearly had difficulty in applying it to Ulster, where the 'planter' element included a working-class majority. Some simply erased the Protestant working class from their view of Ulster. Thus Eithne Coyle, president of the republican women's organisation Cumann na mBan and a signatory to the original Republican Congress manifesto, obviously saw the 'reconquest' in atavistic terms: 'We must show these tyrants in the North that the land of Ulster belongs to the real people of Ireland and not to the planter stock of Henry VIII.'[125]

The dominant strain in social republicanism and in the Congress was what Clare O'Halloran has dubbed the stereotype of the hard-headed and practical Unionist who respected plain speaking and would respect republicans who stuck to their principles.[126] While certainly less obnoxious than the planter/bigot stereotype, it was nevertheless based on a failure to engage with the substance of the Unionist movement and state. If the mass of Protestant workers were hostile to the legacy of Wolfe Tone, this was to be explained by their failure to distinguish the secular and non-sectarian nature of republicanism from the sectarianism which had corrupted nationalist politics in Northern Ireland. Thus *An Phoblacht* speculated that, 'If you could succeed in discrediting organised political sectarianism on the Catholic side, the Orange Order would not long survive.' It attacked Joe Devlin, the leading northern nationalist and MP for West Belfast, for his role in the Catholic organisation the Ancient Order of Hibernians, and the main Catholic daily, the *Irish News*, claiming that, 'For nationalism that paper substitutes Catholicism; for Imperialism it substitutes Protestantism, fanning the flames of sectarianism and keeping the Catholic and Protestant exploited in disunity.'[127] Such recognition of the role of sectarianism in nationalist politics represented one of the more honest and attractive features of social republicanism, but it still functioned to sustain a political strategy which ultimately failed to come to terms with the fact that, for many republicans, nationality and Catholicism were integrally linked and that 'secular' republicanism was very much a minority creed.

The onset of the Great Depression and the sharp increases in unemployment in the heartlands of the Protestant working class formed the basis for a new optimism about the possibilities of winning Protestant workers to 'anti-imperialist politics'. In an address to 'the men and women of the Orange Order' on 12 July 1932, the Army Council of the IRA informed the Protestant workers that, because of the world depression, Britain was no longer able to support the economy of Northern Ireland and that their future was therefore bound up with the rest of the Irish people: 'The industrial capacity, and training of you, industrial workers of North-East Ulster ensure for you a leading influence and place in the economy and life of a Free Irish Nation.'[128] How the export-oriented shipbuilding, engineering and textile industries of Belfast would be integrated into an autarkic social republic was not explained. The superficialities of the address would be sustained by the outbreak of serious working-class discontent during the Belfast outdoor relief strike and accompanying riots in October. As Protestant and Catholic workers campaigned and rioted together, social republicans proclaimed the beginning of an historic shift in Protestant allegiances. George Gilmore, a republican from a northern Protestant background, described the outdoor relief strike as 'the most important event in that city for centuries'. Here there is a clear repetition of Connolly's tendency to see in every serious strike involving Protestants the beginning of a break with Unionist ideology. For republicans of the left and right, Unionism was a reactionary ideology whose mass base had to be explained by assuming a Protestant working class blinded to its own interests. Conversely, any sign of even a limited economic and social awareness was read as the beginning of the end of Unionism.[129]

The Republican Congress would make much of the need to involve the newly awakened Protestant working class in 'anti-imperialist activities'. Its paper claimed that 'The advance of the vanguard of the Protestant workers into active struggle for the Workers' Republic is no longer a matter for day-dreaming. It has taken place.'[130] Congress supporters made much of their ability to bring a contingent of Protestant workers from the Shankill Road to the 1934 Wolfe Tone commemoration march at Bodenstown and of their success in establishing local sections of the Congress in Belfast. It was certainly an achievement to get even 'two lorry loads'[131] of Protestant workers to a traditional Republican occasion, but then, as before and since, the actions of small groups and individuals were assigned a wholly spurious representative significance. These few Protestants were then used to shore up an approach to the mass of Protestant workers which, if they were aware of it, evoked only hostility.

O'Donnell could claim in Dublin that a 'great awakening' was taking place amongst Protestant workers. But economic discontent and even dissatisfaction with the Unionist regime hardly justified his claim that, 'Workers of non-nationalist stock are realising that their place is in a united front with their comrades in the south.'[132] The dominant strain in the coverage of the north in the *Republican Congress* was to emphasise that economic class consciousness was not enough, that Protestant workers had to move beyond the politics of the Northern Ireland Labour Party. 'The main weakness of anti-imperialist activities in Belfast working-class organisations has been a shying away from the national struggle for freedom.'[133] In an address to trade unionists in the Independent Labour Party hall in Belfast, O'Donnell attacked the NILP for

> dodging the Republican issue ... the working-class movement in the North-East has weakened the whole national struggle by its failure to see that its own freedom is inseparably bound up with the unity and freedom of an Irish Workers' Republic.[134]

In the face of developments like the sectarian riots in 1935, this incapacity to gauge the depth of Protestant working-class antagonism to 'the national struggle' could only sustain its optimism by more frantic attacks on the 'pro-imperialist' leaders of the northern labour movement and the reactionary and sectarian role of the IRA leadership in Belfast.

Prior to the outdoor relief riots, *An Phoblacht* had criticised northern republicans for being little more than a Catholic defence force and making no attempt to establish contacts with Protestants. Belfast republicans were said to be 'on the whole possessed of a bigotry that is dangerous to the cause they have at heart'.[135] The failure of the Belfast IRA to get involved in the outdoor relief strike as an organisation was also attacked by O'Donnell, who claimed that they had been encouraged to make contacts with the Protestant working class:

> But always the reply was a thousand and one good reasons why it could not be done. Even on the eve of the ODR workers' uprising the local OC pooh-poohed the idea that such a development was likely.[136]

It was true that, except for a small number of socialist-inclined volunteers and a small number of Protestant IRA men, the Belfast organisation was not fertile ground for social republicanism. Its concerns were predominantly military and geared towards its role of communal defence. As O'Donnell bluntly put it: 'We haven't a battalion of IRA men in Belfast; we just have a battalion of armed Catholics.'[137] To claim, as the Congress did, that, 'The erection of the border was made possible by the separation of the Republican movement from the working class movement,'[138] was, however, greatly to exaggerate the role of these negative features of Belfast republicanism.

The failure to achieve the Republic was explained away on the republican left by various failures of leadership – the 1919 failure to support the demands of the small farmers and landless men, or the Belfast IRA's lack of proselytising activity amongst the Protestant workers. That the problem lay in the objective was never raised as a possibility. Social republicanism emerged as a strategy evolved to overthrow the Treaty settlement. Its use of the language of class and its attempt to link republican objectives to social and economic issues did have some real effects. Most crucially, it ensured that Fianna Fáil sounded the note of agrarian radicalism in 1932, but although it could play a role in pushing Fianna Fáil to the 'left', it could

achieve little more. Attacks on de Valera in power only alienated its rural constituency, which feared 'socialism'. Left republicans had the weakest of roots in the southern working class
and only illusions about Protestant workers. The Congress
would split and disappear, divided between a majority led by
O'Donnell, who still held to the strategy of mobilising the
masses by demonstrating that only an economically and socially
radical strategy could achieve traditional republican objectives,
and a minority led by Michael Price and two of Connolly's children, who argued that only a specifically socialist objective
could ensure the support of the Protestant workers of Ulster.

The majority position completely failed to take account of
the fundamental change that Fianna Fáil's victory had brought
about. Before that, it was possible to argue for a radical republican movement to force Fianna Fáil to the left or even to displace the party altogether. With the resources of state power, de
Valera had proved able to siphon off large elements of the
republicans' constituency. It was much more difficult to
mobilise an 'anti-imperialist' united front when the government could not be so easily portrayed as a reactionary pro-
British rump.The minority position failed to attract because of
the manifest difficulties facing any exponent of a 'Workers'
Republic' in a state where the headquarters of the tiny
Communist Party had recently been burned down by a cleri-
cally-inspired mob. Nevertheless, its supporters made some
highly pertinent criticisms of the arguments of O'Donnell and
Gilmore. These had emphasised that the only principled
approach to adopt in Northern Ireland was to put the republican position straight to Protestant workers:

> It is harder to go among Protestant workers and insist that they
> must team up with the Republican masses against British
> Imperialism than to go under the banner of a Workers'
> Republic.[139]

In response, it was argued not simply that such propaganda
would get nowhere in Belfast, but even more significantly, that
the continued affiliation to republican objectives would tie the
movement to some of the most reactionary Catholic integrative political currents in the south. In an astonishingly pre-
scient attack on the proponents of a republican united front
strategy, Michael Price recalled a recent bellicose statement by

Seán T. O'Kelly, a Fianna Fáil Cabinet minister, threatening to impose the Republic on the north by force of arms and an offer by O'Duffy, the Blueshirt leader, to sink his differences with de Valera in a common campaign against Ulster. 'The united front movement might lead them to become involved in an attempt to make positive the jurisdiction of an all-Ireland Republic.'[140] It would in fact be the IRA, not the Congress, that would soon be involved in such a campaign. The social republicans had greatly exaggerated the radical potentialities of the rural and urban masses and were unable to combat the absorptive capacity of Fianna Fáil's populist nationalism to which they had contributed. On the issue of Protestant Ulster, social republicanism had failed utterly to escape the iron cage of nationalist assumptions and, while they might look with dismay at the subsequent IRA attempt forcibly to 'complete the national revolution', O'Donnell and his supporters would continue to judge all issues by their relationship to an objective they happily shared with the most conservative and militaristic elements of the IRA.

Notes

1. Dorothy Macardle, *The Irish Republic*, London 1968, p.772.
2. Ibid.
3. Michael Hopkinson, *Green Against Green: A History of the Irish Civil War*, Dublin 1988, p.268.
4. Ibid., p.7.
5. Sinn Féin received 27 per cent of the poll and 44 seats, Cumann na nGaedhael received 38.9 per cent of the vote and 63 seats: E. Rumpf and A.C. Hepburn, *Nationalism and Socialism in Twentieth-Century Ireland*, Liverpool 1977, p.88.
6. *An Phoblacht*, 22 January 1926, quoted in Richard Dunphy, 'Class Power and the Fianna Fáil Party: A Study of Hegemony in Irish Politics 1923-1948', unpublished DPhil thesis, European University Institute, Florence, 1988, p.91.
7. J. Bowyer Bell, *The Secret Army*, London 1972, pp.70-1.
8. Information on O'Donnell is from Grattan Freyer, *Peadar O'Donnell*, New Jersey 1973, Michael McInerney, *Peadar O'Donnell: Irish Social Rebel*, Dublin 1974, and Uinseann MacEoin, *Survivors*, Dublin 1980. The most comprehensive account of O'Donnell's role can be found in Richard English, *Radicals and the Republic: Socialist Republicanism in the Irish Free State 1925-37*, Oxford 1994.
9. Quoted in James McHugh, 'Voices of the Rearguard: A Study of *An Phoblacht*, Irish Republican Thought in the Post-Revolutionary Era 1923-1937', unpublished MA thesis, University College, Dublin, 1983, p.64.

10. Freyer, op.cit., p.30.
11. McInerney, op.cit., p.81.
12. MacEoin, op.cit., p.25.
13. Peadar O'Donnell, *There Will be Another Day*, Dublin 1963, p.11.
14. Seán O'Faoláin, *De Valera*, London 1939, p.167.
15. Deirdre McMahon, *Republicans and Imperialists*, New Haven and London 1984, pp.38-41.
16. O'Donnell, op.cit., p.22.
17. *An Phoblacht*, 3 October 1931.
18. C. Desmond Greaves, *Liam Mellows and the Irish Revolution*, London 1971, p.313.
19. Ibid. p.364.
20. O'Donnell, op.cit., p.10.
21. *An Phoblacht*, 12 November 1927.
22. David Howell, *A Lost Left*, Manchester 1986, p.79.
23. *An Phoblacht*, 25 March 1927.
24. Brian O'Neill, *The War for the Land In Ireland*, London 1933, p.14.
25. Terence Brown, *Ireland: A Social and Cultural History*, Glasgow 1981, p.97.
26. *An Phoblacht*, 17 September 1927.
27. Ibid., 17 December 1927.
28. *Nation*, 9 April 1927.
29. When he was acquitted of charges arising out of the Donegal agitation, the *Nation* congratulated him: 'We hope his example will give heart to leaders and people to put new vigour into the fight against the starvation and emigration party of the Free State.' 16 April 1927.
30. Seán Cronin (ed.), *The McGarrity Papers*, Tralee 1972, p.141.
31. *Nation*, 9 July 1927.
32. Ibid., 3 December 1927.
33. Ibid., 28 January 1928.
34. Ibid., 24 December 1927.
35. O'Donnell, op.cit., p.85.
36. *An Phoblacht*, 24 March 1928.
37. O'Donnell, op.cit., p.79.
38. *An Phoblacht*, 18 February 1928.
39. O'Donnell, op.cit., p.108.
40. The composition of the provisional organising committee of the Anti-Tribute League is in the Colonel Maurice Moore *Papers on Land Annuities*, National Library of Ireland 105060. The counties represented were Galway, Clare, Leitrim, Cork and Donegal.
41. *An Phoblacht*, 3 November 1928.
42. Lord Longford and T.P. O'Neill, *Eamonn De Valera*, Dublin 1970, p.261.
43. *Nation*, 13 July 1929.
44. Ibid., 19 October 1929.
45. *Connaught Telegraph*, 22 February 1930.
46. *An Phoblacht*, 28 June 1928.
47. *Nation*, 28 January 1928.
48. *Mayo News*, 14 January 1933.
49. Ibid.
50. Ibid.
51. Ibid., 10 January 1931.

52. Ibid., 6 February 1932.
53. *An Phoblacht,* 29 April 1927.
54. O'Donnell, op.cit., p.112.
55. Ibid., p.116.
56. *An Phoblacht,* 16 April 1928.
57. Bowyer Bell, op.cit., p.98.
58. T.P. Coogan, *The IRA,* London 1987, expanded edition, p.85.
59. *An Phoblacht,* 5 January 1929.
60. Commission of Inquiry into Banking, Currency and Credit, *Report P No. 2628,* Dublin 1938, p.24.
61. O'Donnell, op.cit., pp.118-9.
62. Ibid., p.131.
63. Bowyer Bell, op.cit., p.84.
64. The 1926 estimate is from Bowyer Bell, op.cit., p.76. The 1929 estimate is from a Department of Justice memorandum which quotes a police estimate of 1,300 officers and 3,500 volunteers, not including Cumann na mBan and Fianna Éireann. State Paper Office, 'Anti-State Activities, April 1929-October 1931', *5864 B.*
65. McHugh, op.cit., p.175.
66. 'Anti-State Activities.' *5844A.*
67. *An Phoblacht,* 5 April 1930, and M. Milotte, *Communism in Modern Ireland,* Dublin and New York 1984, p.98.
68. 'Anti-State Activities.' Memorandum regarding Activities of Certain Organisations, January 1931, *5864B.*
69. *An tOglach,* July 1931, included in *5844A.* Twomey wrote to McGarrity of 'the extraordinary growth of the volunteer movement' in June 1931, quoted in Dunphy, op.cit., p.184.
70. Letter from O'Duffy to secretary of Department of Justice, 27 July 1931, *5844A.*
71. Ibid.
72. *An Phoblacht,* 27 June 1931.
73. See Austen Morgan, 'Connolly and Connollyism: The Making of a Myth', *Irish Review,* No. 5, 1988.
74. Seán Cronin, *Frank Ryan,* Dublin 1980, p.34.
75. *An Phoblacht,* 3 October 1931.
76. Ibid.
77. He would maintain his republican credentials for a while at least. Thus the Department of Justice informed de Valera in January 1937 that he was one of two TDs, the other being Dan Breen, and a Senator who were at the burial of an IRA man in Tipperary when six men illegally discharged three volleys of shots over the grave. 'Anti-State Activities' *5864C,* 24 January 1937.
78. O'Donnell, op.cit., p.121.
79. Quoted in MacEoin, op.cit., p.6.
80. Ibid.
81. Dermot Keogh, 'The Red Scare' in J.P. O'Carroll and J.A. Murphy (eds), *De Valera and His Times,* Cork 1983, p.140.
82. Seán Cronin, *Frank Ryan,* p.36.
83. It was published as *For or Against the Ranchers? Irish Working Farmers in the Economic War,* Westport 1932.

84. *Mayo News*, 10 October 1931.
85. Charlotte H. Fallon, *Soul of Fire: A Biography of Mary MacSwiney*, Cork and Dublin 1986, p.151.
86. *Mayo News*, 24 October 1931.
87. McHugh, op.cit., p.418.
88. Ibid., p.222.
89. *Mayo News*, 17 October 1931.
90. Ibid., 10 October 1931.
91. *Round Table*, Vol.xviii, May 1928.
92. *An Phoblacht*, 19 November 1927.
93. M.A.G. Ó Tuathaigh, 'De Valera and Sovereignty' in O'Carroll and Murphy (eds), op.cit., p.67.
94. Cronin, *The McGarrity Papers*, p.166.
95. Letter from Fianna Fáil to the IRA Army Council in the immediate aftermath of the 1932 election victory quoted in ibid., p.152.
96. *Irish Times*, 10 January 1937.
97. McHugh, op.cit., p.80.
98. Cronin, *The McGarrity Papers*, p.152.
99. John Bowman, *De Valera and the Ulster Question*, Oxford 1985, p.126.
100. Hopkinson, op.cit., p.34. and Cronin, *The McGarrity Papers*, p.153.
101. Bowman, op.cit., pp.124-5.
102. MacEoin, op.cit., p.33.
103. See P. Bew, E. Hazelkorn and H. Patterson, *The Dynamics of Irish Politics*, London 1989, Chapter 2.
104. *Republican Congress*, 5 May 1934.
105. Ibid., and 6 October 1934.
106. George Gilmore, *The Irish Republican Congress*, Cork 1974, enlarged edition.
107. Quoted in ibid., p.35.
108. Ibid., p.36.
109. O'Donnell, *For or Against the Ranchers?*, p.5.
110. *Republican Congress*, 12 May 1934.
111. Ibid., 22 September 1934.
112. Ibid., 12 May 1934.
113. *Mayo News*, 30 June 1934.
114. *An Phoblacht*, 7 July 1934.
115. Gilmore, op.cit., p.34.
116. Ibid., pp.37-8.
117. Quoted in *Republican News*, 7 June 1975.
118. Freyer, op.cit., p.36.
119. *An Phoblacht*, 26 November 1927.
120. O'Neill, op.cit., p.14.
121. McHugh, op.cit., p.208.
122. On the split, see Charles McCarthy, *Trade Unions in Ireland 1890–1960*, Dublin 1977.
123. *An Phoblacht*, 4 August 1928.
124. Ibid., 23 February 1929.
125. Ibid., 24 June 1932, quoted in McHugh, op.cit., p.451.
126. Clare O'Halloran, *Partition and the Limits of Irish Nationalism*, Dublin 1987, p.42.

127. McHugh, op.cit., p.449.
128. *An Phoblacht*, 16 July 1932.
129. On Connolly and the Protestant working class, see Henry Patterson, *Class Conflict and Sectarianism*, Belfast 1980.
130. *Republican Congress*, 23 June 1934.
131. O'Donnell's description is given in R. Munck and B. Rolston, *Belfast in the Thirties: An Oral History*, Belfast 1987, p.183.
132. *Republican Congress*, 16 June 1934.
133. Gilmore, op.cit., p.36.
134. *Republican Congress*, 12 May 1934.
135. *An Phoblacht*, 20 August 1932.
136. *Republican Congress*, 18 August 1934.
137. Quoted in Munck and Rolston, op.cit., p.184. During the 1932 outdoor relief riots in Belfast, Tommy Geehan, the Communist leader of the agitation on levels of outdoor relief, asked for the protection of the IRA at meetings and marches. The request was refused, to the annoyance of social republicans in Dublin. See Margaret Geehan, 'The Activities of the Belfast Revolutionary Workers' Groups', unpublished BA dissertation, University of Ulster at Jordanstown, 1988, pp.28-9.
138. *Republican Congress*, 12 May 1934.
139. Ibid., 6 October 1934.
140. Ibid., 13 October 1934.

3 In de Valera's Shadow

For almost thirty years after the collapse of the Republican Congress, physical force separatism was the overwhelmingly dominant form of republican activity. The Congress's debacle was used to reinforce traditionalist nostrums concerning the futility of 'politicisation', while in reality the leadership of the IRA was content to accept de Valera's objectives as legitimate, reserving a continued role for the IRA simply by emphasising the need for an intransigent point of pressure to ensure that the risks of Fianna Fáil vacillation were minimised.

But as de Valera pressed ahead with creating a state that would satisfy the republican aspirations of broad swathes of the population, the IRA pretensions to the status of an alternative leadership became increasingly ludicrous. Membership of the IRA, which had soared in 1931-32, fell to 7,358 in 1935 and 3,844 a year later. In the same period the membership in the Dublin almost disappeared, falling from 490 in 1934 to 93 in 1936.[1] The collapse in the Dublin membership reflected the specific effects of an increasingly hard government line against the last vestiges of IRA 'radicalism' – its intervention in a transport strike in Dublin in March 1935, when volunteers sniped at army lorries used to replace trams and shot policemen.[2] As the situation in Spain moved towards civil war, a wave of anti-communist feeling developed in Catholic Ireland, with Dublin most liable to its irruptions. At the 1936 Easter commemoration march, contingents from the Communist Party and the remnants of the Republican Congress were stoned by the crowd.[3] A substantial number of left-wing IRA men were among the 400 or so Irish who fought for the Republic in Spain.[4]

The IRA leadership was increasingly dominated by those who saw the key to the 'Republic' in a military campaign in either Northern Ireland, Britain or in both. Fianna Fáil would be forced to complete the national revolution, not, as the Congress had predicted, through the activation of a grass-roots radical coalition but by armed action which would rekindle popular nationalist sentiment and force a confrontation with Britain. In part, of course, the IRA had little choice. Its very existence required at least the prospect of action. By 1936 it was clear that military activity in the south would invite a quick and predictable response from de Valera. After a number of IRA armed attacks on opponents, culminating in the murders of a retired Vice-Admiral in Cork in March 1936 and a policeman in April, the government proscribed the IRA and arrested many of its leaders, including the Chief of Staff, Moss Twomey.[5] For one of Twomey's successors, Sean Russell, an archetypal anti-political republican, there was no feasible way of shaking Fianna Fáil and the Treaty settlement except through exemplary violence *outside* the Free State, which he mistakenly assumed de Valera would have more difficulty in repressing.

In 1937 Sean MacBride, Chief of Staff and the main political intelligence remaining in the leadership after the Congress schism, accepted de Valera's new constitution with its 'de jure' claim to jurisdiction over the 32 counties as fulfilling most of the republicans' objectives. Any remaining national goals could be achieved peacefully, and thus, he declared, the IRA had no further role.[6] In marked contrast was the bitter denunciation uttered by the *Irish Democrat*, a paper produced by the remnants of the Republican Congress: 'De Valera has sanctified the property system arising from the Elizabethan, Cromwellian and Williamite Conquest with religious phrases.' But still O'Donnell and another prominent social republican who had returned temporarily from the Spanish war, Frank Ryan, counterposed to Fianna Fáil conservatism an abstract appeal for an all-Ireland conference of 'Separatists and Labour bodies' to restore the unity destroyed by the Treaty. This coalescence of an appeal to nation and class had as its premiss a real popular commitment to a progressive 32-county republic: 'We accuse the Fianna Fáil government of this: in a time of trial for the Nation, they ask less of the people than the people are eager and able to achieve.'[7]

That there was considerable and growing dissatisfaction with the limits of the post-1932 reforms, particularly in the country-side, would very soon become clear. But this dissatisfaction, while it might hold out possibilities of changing political align-ments *within* the southern state, could not shake the broad pop-ular sympathy for de Valera's movement towards a truncated but nevertheless effective form of sovereignty.

Popular aspirations for a full 32-county republic and a more egalitarian economic and social order may well have existed, although it was undoubtedly an exaggeration to claim that, 'The 1916 Proclamation was always read to promise a triumph of the poor over the small group of rich men who trafficked in their misery.'[8] But such aspirations could not easily be made the basis for an alternative national strategy to that of Fianna Fáil. This was not simply because, as essentially Irish Catholic aspirations, they had no appeal to the obdurate Protestants of Ulster; more fundamentally, they shared with Fianna Fáil the assumption that the attainment of full political sovereignty made the economic and social regeneration of Ireland a sim-ple matter of governmental will. This ingrained nationalist commonplace linked de Valera and many of his most bitter critics. By the end of the 1930s the limits of Fianna Fáil policies for economic and social regeneration were becoming clear:

> The great leap forward did not materialise. Emigration and rural depopulation were not halted. The link with sterling was maintained. The free flow of capital and labour between Ireland and Britain was not interfered with. Full-blooded pro-tectionism was being strongly diluted by the late thirties. Between the Coal-Cattle Pact of 1936 and the Anglo-Irish agree-ment of 1938 Ireland's trade pattern was returning to 'normal'; that is to say the economy of the Irish state was being reinte-grated into the larger trading economy of the neighbouring state.[9]

But just as the IRA militarists were trapped in a prison-house of assumptions centring on the notion that the two states had evolved from 'betrayal' – from the twists and turns of human desires and weaknesses rather than any factors of a more struc-tural nature – the remnants of social republicanism were trapped in the assumption that the manifest inequalities and oppressions of Irish life could be cured through a more radical, nationalist, political coalition, using the state to institute the socialist republic they claimed was implicit in 1916.

A striking characteristic of both the IRA and social republicanism throughout this period is that, whether 'left' or 'right', its focus was on completing the revolution by action, military or agitational, that would impose itself on the state governed by Fianna Fáil. In the dispute over whether a military campaign should be aimed at Britain or Northern Ireland, the proposal for a northern focus came from the veteran IRA leader Tom Barry from Cork. He proposed an attack across the border to seize a northern town, hold it as long as possible and withdraw, having, it was hoped, roused the population and forced the issue of partition upon a reluctant de Valera.[10] The rejection of this plan, which led to Barry's withdrawal from the IRA, had nothing at all to do with arguments against it from the IRA in Northern Ireland. As Bowyer Bell has noted of the IRA leadership from the 1920s to the 1940s:

> Despite the size and enthusiasm of the IRA in the Six Counties, the north had played only a minimal part in the leadership of the IRA. Rarely had a northerner served on GHQ [General Headquarters Staff] much less the Army Council, and rarely had the Dublin leadership given consideration to the problems of the north.[11]

Just as, for a brief period, an exaggerated view of the effects of the Great Depression on the Protestant working class had led the social republicans to accord the north a privileged place in their strategy for 'reconquest' of Ireland as a whole, so now a military campaign in Northern Ireland was proposed on the basis of little interest in, or knowledge of, conditions in the North, for what was essentially a southern purpose. The defeat of Barry's proposal may have reflected some residual distrust of the more sectarian and 'defenderist' aspects of the northern IRA, particularly in Belfast. Given the barrenness of the strategy that was decided upon, however, this appears doubtful. Rather, the debate over the objectives of the military campaign illustrates that the leadership regarded itself as still being potentially a major force in Irish political life. It had failed utterly to understand de Valera's effective closure of anti- Treaty aspirations.

Throughout the 1940s and 1950s, the attempt to relate republicanism to the realities of Irish life went on outside the

IRA. Absorbing the remaining members of the 'government' of the Second Dáil in 1938,[12] the IRA under Sean Russell's leadership 'declared war' on England and launched a campaign of sabotage and terror which confirmed its increasing marginalisation in Ireland where, buttressed by the massive popularity of his policy of neutrality, de Valera could take stringent measures to repress the IRA with little fear of popular repercussions. Military courts, internment and a small number of executions and deaths from hunger strikes, together with the predictable internal bickerings and charges of 'betrayal' born out of patent failure, had effectively destroyed much of the organisation by 1945. In February 1939 Russell had established contact with the German intelligence organisation, Abwehr II, which was to send agents to Ireland to encourage IRA activity in the north aimed at disrupting the British war effort. In May 1940 he arrived in Berlin, where he met prominent Nazis including Joachim von Ribbentrop, the Foreign Minister, and received training in sabotage. He was being transported back to Ireland by submarine when he took ill and died. Russell's intrigues with Germany, which came to nothing, were not uniformly popular in the south, where some IRA men looked askance at contacts with the Nazis.[13] In the north, the dominant response was to welcome anything that might lead to British defeat. Those few Belfast IRA men who had been touched by the 1930s radicalism could only look on in amused contempt as their comrades in jail jubilantly plotted the eastward march of the German army into the Soviet Union.[14]

Towards a Border War

Defeat and marginalisation would teach no lessons. Neither would the increasing evidence of rural and urban discontent with the de Valera dispensation. Dissatisfaction with the limited nature of Fianna Fáil agrarian reforms and their failure to deal seriously with the continuing problems of under-employment and emigration in the west was expressed in the temporary success of a western peasants' party, Clann na Talmhan (Children of the Land) founded in 1938. It won 11 per cent of the vote and fourteen seats in the Dáil election of 1943. The limits of the industrial policies of tariff protection and job creation were also clear by the 1940s, and in the 1943 election the Irish

Labour Party substantially increased its vote – from 10 per cent to 15 per cent – almost doubling its Dáil representation from nine to seventeen.[15] Although this advance would be soon checked by a major split, fuelled by nationalism, antagonism to British-based unions and anti-communism, in both the Labour Party and the Irish TUC, there was clear evidence that the material existed for a radical attack on Fianna Fáil.[16]

When it came, it was led by the ex-IRA leader Sean MacBride, who founded a new party, Clann na Poblachta (Family of the Republic) in 1946. Rumpf and Hepburn summed up its fundamental dynamics as expressing

> the dissatisfaction of the more constructive members of the younger generation of Republicans, both with the growing conservatism and machine politics of Fianna Fáil and with the arid brutality which had characterised the IRA.[17]

Its specific policies on the economy – repatriation of Irish capital invested abroad, breaking of the monetary link with sterling, substantial government investment to stimulate a depressed economy – resembled a revamped radical Fianna Fáil platform of the 1920s. Its achievement of 13 per cent of the vote and ten seats in the Dáil in 1948 was a central factor in displacing Fianna Fáil from office for the first time since 1932. However its acceptance of places in a coalition government which included the anti-republican Fine Gael only alienated many of its supporters. More fundamentally, it demonstrated the problems for any political party in the southern state which combined its appeal to social radicalism with an inchoate hope that, just as it was possible for a Dublin government to take a more active role in dealing with unemployment, poverty and disease, so it was open to it by a simple act of will also to 'solve' the national question.

The result of MacBride's brief irruption into mainstream politics was a self-interested scramble for nationalist credentials between the coalition parties and Fianna Fáil, manifested in the declaration of a Republic in 1948 and the launching of an all-party Anti-Partition Campaign. This campaign, with its origins in the dynamics of inter-party competition in the south, highlighted the 'affront' of partition in an intense propaganda onslaught in Ireland and abroad, but failed miserably, though predictably, to alter the situation. Its effect on the

IRA, however, was substantial.

The initial success of Clann na Poblachta encouraged the remnants of the IRA (in 1948 the 'General Headquarters Staff' estimated that the organisation had 200 activists and some hundreds of sympathisers[18]) to equip themselves with a political arm by re-establishing the link with Sinn Féin – by taking over the moribund organisation. This politicisation had two notable characteristics. The first and more important was to be the clear subordination of the political organisation to the IRA Army Council. At an Army Convention in 1949 a resolution was passed instructing the IRA to infiltrate and take control of Sinn Féin.[19] The second was the staggering backwardness of its economic and social programme.

The 'National Unity and Independence Programme' of Sinn Féin referred to a 'reign of social justice based on Christian principles'. These were the corporatist vocational principles which had so enamoured the Blueshirts and the Catholic hierarchy in the 1930s and which Fianna Fáil, to its credit, eventually rejected.[20] In the late 1940s, they had been narrowed down to the matter of intense Church opposition to any attempt to 'import' the 'socialistic' welfare state from the United Kingdom. It was the attempt by the radical Minister of Health, Noel Browne of Clann na Poblachta, to provide free health care for pregnant women and nursing mothers which would destroy the coalition and MacBride's new party.[21] In this crucial conflict between a government minister and the Catholic hierarchy, the republican movement's position was an implicitly miserable one. While the Unionist government in the north was able to use the 'Mother and Child' affair to intensify its depiction of the Republic as priest-ridden and backward, Sinn Féin, now the mouthpiece for an organisation which had decided in 1948 to prepare for a military campaign against the 'occupied Six Counties',[22] declared itself for vocational principles and against the welfare state.[23] The new monthly paper of Sinn Féin, the *United Irishman*, swore its fidelity to the republican saint Wolfe Tone and his objective of destroying English rule by 'unity of Protestant, Catholic and Dissenter'. At the same time, however, it persisted in the characteristic Catholic nationalist fixation with the supposed power of southern Freemasonry,[24] and was content to reject blithely such manifestations of the 'British link' as the welfare state, which was massively popular with the Protestant working class.

Most IRA members were, of course, little interested in social philosophy, Marxist, Catholic or otherwise. Most would have been practising Catholics with no time for politics, particularly if they were tainted by 'communism' (a capacious term in post-war Ireland). Like their Chief of Staff, Tony Magan, they were dedicated to a republican ideal narrowed down to reunification by physical force. There were exceptions to this general rule, and some of these would play a key role in the 1960s. In a book which recalls one of the darkest and most arid periods for the IRA – the 1939-1940 bombing campaign in England – Brendan Behan claims to have declared to his captors that he had come over 'to fight for the Irish Workers and Small Farmers Republic'.[25] He typically differentiated his own variety of republicanism from those of

> your wrap-the-green-flag-round-me junior civil servants that came into the IRA from the Gaelic League, and were ready to die for their country any day of the week, purity in their hearts, truth on their lips, for the glory of God and the honour of Ireland.[26]

Behan's working-class background in north Dublin was shared with a friend, Cathal Goulding, who had joined Fianna Éireann – the junior wing of the IRA – in 1937 at the age of eleven. Goulding's grandfather had been a member of the Invincibles – the group responsible for the murder of the two most senior British officials in Ireland in 1882 – and his father and uncle had both been in the IRA. His father was a house-painter who, like many anti-Treatyites, found it extremely difficult to get work in the aftermath of the Civil War because of hostility from many employers. He set himself up as a self-employed contractor and his son would combine work as a painter and active membership of the IRA. Both his parents had been sympathetic to social republicanism, and Austin Stack's pamphlet 'The Constructive Work of Dáil Éireann', outlining the 'responsible' attitude taken by the First Dáil to divisive land and labour issues, was used as a primer on the dangers of reactionary degeneration within the republican movement.[27]

Class consciousness, however, was not to act for Goulding as a solvent of republican intransigence and militarism until the collapse of the IRA's next military campaign. In Dublin, at least, it was possible for traditions of working-class militancy to

influence some members of the IRA, even in its most militarist
and reactionary period. In Goulding's north Dublin, James
Larkin, the charismatic leader of the 1913 lock-out, had been
elected to the Dáil in 1928 with over 8,000 votes as a candidate
of the Irish Workers' League which he had founded as the Irish
section of the Communist Third International.[28] Yet such class
consciousness tended to be sublimated into a militaristic
intransigence and self-justifying belief that the fundamental
mistake of people like O'Donnell and Gilmore was to take
action that put them outside the 'army', and that ultimately the
task was to win the IRA to radical politics. This formidable task
was made no easier by the fact that these faint echoes of the
Congress debates were soon drowned out by strident anti-
partitionism.

In the late 1930s and 1940s the IRA was composed predominantly of people whose focus was still on the Civil War and the
subsequent divisions and redivisions of anti-Treatyism. For all
its often barren bitterness, it still had a capacity, especially in
its urban form, to express a deep, intransigent opposition to
the Irish state. From 1949 onwards, as the anti-partition campaign dominated public life in the south, a new generation of
IRA members emerged whose focus was largely an extreme
variant of official propaganda. The new members who flocked
into Sinn Féin, and thence to the IRA, had received their for-
mative political education not from the stock republican lita-
nies of the evils of 'Free Statism' but from the leaflets and pamphlets on the evils of partition produced by the southern state.
For Tomás MacGiolla, later president of Sinn Féin, political
education began with a massive all-party rally held in
O'Connell Street in 1949 to condemn the passage of the
Ireland Act at Westminster as an 'iniquitous' solidification of
partition. The 'national question' became identified with the
ending of the British-supported 'Orange State' thanks to the
thorough and well-produced pamphlets detailing Unionist discrimination and gerrymandering which the all-party campaign
had produced.[29] Then came the collapse of the coalition government and the return in 1951 of a lacklustre Fianna Fáil
administration whose energies were totally absorbed in an
unimaginative response to the Republic's burgeoning economic crisis. For many like MacGiolla, enthused and mobilised
in 1949-50 and observing the lack of results from the campaign
of the constitutional parties, membership of Sinn Féin was a

natural progression, as was support for the armed assault on
Northern Ireland to which the IRA had been committed since
1948.

Republicans could not have been unaware of the massive crisis of the Republic's domestic economy in the mid-1950s, when
unemployment rocketed and emigration levels reached and
surpassed their worst pre-independence levels. However these
developments were treated not as evidence of the bankruptcy
of de Valera's ideals of economic autarky but rather as signs
that 'Free-Statism' could only corrupt and violate what were
essentially sound principles of national development. Thus
while the crisis impelled Fianna Fáil to jettison the economics
of Sinn Féin and to reintegrate the Republic into the world
economy, it confirmed the republican movement in its full-
blooded protectionism. MacGiolla and other republicans
watched trains arrive in Dublin's Westland Row station from
the west of Ireland, packed to capacity with those who were
going straight on to the mailboats at Dun Laoghaire and emigration. They gave out leaflets at rallies of the unemployed in
O'Connell Street.[30] The message was the consoling one that
until the 'British occupation' of the Six Counties was ended the
economic depression would not be ended – a prediction that
would prove more damaging to the IRA in the Irish Republic
than the predictable failure of its armed campaign in Northern
Ireland, which was launched at the end of 1956.

Idealism and Sectarianism in the 1956 Campaign

Within less than a year of its launch, the border campaign had
clearly failed, and for reasons that were predicted before it
commenced, yet it dragged on from 1956 to 1962. The delay in
launching the campaign, which had caused much dissatisfaction in the ranks and led to a couple of anticipatory splinter
attacks in Northern Ireland, reflected a debate inside the IRA
leadership over the viability of a guerrilla campaign in the
midst of a hostile majority population. As an alternative to a
guerrilla campaign, some leaders suggested a longer-term strategy: first, sabotage of transport and communications to bring
everyday life to a standstill and, second, preparation of the
nationalist population for a civil disobedience campaign. The
latter, it was calculated, would provoke repression from the

police and the B Special constabulary (which was particularly unpopular among Catholics) and provide the space for the IRA to emerge as a 'people's' defence force.[31]

Instead it was decided to opt for Seán Cronin's Operation Harvest, a plan for a guerrilla campaign waged initially by 'flying columns' from the south which would sabotage communications, destroy police barracks and ultimately create 'liberated areas'. Cronin, a Kerryman and ex-member of the Free State army who had recently returned from the United States, was a forceful personality and the acceptance of his strategy seems to have owed as much to the energy and conviction with which he argued it as to any more substantial factor. It was sadly lacking any grasp of northern realities. Indeed, one of its attractions was precisely its effective suppression of the dynamics of northern sectarianism. For as long as the IRA's activities were focused on creating 'liberated areas' in some of the predominantly Catholic borderlands of Northern Ireland, the question of the repercussions of such activities on Catholic-Protestant relations, particularly in the sectarian cockpit of Belfast, could be ignored.

The IRA Army Council was also well aware that action in the north was necessary to undermine support that had emerged for heretical anti-abstentionist ideas amongst some republicans. The key figure was Liam Kelly, an IRA man from Pomeroy in County Tyrone. Influenced by the formation of Clann na Poblachta, and particularly by Sean MacBride, Kelly persuaded a majority of Tyrone republicans to support the idea of a new political organisation, Fianna Uladh (Soldiers of Ulster) and a new military organisation, Saor Uladh (Free Ulster). Kelly agreed with MacBride that the 1937 Constitution should legitimise the southern state, particularly now that the coalition had taken the Free State out of the Commonwealth and established a Republic in 1948. As a consequence he argued for an end to abstentionism in the south and a concentration of republican effort against the state of Northern Ireland. Expelled from the IRA in 1951 for planning an operation without authorisation, he was elected to the Stormont parliament for Mid-Tyrone in 1953. His support base by then extended to Derry and Belfast, where some younger republicans – including a later leader of Official republicanism, Billy McMillen – were attracted by his mixture of political and military activism. Jailed for making 'seditious statements', Kelly was nominated by MacBride and elected to the Irish Senate in 1954. His release from prison in August 1954 was the occasion of a serious riot in Pomeroy, when thousands of his supporters clashed with the RUC. In November 1955 Saor Uladh attacked the RUC station at Roslea, County Fermanagh, and in November 1956 Saor Uladh and another splinter group attacked six customs posts along the border with the Republic.[32]

These developments made inevitable some sort of 'decisive' response from the IRA. The Army Council was no doubt encouraged by the 1955 Westminster election results. Two IRA arms raids on army barracks in Armagh and Omagh in 1954, the second of which led to the capture and imprisonment of eight IRA members, had done much to restore republican morale. In the election Sinn Féin contested all twelve Ulster constituencies, half of them with men in prison for the Omagh raid. The result was the largest anti-partition vote since the formation of the state – 152,310 votes – and victories in Mid-Ulster and Fermanagh-South Tyrone.[33] Interestingly, the only constituency with a large Catholic population in which the Sinn Féin candidate did not perform well was West Belfast. Here Sinn Féin's neglect of economic and social issues ensured that it trailed behind an Irish Labour Party candidate – the Catholic working class would remain wedded to various versions of labourist and republican labour politics until the late 1960s.[34] Meanwhile Cronin's strategy would direct the IRA's attentions to the redoubts of intransigent rural republicanism in the border areas and north Antrim.

On the night of 12 December 1956 Operation Harvest began and approximately 150 men were involved in attacks on ten different targets in Northern Ireland. By its end six members of the RUC and eleven republicans were dead, a relatively small number by comparison with the 1970s and 1980s, but a significant loss of life in the atmosphere of the time.[35] Its highpoint was the abortive attack on Brookeborough RUC station in Fermanagh in January 1957. Like all the 'flying columns', that which attacked Brookeborough was composed of IRA men from the south with only the skimpiest knowledge of local conditions. Two of the group, Sean Garland from Dublin and Daithi O'Connaill from Cork, would play crucial and conflicting roles in post-1962 republican rethinking. The key figures in the attack would be the two IRA men who were killed during it – Sean South and Feargal O'Hanlon. The deaths of two young idealists – as they were widely perceived in Catholic Ireland – resulted in a powerful spasm of public emotion:

> When the bodies of South and O'Hanlon were carried across the border, their transmutation from young men into martyrs began. There began a week of all but national mourning. Crowds lined the route of South's funeral cortege to Dublin . . . Town Councils and County Corporations passed votes of sympathy.[36]

In the general election which occurred soon after, Sinn Féin's nineteen candidates received just over 5 per cent of the vote and it had four TDs elected. These were unexpected victories but, as Rumpf and Hepburn noted, the result was 'ultimately insignificant'.[37] Mass concern over the coalition government's lack of response to a massive economic crisis was the decisive issue in giving de Valera a last impressive election victory. In 1956 he had made it clear to emissaries from the IRA who had asked for his co-operation or connivance in the planned campaign that he thought partition could not be ended by force.[38] As the futile campaign sputtered on, producing only internment (eventually over 250 people were interned in Northern Ireland) and a massive mobilisation of the police and 13,000 B Specials,[39] interest and sympathy evaporated. In July 1957, after the IRA had killed an RUC man in County Armagh, internment was introduced in the Republic and nearly 200 were rounded up.[40] Catholic disillusionment was plain in the Westminster election in October 1959 when the Sinn Féin vote slumped by more than half.[41] In the Republic the Sinn Féin vote in the 1961 general election declined to 36,393 for 21 candidates – 3 per cent – and only one was elected.[42]

The IRA's Army Council had addressed an appeal to the Protestants of Northern Ireland to support the independence movement, in the very midst of its military campaign.[43] The exotic futility of this gesture should not obscure the nagging doubts and suspicions which some southern republicans had about a too-direct mobilisation of the forces of grievance and traditional animosity which existed in the Catholic population in the north. It is still unclear whether, as some claim, a decision was made not to include the Belfast IRA in the campaign, so as to avoid the possibility of sectarian conflict,[44] or whether Belfast's non-involvement reflected fears that its personnel were too well known to the police.[45] What is clear is that the order from the IRA GHQ that all possible steps had to be taken to avoid shooting members of the part-time Protestant constabulary – the B Specials – was intensely unpopular with northern IRA men and their sympathisers.[46] Regarded by the government and the Protestant population as the 'eyes and ears' of the state, with a detailed knowledge of their Catholic neighbours, the Specials were the focus of much fear and animosity. Attacks on the Specials were opposed on the basis that their deep roots in local Protestant communities would ensure that such attacks would provoke bitter sectarian animosities. As the IRA campaign reeled under its own futilities and the introduction of internment north and south, some began to query the wisdom of excluding action that would at least restore flagging Catholic interest and support.

Ironically, it was Seán Cronin, whose original plan had effectively marginalised the appeal to Catholic communalism, who in 1959 appeared willing to contemplate the risky venture of a Belfast campaign. By then the leadership was bitterly divided over whether the campaign should be called off, with Cronin to the fore in pressing for its continuance. He hoped to ensure revival through a sharp change in focus from the border areas to Belfast. Sean Garland, a survivor of the campaign's most martyrogenic action, the attack on Brookeborough RUC station, was chosen to mobilise the Belfast IRA. Disguised as a Glasgow university student but largely ignorant of the city and its republican sub-culture, he had just enough time to discover widespread demoralisation before he was arrested and gaoled in the Crumlin Road prison, where his mission was received with sullen resentment by the many IRA prisoners who regarded the campaign as by then an obvious and definitive failure.[47]

For some in the Belfast IRA, the failure of 'Operation Harvest' stemmed directly from its fastidiousness. As the national leadership settled its divisions by intrigue – Cronin was displaced by an organised letter-writing campaign from Irish-America which used anti-communism and other disreputable charges against his radical American wife[48] – the remaining republicans in Crumlin Road speculated on what, if anything, their future might be. Attempts to politicise such discussion were received with hostility.[49] More typical would have been the jocular remark of a future leading Belfast Provisional, that a military campaign of the 1956 sort was 'no use' and that the only way forward was to 'shoot a lot of priests and ministers', thus ensuring a strong communal base for the IRA in the resulting sectarian polarisation.[50] Such sentiments reflected a stubborn reality of the northern situation which the idealist rhetoric of 'Wolfe Tone' republicanism found hard to recognise, let alone deal with.

Notes

1. Seán Cronin, *The McGarrity Papers*, Tralee 1972, p.166.
2. J. Bowyer Bell, *The Secret Army*, London 1972, p.150, and M. Milotte, *Communism in Modern Ireland*, Dublin and New York 1984, p.236.
3. T.P. Coogan, *The IRA*, London 1987, p.112.
4. Bowyer Bell, op.cit., p.164.
5. Ronan Fanning, 'De Valera and the IRA 1923-1940' in J.P. O'Carroll and J.A. Murphy (eds), *De Valera and His Times*, Cork 1983, p.166.
6. Seán Cronin, *Frank Ryan*, Dublin 1980, p.175.
7. *Irish Democrat*, 8 May 1937.
8. Ibid.
9. M.A.G. Ó Tuathaigh, 'De Valera and Sovereignty' in O'Carroll and Murphy (eds), op.cit., p.70.
10. Coogan, op.cit., and J.A. Murphy, 'The New IRA 1925-62' in T.D. Williams (ed.), *Secret Societies in Ireland*, Dublin and New York 1973, p.158.
11. Bowyer Bell, op.cit., p.166.
12. Murphy, op.cit., p.166.
13. Seán Cronin, *Frank Ryan*, pp.182-90.
14. Interview with Jack Brady. The pro-Nazi orientation of many republicans was still expressed even after the end of the Second World War. In 1948 an Irish-American visited Dan Breen, the legendary IRA man whose unit had initiated the War of Independence with the killing of two RIC men at Soloheadbeg. He was taken aback to see two pictures of Adolf Hitler on the walls of his hero's study. As Breen explained to the shocked American, 'He fought for freedom but not for democracy.' John S. Monagan, 'An Irishman's Diary', *Irish Times*, 24 February 1997.
15. Peter Mair, *The Changing Irish Party System*, London 1987, p.24 and E. Rumpf and A.C. Hepburn, *Nationalism and Socialism in Twentieth-Century Ireland*, Liverpool 1977, p.149.
16. See Charles McCarthy, *Trade Unions in Ireland 1894-1960*, Dublin 1977.
17. Rumpf and Hepburn, op.cit., p.145.
18. Bowyer Bell op.cit., p.290.
19. Coogan, op.cit., p.293.
20. Ibid., p.331. On vocationalism, see Joe Lee, 'Aspects of Corporatist Thought in Ireland: the Commission on Vocational Education, 1929-43' in A. Cosgrove and D. McCartney (eds), *Studies in Irish History*, Dublin 1979.
21. See Noel Browne's autobiography, *Against the Tide*, Dublin 1986.
22. Bowyer Bell, op.cit., p.292.
23. Coogan, op.cit., p.330.

24. Ibid. p.332.
25. Brendan Behan, *Borstal Boy*, London 1967, p.13.
26. Ibid., p.86.
27. Interview with Cathal Goulding and a long and useful interview with Goulding in the *Starry Plough*, the Official Republican paper in Derry, Easter 1972.
28. Richard Dunphy, 'Class, Power and the Fianna Fáil Party: A Study of Hegemony in Irish Politics 1923-48', unpublished DPhil thesis, European University Institute, Florence, 1988.
29. Interview with Tomás MacGiolla.
30. Ibid.
31. Murphy, op.cit., p.162.
32. On Liam Kelly, see Michael Farrell, *Northern Ireland: The Orange State*, London 1976, pp.205-6, 213 and 219-20; Coogan, op.cit., pp.360-1 and interview with Paddy Joe McClean.
33. Figures from Farrell, op.cit., p.209. The established pattern in elections in Northern Ireland from the 1920s was for the constitutionalist Nationalist Party to contest elections for the Northern Ireland parliament and for Sinn Féin to contest Westminster elections – Rumpf and Hepburn, op.cit., pp.183-4.
34. Farrell, op.cit., p.224. The Irish Labour Party began an attempt to organise in Northern Ireland after the decision of the Northern Ireland Labour Party in 1949 to come out clearly in support of the link with Britain. A republican-socialist group then seceded from the NILP and became the basis for the extension of the ILP. Rumpf and Hepburn, op.cit., pp.190-1.
35. Coogan, op.cit., p.384.
36. Bowyer Bell, op.cit., p.353.
37. The victories were in the border constituencies of Monaghan and Sligo-Leitrim; in adjacent Longford-Westmeath and in South Kerry, a stronghold of traditionalist republicanism; Rumpf and Hepburn, op.cit., p.153.
38. Lord Longford and T.P. O'Neill, *Eamon de Valera*, Dublin 1970, p.445.
39. Farrell, op.cit., p.216.
40. Ibid., p.218 and Bowyer Bell, op.cit., p.360.
41. Farrell, op.cit., p.220.
42. Bowyer Bell, op.cit., p.392.
43. *Republican Manual of Education: Part Two – Historical*, Dublin n.d., p.34.
44. Interview with Tomás MacGiolla.
45. Bowyer Bell, op.cit., p.383.
46. Interviews with Francie Donnelly and Sean Garland.
47. Interview with Sean Garland.
48. Interviews with Cathal Goulding and Sean Garland.
49. Interview with Francie Donnelly.
50. Quoted by Jim Sullivan in interview.

4   A Limited Reassessment:
The IRA after 1962

In June 1963 an incident occurred in Belfast which epitomised the contradictory impulses at the heart of republicanism as it sought to recover from the failure of the border campaign. A march was to be held to celebrate the 200th anniversary of Wolfe Tone's birth. It was part of a series of activities organised by the Wolfe Tone Society, which had emerged from discussions between Cathal Goulding, Seán Cronin and Dick Roche in Dublin and a small group of republicans, nationalists and labourites there and in Belfast.[1] In Belfast, the urge behind the Wolfe Tone Society – to create a broad coalition of 'progressive' and 'nationally-minded' forces – ran up against the brutal wall of communal assertiveness. The Belfast IRA had been asked to act as a colour party, but when the police forbade the carrying of an Irish tricolour, the IRA commander in Belfast, Billy McKee, assented. This decision was bitterly contested by the bulk of Belfast IRA men and, despite Goulding's attempt to mediate, McKee was forced to resign and was replaced by Billy McMillen. A march inspired by a strategy apparently aimed at building a new 'anti-imperialist' alliance to include at least a section of the Protestant community would in fact herald a period of intensifying conflict between the police and republicans on an issue which could reinvigorate communal solidarity amongst Catholics but left even progressive Protestants cold.[2]

Goulding was now Chief of Staff of the IRA, his reputation for leftism notwithstanding. Imprisonment in England during the first three years of the border campaign meant that he was

untainted by its failure and in any case, the general demoralisation was such that no one else wanted the job.[3] The Army
Convention in 1962, at which his tenure commenced, marked
the beginning of a process of assessment of the state of the IRA
and a reassessment of the history of the republican movement.
For Goulding, such a reassessment meant, in part, a return to
the debates of the inter-war period, with the aim of reconsti-
tuting the IRA as a vanguard of social republicanism. It was in
this context that he made overtures to intellectuals outside the
IRA. The nature of this external input has been the subject of
bitter controversy, but little useful information or analysis has
been forthcoming. The split in the IRA and Sinn Féin in 1969-
70 would see Goulding's opponents claim that he had allowed
'Marxists' to take effective strategic direction of the republican
movement. These claims have been somewhat uncritically
repeated in Bishop and Mallie's history of the Provisionals.[4]
What was the significance of these external influences?

The two key individuals involved in this process were
Anthony Coughlan and Roy Johnston. Both had lived in
England and been involved there in the activities of the
Connolly Association, which had emerged from the disintegrating Republican Congress. A London branch reconstituted
itself as a Connolly Club, and this was subsequently revived by
an influx of Irish International Brigaders.[5] Its monthly paper,
the *Irish Democrat*, had been edited since 1947 by Desmond
Greaves, a member of the Communist Party of Great Britain
and author of a major, if tendentious, biography of Connolly.[6]
Under his leadership the Connolly Association concentrated
on organising among Irish emigrants with two principal aims:
'first their own defence, second the freedom of their country'.[7]
It also sought to influence the British labour movement away
from what was seen as its dangerous mixture of apathy and pro-
Unionism on the Irish question.

During the border campaign the Connolly Association concentrated on attacking the Unionist government for interning
republicans and began to press the British government to use its
power under the Government of Ireland Act to legislate for civil
rights in Northern Ireland.[8] As early as 1955, the *Irish Democrat*
had put forward the idea of a civil rights campaign as the way to
shatter Ulster Unionism.[9] For a year in 1960-61 Coughlan acted
as a full-time organiser for the Connolly Association, promoting
'anti-Unionist political activity in Britain',[10] including a march

from London to Birmingham to raise the issue of British acquiescence in Unionist rule.[11] A graduate of University College,
Cork, who had been in London from 1958 doing post-graduate
work, Coughlan returned to a lectureship in social administration in Trinity College, Dublin, in 1961. He was a fervent republican in the sense that he saw the central issue of Irish politics as
the completion of the national revolution. He believed, however, that this could not be achieved by the physical force tradition but only by the creation of a broad national coalition in
which the labour movement would play a central role. The
objective of this movement was 'real' independence, not socialism. In Northern Ireland the objective would be to destabilise
Unionism by reforms which would detach enough Protestants
from the Unionist Party to create a 'progressive' coalition:
'Stormont could then be used against imperialism,' to quote his
friend and mentor Greaves.[12]

Coughlan was invited to join the Wolfe Tone Society in 1964
when it was decided to maintain it as a permanent 'think tank'
of 'active people with roots in the language, trade union, co-
operative, republican and other organisations'.[13] The Wolfe
Tone Society was to provide the intellectual resources for a unification of 'the bulk of the radical-minded elements in the
existing trade union and republican movement' in a new revolutionary political organisation.[14] Goulding and Cronin had
played a role in initiating the Wolfe Tone Society, but its subsequent development was not heavily influenced by the IRA. In
fact, the IRA was undergoing a parallel process of development
in which some of the central ideas propagated by the Wolfe
Tone Society were to play a crucial if controversial role.

Coughlan's ideas on the economic conjuncture and subsequently on the reform of Stormont had considerable influence
on the IRA's reassessment. Although he made a direct contribution to the Army Council's discussions on future strategy, he
was determined to maintain a position of independence and
refused all requests to join the organisation.[15] The person
responsible for bringing such ideas directly into the IRA's internal education programme was Roy Johnston. From a middle-
class Dublin Protestant background, Johnston had a science
doctorate from Trinity College, Dublin. In England between
1960 and 1963 he had been active in both the Communist Party
and the Connolly Association.[16] On returning to Dublin he
joined the Wolfe Tone Society, but, unlike Coughlan, became

deeply involved in the IRA's re-orientation. Goulding had met him in the Wolfe Tone Society and was impressed with his abilities. Goulding was unburdened by the common IRA disdain for 'civilians' and, with a background which predisposed him to social republicanism, he was eager for Johnston to play an active role in internal discussion and education. It was possible for individuals to join Sinn Féin and not be a member of the IRA, but the clear subordination of the 'political wing' to the army meant that 'real' membership of the republican movement dictated membership of the IRA. For this reason, Johnston joined the IRA, and it was this, and in particular his role in the education of volunteers rather than his position as education officer for Sinn Féin, that caused intense disquiet among more traditional members.[17]

Goulding appears to have had a largely instrumental attitude to people like Coughlan and Johnston and to his generally good relations with Irish Communists, particularly those in Belfast. He would later observe of this period that, 'Most of our people were very naïve about making political demands.'[18] The IRA needed to import some theoretical assistance for its rethinking process. However he also believed that such ideas would be relatively easily harnessed to the principal purpose:

> We knew that if we were to retain the leadership of the movement, and maintain the movement itself as a revolutionary organisation, we would need to have a policy for the next phase of the fight against British imperialism in Ireland.[19]

The long severance between the IRA and social republicanism dictated that this tradition had to be reappropriated from largely external sources, but for Goulding this would create the conditions not for the demise of the IRA but for its reconstitution as armed guarantor of the social and political gains of a revolutionary popular movement. For all its dramatic effects in the 1960s, the new thinking was in central respects traditionalist.

Regressive Modernisation

There was much that was critical and innovative in the approach of Coughlan and Johnston. In particular there was an emphasis on the republican movement's intellectual bankruptcy. In a key

analysis, Coughlan emphasised the need for theory: 'It is time
that Irish republicans began to take ideas and theory seriously.'[20] Republicanism had proven itself incapable of developing 'the substantial body of theoretical writing' of the major
Irish revolutionaries of the past and applying it to contemporary
circumstances. As a result it had no engagement with some of
the most crucial questions of contemporary politics:

> We ask where has the republican movement put forward an
> authoritative criticism of the Second Programme of Economic
> Expansion of the Fianna Fáil party as it leads Ireland back
> towards economic union with Britain? [In 1964 the Fianna Fáil
> government published its Second Programme of Economic
> Expansion to continue the process of trade liberalisation and
> attraction of foreign capital begun with the First Programme in
> 1959.] Or of the reasons for the failure of the Irish cultural and
> language movement to achieve more success in the past forty
> years than it has in fact done? Where is the ruthless analysis of
> the failure of either republicanism or labour to significantly
> influence government policy in the 26 Counties since the
> southern state was founded?[21]

Although there is no doubting the radical and progressive
intent of this approach and its desire to demilitarise the republican movement – 'Superior ideas are more effective than
armies in that the changes they bring about are more permanent'[22] – it was ultimately limited by its traditionalist ideological horizon. This was set out most clearly in the constitution
of the Wolfe Tone Society, which as a description of 'Ireland
Today' said little with which a leader writer in the *Irish Press*
(the pro-Fianna Fáil daily) would have disagreed:

> The Irish people, north and south, are one nation sharing com-
> mon history on a common territory . . . No real conflict of inter-
> est exists between any section of the common people, either
> between different sections of the people of the north, or
> between north and south. Propaganda which depicts imaginary
> causes for division, which fosters artificial conflicts, or which
> exaggerates regional differences in character in order to justify
> the political division of the country, is false propaganda . . . The
> partition of Ireland is inimical to the interests of all Irish peo-
> ple; is the cause of all the exceptional political and economic
> problems from which Ireland has suffered for the past 40 years
> and today is the main barrier to the solution of those problems

... Economically ... partition is responsible for Ireland's excep-
tional problems of unemployment and emigration ... The basis
of partition in the Six Counties is an artificially fostered sectarianism, an anti-Catholic prejudice and bigotry which has become
identified with the state system ... without which the system
could not survive and without which there would be no reason
for its existence ...[23]

The traditional nationalist assumptions of one nation, 'artifi-
cial' divisions implanted by Britain, the identification of the
popular basis of Ulster Unionism with sectarianism, the identification of reform as a prerequisite for winning Protestants to
the cause of national independence were thought to have a
renewed and radical significance precisely because Fianna Fáil
was in the process of openly and flagrantly betraying them for
the first time.

In the debate that split the Republican Congress, O'Donnell
had claimed that the slogan of a 'Workers' Republic' would
allow de Valera to continue to hegemonise workers and small
farmers by identifying Fianna Fáil with 'the Republic'. The real
task was to demonstrate to the masses not that de Valera was
not a socialist but that he was not a real republican. The difficulty in the 1930s was that the Economic War, the adoption of
protectionism and other development policies by Fianna Fáil
allowed it to maintain a claim to continuity with traditional
republican objectives. Now, it was claimed, the conditions for a
united front of republicans and trade union and small farmers'
organisations against Fianna Fáil were much more favourable.
Crucial here was the break with the protectionist measures of
the 1930s, which the Fianna Fáil government of Seán Lemass
had initiated at the end of the 1950s in response to the grave
economic crisis.[24] The gradual phasing out of protectionism,
the vigorous attempts to attract foreign capital and the preparation of Ireland for EEC membership simply signified the
final capitulation of Fianna Fáil:

Whereas de Valera's efforts at economic independence were
half-hearted ... at least some effort was made during the 1930s
and 1940s to weaken some of the links with Britain. But Lemass
has given up the effort entirely. And between de Valera's compromise and Lemass's capitulation there is difference enough
to justify Britain in turn changing its tactics.[25]

Now that the leadership of Fianna Fáil had acquiesced in 'their present ignominious role of local managers for imperialism', Britain had been encouraged to change its strategy towards Ireland as a whole. Partition was no longer the best possible way of keeping the country in a weak and dependent position; Lemass's capitulation had encouraged Britain to seek a more radical constitutional change, of which the Anglo-Irish Free Trade Agreement in January 1966 was seen to be a portent: 'Britain now hopes to snare Lemass back into the United Kingdom. The Free Trade Agreement will do the trick.'[26]

The basis for speculating about such a drastic possibility was not argued out at any length. A Sinn Féin document prepared by Johnston's Education Department pointed to Britain's economic problems as a symptom of 'deep crisis': 'The imperialist power . . . [is] finding it increasingly difficult to maintain the huge profits it has been drawing from the neo-colonial exploitation of its former empire.'[27] In such a situation, 'Britain will be increasingly anxious to weld Ireland more tightly to her side as a secure neo-colony.'[28] Fianna Fáil's economic 'capitulation' was seen as the basis for a total reversal of classical republican objectives and it was now denounced as a 'Unionist' party. The opportunities had never been greater for a broad anti-imperialist alliance in the Republic to challenge the hegemony of 'anti-national ideas and theories' which had as their hallmark 'the abandonment of the aims of the 1916 men and the republicans of the past as "impractical" and impossible of attainment in the world of today'.[29] This alliance would reflect the interest of the mass of the people, 'the workers and small farmers and those sections of small business and the intellectuals who are adversely affected by the domination of British and foreign capital in Ireland'.[30]

At the centre of what Sinn Féin would label its 'economic resistance' campaign was the notion that a 'truly' republican government could use its sovereignty to establish 'real' economic independence. The proposals were largely a résumé of past critiques of the timidity of de Valera's policies in the 1930s, in particular his failure to control the movement of Irish capital abroad and to repatriate Irish capital invested abroad by banks, insurance companies and individual Irish investors.[31] A certain novelty was achieved by the attachment of the idea that, in a world of decolonisation and old and new 'anti-imperialist' powers, Ireland could count on what, in coy deference to the strength of anti-communism, republicans referred to as 'mighty friends'.[32]

While such ideas certainly provided republicans with a broader set of strategic options than had been current in the 1940s and 1950s, their ultimate capacity to assist in the modernisation of the movement was limited. This was not, as some of their opponents would claim, because they were 'foreign' or 'Marxist'. It was the case that the two small Communist parties on either side of the border had in 1962 adopted programmes which contained many similar themes, particularly on the need for 'anti-imperialist' alliances against the Fianna Fáil 'sellout'.[33] But both the Communists' programmes and the core ideas of republican rethinking were deeply dependent on the pre-given categories of nationalist thought – particularly that unfulfillable quest for 'real' independence, which assumes that political will can compensate for the realities of a small island with (relatively) tiny resources. The most striking characteristic of the thinking of the period is its capacity to deny the significance of certain massive realities upon which a 'Marxism' less influenced by nationalism would have paused to reflect.

Centrally, the republican analysis failed even to begin to comprehend the appeal of the new economic policies to the working class. In terms that echoed O'Donnell's disdain for the labour movement, the trade unions were castigated for their narrow concern with wages and conditions: 'Only a militant trade union movement with a national consciousness . . . can work towards the expansion of employment opportunities and control over the export of Irish capital.'[34] The absence from the recent Irish Trade Union Congress of any resolution expressing opposition to the Anglo-Irish Free Trade Agreement was noted, as was the general failure to oppose the 'economic capitulation' of the Fianna Fáil government.[35] Completely absent was any recognition that the policies of economic liberalisation, while they threatened indigenous industry, built up behind tariff walls since the 1930s, held out the promise of new employment by foreign capital. For devotees of economic nationalism, such employment was a sign of dependence and did not enter their calculations as anything else but an indication of national decadence. This blinded them to the popularity of the new policies with large sections of the working class which saw them as the only way out of the morass of the 1950s. The concern with the 'anti-national' aspects of the new policies also blinded the republican movement to the increasing role that the state itself would play under the new economic programmes in generating employment through an expanded public sector.[36] Thus the post-1962 'turn to politics' was accomplished under the direction of types of thinking that would prove to be out of touch with key realities of political and economic life in the Republic. On the other hand, the new emphasis on challenging 'British imperialism' through the development of a broad coalition mobilised on a range of political, economic and cultural issues, did have radical and, for many, unsettling implications for the role of the IRA.

Towards an Army of the People

An editorial in the Wolfe Tone Society's newsletter, *Tuairisc*, in the year of the fiftieth anniversary of 1916, challenged

> the illusion still current in some pockets of the Republican movement that a simple-minded armed struggle against the British occupation is alone sufficient to generate sufficient popular support to complete the national revolution.[37]

These 'pockets' of illusion were, in fact, far from residual elements in the IRA. Goulding was keenly aware that any rethinking must maintain a role for the IRA as a military organisation. He subsequently described the situation:

> We had on our hands trained physical force revolutionaries who were, to some extent, still armed. They would decide for themselves what would happen next, if we didn't decide for them.[38]

As the conception of anti-imperialist activity was broadened, there was a clear necessity to devise a role for the IRA which was subordinated to this broader strategy while not stampeding those in the organisation who saw it first and foremost as an army. An IRA document produced in the early 1970s gave one version of how this process had transformed 'an army of militarists, rigid and inflexible, and geared only for a military campaign against British forces in Ireland', into a 'revolutionary army, an army of the people, capable of developing and exploiting a revolutionary situation for the benefit of the people'. It was no longer an elitist force divorced from popular struggles, but existed to 'assist the people in what is THEIR liberation struggle'.[39] As will become apparent, this was a rather romanticised description of the role of the Official IRA in defending Catholic ghettos in Northern Ireland and 'retaliating' against the British Army. It was a 'people's army' with no actual relation to the bulk of the population in the two Irish states other than that of assertion. But this role was not in fact one for which the rethinking of the 1960s had wished to prepare. Until 1969 the role of the IRA was increasingly defined as that of ultimate 'guarantor' of the gains of popular struggles.

The first major result of the rethinking was a nine-point programmatic statement put to a special Army Convention in 1964. The points included involvement in economic and social agitations, the creation of a national liberation front of republicans, trade union and small farmers' organisations and other radical groups, and, most controversially of all, the end of abstention from both the Irish and British parliaments.[40] All except the last, which the Army Council had recommended be rejected, were accepted. Such new commitments sat uneasily in relation to the IRA's traditional military role. Implicit in a number of important republican documents of the period, however, is an attempt to maintain the IRA's primacy while transforming its most fundamental functions.

Thus in the Sinn Féin document 'Lessons of History' a key element for the success of the 'national revolution' was said to be 'an organised body of men, prepared to resort to arms if necessary and therefore subject to discipline.'[41] Yet this was only one of four factors identified as crucial; the others were:

the existence of a body of theoretical thought; the extent to which the interest and political and social outlook of the 'men of no property' predominate in the national independence movement; a political crisis for imperialism.[42]

The resort to arms was clearly envisaged as the ultimate defence of a popular movement's gains in an 'anti-imperialist struggle', and even then was not declared inevitable. The primary role of the IRA was clearly political: 'rousing the consciousness and understanding of the common people'.[43] An IRA document captured by the police in the Irish Republic in May 1966 gives a clear idea of the problems this policy was encountering and the radical implications that were by then being confronted. Little progress had been made in developing Sinn Féin as a relatively independent political organisation and most educational work was being carried on inside the IRA.[44] Recruits to the movement joined for traditional reasons and the methods of training them did little to discourage 'militarist' thinking. There was a need to change the emphasis away from arms and battle tactics to 'social and economic objectives':

> It is felt that a recruit graduating from recruits class finds that there is a lot of unromantic and possibly boring work to be done before he gets a chance to use his military training. This accounts for the high turnover in membership at present.[45]

Recruits needed to be clear that military activity was to be geared to backing up and consolidating 'revolutionary action initiated legally'.[46]

The document, which the IRA denied had ever been adopted as policy,[47] indicated the general direction of the new thinking. Most disturbing for some would have been its proposed 'Organisational Principles'. Thus it was argued that the 'basic movement will be a political national and social revolutionary organisation with an open membership and legal existence'.[48] At a time when the republican movement was struggling to recover from the collapse of the military campaign and hold together a depleted membership, some of the proposals were grandiose. For example, the new political organisation was envisaged as leading a 'vast and diversified movement under the Republican umbrella', including trade unions, co-operatives, tenants' associations and youth groups.[49] At their heart was the aspiration to use such an expansionary perspective as a means of justifying a radical transformation in the role of the IRA. The vanguard role of the IRA in the republican movement, although linked to its continuing military function, was now defined differently. It was the wider movement's 'backbone', composed of the 'best and most conscious members . . . the most advanced elements'.[50] Its leadership principle was thus being transformed from the military idealism of traditional Fenianism into a semi-Leninist one.

If the movement was to be radically politicised in this way, there were also clear implications for the existing hegemony of the IRA. As the document noted, 'The current position that the [Sinn Féin] Árd Fheis is a rubber stamp for the Convention is an imposition on the many sound people in SF.'[51] In the interim the Army Convention would continue as the effective policy-making body, but this role would be attenuated 'as the basic policy decisions are seen to be made correctly and openly by the National Conference'. It was envisaged that the role of the Army Convention would ultimately be downgraded to that of a 'specialist conference of certain people in the Movement for examining technical problems connected with the military aspect of the revolution'.[52]

Such ideas were seen by many members of the IRA as subverting the very existence of the physical force tradition. They certainly raised an old conflict between champions of self-referential military action to arouse the masses and those who stressed the need for popular mobilisation as a preliminary to the use of force. None the less, even the most militant proponents of the second position, like Goulding, were in no doubt that the trickle of people who were joining the IRA in the period between 1963 and 1967 had for the most part joined in the hope of another campaign. Consequently, although Goulding could, in moments of exasperation, startle his volunteers with unguarded declarations of the effective redundancy of the IRA,[53] it was believed that the road to politicisation entailed a compensatory range of military activities. The blowing up of Nelson's Pillar in Dublin in 1966 has encouraged the idea that these activities were essentially frivolous diversions for the bored volunteer. In fact, the strong resistance to the new direction ensured that more serious activities had to be contemplated. In 1964 a plan for an arms raid on a Territorial Army barracks in Newry was only aborted at the last moment when a local guide did not turn up.[54] The document seized by the police in 1966 included a military plan for another northern campaign, which would eschew 'classical guerrilla type operations' of the 1956 type and instead 'learn from the Cypriots and engage in terror tactics only'.[55] The seizure did not put a stop to the planning of activity in this area. In 1966 a special military council was established by the Army Council with the task of planning a new northern campaign, and a member of the Army Council went to England to set up a network of support for such a campaign.[56]

Such developments reflected Goulding's approach to introducing change in the republican movement, which was to seek to maintain maximum unity, bringing as many traditionalists along as possible. His implicit point of reference was O'Donnell and the Republican Congress. By moving outside the IRA and refusing the task of struggling for change from within, the Congressites had condemned themselves to nullity. For Goulding the only way forward was within the 'Official Army'.[57] This necessitated the maintenance of a commitment to 'armed struggle', the more strongly because the main thrust of the new policies and, in particular, the use of 'outsiders' like Coughlan and Johnston in discussions of strategy and in internal education, had provoked fierce resistance.[58] Yet the contradictions were painfully clear. In an interview with the main Belfast evening paper, Goulding claimed that the IRA had no immediate military plan and repudiated past unilateral militarism: 'We want to have the bulk of the people with us.' Most crucially, he explained that he wanted 'to try and get through to the Protestant working class'.[59] For Goulding, any real prospect of a new campaign was unthinkable before there had been radical political and ideological developments in the Republic and Northern Ireland. But as long as the new thinking was confined to paper and declarations, the IRA had nothing to offer its members as an attractive alternative to the inevitable hankering for 'real' action. In this context the creation of a structure for planning a new campaign in the north was only a slightly more sophisticated variant of the activities which the local readerships of the IRA embarked on as a means of maintaining or recuperating morale.

The local commander in Belfast, Billy McMillen, was aware of the criticisms of a number of veteran republicans who had left the movement since 1963. Himself initially hostile to the new direction, and eager to convince rank-and-file members that the increased involvement in politics would not make them redundant, he ensured that not only was the training of new recruits solely a military matter, but that scope was provided for its exercise.[60] McMillen was able to build up the membership of the Belfast IRA from a tiny 24 in 1962 to around 120 by 1969, thus allowing the creation of three 'battalions', centred on the 'Third Battalion' based in the Lower Falls area, where McMillen and his 'adjutant' Jim Sullivan had formidable popular reputations.[61] He would later claim that the 'selective' use of force was crucial in allowing the IRA to maintain itself and expand during the period.[62] Certainly the young Catholics who did join the IRA at this time were largely uninfluenced by the post-1962 rethinking.

After the Divis Street riots during the 1964 Westminster election, which were provoked by the RUC's removal of a tricolour from the window of a shop being used as a Sinn Féin election headquarters for McMillen, the West Belfast candidate, a couple of dozen recruits were made.[63] For McMillen, the 'patriotic fervour' generated by the riots and motivating these young IRA men was an unalloyed blessing for the republican movement in the city. For those who joined, 'politics' and the republican movement were often opposing universes,[64] and clandestinity, gun lectures and instructions for destroying telephone kiosks and pillar boxes the centre of revolutionary activity.

As the pace of IRA political involvement in the Republic accelerated in 1967, McMillen and the Belfast leadership insisted that they be allowed a 'happy blend of political agitation and military activity'.[65] Well after the IRA's Army Council had decided to promote a civil rights campaign in Northern Ireland as the best possible way of undermining the Unionist Party's hegemony and getting through to the Protestant working class, the Belfast IRA launched a series of large fire-bomb attacks on Territorial Army bases in Belfast and Lisburn.[66] Goulding saw the Belfast IRA in terms which recall the dismissive attitude of earlier IRA radicals to the 'reactionaries' in the Belfast movement. The resistance of the Belfast leadership to the new thinking was explained by the fact that the movement there was dominated by 'Catholic bigots'. Goulding often found it more congenial to glean his information about conditions in the north from local Communists with whom he was friendly. Echoing the Republican Congress's criticism of the Belfast IRA's lack of connection with the Protestant working class, he attached a perhaps exaggerated significance to the Protestant working-class credentials of some members of the Communist Party in Belfast. His lack of rapport with the leadership of the Belfast IRA was made apparent in some of his trips to the city when he would meet local Communists and return to Dublin without contacting the IRA leadership.[67] This recoil from republican Belfast was an unconscious recognition of the terrible obstacles which the sectarian realities of Ulster posed for even a modernised republican project.

The fundamental dynamic envisaged in the rethinking had been one of a build-up of agitational coalitions to rescue the

IRA from the self-imposed isolation of a physical force campaign in Northern Ireland. Much of this new dynamism was
expected to develop in the Republic, and this would pull the
organisation away from a militarised fixation on the northern
state. Yet almost exactly three years after the Army Council
decided on support for a gradualist campaign of civil rights
reforms in the north, the northern situation would deal a
major blow to the whole Goulding strategy. No adequate
understanding of the division of the republican movement and
the subsequent decades of violence is possible without an
appreciation of the assumptions and limitations of the IRA's
northern strategy.

Civil Rights and Abstentionism

In August 1966 a meeting of members of the Wolfe Tone
Society was held in Northern Ireland at the Maghera home of
Kevin Agnew, a prominent republican. Goulding was present,
but it was a young graduate from Cork, Eoghan Harris, who
had been recruited into the Wolfe Tone Society by Goulding,
who read a paper agreed by the IRA Army Council on a civil
rights strategy for Northern Ireland.[68] The replacement in
1963 of the geriatric Unionist Prime Minister, Lord
Brookeborough, by Terence O'Neill and the latter's adoption
of certain modernising themes had encouraged some hopes of
reform of the sclerotic Protestant regime. Then came the 1964
election victory of Harold Wilson, who had publicly proclaimed
his desire to force change on the Unionist regime. The work of
Dr Conn McCluskey and his wife in Dungannon, who since the
early 1960s had publicised discrimination against Catholics in
jobs and housing, and founded the Campaign for Social Justice
in 1964, clearly demonstrated the existence of a reformist
agenda. But the failure of either O'Neill or Wilson to deal with
these injustices created conditions of growing Catholic frustration which republicans could hope to mobilise. At the same
time the fact that O'Neill's largely cosmetic modernisations
had provoked intense intra-party disputes, and that he was
already being attacked by the emerging Protestant populist Ian
Paisley for 'betrayal' of Loyalist interests, demonstrated the difficulties awaiting any strategy that depicted a reformist agenda
on civil rights as a means of forging popular alliances between

even just parts of the Catholic and Protestant working class.

The paper Harris read was in fact closely based on a long article by Coughlan which was published that month in *Tuairisc*. Through his activities in the Connolly Association and the influence of Desmond Greaves, Coughlan had come into contact with a perspective which regarded civil rights issues as the Achilles' heel of Unionism.[69] The issue had assumed an even more crucial significance, it was argued, because of a transformation in British strategy towards Ireland:

> The far-seeing leaders of British imperialism saw that the bright young men of Fianna Fáil might prove a better bet for preserving British influence in Ireland than the bigoted fanatics of the North.[70]

As part of the British master-plan to 'snare Lemass into the United Kingdom', the Northern Ireland Prime Minister, Terence O'Neill, had been ordered to play down discrimination and provide a cosmetic modernisation of his regime.[71] The opportunity thus existed to use his thawing of political life to press for a much more thorough-going set of reforms:

> The Unionists should be squeezed by popular demands from the disenfranchised, the gerrymandered, the discriminated against, the oppressed Catholic and nationalist minority within the North itself, demands for reforms, for civil rights, for genuine democracy and opportunities for free political expression.[72]

The 'most progressive' outcome would be the releasing of the energies of 'the people', which was then defined as the Catholics and the Protestant working class. The analysis was characterised by its fundamental optimism about the likely response of Protestant workers to the development of civil-rights agitation: 'If things change too much the Orange worker may see that he can get by alright without dominating his Catholic neighbour.' The emergence of Paisleyism was recognised, as was the possibility that he would overthrow O'Neill, but this was dismissed as unlikely. The reasons provided demonstrate the distance that separated even the most progressive and intelligent republican analysis from a serious grasp of Unionism:

If Paisley and his followers are opposed by both the British government and the main Unionist leadership, who have switched
their policy, how can he possibly win? Britain has changed its
tactics relating to Ireland as a whole, consequent on the Dublin
government's capitulation. The Orange card is no longer as useful as it was. At present the Orange rank and file in the North
don't know what has happened. They are in a state of deep
doubt and confusion and Paisley is the only one who has come
forward as a guide. But the old certainties of anti-Catholicism
and bigotry peddled by Paisley no longer suit imperialism as
well as they did in the past. The Orangemen are being sold
down the river and they do not know it. For years the basic fundamental of their faith has been their trust in Britain. Whatever
they did, Britain would stand by them and back them up. But if
this rock of faith is removed, if Britain betrays them – what
then?[73]

The long-term prospect was seen as one in which republicans could break through to the Orange masses and explain
imperialism's real motivation, thus liberating them at last from
their illusions and allowing them to join the national struggle.
This undoubtedly serious commitment to winning Protestants
through a process of political reform, and the stated opposition to Catholic sectarianism and any resort to violence, could
not compensate for the unreconstructed assumptions that survived from the traditional nationalist project. Centrally, the
internal dynamics of the Unionist movement were overlooked
in favour of a largely external explanation. Orangeism was seen
as a phenomenon that existed for the convenience of the
British state, when the latter changed its strategy, the basis for
Orangeism was effectively removed. From James Connolly
through to Árd Fheis speeches by leading Provisionals, and
including the main theses of constitutional nationalism as set
out in 1984 in the New Ireland Forum Report and constantly
repeated by John Hume, there is an unbroken thread of analysis to which the modernising republicans in the 1960s maintained fealty. It is that Unionism's substance is the British 'guarantee'; if British support is removed, Ulster Protestants will
wake up to their real interests.

In the two years between the Maghera meeting and the first
civil rights march from Dungannon to Coalisland in August
1968, the Wolfe Tone Society, northern republicans and some
Communist trade unionists assumed the key role in the

creation of the Northern Ireland Civil Rights Association (NICRA) in January 1967.[74] In this period, the main concern of the IRA leadership remained the development of the movement in the Republic, where there was, by 1967, clear evidence of a crisis. Although the special IRA convention in 1965 had accepted the bulk of the leadership's recommendations for change, there had been considerable resistance to their implementation. As a result, there was a feeling of disarray and demoralisation in the movement. A meeting of the leaders of IRA units throughout Ireland in August 1967 assessed the state of the movement in terms of membership, finance, arms and political development. It was a depressing stock-taking:

> They suddenly realised that they had no movement at all. They only thought they had a movement ... the circulation of the *United Irishman*, for example, which in 1957-59 had been in the hundred thousand bracket had fallen to fourteen thousand.[75]

The way out of this state of affairs lay in a more intense propagation of the new policies. Thus the 1967 Sinn Féin Árd Fheis, in line with a previous decision by the August IRA gathering, amended the party's constitution to define its aim as the establishment of a Socialist Republic.[76] That year would also see the organisation establish a number of citizens' advice bureaux and, most importantly, the Dublin Housing Action Committee, which quickly mobilised a considerable popular constituency through a campaign which focused on the contrast between the housing crisis and the unprecedented level of office building in the city.[77]

A crucial factor in republican calculations was the emergence of the Irish Labour Party as a significant political force in urban areas, and particularly in Dublin. In the 1960s the Labour Party made significant gains in seats and membership in Dublin, and in the process shifted away from the staid conservatism which had characterised it in the 1940s and 1950s.[78] The improving economic conditions in the Republic, associated with Lemass's liberalising policies, resulted in a decline in emigration and an upsurge of industrial militancy.[79] The disintegration of de Valera's Ireland released Labour from its traditionally timid public poses; for the first time since the 1930s, Labour politicians could publicly identify their objectives as socialist. The progress made by the Labour Party in Dublin was an important consideration in Fianna Fáil's unsuccessful attempt to secure popular endorsement for a constitutional amendment to abolish proportional representation in 1968.[80] Although the dominant tendency in the IRA and Sinn Féin leadership favoured the creation of a broad national liberation front, including trade unionists and Labour Party members, there was no shift in the traditional republican disdain for the leadership of the Labour Party, and the growth of support for the Labour Party was deeply disturbing to the architects of the new policies.

The position was set out clearly in a major article, 'The Dilemma of Sinn Féin', in the November 1968 issue of the *United Irishman*:

> The organisation [SF] has grown and developed in the last few years. Yet its impact is still marginal. The radical position which it had been carving out for itself will not be easily established in the face of the growth of Labour, backed by the trade union movement. This is in fact the core of Sinn Féin's present dilemma. It is not Fianna Fáil or Fine Gael which need worry Sinn Féin, but the fact that Labour has a ready-made broad base in the trade union movement. It is the lack of a corresponding base that is Sinn Féin's major problem. Two radical movements are not feasible on a small island. The relation of Sinn Féin to the trade union movement and also to the Labour Party is the hitherto unresolved problem for Sinn Féin. Campaigns such as that on housing are only of a limited value if the political advantages are going to be picked up by Labour.

In 1967-68 Sinn Féin and the IRA would emphasise their involvement in an 'economic resistance campaign'. Some of these activities, like the IRA's destruction of buses used to ferry strike-breakers in an industrial dispute involving an American company in Limerick, its blowing up of a foreign-owned oyster boat and its attacks on farms owned by foreigners, served to demonstrate that for republicans the function of all economic and social agitation was to reassert the 'national dimension' which the trade union movement and the Labour Party neglected.[81]

In an article provoked by the recent influx into the Labour Party of a number of university-based intellectuals, most prominently Conor Cruise O'Brien, Roy Johnston warned those who saw in this the prospect of Labour's radicalisation. People like O'Brien would not accomplish the essential task facing Labour, which was to 'clarify its ideas and policies on all aspects of the national and social questions, involving its whole membership in the study ... of the socialist ideas of James Connolly'.[82] For Johnston, the Labour leadership was exposed in its true colours by the telegram of congratulation it had sent to Harold Wilson after his 1966 victory, so demonstrating its disregard for the British party's 'manifest imperialist record'. The influence of people like O'Brien would in fact make the Irish party more like the British, and the best that could be expected from that was a '1945 type victory, giving a government that can be controlled by the large property owners behind a façade of socialist words'. That Johnston could dismiss the substantial achievements of the Attlee administration, particularly in welfare policy, indicated not so much ultra-leftism as a typical republican disdain for economic and social reforms that left the 'imperialist' link unquestioned. Nevertheless, precisely because the Labour Party was growing and even winning support from young radicals in the universities, the question of Sinn Féin's self-imposed political marginalisation by its abstentionist policy took on a new and controversial significance.

By the time the 1968 Sinn Féin Árd Fheis took place, the police attacks on the second civil rights march in Derry on 5 October had propelled the northern question into the centre of politics in both Britain and Ireland. In both marches northern republicans had played a central role as stewards and participants – in the confrontation with the police in Derry they had ensured that the front line of dignitaries and MPs was pushed into the police line. The emergence of a mass civil rights movement seemed to offer rich opportunities, which Goulding and his supporters in the leadership were eager to seize. In his presidential address, Tomás MacGiolla described October 1968 as 'historic', linking the civil rights explosion with the defeat of Fianna Fáil in the referendum on proportional representation – a blow from which he incautiously predicted Fianna Fáil would never recover. The implication was clear; in both states the traditional parties of government were in disarray, and in Northern Ireland the Nationalist Party too had been discredited by the civil rights mobilisation. A political space had opened up and republicanism had a unique opportunity to move into it.[83] Nevertheless, the leadership was unsure of its ground, however optimistically MacGiolla described the political possibilities. The adoption of the commitment to a socialist republic, even as sanitised by the qualification 'in accordance with the Democratic Programme of the First Dáil',[84] had caused some disquiet amongst older and more traditional republicans. MacGiolla was at pains to quell their fears:

> Socialism has nothing to do with either atheism or totalitarianism, as is evident from even a superficial reading of Connolly. Neither is it a philosophy which must be imported. It is part of the republican tradition since the founding of the United Irishmen.[85]

In a speech earlier in the year Sean Garland who, because of his role in the Brookeborough raid, combined military credibility with strong support for the Goulding line, had referred to 'mealy-mouthed sentimentalists' who wished to 'preserve the movement as traditionally constituted', and warned that the movement must be prepared for any 'structural or organisational changes' necessary to obtain its objectives.[86] At the 1968 Árd Fheis, however, he proposed an amendment to the resolution calling for a constitutional change to allow elected representatives to take their seats in the Republic's parliament. Garland's amendment called for the creation of a Structure Commission, 'representing both branches of the movement', to examine how 'the new political situation in the south' could be turned to the advantage of republicanism.[87] The purpose of the commission was to avoid a bitter debate and the possibility of a split. By postponing a decision on the abstention issue for another year, it was hoped that resistance could be marginalised. There was some disquiet that some of the anti-abstentionists, particularly the energetic and articulate Seamus Costello from Bray, an Army Council member and prominent Sinn Féin activist, were unnecessarily abrasive and had needlessly alienated some of the traditionalists, who, it was thought, might ultimately have been won over or neutralised.[88] Costello's passionate contribution in support of the amendment served only to convince traditionalists that it was a manoeuvre to ensure their defeat, a feeling that the report of the commission did little to undermine.

The wording of the amendment and the report, when it was

published in March 1969, made clear the degree to which the dominant section of the leadership saw the main axis of progress as a southern one. The report, *Ireland Today and Some Questions on the Way Forward*, maintained that while,

> The Six Counties are the key to English control, the 26 Counties are the area in which the greatest anti-imperialist unity is possible and where there is most experience of the economic laws of neo-colonialism in operation . . .[89]

There was a section on the class structure of the north, which contained an evaluation of the progress of the civil rights movement. Here the deductive optimism of Coughlan's 1966 analysis was maintained, despite the evidence of increasing sectarian polarisation, particularly after the Peoples' Democracy's 'long march' from Belfast to Derry in January 1969. The growth of support for Paisley was recognised but dismissed:

> This is not the English strategy: they want integration of the whole of Ireland with the UK, under the control of a puppet regime constructed from the O'Neill brand of Unionism and the Lemass/Lynch brand of neo-Unionism.[90]

The classical fixation of republicanism with 'England' as the source of all Irish ills had the effect of blinding the republican leadership to the rapidly deteriorating situation in Northern Ireland. The document envisaged the achievement of the objectives of the civil rights movement and the development of a situation in which the way was open 'for the linking of the economic demands to the national question'. The disintegration of Unionism would enable sections of the Protestant working class to be won from the Northern Ireland Labour Party and ultimately towards 'the framework of an all-Ireland movement for the achievement of a 32-county democratic republic'.[91] The victory of a number of civil rights candidates in the Stormont election in February 1969 was hailed as demonstrating that 'the Six County people' were prepared to support a radical alternative to Unionism on a non-sectarian basis. The defeat of the candidates of the old Nationalist Party, on the other hand, was seen as demonstrating the innovative and disruptive effects of the civil rights marches. However the document simply ignored those features of the electoral returns which showed the major crisis that was developing within the Unionist state and party. O'Neill, whose victory over Paisley had been defined as most likely, was increasingly beleaguered and would soon resign. The Northern Ireland Labour Party would see its electoral base disappear, but not to the advantage of a new progressive republicanism. As 1969 progressed, the analysis of civil rights and Northern Ireland which had underpinned the new political line of Goulding's leadership would diverge ever more markedly from the realities of the northern crisis.

Ireland Today depicted the gradual development of a 'broad anti-Unionist and anti-imperialist alliance' in the north, which would eventually link up with a similar alliance in the Republic. The fundamental difference was that while in Northern Ireland the process of civil rights reforms had to be accomplished before 'anti-imperialist' issues could be raised, such issues were seen to be at the heart of current politics in the Republic. The central question in the document was that of the leadership of the anti-imperialist alliance, the 'national liberation front', in the Republic. Here it was asserted that the republican movement represented 'the great mainstream of the national and social revolutionary tradition', while the Labour Party's tradition was condemned as one of 'national and social compromise'.[92] Yet it was also clear that the commission was aware of the realities of a situation where republicanism had no comparable influence to that of the Labour Party in the urban, particularly Dublin, working class.

In what was probably the most open and extraordinary admission of weakness, the document pointed out that the membership of the republican movement in Dublin was not much greater than that of the Irish Workers Party (as the Communist Party in the Republic was then known), and that Dublin sales of its *Irish Socialist* were comparable to those of the *United Irishman*.[93] The new politicised and agitational style of republicanism was helping develop a radical ambience in the Dublin universities (which were influenced by the international militancy of 1968) but so far this had benefited the Labour Party: 'There is a steady stream of young radicals into the 26-county Labour Party. These would come to us if we were more credible.' As long as the republican movement could only use its resources as a radical and agitational group to the left of the Labour Party, it risked forcing the 'opportunist'

Labour leadership into a fake radicalism which would reap the benefits of republican efforts.[94] Only a decision allowing Sinn Féin to get candidates elected and participating in the Dáil would allow the party to challenge the Labour Party for the leadership of the urban working class.

Some of the ways in which the idea of a national liberation front was presented in the document provided its opponents with easy and lurid targets – particularly the positive attitude adopted towards work with the Communists. Given Johnston's and Coughlan's association with Greaves and the Connolly Association, charges of a 'red' infiltration were predictable. Anti-communism was not the only reason for the subsequent split. Much of the opposition to the document arose from the fear that behind the rather speculative proposals for popular alliances north and south lay another internally radical agenda centred on the future role of the IRA. *Ireland Today* contained a number of proposals for organisational change, of which the central one was for 'the integration of the existing movement into a unified whole'.[95] Although it made some gesture to traditionalists by stating that 'the historic link with the Republican government, at present vested in the Army Council, must be preserved', the core proposal was for a 'single-unified leadership'. This integration of the 'military' and 'political' leaderships seemed to imply the effective marginalisation of the IRA. Of course there was a very large degree of overlap between the leadership of Sinn Féin and that of the IRA – given the history of the effective subordination of the one to the other, this was hardly surprising. Yet the document clearly envisaged that the main business of the new unified leadership would be political – the attempt to develop the national liberation front. Thus, in a section dealing with the various 'specialist functions' to be represented at the meetings of the Ard Chomhairle (executive committee) of the unified organisation, 'action groups concerned with the physical defence of the people' came last, after 'commemorations, youth work, trade unionists' groups, farmers' groups and the *United Irishman*'.[96] Such a rebaptism and downgrading of IRA activity was bitterly resisted by those who saw in the developing northern crisis a very different road to the rebirth of republicanism.

Abstentionism was not a point of principle for all those who were to challenge Goulding's leadership at the end of 1969. Indeed, Kevin Mallon, who later became a leading Provisional, had been one of a group of six prominent Tyrone republicans who resigned from the movement at the beginning of 1969 in protest at the failure to get rid of abstentionism.[97] Many northern republicans were willing to consider any tactic that maintained pressure on the Unionist regime and brought a crisis nearer. However that crisis was seen to hold the possibility of a new and successful military campaign, and as 1969 progressed the gradualism of the original civil rights strategy, essential to its objective of winning Protestant support, was confronted with communal upsurges that undermined its basic premisses.

The main premiss was the vulgar Marxist assumption that as the Republic was breaking with protectionism, the British interest in partition had gone and, with it, the fundamental force supporting Loyalism. Once it became clear to the Protestant working class that it was being betrayed by the state on which it had lavished its deluded loyalty, a real political realignment was possible. Since Britain no longer had an interest in partition, any move towards the abolition of the Stormont parliament and the imposition of direct rule from London had to be resisted, as meaning unmediated control of the North by imperialism. As the crisis of the Northern Ireland state deepened, the response was to intensify demands for Britain to use its powers under the Government of Ireland Act to enforce reforms of the Stormont regime. In fact, because the republican tradition had always underestimated the relative autonomy of Unionism as a political force, it was now incapable of recognising that the institutional manifestation of that autonomy – the Stormont regime – was disintegrating under internal and external pressure for change, and that this disintegration was fraught with massive possibilities of communal violence. By externalising the sources of the intractable sectarianism of Northern Ireland, the dominant republican analysis, particularly as put forward by Coughlan, appeared increasingly lacking in credibility in the Catholic ghettos of the North.

The *United Irishman* warned of 'dangerous illusions' among some supporters of the civil rights movement. The core illusion was to see the main enemy as the 'Orange Order and the local Unionist junta'. These could not remain for long if 'English' support was withdrawn. The main enemy was 'English imperialist rule which has used religious sectarianism to delude generations of Protestant workers that in some way Irish democracy is the enemy'.[98] The way to end such domination was by forcing the imperialist power to legislate for democratic reforms in Northern Ireland; a reformed Stormont was the only way of releasing Protestant workers from their illusions. There was, of course, a fundamentally attractive impulse here – to move politics forward through peaceful political and ideological struggle aiming at Protestant-Catholic unity. In an Easter 1969 address in Belfast, Sean Garland had declared that if the civil rights movement was to succeed it would have to recreate the unity of purpose between Protestant and Catholic workers seen in the 1907 dock strike and the 1932 outdoor relief agitation. However, he then went on to define the role of republicans in the civil rights movement as to press on with the primary task 'of ending British domination of our country'.[99] As in the 1930s, left-wing republicans were convinced that a successful national-liberation struggle had to win substantial Protestant working-class support. They once again tended to see in their more traditional comrades, particularly in Belfast, one of the major obstacles to this objective, but these undoubtedly positive impulses could not compensate for their basic tendency to treat popular Unionism as a superficial imposition on what would otherwise be an integral part of 'the Irish people'.

The republicans' problems in relation to the Protestant majority in the north would be sharply intensified by the unresolved question of what exactly the role of the IRA should be. And as the possibility of severe communal conflict increased in 1969, the exact nature of the IRA's capacity became a major issue not simply for the republican movement but for sections of the ruling party in the south.

Fianna Fáil and the IRA

In a speech to a conference of the Republican Clubs (due to a government ban on Sinn Féin in the mid-1960s, this was the name of the political wing of the movement in Northern Ireland) held in Carrickmore, County Tyrone, in July 1972, Tomás MacGiolla provided a very comprehensive, if Manichaean, account of how what was by then the Official republican movement understood the major political and military developments since 1969. He emphasised the 'revolutionary' significance of the civil rights mobilisation:

There was no way by which the Stormont or British government could defeat the people's demands or break their unity and determination . . . the Dublin government had lost all influence and control of the situation since the eclipse of the Nationalist Party in the spring of 1969. Control of events and the leadership of the peoples' struggles was in the hands of the republican movement, although many other forces were also at work.[100]

The 'forces of imperialism' had then intervened to change the character and course of the struggle, initially through the encouragement of sectarian confrontations. The intense communal violence, which began in Belfast on 13 August,

> was no spontaneous communal riot or uprising by the Protestant people against their Catholic neighbours. It was organised by the forces of the state following a political decision at the highest level.

While the Stormont regime and its British controllers were held responsible for the August violence, it was the Fianna Fáil regime that was made to bear prime responsibility for reactionary developments on the Catholic side:

> The republican movement and the civil rights movement had set their faces against sectarianism and the Ancient Order of Hibernians and Nationalist Party were dead. So a new Catholic sectarian force was needed . . . As early as February the Dublin government had begun their part of the imperialist plan by making their first contacts with republicans and civil rights workers in the north. Following the August pogroms they intensified their work on much more fertile ground. By concentrating on those republicans and ex-republicans who saw their role as Catholic defence groups and by playing on their latent sectarianism and militarist desires, they created a split amongst republicans in Belfast and offered money and guns to those who would reject the leadership of the republican movement.[101]

The claim that Fianna Fáil was attempting to split the republican movement had appeared in the *United Irishman* as early as November 1969, in a story claiming to be based on two months of investigations. After the split, it became a staple of Official attacks on the Provisionals that they were the creatures of Fianna Fáil. MacGiolla's Carrickmore speech is simply a polished and

comprehensive example of this; Rosita Sweetman's widely publicised book, *On our Knees: Ireland 1972*, which was written from a
clearly pro-Official perspective, also emphasised the supposed
role of Fianna Fáil. In their recent substantial history of the
Provisionals, Bishop and Mallie dismiss the Official account:

> The theory of a government-inspired conspiracy to remove the
> dangerous leftists of the new IRA and replace them with the
> manageable stooges of the old tradition is characteristically fan-
> ciful and vain.[102]

While some of the Official analysis deserves the charge of
being fanciful, the role of a *faction* within Fianna Fáil cannot be
so easily dismissed.

The central weakness in Official analysis of the factors leading to the split was its incapacity to acknowledge the significance of the communal polarisation in Northern Ireland in
1969. As the Scarman Tribunal subsequently commented:

> While the Catholic minority was developing confidence in its
> power, a feeling of insecurity was affecting the Protestants. They
> became the more determined to hold their traditional summer
> parades, particularly those in Londonderry and Belfast. In these
> circumstances sectarian conflict was to be expected.[103]

The IRA, particularly in Belfast, was inevitably affected by this
polarisation. During serious riots in Derry in April police discipline disintegrated and a Catholic, Samuel Devenny, was seriously injured by the RUC and later died.[104] This served to
intensify popular Catholic hostility to the police, already significant after major riots in Derry in January 1969. In response to
the April disturbances, the Belfast IRA attacked several post
offices in the city with the aim of diverting police resources
from Derry.[105] Such actions were inevitably used by the
Unionist government in its claims that a more sinister subversive purpose lay behind the civil rights mobilisation.[106] In fact
the Belfast IRA was pitifully inadequate in its preparations for
any such role, with a membership of not much more than 100
and a grand total of 24 weapons.[107] After anti-police riots in the
Ardoyne, a largely Catholic district in North Belfast, the IRA
came under strong communal pressure for 'defensive' action.
Such pressure was initially resisted by McMillen.[108] However as
sectarian confrontation intensified in July, particularly in the
Ardoyne and at the Unity Flats complex at the bottom of the

Shankhill Road, such abstinence came under increasing pressure from within republican circles.

At the minimum, Belfast republican traditions – and popular memories of the IRA's role in communal defence during the violence at the formation of the state and the sectarian riots of 1935 – demanded that the IRA take on a similar role for the Catholic communities in which it was based. In July IRA members were called together and told that they would have to defend Catholics in the Unity Flats area.[109] At this time the Ardoyne and Unity Flats were part of the IRA's First Battalion area, but the realities of numbers and arms mocked the nomenclature. This battalion was supposed to cover north Belfast – the Ardoyne, the New Lodge Road and Oldpark area – as well as two other small Catholic ghettoes, the Markets and the Short Strand. It had fewer than 40 members and scarcely any weapons.[110]

McMillen, himself a late and reluctant convert to the new policies,[111] was well aware of the criticisms that many older republicans in Belfast were making of the move away from traditional concerns. Some of the critics were people like Joe Cahill, who had left the organisation soon after the new emphases became apparent.[112] Others had remained but continued to voice their opposition. Jimmy Steele was the pre-eminent republican veteran in Belfast, his status derived from a leading role in the IRA and the more than twenty years in prison that had resulted from this. He took the opportunity of the reinterment of Barnes and MacCormack – two IRA men executed in England during the 1940s campaign – to launch a bitter and comprehensive attack on the direction the movement had taken since 1962. The speech, given at Mullingar in July 1969, enraged many of the national leadership pres-ent and Steele was suspended from the movement. This had a catalytic effect in Belfast, where it encouraged many of those who opposed the new policies to intensify their opposition.[113]

Support for the national leadership was concentrated in the Lower Falls area, where McMillen and Sullivan reigned supreme in the republican subculture. It was here as well that most of the meagre resources of men and weapons were concentrated. In large swathes of Catholic west and north Belfast, the dominant republican notables were hostile to Goulding's leadership. In Andersontown, the Drumm family and Leo Martin exercised influence; in Clonard, the Hannaways and

Francis Card, although until the split itself Goulding and his supporters considered Card an ally;[114] in Ballymurphy, Joe Cahill and Gerry Adams's family.[115] Some of these figures had remained active, many had dropped out, but their recognised role and status in their fiercely localistic communities gave them a major resource when the prolonged and serious violence erupted in August 1969.

The IRA leadership in Belfast was increasingly ground down between two conflicting impulses – to aid and assist in the development and intensification of the civil rights demands or to become the armed defenders of Belfast Catholics. The first impulse, which arose from the belief that a sectarian state was no longer in the interests of 'imperialism', was now compromised by the rise to dominance of forces which the analysis had proclaimed historically redundant. This would lead to a simple inversion of the original position. Now it would be argued that because of the threat of a united people, 'imperialism' had turned to the revival of sectarian animosities in order to defend its interests. In a few months the *United Irishman* would shift from emphasising the irrationality of Paisleyism for the British state's strategy of a modernised Ireland reintegrated in the UK to claiming that, 'Civil war is Britain's aim.'[116]

The large-scale communal violence of August 1969 was the most disturbing evidence to date of the limits of the IRA's civil rights strategy. It had been recognised that a Protestant backlash was possible, but this had been downplayed. When it occurred, the unresolved issue of what would be the IRA's military role inevitably came to the fore. That a reform of the Northern Ireland state, especially if partly impelled by a largely Catholic mobilisation, would generate severe tension and possibly violence, was hardly unpredictable. The IRA's lack of preparedness reflected not simply the weakness of its strategic analysis but also a recoil from the implications of what communal violence would mean for its objective of reaching the Protestant working class. Many regarded such fastidiousness as the sign of ultimate degeneracy. For as the northern crisis erupted, it briefly, if powerfully, encouraged a widespread feeling that the 'unfinished business' of 1918-23 was on the agenda again. The Officials exaggerated the role of Fianna Fáil, but they did not imagine it.

The communal violence in Belfast on 14-15 August was the first major outbreak since 1935 and the most intense since the

violence that attended the formation of the Northern Ireland
state in 1921 and 1922. It clearly surprised the leaders of the
civil rights movement as well as the IRA. The chairman of the
NICRA, Frank Gogarty, told the Scarman Tribunal:

> We all on the executive underestimated the strength of militant
> Unionism at this time, and had we foreseen the holocaust which
> did occur in mid-August we most certainly would not have
> entered on such an enterprise as we did.[117]

He was referring to the decision made by the NICRA executive
on 13 August to organise demonstrations throughout
Northern Ireland to relieve pressure on the Catholic population of the Bogside in Derry, who were in the second day of bitter rioting against the police, following the traditional
Apprentice Boys' Parade on 12 August.[118] The executive had
intended to exclude Belfast from its plans precisely because of
fears of sectarian confrontation, but as Scarman noted: 'We
have no doubt that some activists, so far from accepting the
decision, did co-operate with some in Londonderry to call for
demonstrations in Belfast.'[119]

The IRA in Belfast had no qualms about initiating action to
relieve the Bogside. The first public manifestation of this was a
march to Springfield Road RUC station to hand in a petition
against police brutality in Derry. This was organised by the IRA:
the man who handed in the petition (referred to by Scarman
as 'Malachy' Doran[120]) was a young volunteer, Anthony Doran,
and he was accompanied at the head of a large crowd, which
sang the Soldier's Song and carried an Irish tricolour, by Joe
McCann, another recent recruit, who was soon to acquire near-
legendary status as an Official IRA leader. Before organising
the march, the volunteers had prepared a sizeable number of
petrol bombs for the subsequent anti-RUC riot.[121] This one
incident crystallises the dilemma of the national IRA leadership. Their representatives on the NICRA executive supported
the decision not to involve Belfast, but the Belfast leadership
was in the forefront of activities which, at the very least, helped
to exacerbate an atmosphere of fevered communal fears and
animosities.

Gerry Adams has spoken of two separate, if overlapping agendas, being followed by republicans at the time: 'One group was
intent on exposing the irreformable nature of the Six County

state: the other was following a gradualist approach to reform the state.'[122] This is a useful but overneat description of a situation in which dividing lines were not so clear-cut and the 'two agendas' were often in confusing interaction in the same people. The policy of *Ireland Today* had, after all, envisaged that civil rights would create the conditions for the subsequent raising of the issue of national rights. In conditions of intensifying crisis for the Stormont regime, many supporters of the civil rights strategy would see no real contradiction in activities that more directly confronted the state. A small group like the IRA in Belfast, whose leadership was only very recently converted to the need for 'politics' and whose rank and file had as yet had virtually no political education,[123] was faced with an accelerating political crisis which by its nature encouraged a traditional response.

Just before the eruption of violence in Belfast, the Prime Minister of the Republic, Jack Lynch, had made a television broadcast in response to the rioting in Derry. He claimed the Stormont government was no longer in control of the situation, described the violence as the result of decades of Unionist rule, demanded the introduction of a UN peace-keeping force and requested the British government to enter into negotiations on the constitutional position of Northern Ireland.[124] With its portentous, if ambiguous, declaration that 'The Irish government can no longer stand by and see innocent people injured and perhaps worse,' the broadcast contributed powerfully to the mixture of fear and expectation that gripped the Catholics of Belfast in the subsequent weeks.

The death toll in the two days and nights of intense rioting in Belfast was seven: five Catholics and two Protestants. Four of the Catholics were killed by police gunfire[125] and, as Scarman commented, 'The absence of any sustained heavy shooting by civilians ... was a feature of the disturbances.[126] In a subsequent comment on earlier pressure which the IRA had come under to use weapons in the defence of Catholic areas, Billy McMillen explained:

This we were reluctant to do as we realised that the meagre armaments at our disposal were hopelessly inadequate to meet the requirements of the situation and that the use of firearms by us would only serve to justify the use of greater force against the people by the forces of the Establishment and increase the danger of sectarian pogroms.[127]

Here a very realistic estimate of the possibly disastrous effects
of IRA armed action co-exists uneasily with the notion that
such a disaster might be less likely if the IRA had more arms
than it then possessed. The evidence given to the Scarman
Tribunal fully supports McMillen's qualms about the use of
weapons. On the night of 14-15 August the use of IRA guns in
the Lower Falls, in a situation of inter-communal rioting, simply served to incense the Protestant crowds and encouraged
the RUC to introduce armoured cars with heavy machine-
guns.[128] Given the intensity of communal feelings by 13 August,
serious disturbance was likely in Belfast. However, the frenzied,
systematic burning of Catholic houses in the Lower Falls,
Clonard and the Ardoyne was not inevitable. The IRA's use of
guns contributed powerfully to the remorseless intensity of the
Protestant onslaught in these areas.

It was therefore merciful that the IRA's resources were so
pitiful. In the Lower Falls – the heart of IRA resistance and
strength – there were thirteen weapons in all, including a sub-
machine-gun and a couple of rifles.[129] It was these that were
used in what Scarman referred to as the only 'sustained heavy
shooting by civilians',[130] when IRA members occupied a primary school building for an attack on a Protestant mob. In the
Ardoyne there were no IRA arms at all – four weapons had
been sent in some time previously but due to the disorganisa-
tion of the local republicans they had subsequently been withdrawn.[131] The Short Strand, a small Catholic ghetto in East
Belfast, had no weapons either, and after 14-15 August the IRA
leadership was able to despatch only seven volunteers and two
defective pistols for the defence of this area.[132] There was,
however, little evidence of McMillen's initial qualms about the
use of weapons in the passionate and semi-euphoric atmosphere that existed in the working-class heartlands of Catholic
Belfast in the aftermath of the August violence. Barricades had
gone up, citizens' defence committees were created and the
intense sense of communal solidarity would admit no nuances
in the depiction of the two days and nights of violence as a
pogrom launched jointly by the police and Protestant mobs on
an ill-defended population. Catholics had so obviously borne
the brunt of the violence in lives and property, and distrust of
the government and the police was so intense, that many people became locked into a sense of communal righteousness
that allowed only one disastrous conclusion: August 1969 was a

product of the defencelessness of Belfast's Catholics.

This profound communal feeling was to have irresistible effects on the IRA, in part at least because of the way it was taken up and refracted back on Belfast by an important current in the Fianna Fáil government. The development of the civil rights movement, the crisis in the Northern Ireland state to which it massively contributed and the onset of serious violence brought the 'national question' back into the centre of the southern government's concerns. As *the* republican party, with the first of its constitutional aims being 'to secure the Unity and Independence of Ireland as a Republic', Fianna Fáil faced a potentially explosive problem when serious disorder developed in Derry and Belfast. For a while it appeared that the whole 1921 settlement, which it had denounced for decades, was disintegrating. This inevitably raised the question of what Fianna Fáil strategy should be in such an eventuality.

Seán Lemass (Taoiseach from 1959 to 1966) had reconstituted Fianna Fáil's approach to Northern Ireland by emphasising the need to create the economic and social conditions in the Republic which would make unity a more attractive notion for northern Protestants. Under Lemass and his successor, Jack Lynch, the focus of concern in Northern Ireland was the need for internal reform as a prerequisite for the essential transformation of attitudes which would allow a majority of Protestants to reconsider their British affiliations. Both maintained their formal fidelity to the notion that partition was wrong: 'a deep throbbing weal across the land, heart and soul of Ireland' was how Lynch described it at the 1970 Fianna Fáil Árd Fheis. There was, however, no question of encouraging the notion that partition could be eliminated by some simple policy option like British withdrawal or that there was any way around attempting to persuade Unionists to alter their attitudes to unity.[133]

The northern crisis was a major check to this process of modernisation. It stimulated a strong upsurge of traditionalism, and not simply in those parts of the Republic like the border areas and the west where fundamentalist attitudes were strongest. There was a wave of sympathy for the victims of what was commonly perceived as a state-sponsored pogrom, and demands for strong government action to defend northern Catholics. After the August violence representatives of the various citizens' defence committees, including many prominent republicans, travelled to Dublin to demand aid, which often meant military training and guns.[134]

In the Cabinet, a group led by Charles Haughey, Minister of Finance and Neil Blaney, Minister of Agriculture, pressed for a more decisive response than that favoured by Lynch. Despite this, when the government decided to create a distress fund for the victims of northern violence, it was left to Haughey to decide on the size of the fund, and he was given effective autonomy in allocating these resources. Haughey and Blaney were also key members of a committee set up to improve the government's profoundly inadequate knowledge of what was going on in Northern Ireland. In May 1970 Lynch sacked Haughey and Blaney, who were subsequently tried and acquitted on charges of attempting to import arms illegally. The evidence from their trial, a subsequent investigation by the Dáil Public Accounts Committee and the impressions of some of the participants in the crisis, indicate the development of a para-state apparatus for involvement in Northern Ireland through an attempt to influence the main lines of development of Catholic insurgency.[135]

This approach involved military intelligence officers, public employees on secondment, businessmen allies of Fianna Fáil and at least one prominent Irish journalist. A major aim was to ensure that the various defence committees were led by reliable people, so that they would be single-minded in their role as a Catholic defence force and as insulated as possible from some of the more radical currents which were perceived to have developed in the civil rights movement. One cause for concern here was the degree to which northern republicans had been infected by the new politics of the IRA national leadership. The cabinet, through the Justice Department and the Special Branch, had been given an exaggerated version of the supposed threats of radical subversion which existed in the south. While much of this concerned the 'Marxist' takeover of the Labour Party, there was serious disquiet about the influence of 'communists' on the IRA leadership.[136] If arms and military training were to be provided for members of the defence committees, it was necessary to ensure that northern republicans who would be at the core of any 'defence' activity were not under the influence of the 'reds' in Dublin.

Neil Blaney, as a Donegal TD, was closely in touch with the situation in Northern Ireland and had made an approach to

Francie Donnelly, the IRA commander in neighbouring South Derry, in the spring of 1969. The contact was renewed after August when, at a meeting in Donegal, Blaney sounded him out on the numbers available to defend the area and the number of weapons available. A car and a weekly wage were also offered if Donnelly would act as an organiser.[137] The contacts were reported to Goulding, who encouraged their continuation, for by now it was clear that there was a likelihood of substantial resources being channelled to forces hostile to his leadership. In early October Donnelly attended a meeting in the Shelbourne Hotel, Dublin. Two prominent businessmen and supporters of Fianna Fáil attended, one of them an ex-member of Saor Uladh. Others in attendance were a journalist who was to play an active role in the Fianna Fáil intervention in the north and a recently elected civil rights MP. The possibility of acquiring arms and moving them to the north was discussed, but there was a condition: that the IRA in the north set up a separate northern command, independent of the 'communists' in the southern leadership.[138] Soon after this Donnelly, whose farm was in Maghera, County Derry, was visited by Charles Haughey's brother Padraig and others. In his struggle to win the leadership of Fianna Fáil, Haughey would make much of the northern roots of his republicanism. His father's family were from Swatragh in the south of County Derry, a few miles from Maghera. They discussed the situation and left £200 'to help you out'.[139]

In Belfast the various defence groups created in the barricaded Catholic ghettoes in the aftermath of the violence were often led by republicans who had resisted the new direction or dropped out in disgust. It was to people like these that the Haughey-Blaney group looked for the basis of their intervention in Northern Ireland. Captain James Kelly, the military intelligence officer who played a central role in the affair, had made contact in September with a number of crucial figures in Belfast, including the Republican Labour MP for a Stormont constituency which included the New Lodge Road, Paddy Kennedy. Kennedy was on friendly terms with many leading Belfast republicans, particularly of the traditional variety. After the violence there was a scramble by the various republican factions for southern support. Goulding's supporters in the leadership of the Belfast IRA asked a Belfast Catholic politician to make contact with Blaney about their pressing need for arms 'for the defence of the people'.[140] The politician met Blaney and returned with promises of an arms shipment and offers of men, including an explosives expert.[141] Like much else that would be promised, none of this materialised, and it gradually became clear to the Goulding loyalists that assistance from the south was being directed elsewhere. Initially, some money was channelled their way, including £1,000 of a promised £3,000 from some prominent businessmen in County Louth who had been contacted by a friend of Blaney.

Within a month or so of the August violence, however, it was being made clear to the leadership of the Belfast IRA that a condition for assistance was a break with the Dublin leadership. By then the Blaney-Haughey group had direct representation on the Central Citizens' Defence Committee (the body with representatives from all the areas which had barricaded themselves in August) in the person of Hugh Kennedy, an employee of Bord Bainne, the Irish Milk Marketing Board, which was a responsibility of Blaney's Ministry of Agriculture.[142] Kennedy became 'public relations officer' for the CCDC. He worked in close liaison with two prominent republican brothers from the New Lodge area, John and Billy Kelly. Both had been imprisoned during the 1956 campaign and had drifted out of active involvement after 1963. Now both would play a key role in mobilising anti-Goulding sentiment in Belfast.

Initially, an attempt was made to win over the existing leadership. Hugh Kennedy arranged a meeting between Jim Sullivan – representing the Belfast 'brigade staff' – and an *Irish Press* journalist in a Belfast hotel. The journalist told Sullivan that resources would be available and set up a meeting in the Republic involving Sullivan, Captain Kelly, Haughey and Blaney. Here it was agreed that a bank account would be opened in Dundalk to allow the transfer of money for guns to begin.[143] Goulding himself was approached by Captain Kelly, who informed him that he was still regarded as a 'sound' republican who had been fooled by a clique which was basically loyal to the Communist Party of Great Britain, which was in fact itself infiltrated by British intelligence agencies. He was asked to break with this group and concentrate his movement's resources on the north. If this was done, it was promised, he would receive aid and assistance, including the training of northerners at army bases in the Republic.[144]

Faced with the strong possibility that such assistance would go to his opponents, Goulding did not rebuff the overture.

Soon after this he was contacted by a priest working in the Irish Centre in London who told him that money could be made available for the purchase of arms if it could be guaranteed that they would only be used in the north. Goulding travelled to London where the priest's contact turned out to be Padraig Haughey. Goulding asked for £50,000 and was given £1,500 on account.[145]

But the animosity towards Goulding's leadership in Belfast was so great that the original attempts to negotiate with McMillen and his supporters soon gave way to a decision to overthrow the local leadership. In late September, a meeting of the Belfast staff of the IRA was broken up by the intervention of a group of armed men. It included some of the most prominent older critics of the new policies – Jimmy Steele, Billy McKee, Joe Cahill and Jimmy Drumm – and the Kelly brothers. McMillen, while making it clear that he would not accede to their demand that he resign as commander of the Belfast IRA, did formally accept their other demands: for representation in the Belfast leadership and for a break with the Dublin leadership.[146] From September there was a de facto split in the IRA in Belfast. McMillen and his supporters maintained a secret affiliation with Goulding and entered into prolonged negotiations with Captain Kelly to try to extract resources for arms. It was becoming clear, however, that Fianna Fáil support was being directed towards areas where their opponents were increasingly dominant.

In October, a new paper began publication, funded directly from the money the Lynch government had decided to make available for relief of distress. The *Voice of the North* was edited by Seamus Brady, a former speech writer for Blaney and an employee of the Propaganda Unit established by Lynch's government to put the Irish case on the north internationally.[147] Its board of management included Hugh Kennedy, John Kelly and the veteran Derry republican Sean Keenan.[148] Its ideology was bitterly anti-communist, its accent traditionally Catholic and nationalist. In the New Lodge area, where the Kelly brothers increasingly dominated the IRA, the house of a younger brother became the centre for the distribution of the *Voice of the North* in the city.[149] In areas like New Lodge and the Ardoyne, where the small IRA units were swamped by a wave of young Catholics eager for military training, a strong nucleus for the Provisional IRA was in existence by December 1969.

The Goulding loyalists in Belfast were aware that a combination of the large influx into the IRA after August and the new assertiveness of their critics, behind whom stood powerful backers, represented a threat. However a certain complacent contempt for many of the people involved in the 'coup' in September – because of their having dropped out after 1962 – contributed to a tendency to underestimate the seriousness of what was involved. One illustration of problems faced was the discovery that, although no money had been paid into the bank account opened in Dundalk, a substantial sum of money from the government's distress fund had been paid into an account in Clones in the Republic. Money could be drawn from this account on cheques signed by one of three prominent Belfast Catholics, including a Belfast politician. One of the others informed McMillen about the account and also about a decision to exclude those in the IRA leadership who were still suspected of supporting Goulding. As a result the politician was 'arrested' by the IRA and made to sign a cheque for £2,000 which was then cashed by a volunteer. He was made to repeat the operation a week later. It was perhaps because of this that the Clones account was closed in November and the money transferred to a Dublin bank.[150] Money would continue to find its way into the hands of Goulding loyalists in Belfast until January 1970, but usually in sums of considerably less value – £200 at the end of January 1970, for example – and they were convinced that their rivals were receiving the bulk of the 'relief' money.[151]

Bishop and Mallie dismiss too categorically the role of Fianna Fáil in the events which led to the formation of the Provisional IRA. Later statements about the role of Fianna Fáil from the Officials may well have exaggerated the threat to the political system in the Republic which the intervention was supposedly designed to head off, and it is also true that the August events would inevitably have provoked a communalist upsurge beyond the bounds of the IRA's existing strategy. Ruairí Ó Bradaigh, a leading anti-Goulding figure and the first president of Provisional Sinn Féin, would subsequently play down the Fianna Fáil connection: 'Their split with the IRA was not the result of Blaney intrigue, but of rank and file exasperation for the IRA Executive's unpreparedness last summer.'[152] It is undoubtedly the case, however, that the vigour and self-confidence of Goulding's challengers was stimulated by the knowledge that they, and not the discredited 'reds', had a serious prospect of material and ideological assistance.

Notes

1. Interviews with Anthony Coughlan, Roy Johnston and Cathal Goulding; see also *Tuairisc: Newsletter of the Wolfe Tone Society*, No. 6, June 1966.
2. Liam McMillen, *The Role of the IRA 1962-67*, Dublin 1976, p.3.
3. Interview with Cathal Goulding.
4. Patrick Bishop and Eamonn Mallie, *The Provisional IRA*, London 1987, p.35.
5. C.D. Greaves, *Reminiscences of the Connolly Association*, 1978 no place of publication, p.16.
6. Ibid., p.23.
7. Ibid., p.28.
8. Ibid. p.30 and letter from Anthony Coughlan to Bob Purdie, 12 August 1988 concerning Purdie's 'Was the Civil Rights Movement a Republican/Communist conspiracy?', *Irish Political Studies*, Vol. 3, 1988. Copy of letter courtesy of Anthony Coughlan.
9. Coughlan letter.
10. Ibid.
11. Greaves, op.cit., p.31.
12. Ibid., p.32.
13. Constitution of Wolfe Tone Society adopted at a meeting in Dublin, 25 July 1964, courtesy of Anthony Coughlan.
14. *Tuairisc*, No. 6, June 1966.
15. Interviews with Sean Garland and Anthony Coughlan. Coughlan successfully sued the publishers of Mallie and Bishop for their allegation that he was an IRA member.
16. Roy Johnston, 'Why I Quit Sinn Féin', *Sunday Press*, 23 January 1972.
17. Interview with Cathal Goulding.
18. Ibid.
19. Cathal Goulding, 'The New Strategy of the IRA', *New Left Review*, No. 64, November/December 1970, p.51.
20. 'Our Ideas', *Tuairisc*, No. 7, 31 August 1966.
21. Ibid.
22. Ibid.
23. Constitution of Wolfe Tone Society.
24. This is discussed at length in Paul Bew and Henry Patterson, *Seán Lemass and the Making Of Modern Ireland*, Dublin 1982.
25. 'Our Ideas'.
26. Ibid.
27. Sinn Féin, *The Lessons of History*, Dublin 1970, first published September 1967.
28. Ibid.
29. 'Our Ideas.'
30. Sinn Féin, op.cit.
31. The demand to break the link with sterling and repatriate Irish capital

abroad was a long-standing one – it featured in submissions to the Irish Banking Commission in the 1930s and was raised again by Clann na Poblachta. It was a central feature in 'Our Ideas'.

32. Sinn Féin, op.cit.
33. M. Milotte, *Communism in Modern Ireland*, Dublin and New York 1984, p.236.
34. 'Our Ideas.'
35. Ibid.
36. See Bew and Patterson, op.cit., Chapter 6.
37. *Tuairisc*, No. 6, June 1966.
38. Goulding, op.cit., p.51.
39. *The IRA Speaks in the 1970s*, Dublin 1972, p.10.
40. Goulding, op.cit., p.53 and Rosita Sweetman, *On Our Knees: Ireland 1972*, London 1972, p.142.
41. Sinn Féin, op.cit.
42. Ibid.
43. Ibid.
44. The document was printed as an appendix to the Inquiry of Lord Scarman, 'Violence and Civil Disturbances in Northern Ireland in 1969', *Report of a Tribunal of Inquiry*, HMSO Belfast, Cmnd 556, 1972, Vol. 2, p.45.
45. Ibid., p.46.
46. Ibid.
47. Ibid., p.52.
48. Ibid., p.46.
49. Ibid., p.47.
50. Ibid.
51. Ibid.
52. Ibid.
53. Interview with Cathal Goulding.
54. Interview with Sean Garland.
55. Scarman, op.cit., p.50.
56. Interview with Sean Garland.
57. Interview with Cathal Goulding.
58. Ibid.
59. 'The Mind of the IRA', *Belfast Telegraph*, 16 February 1966.
60. Information on McMillen's role from Sweetman, op.cit., from the pamphlet *Liam McMillen: Separatist, Socialist, Republican*, Dublin 1976, and interviews with Cathal Goulding, Jim Sullivan, Kevin Smyth and Seamus Lynch.
61. Liam McMillen, *The Role of the IRA 1962-67*, Dublin 1976, pp.2 and 10, and P. Beresford, 'The Official IRA and Republican Clubs in Northern Ireland 1968-74', unpublished DPhil thesis, University of Essex, 1975, p.247.
62. McMillen, op.cit., p.1.
63. Ibid., p.5.
64. Interviews with Kevin Smyth and Seamus Lynch.
65. McMillen, op.cit., p.8.
66. Ibid. and interview with Jim Sullivan.
67. Interview with Cathal Goulding.

68. Interview with Eoghan Harris.
69. Anthony Coughlan, letter to Bob Purdie.
70. 'Our Ideas'.
71. Ibid.
72. Ibid.
73. Ibid.
74. Purdie, op.cit.
75. Goulding, op.cit., p.55, and Sean Garland, 'The Lessons of History', *United Irishman*, June 1971.
76. Ibid. and *United Irishman*, December 1968.
77. Carol Coulter, 'A View from the South' in Michael Farrell (ed.), *Twenty Years On*, Dingle 1988, p.108.
78. Michael Gallagher, *The Irish Labour Party in Transition 1957-82*, Manchester and Dublin 1982.
79. See Bew and Patterson, op.cit., Chapter 6.
80. See Paul Bew, Ellen Hazelkorn and Henry Patterson, *The Dynamics of Irish Politics*, London 1989, Chapter 4.
81. *The IRA Speaks in the 1970s*, Dublin 1972, pp.3-6.
82. 'Conor Cruise O'Brien and Labour', *United Irishman*, January 1969.
83. Ibid.
84. Ibid., December 1968.
85. Ibid., January 1969.
86. Speech at Bodenstown quoted in *United Irishman*, April 1971.
87. *United Irishman*, January 1969.
88. Beresford, op.cit., pp.112-4, and interviews with Cathal Goulding and Sean Garland.
89. Republican Education Department, *Ireland Today and Some Questions on the Way Forward*, March 1969, p.5.
90. Ibid., p.4.
91. Ibid., p.5.
92. Ibid., p.15
93. Ibid., p.8.
94. Ibid., p.15.
95. Ibid., p.20.
96. Ibid.
97. Beresford, op.cit., p.114.
98. *United Irishman*, May 1969.
99. Ibid.
100. Tomás MacGiolla, *Carrickmore Speech*, Dublin 1973.
101. Ibid.
102. Mallie and Bishop, op.cit., p.99.
103. Scarman op.cit., Vol. 1, p.6.
104. Ibid.
105. Ibid., pp.21-2.
106. Thus the Unionist Prime Minister in the Stormont parliament on August 14 1969: 'This is not the agitation of a minority seeking by lawful means the assertion of political rights. It is the conspiracy of forces seeking to overthrow a government, democratically elected.' Quoted in Scarman op.cit., p.10.
107. McMillen, op.cit., p.10.

108. Ibid., p.11.
109. Interview with Seamus Lynch.
110. Beresford, op.cit., p.247.
111. See his interview in Sweetman, op.cit., p.195: 'We resisted it tooth and nail. We used to spend hours at meetings trying to come up with ideas and excuses as to why we shouldn't become involved in this type of political activity.' Interviews with Jim Sullivan and Cathal Goulding.
112. Interview with Jim Sullivan.
113. Interviews with Seamus Lynch and Jimmy Drumm.
114. Interview with Cathal Goulding.
115. Beresford, op.cit., p.266, and interviews with Jimmy Drumm, Seamus Lynch and Jim Sullivan.
116. *United Irishman*, October 1969.
117. Scarman, op.cit., Vol. 1, p.12.
118. Ibid., p.9.
119. Ibid., pp.9, 119 and 120.
120. Ibid., p.121.
121. Interview with Seamus Lynch.
122. Gerry Adams, 'A Republican in the Civil Rights Campaign' in Farrell (ed.), op.cit., p.46.
123. Interviews with Kevin Smyth and Seamus Lynch. The Republican Clubs had been formed to get around the northern government's ban on Sinn Féin. Young volunteers like Adams and Lynch were ordered to go to a meeting to elect the first NICRA executive and vote for a list of names given to them in advance; there was some resistance to being ordered to vote for Communist Party members.
124. Printed in full in Scarman, op.cit., Vol. 2, pp.43-4.
125. Ibid., Vol. 1, pp.9-10.
126. Ibid., p.14.
127. McMillen, op.cit., p.11.
128. Scarman, op.cit., pp.133 and 159.
129. Interview with Jim Sullivan.
130. Scarman, op.cit., p.14.
131. Interview with Jim Sullivan.
132. Interview with Seamus Lynch.
133. Jack Lynch's speech is quoted in Geraldine Kennedy, 'The Thoughts of Chairman Jack', *Magill*, February 1978, p.29.
134. *Resistance*, a special issue of the *United Irishman* produced in the aftermath of the August violence, reported a speech by Paddy Devlin, NILP MP for the Falls constituency, given at the GPO in Dublin: 'We need guns was Paddy Devlin's unabashed cry – Don't abandon us.'
135. For a balanced analysis of the 'Arms Crisis' see T.R. Dwyer, *Charles Haughey*, Dublin 1987, pp.72-100. For participants' views, see Kevin Boland, *Up Dev!*, Dublin n.d., pp.142-9 and James Kelly, *Orders for the Captain*, Dublin 1971.
136. The chief civil servant in the Republic's Department of Justice recalled a memorandum which he encouraged his minister to circulate to the government in July 1969. It gave an analysis of the IRA and 'emphasised again that the time had become opportune to drive a wedge between the rural members – the old faithful – and the doctrinaire republicans,

mainly based in Dublin, who were sedulously propagating the gospel of a "Workers' Socialist Republic".' Quoted in 'The Berry Papers', *Magill,* June 1980, p.50.

137. Interview with Francie Donnelly and Cathal Goulding.
138. Information is derived from a tape-recorded conversation of three leading Officials involved in dealings with Fianna Fáil. The three were Goulding, McMillen and a prominent Belfast Official, Malachy McBurney. The tape, *1970 Discussion,* formed the basis for the anonymous 68-page pamphlet, *Fianna Fáil and the IRA,* which was issued in the early 1970s with no place or date of publication. It was on sale for a while in the Official bookshop in Dublin and from their paper-sellers. However it was declared a 'seditious document' and its possession made a criminal offence. Fortunately, a few copies survive.
139. Interview with Francie Donnelly.
140. *1970 Discussion.*
141. Malachy McBurney in ibid.
142. See Beresford, op.cit., pp.204 and 229.
143. Interview with Jim Sullivan and *1970 Discussion.*
144. Interview with Cathal Goulding.
145. Interview with Cathal Goulding and *Fianna Fáil and the IRA,* p.24.
146. *1970 Discussion.*
147. Kelly, op.cit., p.8 and *Fianna Fáil and the IRA,* p.31.
148. Beresford, op.cit., p.204.
149. Interview with Seamus Lynch.
150. *1970 Discussion* and Kelly, op.cit., p.19.
151. *Fianna Fáil and the IRA,* p.34.
152. Quoted in Conor Cruise O'Brien, *States of Ireland,* London 1972, p.81.

5   The Officials:
Regression and Development,
1970-1977

An extraordinary IRA 'General Army Convention' was held in early December 1969 to take decisions on the report of the Structure Commission established by the 1968 Sinn Féin Árd Fheis. Those who were opposed to the ending of abstentionism later complained of the deliberate failure to pick up delegates known to be opposed to change. Even some of those in support of the motion had doubts about the wisdom of pushing on with the abstention debate after the exacerbation of divisions within the IRA caused by the violence in the North. The vote in favour of ending abstentionism was 39 to twelve, and when the result became clear Sean MacStiofain, soon to be Provisional Chief of Staff, burst into tears declaring, 'This is the end of the IRA.'

MacStiofain – who, as John Stephenson, an English-born IRA man, had been jailed with Goulding in 1953 for a failed raid on the armoury of an English public school – had been appointed Director of Intelligence in 1966. Goulding had admired his energy and his disciplined and systematic approach to work while scorning his traditionalist attitude to politics. MacStiofain, a vehement critic of Roy Johnston's role, had been suspended for six months in 1964 for refusing to circulate an edition of the *United Irishman* in which Johnston criticised the practice of reciting the rosary at republican commemorations. After the December convention he had immediately set about organising an alternative 'Provisional Army Council'. It could look for support to the very substantial dissident elements in Belfast and to many prominent traditionalists throughout Ireland. At this level its most crucial members were Daithi O'Connaill and Ruairí Ó Bradaigh. Both had been active in the 1956 campaign – O'Connaill had taken part in the ill-fated Brookeborough raid and served on the Army Council in 1962. At that time O'Connaill had been in favour of ending abstentionism, but then he had drifted out of the movement, disillusioned by its 'communist' links. A carpentry instructor with the Republic's Board of Works, he had been in Donegal in 1969 and had approached Goulding with an offer to become active again. He was made OC in Donegal, a decision which Goulding was to come to regret bitterly. Ó Bradaigh had been Chief of Staff for the last two years of the Border campaign. A school teacher, his devout Catholicism produced a marked distrust of the 'extreme socialism' which he thought Johnston was pushing, and he was a fierce opponent of moves to end abstentionism. Ó Bradaigh and O'Connaill would provide the core of Provisional ideology and strategy until the late 1970s.

Both the Provisional, and what was now being referred to as the 'Official' IRA under Goulding, mobilised their supporters for the forthcoming Sinn Féin Árd Fheis. As an Official pamphlet would later describe it, in the interval between the IRA convention and the Árd Fheis, 'The scramble for delegates was only equalled by the scramble for dumps [of arms].' On 10 January 1970 the largest Sinn Féin Árd Fheis since the 1920s met at the Intercontinental Hotel in Dublin. The first major debate centred on the proposal for a National Liberation Front, which was carried by a large majority. The debate on a resolution to remove 'all embargoes on political participation in parliament' from the constitution of Sinn Féin was bitterly polarised. For those like Ó Bradaigh and the veteran republican from Leitrim, John Joe McGirl, who had been a Sinn Féin abstentionist TD between 1957 and 1961 and a close friend of both Cathal Goulding and Sean Garland until the late 1960s, the case was a moral, almost theological one. Two generations of republicans had made sacrifices, and some had died, in the struggle to defend the 'legitimacy' of the Second Dáil against the Treaty settlement and the 'Partition statelets' which had emerged from it. 'Politicisation' would mean gradual absorption into the state structures based on this settlement – Sinn Féin, it was argued, would go the way of Fianna Fail and Clann na Poblachta. For their opponents such arguments simply condemned republicanism to a declining existence on the margins of Irish political life. Although the resolution was passed, it failed by nineteen votes to get the two-thirds majority necessary for an amendment to the constitution. However by the end of an emotional and charged four-hour debate, many on the majority side were determined to press the issue to breaking point. Finally, a northern delegate proposed a vote of confidence in the leadership of the IRA – which the previous December had already accepted the proposal for an ending of abstentionism, a decision subsequently endorsed by an IRA Convention at which the Belfast IRA, in a semi-detached relation since the 'coup', was not represented. At this point MacStiofain and a third of the delegates walked out to found an alternative Sinn Féin.[1]

The first statement issued by the Provisionals after the split at the Sinn Féin Árd Fheis, on 11 January 1970, gave five major reasons for their walk-out. The first was the prospect of recognition of the three parliaments, which would 'change a National Movement into yet another political party seeking votes at all costs'. This was linked to the proposal for a National Liberation Front with other radical groups, which was portrayed as the product of the influence of 'infiltration and take-over' by those who had joined the movement from the Irish Workers' Party, as the Irish Communist movement was then known, to push 'an extreme form of socialism'. They attacked 'repressive' internal methods, which included expelling branches in North Kerry and Sligo which opposed the new line, disbanding the Cumann na mBan organisation for the same reason, and expelling leading veteran republicans like Jimmy Steele and Sean Keenan. The Goulding leadership, it was argued, had 'let down' the North: 'The leadership of the movement was obsessed with the "Commission" . . . preparations for the defence of our people did not receive the necessary attention.' There was particularly strong criticism of the opposition to the abolition of Stormont:

> We find absolutely incomprehensible from any republican stand-point the campaigning in favour of retaining the Stormont parliament . . . In any future struggle for freedom it would surely be preferable to have a direct confrontation with the British government on Irish soil without the Stormont junta

being imposed. In any event, the taking away of the Orange Order's power block would surely be a step forward rather than backward.

The new organisation immediately dismissed any notion of healing the split: 'There can be no question of rapprochement or of meetings with those who are opposed to us.'[2] In the following month's issue of the *United Irishman*, which dealt with the Árd Fheis the editor, however, took a much more conciliatory attitude towards those who had walked out. He had warned those most militantly in favour of getting rid of abstentionism that,

A two-thirds majority, instead of isolating the reluctant third might eventually isolate the two-thirds from the mainstream of republican opinion, that the vote of the Árd Fheis might not reflect the real state of opinion on this issue.[3]

The editor's 'personal view' was critical of younger delegates, particularly those who had been active in the civil rights movement in the north, who 'could see no virtue in marking time to avoid a split' and who needlessly antagonised those with doubts about participation by labelling them as inactive reactionaries. This reflected the concerns of some in the leadership, including Goulding and Garland, who had favoured a more gradualist approach to the abstention issue and who resented the abrasiveness of people like Seamus Costello and the former editor of the *United Irishman*, Tony Meade. The latter, in canvassing for the new policies, had not hesitated to label all signs of equivocation as evidence of 'constipated thinking'.[4] Garland and Goulding would continue to believe that many sincere republicans had been pushed into the Provisionals by what Garland would subsequently term a 'combination of unfortunate errors on the part of some people'.[5]

The Official leadership was convinced that many of the dissidents could be won back, that they were the unwitting dupes of an alliance between a group of superannuated reactionaries stimulated by the August violence and the Blaney-Haughey faction in Fianna Fáil. The January issue of the *United Irishman* had warned of the most determined attempt in recent years by the *Sunday Press* and the *Irish Press* to cause disruption within the ranks of the movement'. As the then editor of the *Irish Press*,

Tim Pat Coogan, admits in his own history of the IRA, produced just after the split, the news of the IRA Convention vote against abstentionism had been leaked to the *Sunday Press*, and both papers gave the issue, and divisions in the Republican movement, much coverage as the Árd Fheis approached. This coverage reflected the established concern of sections of the Fianna Fáil leadership about Communist influence on the Army Council. Coogan symptomatically described the NLF proposal as coming very close 'to giving Moscow a voice in the Irish national movement for the first time in history'.[6] The *United Irishman* had warned that the press campaign was all part of the Fianna Fáil strategy of

> binding this country closer to British imperialism. Only a united, alert and growing republican movement in the 1970s can save the Irish nation from a future worse than that which followed the Act of Union.[7]

The Official IRA's Easter statement in 1970 continued to emphasise the need to end the division in the face of the 'real' enemy:

> A division in republican ranks helps only Ireland's enemies: British imperialism, Unionism and Free Statism. This decade may well decide the future of the Irish nation for decades to come. It may well decide whether or not there will be an Irish nation. In this perspective, our internal difficulties on tactical questions are of small importance, however large they may seem in people's minds at present.[8]

The Army Council called for the utmost efforts to 'achieve unity in our ranks' and claimed that the Officials would continue to avoid controversies that might deepen divisions and would 'direct all our shafts at the enemy'. If immediate unity was impossible, there should at least be 'maximum co-operation in the struggle for the emancipation of our people'. Such calls continued to be made into 1971. In February MacGiolla, in response to 'British Army provocation' and growing violent conflict between Officials and Provisionals in Belfast, called on all those opposed to 'the British army and British rule' to unite 'or at least co-operate with each other'. He made it clear that he was calling not for organisational fusion but 'co-operation and unity of action where possible'.[9] At the Officials' Easter

Commemoration parade in Belfast in 1971 Garland made another appeal to his 'former colleagues' to unite 'in the attempt to restore the land of Ireland to the people of Ireland'.[10]

The lack of response to such appeals reflected in part the intense competition between the two organisations in Belfast; despite the fact that a post-August influx soon ensured the Provisionals an easy numerical predominance, the Officials also began to recruit substantially in a number of areas, particularly the Lower Falls, where the pre-eminence of McMillen and Sullivan was unshaken by the split. The *United Irishman* was to claim that the loss of membership due to the split was made up in six months and that by the end of 1970 the membership had increased by 40 per cent.[11] The northern crisis certainly provoked a broad, if inchoate, republican sentiment throughout Catholic Ireland, which resulted, among other things, in large crowds marching on the Official headquarters in Gardiner Place demanding guns and transport to the North.[12] Sales of the *United Irishman* soared to 70,000 in the early 1970s.[13]

In Belfast the bulk of the membership had stayed with the Officials, although it was now clearly dwarfed by those who had joined the Provisionals as a response to the August violence. The Belfast leadership of the Officials regarded the Provisionals with a mixture of contempt and bitter animosity. The role of 'ex-members' like the Kelly brothers and Joe Cahill defined the nature of the Provisionals for Officials like Jim Sullivan. Although he was unable to persuade McMillen of the need to eliminate physically the leadership of the Provisionals in the city, Sullivan lost no opportunity in attempting to establish the Officials' military credentials in as many areas as possible. The pre-August Officials did not take the Provisionals seriously as potential competitors. They were seen as 'a collection of Glasgow Celtic supporters, backward nationalists, people on the make and general ne'er-do-wells'.[14] The Officials would pride themselves on maintaining a serious attempt to screen and educate the increasing numbers who applied to join the IRA, and would compare this with the Provisionals' promiscuous intake of those infused with a Catholic defender mentality.[15] Subsequent evaluations of the period, however, stressed the many negative effects of the Officials' northern expansion in the years immediately following August 1969. In 1975

Sean Garland gave a stringent assessment of the effects of the northern crisis:

> The Six County situation has, since 1969, dominated the attention of the movement despite many efforts on our part to bring the struggle back to basics, by attempting to raise issues which require the involvement of the mass of the people, we have been unable to do so . . . The imbalance that the Six County situation creates in the entire country has been one of the greatest difficulties we have had to face and fight. After internment we found ourselves gradually getting involved in military activities, as a reaction to the British army and also, in some cases, as competition with the Provisionals . . . Without doubt over the past years we attracted many unreliable elements to our movement, opportunists, ultra-leftists, criminals and plain unadulterated madmen. It has taken us much effort to retain our fundamental struggle and to shake off these unstable elements.[16]

These reflections on the undesirable effects of the shift in the strategic axis of the Official movement brought on by the northern crisis and its militarising consequences need to be amplified by a consideration of the central defects of the Officials' analysis of the crisis, which made creeping militarisation difficult to contain.

The Freedom Manifesto – Social Republicanism in Crisis

The 1970 Árd Fheis adopted a 'Freedom Manifesto' which was supposed to be the strategic basis for the creation of the National Liberation Front. For all the charges of 'extreme socialism' and 'communism' which the Provisionals were to level at the Officials, the most striking characteristic of the manifesto is its emphasis on the centrality of the national question. All reforms and advances, whether in the area of civil rights or economic and social conditions, must help to 'weaken imperial control . . . The need to reunify the nation dominates the immediate horizon. No demand should be formulated without this in mind.'[17]

Despite the importance accorded to the national question, the section on the Six Counties continued to put the civil rights issue at the centre of demands. The relationship of civil rights to the Protestant working class was the source of major problems for the manifesto. It recognised that support for civil rights demands was confined to a 'tiny politically conscious minority' of Protestants in the trade union movement. Support for the 'national demand for unity' was recognised to be even slighter, although the startling claim was made that there was still less support for social demands amongst Protestant workers. This was because of the 'elite position' in the job market which Unionist Party patronage had given Protestant workers. There could be no progress on social issues until this patronage system was destroyed. The process of destruction was identified with the campaign to force the British government to reform the political system in Northern Ireland. The Official analysis, however, was so fixated on the supposed British 'master-plan' to reintegrate the Irish Republic into the United Kingdom that the very radical import of a demand for the destruction of the existing sectarian state apparatuses was neutralised by the insistence that this could only be accomplished through the reform of the Stormont system and not by its abolition. Direct rule was passionately opposed on the grounds that it brought the North under tighter 'imperial' control – at least Stormont was run by Irishmen.

The strategy of pushing for the reform of the Stormont regime and opposing demands for its abolition was a difficult one to explain to many northern Officials, let alone to the Catholic communities in which they operated. Even those with fewest regrets about the split with the Provisionals found it difficult not to see the plausibility of the Provisional charge that they were attempting to reform the irreformable.[18] Goulding, who had had his own difficulties with the strategy, was ultimately convinced by Coughlan and Johnston. As in the past, it was tempting to explain the failure of strategic calculations in Dublin by referring to the recalcitrant material that had to be worked on in the North – in an interview in 1972 Goulding mentioned as one of the problems the Officials faced the fact that, 'In the North every Catholic youth is a Provo at heart.'[19]

At the heart of the Official analysis was an implicit recognition of the depth of communal polarisation, the implication of which was certainly that only gradual incremental change was possible. This allowed some realistic counterpoints to be made to the Provisional contention that once the 'puppet regime' at Stormont was gone, the 'Irish people' would quickly resolve the basic conflict with the British state. It was pointed out, for instance, that the abolition of Stormont would not shatter the Unionist 'power-base': 'Is not the real Unionist power base the determination of one million Protestant Irishmen not to enter a united Ireland?'[20] The Officials had consistently portrayed the essence of the civil rights movement as one of creating conditions which would allow for political differentiation within Unionism. While it was admitted that winning over Protestants, 'even some of them, may seem improbable at the present time', it was pointed out that the civil rights movement had shattered the unity of the Unionist Party and that, 'If proportional representation can be won, divisions in the ranks of Unionism may become institutionalised and can be exploited even further.'[21]

However the very positive aspects of an analysis which recognised the realities of massive internal opposition to a united Ireland, and the consequent need to pursue a process of political development within Northern Ireland, were ultimately nullified by the basic strategic framework of the National Liberation Front, which valued reforms and political development only if they assisted in developing 'a more Irish-orientated framework in the Six Counties within which some of the one million Protestants can be won in time to stand for a United Ireland'.[22]

Direct rule was opposed not essentially, as the Provisionals claimed, because of the 'reformism' of the Officials – after all, direct rule was arguably a better framework for the introduction of reforms than a crisis-ridden and divided Unionist regime – but rather because of a fundamental concern about its effects on the 'Irish nation' as a whole. The abolition of Stormont would represent an important shift towards fulfilment of Britain's new strategy towards Ireland. A speech by Quintin Hogg calling for the institutionalisation of relations between Dublin, Belfast and London and arguing that Fianna Fáil was the best party to institute détente in Anglo-Irish relations was seen as of great revelatory significance:

> People who take the political independence of the 26 Counties for granted are in for a shock. The 26 Counties is economically far more dependent on Britain now than it was ten years ago . . . Political dependence follows economic dependence as night follows day.[23]

A subsequent article in the *Economist* supporting direct rule was used as further evidence of the grand design:

> The Catholics would be guaranteed civil rights, the Protestants would be more secure within the United Kingdom than ever, the 'wild men' on both sides would be isolated. Northern Catholics would have no say in a UK parliament of 640 MPs and Lynch and the British would begin discussions about the Anglo-Irish federation.[24]

The concern with evaluating every specific proposal for change in the North in relation to the Official depiction of 'imperialist' strategy enabled some remarkable resistance to reality to be maintained. When Paisley's Protestant Unionist Party won its first seats at Stormont in April 1970, Sinn Féin issued a statement pointing out that the development of Paisleyism should not be used to justify arguments for direct rule. It alleged a British plan to replace Stormont with interim rule by a commission and to establish a Council of Ireland in which Belfast, Dublin and London governments were to be represented.[25] Such moves would be presented as moves towards a united Ireland, but were in fact aimed at giving Britain greater political control over Ireland as a whole.

In fact, the British state's relationship to Ireland was the reverse of the one posited by the Official analysis. Rather than thirsting to impose direct rule on Northern Ireland as part of a strategy to bring Ireland as a whole further into its sphere of interest, both the Wilson and Heath governments resisted the pressure which the unfolding crisis in Northern Ireland imposed for greater direct involvement. It was precisely this reluctance to remove the convenient buffer of the Unionist government, even after the sending of troops to Northern Ireland in August 1969, that created the best possible conditions for the development of the Provisionals. In the eyes of Northern Ireland Catholics, the reforms introduced in late 1969 were the hostage of a Unionist government under increasing pressure from its own ultras and the Paisleyites to backtrack. British troops would very soon be easily depicted as defenders of a corrupt and disintegrating Unionist regime. Such developments could have been avoided if, as the Wilson government had threatened, Stormont had been abolished at the time the troops were sent in. It was precisely because the dominant policy current in the British state was deeply averse to being sucked back into the 'Irish bog' that a series of disastrous expedients were adopted to keep the Unionists in power, expedients which contributed powerfully to an upsurge of militant republicanism.[26]

For all its undoubted struggle to modernise its politics and ideology, Official republicanism still suffered from that congenital nationalist belief in an unchanging substratum of British interest in Ireland. This resulted in a reading of recent economic history which was the exact reverse of the truth. The Lemassian break with protectionism and the opening of the Irish economy to foreign capital was a result of the bankruptcy of traditional Sinn Féin economic philosophy in the face of an economic crisis of major proportions in the 1950s. Liberalisation of the Republic's economy was no doubt welcome to Britain and sections of its industry, but it implied no concomitant need for a reordering of constitutional relations between Britain and the Republic. The new economic policies were impelled by the crisis of the Republic's economy and, although they were profoundly disturbing for traditional nationalist ideology, they did little to affect the British elite's fundamental lack of interest in Ireland. By presuming a British ruling class with an unchanging outlook and interests, Official republicanism produced an analysis of the northern situation which at times verged on the exotic,[27] and, more fundamentally, was not able to restrain the creeping militarisation of its supporters in Northern Ireland.

Militarisation

As Chief of Staff of the Official IRA, Goulding faced a major dilemma after August 1969 and the subsequent split. But the roots of the dilemma were in the conflict which implicitly existed between politicisation of the republican movement and the continuing existence of the IRA. As Goulding described it, one facet of the problem was that many of those attracted to the republican movement were drawn by its military mystique, but most people who wanted guns 'had no politics, or bad politics'.[28] The existence of the IRA as the dominant wing of the movement had many negative effects: in particular, it created permanent pressure for 'action'. Goulding used a prosaic metaphor to describe the tension in the IRA: 'It was like a grey-hound who is trained to race – you have to let it race or it goes bad.'[29]

Prior to the northern crisis the solution of the dilemma had been seen in developing Sinn Féin, involving members in social, economic and civil rights campaigns and, most importantly, taking a very selective and restrictive approach to recruitment to the IRA, which would only take the most 'politically conscious' members of the movement. Revolution would be redefined away from a fixation on armed struggle towards notions of a popular mass movement which might ultimately need force to defend its gains. In the interim this view enabled important individuals like McMillen to stay loyal, since for all its upgrading of politics and emphasis that there was more to 'anti-imperialist' activity than action against British troops in Northern Ireland,[30] it reserved the implicit leading role for the IRA, filled as it would be with the politically conscious elite of the movement. This, however, was very much a transitional view of the respective roles of politics and force, and it would ultimately prove unsustainable.

By the end of 1971 it was clear that developments in Northern Ireland had disrupted any plans for a change in the nature and role of the IRA. Within four months of the split the Provisionals were involved in a bombing campaign against commercial targets which were often owned by prominent Unionist businessmen. The Provisionals correctly calculated that the bombings would lead to increased pressure on the Unionist government and the British state for a policy of repression. British government acquiescence in the more repressive measures which the Unionist Cabinet declared were necessary to prevent a drain of support to the Protestant ultras, and increasingly hostile relations between British troops and the Catholic communities from which the Provisionals operated allowed the Provisionals to intensify their campaign. They first killed a British soldier in February 1971 and launched an intensive bombing campaign in the summer of that year. Under great pressure from the Unionist government, Edward Heath's Conservative government sanctioned the introduction of mass internment in August 1971. The results were disastrous – prior to internment there had been 34 deaths in 1971; between internment and the end of the year there were 139.

An atmosphere of fevered resentment and anticipation developed in many Catholic ghettos. The dynamics of communal expectations and competition with the Provisionals drew the Officials into attacks on the British Army and, after internment, even more indiscriminate violence.

The British Army's imposition of an arms search and curfew on the Lower Falls soon after the Conservative election victory in 1970 gave the local Officials the opportunity to establish their military credentials in a major gun-battle which entered Official mythology as the 'Battle of the Lower Falls'. This encouraged McMillen and Sullivan to believe that forceful assertion of the defensive role of the IRA would soon recuperate any ground that had been lost to the Provisionals. This inevitably caused friction with the Provisionals, as, for example, when Sullivan brought a group of Officials into Ballymurphy to respond to local complaints of army harassment, to the chagrin of the local Provisionals – among them Gerry Adams – who regarded Ballymurphy as their territory.[31] Such territorial disputes over issues like fund-raising and paper-selling as well as military action soon resulted in violent and brutal conflicts and killings. At the same time the Officials appeared to be happy to justify a 'defensive' role for the IRA, while attributing any polarising effects of violence to the Provisionals' bombing campaign.

As the Provisional bombing campaign intensified in the spring and summer of 1971, with the predictable army response – saturating Catholic areas, house searches, large-scale screenings of the population and so on – the Officials moved from 'defensive' to 'retaliatory' action. In its New Year statement in January 1972 the Official IRA blamed the escalation of its own activities on the 'sectarian bombing campaign' of the Provisionals, 'people who are blinded by bigotry and unable to see who the real enemies of the Irish people are'. This had allowed the British Army to 'escalate their terror tactics', which in turn were held to justify the new 'defence and retaliation' doctrine. At the same time the statement was at pains to emphasise that, 'It has never been and is not now our intention to build a movement to launch a purely military campaign against British forces in the North,' and to deny that it was engaged in a military campaign in Northern Ireland. This denial sounded hollow, especially when set against other lines in the statement that boasted of the 'many casualties inflicted on the forces of imperialism' by the IRA.[32] Armed struggle 'on its own, or as an end in itself', was declared to be doomed to failure. The problem for the Officials was that, as the impetus of the civil rights movement disintegrated and their agitational strategies in the Republic made only limited progress, there was a real danger that their political complement to IRA activities would seem increasingly formal and gestural.

Internment in August 1971, and the substantial increase in violence which it caused, greatly intensified these negative tendencies. While many prominent Officials were interned, the ranks were swelled by new recruits. By the end of 1972 the Officials' membership in Belfast, though still substantially less than that of the Provisionals, was around 800.[33] The distinction between 'retaliatory' and 'offensive' action was always a dubious one and increasingly IRA attacks clearly contradicted the claim that it had 'consistently eschewed all sectarian actions . . . our units will not take action designed to alienate any section of the working class'.[34] In December 1971 the homes of prominent Unionists in the Malone Road area of Belfast were attacked and, in 'reprisal for the destruction of working-class homes by the British forces', the Derry brigade admitted responsibility for the murder of a prominent Unionist politician, Senator Barnhill, shot dead by IRA men who had planned to blow up his home.[35]

In the aftermath of the Bloody Sunday killing of thirteen civilians by British paratroopers, Official militarism reached its nadir. In February 1972 a car-bomb attack on the Officers' Mess of the Parachute Regiment at Aldershot killed seven people, including five women canteen workers and a Catholic priest. Soon after this an attempt was made to murder John Taylor, the prominent Unionist minister, in Armagh, and an RUC sergeant was shot dead by the South Down-South Armagh Official IRA. In Derry the Officials, whose numbers had increased substantially since 1969, combined impatience with the national leadership's emphasis on civil rights with a ready belief in the revolutionary significance of 'armed struggle'.[36] In March they 'executed' a local Catholic accused of spying and in April murdered another Catholic home on leave from the British army.[37] By this time the disastrous implications of militarism were apparent. Roy Johnston resigned from Sinn Féin after the killing of Senator Barnhill, which he portrayed as the culmination of a process in which the balance in the movement had been unhealthily tilted towards a northern fixation with competing with the Provisionals:

> There has always been a difference in the points of view between both areas of the republican movement. The national movement sees Ireland as a whole . . . the northern section only sees one end of it and their feelings are sharp at the moment . . . they will tend to think of a purely military campaign.'[38]

The problems which Johnston's resignation highlighted were increasingly obvious to most people in the national leadership of the IRA and Sinn Féin. Most worrying was the threat posed to the political development of Sinn Féin in the Republic by IRA military activity in Northern Ireland. August 1969, internment and Bloody Sunday had all provoked spasms of emotional nationalism, but these quickly subsided with little evidence of any significant effects on the main lines of political affiliation in the south. As Provisional violence intensified and Protestant paramilitary groups in Belfast launched their own horrifying brand of counter-terror, the Officials' own involvement in northern violence was threatening marginalisation in the Republic. There were real fears of internment,[39] but even more significant was the growing fear that the organisation's preoccupation with the northern crisis was distracting attention from what an IRA statement defined as 'the central and most important issue facing the Irish people today', the proposed referendum on membership of the EEC.[40] EEC membership was portrayed as the culmination of the 'anti-national' economic policies pursued by Fianna Fáil since 1958, the result of which was depicted in apocalyptic terms:

> The loss of employment and livelihoods that would result from entry would mean the final devastation of a devastated people. North and South would face economic ruin and national extinction.[41]

The anti-EEC campaign saw the Officials and Provisionals united with the Irish Labour Party and the left fringe. The result was a major blow to the whole republican project. The people of the Republic voted by five to one for membership.[42] The *United Irishman* had to admit that the result was 'a kick in the stomach for the republican movement . . . The Irish people have rejected the proclamation of 1916 and the principles of national independence and sovereignty.' It drew the reasonable if pessimistic conclusion:

> What happened proves how much hard and patient work there is to be done before we will have convinced the people of either the necessity or more importantly the possibility of socialism.[43]

Throughout 1971 and 1972 leading Officials continued to reiterate the need for mass support for an 'anti-imperialist' strategy based on conditions in Ireland as a whole. As Garland put it, 'The North is not the only battleground.'[44] But attacks on elitism ('the doctrine which sets aside the wishes of the people with the expectation that where militants lead the people are bound to follow') and the emerging theme of 'the revolutionary party of the Irish people'[45] sat uneasily with the actualities of northern military emphases. In one of the earliest speeches canvassing the notion of a 'revolutionary party', Sean Garland also emphasised the need to widen radically the scope of republican activity: 'The struggle is everywhere, in the schools, in factories, in the fields, in the churches.'[46] Of course this was not new; it had been at the heart of the post-1962 rethinking. That it had to be reiterated in such an emphatic way was a sign of the degree to which the movement had regressed under the pressure of the North.

A prolonged and bitter debate in the Official Army Council in May 1972 resulted in the declaration of a ceasefire. There was much opposition from representatives from Belfast; McMillen argued that it would be extremely difficult to impose on the rank and file. His resistance was largely responsible for conditions attached to the ceasefire; the IRA reserved the right to undertake 'defensive' and 'retaliatory' actions.[47] Delegations of Belfast Officials, particularly in areas like the Ardoyne where the Officials were a small minority, came to Dublin to protest that the ceasefire would destroy any remaining credibility they had in competing with the Provisionals.[48] In Derry, where the militancy of the local Officials had checked the growth of the Provisionals, there was bitter opposition to the ceasefire and, in particular response to the intensification of loyalist killings of Catholics, there was pressure for an end to the ceasefire or at the very least for a liberal interpretation of 'retaliatory' action. Such pressure was resisted, but the fact that the ceasefire was not unconditional and that the Official IRA continued to exist would lead to increasingly bitter internal wranglings over the next three years. At the core of the conflict was the ever more obvious incapacity of the strategic framework set out in *Ireland Today* to relate to politics and society in either of the Irish states.

Civil Rights Versus the National Question

The imposition of direct rule was a major blow to the Officials, who continued to argue that it was a retrograde step, even though there was an increasingly clear formalism in their criticisms. Once the familiar charge that it was all part of Britain's broader aim of 'a false unity without independence'[49] had been repeated, the substance of Official demands – ending of internment, anti-discrimination legislation, 'fair and free elections under proportional representation' – could all be reasserted within the new framework. These were defined as 'interim democratic demands' and commitment was still maintained to 'full national unity and social freedom', but there was no mistaking the essential gradualism of the perspective. The major problem for the Officials was the lack of evidence that political reforms would prompt significant numbers of Protestants to the necessary reassessment of national identity. The lack of credibility of gradualist republicanism, together with the fevered expectations aroused by the crisis in Northern Ireland, created the conditions for a major assault on the civil rights component of the *Ireland Today* strategy.

The two key figures were Sean Garland and Seamus Costello. As early as May 1971 Garland had warned of the dangers of playing down the national question. Referring back to the Republican Congress, he claimed that it had failed because of its concentration on 'social questions' and its separation of these from the national question. In fact, this was the exact opposite of what the dominant, O'Donnellite, position had been, but Garland was obviously rewriting history with a purpose. He concluded, in strong implicit contrast with the *Ireland Today* analysis:

> The centuries-old struggle of the Irish people to establish an independent nation is still today one of the most potent

weapons in the revolutionary arsenal, is in fact the one single issue on which all Irishmen can come together.[50]

In marked contrast to this would be the continuing emphasis on the centrality of civil rights in the *United Irishman*, where statements like this were typical: 'The foremost issue for the people of the North is not the national question, but a democratic question of peace, justice and security.'[51]

The editor of the time, Eoin O'Murchu, has given an account of the tensions of the period. A strong supporter of the emphasis given to the struggle for civil rights, he subsequently left Sinn Féin to join the Communist Party. Despite the ceasefire, the continued emphasis on civil rights was not popular:

There was a growing feeling among many of the rank and file that there was a third way – neither militarist nor alliancist, but an individual, and indeed, exclusivist, political republicanism.[52]

He explains this in terms of three factors: a residual anti-Communism in the Officials, which saw the NLF strategy and the civil rights emphasis as Communist-inspired, traditional republican isolationism and distrust of working with other groups and the continued pressure for military action from the North which, given the ceasefire, made it all the more important to emphasise the specifically republican aspect of the movement's strategy.

There was certainly some resentment among the Officials that the Communists tended to see themselves as the hegemonic group in the NLF, providing theoretical leadership and 'experience of working-class struggles'.[53] Johnston's decision to join the Communist Party on resigning from Sinn Féin may well have intensified this. But such feelings, and also the desire to ensure Official leadership of campaigns, would have been shared by people on both sides of the debate over civil rights. The crucial source of the conflict lay in the different responses to the increasing evidence that, contrary to the expectations of the late 1960s, prospects for radical change in Ireland were dim indeed. Part of the necessary ideological baggage which the post-1962 transformation had carried along was a nebulous notion of a coming 'Irish revolution' in which a revamped republican movement would play a central role. Since little serious thought was given to what such a revolution would entail, it was not surprising that for some members, particularly in the North, the disintegration of the Unionist state and the continuing disorder and unrest appeared to create a potentially revolutionary situation.

It was to Seamus Costello, Director of Operations of the Official IRA, that such people increasingly looked for direction. A man whose bitterest opponents would admit that he had qualities of energy, efficiency and practical intelligence, Costello was fundamentally committed to the notion that 'armed struggle' could create revolutionary situations. Although his various proposals for joint action with the Provisionals and for various Official 'spectaculars' in Northern Ireland received little support either at Army Conventions or in the Army Council, the increasing disarray over political strategy provided a favourable environment in which he could continue to press for a return to militarism.

At the IRA Convention in October 1972 the issue of whether the emphasis on civil rights was too 'reformist' was raised and, after clear evidence of divided opinions, was referred back to the local units of the IRA for discussion. In the interim Garland had drafted a document calling for a reassertion of the national issue, and at the reconvened Convention and the subsequent Sinn Féin Árd Fheis, the new emphasis was accepted.[54] This produced unprecedented internal confusion and disarray. The bulk of the IRA and Sinn Féin leadership opposed the change, on the basis that a renewed emphasis on the 'national struggle' would be read as meaning a return to militarism. This was not Garland's intention, but he failed to specify what means were available to raise the 'national question', apart from those being currently used by the Provisionals. Simply to re-emphasise traditional republican values, while engaging in agitations and electoral activity which the Provisionals denounced as reformist, seemed insufficient for those Officials who emerged as Costello's supporters.

In 1973 and 1974 questions of strategy were intertwined with increasing concern for the basic structure of the Official movement. Participation in electoral activity was expanded in both states at local and parliamentary levels. This increased political work raised again the question of the respective roles of Sinn Féin (in the North, the Republican Clubs) and the IRA. Prior to August 1969 it had been possible to hope that the increased involvement in agitations and electoral activity would, of itself, lead to a gradual diminution in the significance of the military organisation. By the time of direct rule such hopes were clearly over-optimistic. In Northern Ireland at least, the IRA still dominated, and the high level of dual membership meant that the Republican Clubs were clearly and practically subordinate organisations. Even after the ceasefire, there was considerable resistance to electoral activity.

In the 1973 local government elections the Republican Clubs had ten of their 80 candidates elected, with an average of 10 per cent of the poll in constituencies contested.[55] The results were hailed as a victory for 'the development of genuine non-sectarian working class politics', but there was little evidence to support this; the fact was that the victories were obtained on an abstentionist platform because of continuing internment in predominantly Catholic constituencies.[56] Moreover, despite the traditionalist aspects of the campaign, there was clear resistance to involvement from some Officials. The *United Irishman* complained that some areas had played little or no part in the campaign:

> This displays a total misunderstanding of the opportunity the elections provided to publicise Republican policy, and is dangerously close to elitism . . . it is felt that the goal of a socialist Republic can be won without the co-operation and understanding of the people.[57]

The resistance was not lessened by the results of the subsequent Assembly elections in which, still fighting on an abstentionist platform, the Republican Clubs had no candidates elected and received a mere 1.9 per cent of the total poll.[58] The undoubtedly attractive and positive note in the Officials' propaganda, stressing the need to reach the Protestant working class, was undermined by the fact that the stated project was to win them to republicanism, albeit of a 'progressive' and class-conscious sort.[59] The lack of reality inherent in this approach made it more difficult to challenge the idea, common amongst Costello's supporters, that the Protestant working class was a privileged stratum that could only be won away from its reactionary politics by the destruction of the northern state.

The nationalism of the *Ireland Today* programme increasingly acted as a major ideological obstacle to the clarification of perspectives necessary for a fundamental break with militarism. For people like Garland, MacGiolla and Goulding, the activities of the Provisionals were anathema, as were Costello's proposals for alliances with them and for an intensified, aggressive posture for the Official IRA.[60] However ideological dependence on the *Ireland Today* analysis would continue into the mid-1970s,[61] and it would be only slowly undermined. In this process it would be the unresolved question of the role of the IRA which would prove decisive in forcing a fundamental reassessment of the whole republican tradition.

By the beginning of 1973, in part because of the ceasefire which had led to the release of many Official internees and also because of the successes of the security forces in actions against the Provisionals, the Officials were for the first time since the split almost as strong as the Provisionals in Northern Ireland.[62] This raised the question of their purpose, particularly given the restraint imposed by the ceasefire. The national leadership complained of

> a dangerous tendency . . . in some areas to equate the national question with the border and British troops . . . we must continuously re-emphasise that the national question . . . is all about the ownership of the wealth of this country.[63]

Nevertheless, the movement's military presence in Northern Ireland was functioning to reproduce the tendency which Garland was criticising.[64]

Garland's 1972 intervention had opened the way for those who wished to read the renewed emphasis on the national question as meaning a break with what a leading Costello supporter referred to as 'the bourgeois reforms' of the civil rights movement. It was now argued that the support for the civil rights strategy meant that, 'the republican movement had fallen behind the people in their revolutionary demands'.[65] The critic, the prominent Derry republican Johnnie White, was proposing an amendment to the main political resolution, which restated the commitment to the NLF strategy, and its emphasis on the fight for reforms. This was seen as a deliberate backtracking on the decision the year before to upgrade the priority of the national question.[66] The supporters of the amendment claimed that the effect of the resolution would be to turn the republican movement into a 'reformist' organisation, ignoring the obstacle that partition represented to progress in Ireland as a whole. As in 1972, the critics of the civil rights strategy also implied that it had led to the failure of the IRA to defend Catholics against the British army and loyalist assassins.[67] Little hope was held out for developing relations with the Protestant working class until partition was ended. Many of these criticisms echoed those the Provisionals had been making since 1969, as did the claim that the leadership of Sinn Féin was 'simply another facet of the Communist Party of Ireland'.[68]

By 1973 key figures in Official Sinn Féin and the Army Council had moved towards new organisational principles as part of a desperate search for the means of disciplining and marginalising Official militarism without provoking another split. Some of these means were the predictable resources of a conspiratorial organisation, like the denial of weapons and training to units of the IRA suspected of 'disloyalty'. As Director of Operations, Costello, the centre of resistance to the dominant line, was, of course, well placed to create an alternative infrastructure.[69] More significant was the attempt to transform the relationship between the IRA and Sinn Féin. In his Bodenstown speech in 1972, Garland had spoken of the need to build a 'revolutionary party', and this was a notion that was increasingly voiced by leading members of Sinn Féin. It was very unclear, however, what relationship this party would have with the IRA. While denouncing Provisional 'terrorism' and its sectarian effects, Garland had added that repudiation of terrorism did not mean there would be no role for the IRA, 'the army of the people', in 'defending the interests of the working class'.[70] For those in favour of the Costello approach, talk of a revolutionary party was seen as disguising a turn to 'social democracy', and there had been substantial opposition to the idea at the 1972 Árd Fheis.[71] A Structure Commission was established and produced a report in August 1973. According to O'Murchu, three positions were argued:

One, the IRA should be abolished forthwith. While this had extensive support, it was felt too blunt, too likely to provoke the split which subsequently happened ... Two, that the IRA's authority as the prime revolutionary force be reasserted. Three, that the IRA be removed entirely from political affairs and Sinn Féin developed as the sole republican political voice with the

implied understanding ... that the IRA would in fact wither
away and disappear without formal abolition.[72]

He claims that no formal position was adopted – the events
of the Costello split in 1974-75 intervening – but that, 'It is reasonable to assume that the third strategy was adopted.'[73] In
fact, there was serious resistance to the third proposal and substantial figures, particularly McMillen, asserted themselves in
favour of the second position. The report of the Structure
Commission had noted the

> feeling of many people in the movement that failure to main-
> tain Group B [the documents referred to the IRA as Group B
> and Sinn Féin as Group A] would create a dangerous vacuum
> which possibly would be filled by the Provos or some other
> group.[74]

The strength of the resistance only persuaded the leadership to
pursue a more gradualist approach. The pressure to maintain
the IRA as the leading core was recognised, but a majority of
the Army Council was persuaded to support a strategy substi-
tuting a form of Leninist for military vanguardism.

To the chagrin of the Derry Officials, influenced by the
Trotskyism which affected much of the student and labour left
in Northern Ireland in the aftermath of 1968, the 1973 Árd
Fheis had passed a resolution committing the Officials to a concept of 'Irish freedom' like that 'presently being built in the
Socialist countries'.[75] The Officials would be represented at the
'World Congress of Peace Forces' in Moscow in October 1973,
and, although the message was a traditional one,[76] the visit symbolised the increasing desire of the Official leadership to adopt
Leninist (or Stalinist, as their opponents labelled them) forms
of organisation.

In 1973 a meeting of the Army Council passed a resolution
committed to transforming the movement into a party, the philosophy of which would be Marxist and the organisational principles Leninist.[77] Such commitments, particularly that to the
creation of a 'revolutionary party' based on democratic centralism, represented in part the feeling of Goulding and
Garland that the phase of ideological apprenticeship to the
Communists was over and that the Officials needed to assert
their independence. At the same time, the recognition of the

very uneven results of the process of internal education, especially given the 'distractions' of northern violence, meant that
the major immediate concern was with organisational rather
than philosophical questions.

An Extraordinary Árd Fheis was supposed to be held to discuss the issues raised in the Structure Commission Report, but
by the time of the 1974 Árd Fheis this had still not occurred.[78]
As in 1969, it appears that Goulding and others who favoured
quite radical changes were unsure about the likely response
emerging from an immediate and open debate. One major
consideration was Costello, who had been suspended from
Sinn Féin for allegedly promoting a secret list of supporters for
election to the National Executive at the 1973 Árd Fheis. He
was subsequently 'court-martialled' and dismissed from the
IRA for undermining the organisation and misappropriation
of funds.[79] It was feared that, as in 1969, 'ordinary decent'
Officials would be swayed by Costello because of the radical
implications of the 'revolutionary party' proposal for the existence of the IRA.

During 1974 a leadership committee carried out a programme of visits to branches throughout Ireland to explain the
implications of the concept of the 'revolutionary party' and to
minimise support for Costello.[80] The subsequent decision, rat-
ified at the 1974 Árd Fheis, to expel Costello from Sinn Féin,
represented more a reaction of the majority of Officials against
any activities that threatened another split than a clear decision
on the future organisational and political direction of the
movement. The difficulties of transforming a movement with
militarist and commandist traditions were immense and often
entailed using very traditional methods to achieve modernising
objectives.

If the organisation which Costello's supporters established in
December 1974, the Irish Republican Socialist Party (IRSP),
had simply been a new ultra-left nationalist grouping, the
Officials would probably have ignored it. But Costello was a
substantial figure in his own right, and had used his considerable organisational abilities to produce the infrastructure for a
new military formation. How the arrival of a new, more 'revolutionary' armed competitor would have been treated by the
Provisionals, had they not been on terms of truce with the
British government through most of 1975, can only be the subject of speculation, but Costello's abrasive role prior to the

1969 split had made him many Provisional enemies.[81] In the event, it was the Officials in Belfast who attempted to eliminate the new organisation's military capacity before it could establish itself.

McMillen, who had been criticised for not acting against the Provisionals in 1969, was determined to ensure that Costello's supporters in Belfast did not use training and weapons acquired in the Officials to set up a rival organisation. He had initially proposed a series of beatings and punishment shootings, which he thought would be sufficient to deter the main Costello supporters and particularly their leader in Belfast, the former student radical Ronnie Bunting, but the view of most of the leading younger Officials who dominated the 'command staff' in Belfast was that more drastic action was needed. Although McMillen successfully opposed a proposal for the killing of Costello, it was decided that those who attempted to take weapons would be killed. The result was a vicious conflict initiated by the Officials in which seven of their members were killed and many others injured as the military wing of the IRSP, the Irish National Liberation Army (INLA) fought back. McMillen himself died and Garland was seriously injured. Over 100 Officials in Belfast joined the IRSP, including the entire IRA unit in the Divis Flats.

As the conflict with the IRSP and its military wing erupted, the Republican Clubs were preparing for elections to the Northern Ireland Convention, the British government's proposed forum in which local parties would discuss possible arrangements for the future internal government of Northern Ireland. On the day of a planned press conference on the organisation's proposals for reform of policing, the Official IRA killed its first leading IRSP member.[82] The killings continued throughout the election campaign and culminated in McMillen's death three days before polling. Leading members of Official Sinn Féin would subsequently complain at press portrayal of the conflict as a 'feud' or 'gang warfare' at a time when the public image of the party was crucial in electoral terms,[83] yet it was clear that a fundamental source of the problem lay not with the 'capitalist press' but with the Officials' still unresolved conception of the IRA's role. The problem returned in October 1975 when the Provisionals launched a concerted series of armed attacks on prominent Officials. When they ended in November, eight members, supporters and relatives had been killed. As Bishop and Mallie note, the Officials 'were efficient at fighting back': seven Provisionals were killed, as was the chairman of the Falls Road Taxi Association, which was a major source of revenue for the Provisionals.[84] The Provisionals' attack was without doubt partly motivated, as the Officials alleged, by the growing unpopularity of the ceasefire their leadership had negotiated with the British: militancy was siphoned off against the Officials.[85] Aggression may also have been encouraged by the fact of McMillen's death and his replacement by a much younger and relatively inexperienced Official. Yet although the Officials clearly felt the aggrieved party, popular perception of the conflict was that it was little different from that with the IRSP. The days of relatively indiscriminate woundings and killings were widely seen in both Catholic and Protestant communities as an internecine republican conflict, and any distinctiveness which the Officials' political strategy sought to establish was correspondingly weakened.

It was this year of violence that provoked the crucial shift in the internal balance within the Officials. McMillen's death removed the last major figure who wanted to maintain the IRA as the vanguard of the movement. A decision symbolic of the shift was the disbanding of Fianna Éireann in 1976. The dominant role of this organisation had been to prepare adolescents for future membership of the IRA. In practical terms, in 1976, it meant nearly 250 youngsters, in Belfast alone, with military training and the build-up of energy and expectation that accompanied it.[86] The replacement of the Fianna with a new wholly political youth movement proved less than successful; many members of the Fianna would not join the new organisation and some joined the IRSP. The decision nevertheless indicated that an era had ended, making clear to all members that the IRA had had its day as an organisation capable of replacing itself across the generations.

The break with republican military continuity would not be open or without some lingering resonances in subsequent incidents. This was particularly the case in Belfast where the years of bitter co-existence with the Provisionals had left their mark: the outlook of many people in the organisation and among its supporters was dominated by the memories of physical clashes with Provisionals and IRSP/INLA members. Loyalty was visceral and deeply overlain with local and familial ties. The Official IRA's arms were never handed in: in 1977 they were used in the last serious confrontation with the Provisionals in which a number of lives were lost.[87] In the same year Seamus Costello was shot dead in Dublin. In 1982 the INLA killed the man whom it claimed was the Official IRA commander in Dublin at the time of Costello's death and had carried out the killing.[88] The Official IRA would continue to have a largely subterranean existence until the end of the 1980s. The Officials' break with militarism was not a clean one, but it was accompanied by increasing evidence of a substantial ideological break with the main tenets of republican ideology.

The Officials and the 'Hidden Ireland'

In his talk on strategy in 1975 Garland had referred to the 'imbalance that the Six County situation creates in the entire country' as one of the major problems facing the movement.[89] In a lecture to the Boston Irish Forum, Tomás MacGiolla depicted the situation in Northern Ireland as a major obstacle to progress in Ireland as a whole. It had served to 'smother all progressive ideas, to weaken the forces of the left and strengthen the right-wing parties to the extent that they are now dominant in both North and South'.[90] The Officials' perspective on Northern Ireland now implicitly accepted the closure of the broader perspectives of the *Ireland Today* document: civil rights leading to the dissolution of Unionism in turn leading to a section of the Protestant working class reassessing its fundamental political allegiances. The positions adopted in 1969 had been reiterated as late as 1974. The British government's proposal's for a power-sharing Executive were opposed. The Sunningdale Agreement signed by the British and Irish governments and the recently formed Executive was denounced as 'a British-imposed solution . . . the beginning of the political integration of the whole of Ireland under a federal government in London'.[91]

The overthrow of the Executive by the Ulster Workers' Council strike in May 1974 ushered in a period of intensifying sectarian violence, and by 1975 it was being argued that the major priority in Northern Ireland was to check the growth of a 'civil war psychosis among a fairly widespread section of the population'.[92] It was necessary to judge all political questions according to the criterion 'do they encourage or distort class politics?'[93] If the Unionists and the constitutional nationalist Social Democratic and Labour Party (SDLP) could come to some arrangement leading to an internal settlement within the framework set out by the British government, this should be supported because it would lead to a lessening of sectarian animosities.[94] This was a sharp break with the previous approach, which had judged all political developments in Northern Ireland according to whether they aided or resisted 'imperialism's' master plan for Ireland as a whole. Increasingly, the whole concept of imperialism which had underlain the Officials' analysis and their continuing fealty to the social republican tradition was put in question.

In February 1977 the *United Irishman* announced the publication of a major document, *The Irish Industrial Revolution* (the IIR), produced by the Research Section of Sinn Féin's Department of Economic Affairs. The IIR, and in particular its first part, 'The Road to Underdevelopment', which provided a broad sweep over the economic history of Ireland from the Penal Laws of the eighteenth century to the 1960s, represented a forceful repudiation of the canon of Irish nationalist history. As Michael O'Riordan, the general secretary of the Communist Party of Ireland, put it in a letter of denunciation sent to all 'fraternal Communist and Workers' Parties', it demonstrated a 'volte-face' by Sinn Féin, which had now repudiated its membership of the 'Irish anti-imperialist movement'.[95] O'Riordan was particularly annoyed by a reference in the IIR to the 'mythical national question'.[96]

Other critics have seen the IIR as the culmination of the 'denationalising' influence of the Economic Affairs Department of Sinn Féin and its Research Section.[97] This department had been created in 1973 after the disintegration of an earlier attempt to develop Sinn Féin's influence in the trade union movement, the Republican Industrial Department. Goulding, who was the prime mover behind both efforts, had brought back an IRA veteran of the 1940s to set up the Economic Affairs Department.[98] Eamonn Smullen had served five years in Portlaoise for membership of the IRA during the Second World War. On his release he had rejoined the IRA in Dublin and had been close to Goulding, sharing a commitment to the idea of the need for political development of a leftist sort. He had been a member of the Dublin Connolly Group, composed mainly of republican ex-prisoners, and in the late 1940s they had often been involved in discussions with Communists and a smattering of leftist students including Roy Johnston. In the early 1950s Smullen had been obliged to go to England to find work. There he joined the Communist Party and became a trade-union activist in the building industry. He maintained his commitment to republicanism and when the northern crisis developed offered his services to Goulding. He was arrested and jailed in England in 1969 after attempting to buy arms.

Smullen set about the task of building up a trade union presence in a single-minded way that soon brought him into competition and conflict with the Communist Party, which resented what was seen as a republican intrusion. Others criticised what was seen as a secretive and conspiratorial style of work, yet it is doubtful whether the success of the Economic Affairs Department in expanding Official influence in some key unions could have been achieved by such methods alone. Smullen's major achievement was effectively to harness the resources of a small but growing group of intellectuals in the Research section. At the core of this group was Eoghan Harris, a former member of the Wolfe Tone Society who was by then a producer with the Republic's broadcasting body, RTE. He and a small group of Official sympathisers in the media and the civil service made the first serious attempt to take stock of the massive changes in the economic and social structure of the Republic since the 1950s. They argued that Lemass's new economic policies, which republicans had denounced, had in fact produced a major shift towards urbanisation and industrial development which held out new possibilities for advance.

For Harris and a number of other key intellectuals, however, such an advance was predicated on a fundamental reassessment of the traditional republican view of Irish history. Harris was undoubtedly a major influence on the development of the Officials in this period. His own massive energy, coupled with a forceful and dominant personality and the Research Section's penchant for secrecy, which often bordered on parody, has ensured that analyses of the ideological transformation of the organisation have focused on personalities to the almost total neglect of broader reasons for change.[99] One sympathetic professional historian noted of the controversial first section of the IIR that it was 'best interpreted as an explanation in socialist terms of some "revisionist" findings by the younger generation of Irish economic historians'.[100] Harris had been a student of the important revisionist historian John A. Murphy at University College, Cork, and the historical section of the IIR is replete with references to the work of the most important modern Irish historians.

At the core of the vehement response from social republican and nationalist traditionalists was the charge that the IIR had eliminated the role of 'British imperialism' in causing Irish economic backwardness and blamed instead the Irish Catholic bourgeoisie for 'refusing' to create an industrial revolution. There is certainly a tendency in the IIR to polemical exaggeration, a bending of the stick too far back in an effort to break with the traditional nationalist focus on 'British imperialism' as the source of all Irish problems.[101] Nevertheless, the essential contribution of the IIR and its real and positive significance was to provide, for the first time, a serious intellectual basis for a break with the *Ireland Today* analysis. It was clear in a brutal and practical sense that the notion of a National Liberation Front and a 'progressive' struggle against British imperialism was a road to nowhere. In ideological and theoretical terms, however, there had been no decisive break with a framework which still tied the Officials to a critique of the Provisionals and IRSP which was concerned to prove that they were not 'real' republicans, a criticism which for all its internal resonance, had no wider appeal, whether to Protestants or, even more critically, to the urban population in the Republic.

The IIR emphasised that the Irish national revolution was a profoundly Catholic and conservative affair with a rural bourgeoisie as its leading class. It demythologised the Land War of the 1880s, long romanticised by left republicans as a heroic struggle of a poverty-stricken peasantry against greedy landlords, and instead emphasised the dominant role played in the Land League by a strong rural middle class which had emerged in the post-Famine years. More disturbing to the whole focus of social republican 'class analysis' since the 1920s was the degree to which the IIR depicted the small farmers as the effective allies of the rural middle class, tied to them by their own intense aspirations for more land and livestock. As the economic historian Cormac O'Gráda pointed out, such an analysis cut the ground from under the core class alliance between workers and small farmers posited by social republicanism from Peadar O'Donnell to the authors of *Ireland Today*.[102]

At the same time as the IIR decisively shifted the focus of radical aspiration to the working class, it challenged the fundamental assumption about Ireland's domination by 'British imperialism'. Again, the rethinking represented the appropriation of an expanding body of academic and serious journalistic analysis of the Irish economy since the 1950s. Such analysis demonstrated that the new economic policies were tending, contrary to the Johnston-Coughlan theses, to lessen the Republic's economic dependence on Britain. The expanding foreign-controlled manufacturing sector, a source of very rapid economic growth in the 1960s and 1970s, was dominated by US, European and Japanese companies. If 'imperialist' domination of the economy of the Republic was still a central concern, it now became dissociated from the 'national question' in a way that was fraught with implications for traditional republican strategy. Imperialism was now acknowledged to have had certain positive characteristics – the influx of multinationals had created a larger working class:

> What happened in the period 1958-75 was that international capitalism had created what 73 years of native capitalist rule had failed to create – a highly organised and militant industrial working class.[103]

Previous attacks on multinational investment were dismissed as reactionary, as was opposition to the EEC.

The 1977 Sinn Féin Árd Fheis, which voted to change the name of the party to Sinn Féin – The Workers' Party, also adopted a political resolution stressing the change in the nature of imperialism: 'The centre of imperialism has moved from Britain to the USA and where British imperialism has declined and lost control it was replaced by American economic and cultural imperialism.'[104] While the exact 'scientific' value of this characterisation may be questioned, its political implication for the republican project was immense. From the social republicans of the inter-war period to the Official republicans in the early 1970s, all the diverse struggles and activities of the movement had been given a fundamental unity by the belief that they were responses to one common enemy which opposed the small farmer in the west and the shipyard worker in east Belfast. The IIR and the new emphasis on US imperialism effectively destroyed such assumptions of the basic unity of all issues, north and south. The criticism of British government policies in Northern Ireland would cease to be based on the a priori assumption that they were an attempt to defend some fundamental 'imperialist' interest in Ireland as a whole. Instead they would centre on specific economic and political reforms whose basic objective was the lessening of division inside the working class.

Although the formal commitment to a 32-county 'secular socialist republic' remained, it would increasingly assume the role of an ultimate aspiration. If at the centre of republicanism as an ideological tradition there is the assumption of an essential 'national being' assaulted and distorted by external intervention, its fundamental incompatibility with Marxism is obvious. For many social republicans, 'Marxism' was a way of tapping new popular constituencies for the national struggle. In the 1970s Marxism was increasingly attractive to leading Officials as a way of justifying in 'revolutionary' terms their policies of demilitarisation and gradualism in Northern Ireland. Marxism's emphasis on the central role of the organised working class in revolutions in capitalist countries could be used as an antidote to the frantic and fevered claims that 'armed struggle' in the North had a revolutionary significance. This functional use of Marxism was, for a while, compatible with an analysis of the Irish situation as a whole which was still fundamentally influenced by nationalist assumptions. As the North moved towards an ever more obvious sectarian impasse, however, it became of prime importance for the very survival of the movement that it redirect its resources to the Republic, where the only possibility of substantial political advance lay. The political prioritisation of the Republic then demanded an analysis which took account of the fact that there was very little evidence that urban workers would welcome any attempt to link agitation on economic and social issues with the 'national question'.

The increasing importance attached to work on a range of economic and social issues in the Republic, and the attempt to develop a trade union presence, was particularly welcome in the Dublin area where, in the aftermath of the EEC defeat, an internal document complained of 'a general malaise and apathy within the movement'.[105] Another complained of 'attempts to escape from the realities of life which the working class of Dublin faced by continually bawling about the "North" or indulging in fantasies of "instant revolution" '.[106]

In 1972 some Dublin members who were not convinced that the Officials were capable of moving decisively in a socialist direction had resigned and formed the Socialist Party of Ireland, and many who remained in the Dublin organisation shared some of the impatience and criticisms of those few who had left. They recognised the possibilities for expansion created by the Irish Labour Party's decision to return to the strategy of coalition, one forsaken in its period of 1960s radicalisation. Even in 1973, the year which saw the Labour Party enter government as a coalition partner of the traditionally right-wing Fine Gael party, the Sinn Féin organisation in Dublin, after 'one of the most bankrupt years in its history'[107] with 300 members, just over half of whom were active in 25 branches, had received 300 applications for membership.[108] The coalition had to face the major implications of the post-1973 international recession. Unemployment increased from 7.9 per cent in 1973 to 12.5 per cent in 1977, and in June of that year the coalition was defeated by Fianna Fáil in a general election.

EEC membership ushered in a period of major crisis for the Republic's traditional industries in a new competitive environment. The Industrial Development Association had estimated that there would be 17,000 job losses in the 1973-77 period. The actual figure was 57,000 in the first three years.[109] In Dublin, in particular, the Officials were able to emerge as the hegemonic group in the left's response to the economic crisis. This was in part the product of the movement's ability to channel its membership in a disciplined way into a number of significant campaigns on high visibility issues, particularly those of resources protection and housing. In the Resources Protection Campaign the issue was the proposal of the Labour Minister for Industry and Commerce, Justin Keating, to allow a multi-national to develop the large zinc and lead deposits at Navan, County Meath. Sinn Féin's Research Section had produced a large amount of material linking the issue to that of the exploitation of off-shore oil and gas reserves and proposing an alternative statist development strategy with greater job-creating capacity.[110] On issues like this and the economic crisis, Sinn Féin members worked with members of the Communist Party and the Liaison Committee of the Labour Left. However such co-operation was short-lived as Sinn Féin became more and more convinced that it was providing the serious intellectual and research capacity and should be in a position to reap the greatest political benefit from this work.[111] It was certainly the case that the contributions of people like Harris and other Sinn Féin members impressed even their critics,[112] and that in this period the Officials emerged with a distinct persona in Dublin as the talented and articulate defenders of a statist strategy of economic development. At a time when the post-1959 policies of economic liberalisation and attraction of foreign capital were faltering in a hostile international environment, there was scope for such an approach. It was particularly attractive to workers in the Republic's large public sector at a time when prominent Fine Gael members of the government were complaining of the 'parasitic' role that the public sector was playing. Defence of the public sector, and demands for its expansion into areas like energy and construction, ensured a growing audience for Sinn Féin's ideas in the public sector unions.[113]

Throughout this period of Dublin expansion in the mid-1970s the movement retained the secretive and conspiratorial side that was a legacy of its history. The input of intellectuals was organised through two secret branches distinct from the ordinary, geographically based ones. Members of these branches were not open members of the organisation and had little if anything to do with the activities of its ordinary members. Justified by reference to the possible victimisation of individuals who had jobs in the media and the civil service, the secret branches tended to restrict serious discussion of major revisions of party policy by the bulk of the membership. At the same time the very traditional republican self-designation of the movement as composed of a dedicated, self-sacrificing elite was now expressed in the transformed terms of the 'revolutionary vanguard' contemptuous of the 'social democrats' in the Labour Party and increasingly determined to displace the Communist Party. The dominant role which Sinn Féin, through its Research Section, played in the mobilisation of a left critique of the coalition's response to the economic crisis, allowed it to attract a substantial number of disillusioned Labour Party supporters.[114] The real, if limited prospects for political advance in Dublin which opened up after 1973 were a major reason for the consolidation of ideological revisionism in the Official movement.

The IIR was the first major documentary evidence that a part of the 'republican tradition' was willing to accept popular opinion when it violated a central tenet of republican faith. The clear evidence of mass support for economic liberalisation, particularly the decisive vote for EEC membership, was a major blow to the social republican project in the Republic. The IIR was the belated recognition of this fact, and in an important sense it marks the departure of the Officials from the social republican tradition.

Notes

1. This account is based on a number of sources – interviews with Cathal Goulding and Sean Garland, *Fianna Fail and the IRA*, pp.51-2, T.P. Coogan, *The IRA*, London 1987, expanded edition, p.428 and Patrick Bishop and Eamonn Mallie, *The Provisional IRA*, London 1987, p.40.
2. 'Where Sinn Féin Stands', a statement issued subsequent to a meeting of the Caretaker Executive of Sinn Féin on January 17 1970. It was subsequently reissued in pamphlet form with the addition of a favourable article from the *New Statesman* by David George as 'These Are the Provisionals', Dublin 1972.
3. 'The Walk Out: A Personal View', *United Irishman*, February 1970.
4. Interview with Cathal Goulding.
5. Interview with Sean Garland; see also his 'What Sort of Unity', *United Irishman*, July 1971.
6. Coogan, op.cit., p.429.
7. *United Irishman*, January 1970.
8. Ibid., April 1970.
9. Ibid., March 1971.
10. Ibid., April 1971.
11. Ibid., February 1971.
12. Interview with Cathal Goulding.
13. P. Beresford, 'The Official IRA and Republican Clubs in Northern Ireland 1968-74', unpublished DPhil thesis, University of Essex, 1975, p.69
14. Interviews with Jim Sullivan and Kevin Smyth.
15. According to a *United Irishman* estimate in July 1970, the Provisionals took 80 per cent of those actively involved in the various Citizens Defence Committees. It should be noted that some Provisional leaders were aware of the problems associated with the influx: interview with Jimmy Drumm.
16. Sean Garland, 'Policy, Strategy and Tactics', a lecture given at an internal Sinn Féin conference at Mornington, County Louth, on 28 and 29 June 1975.
17. *United Irishman*, February 1970.
18. Interview with Kevin Smyth.
19. Interview with Cathal Goulding in Rosita Sweetman, *On Our Knees, Ireland 1972*, London 1972, p.147.

20. *United Irishman*, September 1970.
21. Ibid.,
22. Ibid.,
23. Ibid., March 1970.
24. Ibid., September 1970.
25. Ibid., May 1970.
26. The role of British government policy in creating the best possible conditions for the development of the Provisionals is dealt with at greater length in Paul Bew and Henry Patterson, *The British State and the Ulster Crisis*, London 1985.
27. See an article by Roy Johnston criticising a pamphlet by the People's Democracy leader, Michael Farrell, *The Struggle in the North*. One of his main criticisms of Farrell was the treatment of the Haughey-Blaney-*Voice of the North* group as 'militantly anti-partitionist'. Johnston commented, 'It is not to establish a Fianna Fáil republic, it is to draw out the republican sentiment of people into a civil war situation where it will be smashed so that a federal solution can be imposed by Westminster.' *United Irishman*, January 1970.
28. Interview with Cathal Goulding.
29. Ibid.
30. *United Irishman*, April 1970, IRA Easter statement: 'The IRA is the Army of the People . . . The people must regard it as their own, and not as a remote organisation which is interested in fighting only one facet of British imperialism, her occupation troops. The people of the 26 Counties must realise that British imperialism is as strong in their midst.'
31. Interview with Jim Sullivan.
32. *United Irishman*, January 1972.
33. Interview with Kevin Smyth.
34. *United Irishman*, September 1971.
35. Beresford op.cit., pp.504 and 505.
36. See Eamon McCann, *War and an Irish Town*, London 1980, for a sympathetic Trotskyist view of the Derry Officials.
37. Details from Beresford, op.cit., pp.509-10.
38. Roy Johnston, 'Why I Quit Sinn Féin', *Sunday Press*, 23 January 1972.
39. Interview with Goulding. The Official IRA's own activities in the Irish Republic made some contribution to the problem. Thus in July 1971 it intervened in a long and bitter strike in the Mogul Silver Mines, County Tipperary, against a foreign mining company. A young IRA man, Martin O'Leary, was killed in an unsuccessful attempt to blow up an electricity transformer. At his funeral Goulding provocatively proclaimed, 'When their answer to the just demands of the people is lock-out, strike-breaking, evictions . . . our duty is to respond in the language that brings vultures to their senses . . . the language of the bomb and the bullet.' *United Irishman*, August 1971. Goulding was charged with incitement to violence but when an RTE tape of the funeral oration was finally handed over to the police it was found to be blank and the charge failed.
40. *United Irishman*, April 1972.
41. Ibid.

42. The vote in favour was 1,041,890 (83.1 per cent); against, 211,891 (16.9 per cent). Turn-out was 70.3 per cent. Michael Gallagher, *The Irish Labour Party in Transition 1957-82*, Manchester and Dublin 1982, p.285 note 53.

43. *United Irishman*, June 1972.

44. 'What Sort of Unity', *United Irishman*, July 1971.

45. Sean Garland, speech at Bodenstown, *United Irishman*, July 1972.

46. Ibid.

47. Interview with Cathal Goulding.

48. Interview with Seamus Lynch.

49. IRA Easter statement, *United Irishman*, April 1972.

50. Sean Garland, 'Building Revolution', *United Irishman* May 1971. Garland's increasing disenchantment with the civil rights strategy may have reflected in part the influence of the American Trotskyist, Gerry Foley, who came to Ireland in 1970 and gravitated towards the Officials. He appears to have influenced Garland's views for a time. See his critique of the political weaknesses of the Officials and the alleged danger that this would leave them open to 'the utopian concept of a long democratic stage ahead as proposed by the dismal hacks of the Northern Ireland Communist Party'. Gerry Foley, *Problems of the Irish Revolution: Can the IRA Meet the Challenge?*, New York 1972, p.21.

51. *United Irishman*, September 1971.

52. Eoin O'Murchu, 'The Workers' Party: Its Evolution and its Future', *Irish Socialist Review*, 1982, p.20.

53. Interviews with Tomás MacGiolla and Eamonn Smullen.

54. O'Murchu, op.cit., p.20 and Margie Bernard, *Daughter of Derry: The Story of Brigid Sheils Makowski*, London 1989, p.109 – she claims that Garland and Costello submitted a joint document to the Árd Fheis.

55. Beresford, op.cit., p.757.

56. Liam Barr, 'The Republican Clubs – The Workers' Party in Mid-Ulster 1974-79', unpublished BA dissertation, Ulster Polytechnic, 1980, p.8.

57. *United Irishman*, July 1973.

58. Bew and Patterson, op.cit., p.124.

59. *United Irishman*, July 1973: 'We have a new opportunity to convince the Protestant working class that republicanism is the only way out of the British-created horror.'

60. At one Army Council meeting he proposed the seizure of the Catholic side of the River Foyle in Derry. In 1972 the Provisionals asked for a meeting with representatives of the Official Army Council. Costello was enthusiastic about the meeting's possibilities but when it took place in a church in Gardiner Street, Dublin it turned out that the Provisionals simply wanted to warn the Officials to keep out of 'their war in the North' – interviews with Cathal Goulding and Sean Garland.

61. Sean Garland, 'Policy, Strategy and Tactics' emphasised the need for a National Liberation Front.

62. Beresford, op.cit., p.707.

63. Sinn Féin, *Árd Fheis Report 1973*, p.6.

64. In May 1974 two members of the South Down-South Armagh IRA were shot dead by British soldiers while attempting to place a landmine 'as retaliation for intimidation and harassment of working-class people of

Newry'. *United Irishman,* June 1974.
65. *Irish Times,* 26 November 1973.
66. For the views of a Costello supporter, see Bernard, op.cit., p.114.
67. Ibid.
68. *Irish Times,* 26 November 1973, and *United Irishman,* December 1973.
69. 'He was choking us for the sinews of war' – interview with Cathal Goulding.
70. *United Irishman,* July 1972.
71. Beresford, op.cit., p.767.
72. O'Murchu, op.cit., p.22.
73. Ibid.
74. The documents found their way to the *Belfast Telegraph,* which published an edited version of them on 13 November 1973.
75. *Irish Times,* 26 November 1973. Gerry Foley commented on the Derry Officials, after the killing of Ranger Best, the local youth who had joined the British army, 'It is true that the Derry unit which carried out the execution is not typical of the Official IRA. Among other things, British ultra-leftist and workerist groups have exercised a more marked influence in this area than in other parts of Ireland.' Foley, op.cit., p.7.
76. MacGiolla urged delegates to support the republican demand for withdrawal of British troops. *United Irishman,* December 1973.
77. Interview with one of the members of the Army Council at the time.
78. Sinn Féin, Árd Fheis 1974-75 *Internal Clar* (Agenda). Various branches raised question of why the Extraordinary Árd Fheis on the Report had not been held.
79. For a pro-Costello account, see Bernard, op.cit., p.116.
80. Barr, op.cit., p.12.
81. Interview with Cathal Goulding.
82. Interview with Kevin Smyth.
83. Sinn Féin Árd Fheis *Report* 1974-75, p.2.
84. Bishop and Mallie, op.cit., p.222.
85. 'What better way, the truce leadership thought, to maintain the cease-fire but at the same time allow the madmen to let off steam, than by allowing them to turn their guns on true republicans.' A quote from Official Sinn Féin leaflet, 'Provo Pogrom', Belfast 1975.
86. Interviews with Seamus Lynch and Kevin Smyth. See also Eddie Rooney, 'From Republican Movement to Workers' Party: An Ideological Analysis' in C. Curtin (ed.), *Culture and Ideology in Ireland,* Dublin 1984.
87. Paul Bew and Gordon Gillespie, *Northern Ireland: A Chronology of the Troubles 1968-1992,* Dublin 1993, p.122.
88. Jack Holland and Henry McDonald, *The INLA: Deadly Divisions,* Dublin 1994, p.118.
89. Sean Garland, op.cit.
90. Tomás MacGiolla, *The Making of the Irish Revolution: Strategies and Tasks,* Dublin 1976, p.5.
91. Belfast Republican Clubs Manifesto for the Westminster election, February 1974.
92. Total deaths in Northern Ireland from the 'Troubles', which had climbed from 25 in 1970 to 474 in 1972, dropped to 221 in 1974, but

rose to 244 in 1975 and 296 in 1976. Figures from K. Boyle and T. Hadden, *Northern Ireland: A Positive Proposal*, London 1985, p.14. The reference to civil war is in a lecture by Des O'Hagan, 'Fundamental Policies and Intentions of Organisations Involved in the Current Situation', given at an internal Sinn Féin conference at Mornington, County Louth, 28 and 29 June 1975.

93. Brian Brennan, 'Sectarianism and Class Politics', lecture at Mornington conference.

94. Ibid.

95. Memorandum circulated by Michael O'Riordan, 30 March 1977.

96. The CP was also concerned about the decision of the 1977 Árd Fheis to change name to Sinn Féin – The Workers' Party and the decision to create the Irish Democratic Youth Movement 'as a rival to our Communist Connolly Youth Movement'.

97. Typical criticisms can be seen in Vincent Browne, 'The Secret World of the SFWP: Part 2 Political Lobotomy', *Magill*, May 1982, and in O'Murchu, op.cit.

98. The following is based on interview with Eamonn Smullen, on his unpublished paper 'The Workers' Party and the Communist Party – In What Ways Do They Differ', and on O'Murchu, op.cit.

99. See Ray McGuigan, 'The Making of a Conspiracy', *Magill*, May 1982.

100. Cormac O'Grada, *United Irishman*, May 1977.

101. Eoghan Harris would admit this but defend it as part of a necessary ideological campaign to shift focus from external to internal sources of division in Ireland – interview with Eoghan Harris.

102. *United Irishman*, May 1977.

103. Research Section of the Department of Economic Affairs, Sinn Féin – The Workers' Party, *The Irish Industrial Revolution*, Dublin 1978, p.50.

104. *United Irishman*, February 1977.

105. Secretary's/Organiser's *Report* to Annual General Meeting of Dublin Comhairle Ceanntar, 21 December 1973.

106. Organisers' *Report* to Dublin AGM, 1 December 1974.

107. Ibid.

108. Secretary's/Organiser's *Report* to 1973 AGM and Reorganisation Document 1974.

109. See Paul Bew, Ellen Hazelkorn and Henry Patterson, *The Dynamics of Irish Politics*, London 1989, Chapter 4.

110. See, in particular, Research Section, Department of Economic Affairs, Sinn Féin, *The Great Irish Oil and Gas Robbery: A Case Study of Monopoly Capital*, Dublin 1974.

111. Smullen, loc.cit.: 'Our party contributed the bulk of the research material . . . our research contribution was mostly not credited to us.'

112. See Carol Coulter, 'How They Infiltrated the ITGWU', *Magill*, May 1982: 'The main reason for the success of the infiltration process has simply been that the SFWP-inclined candidates were very often by far the most outstanding applicants for positions – most of them have also proved to be highly competent and diligent.'

113. Research Section, Department of Economic Affairs, Sinn Féin, *The Public Sector and the Profit Makers*, Dublin 1975, reprinted 1976.

114. Nationally the Labour Party vote rose from 185,176 (13.7 per cent) to

186,410 (11.75 per cent) but in Dublin its vote dropped from 78,342 (22.3 per cent) to 74,688 (17.5 per cent). In 1969 its Dublin vote had been 93,430 (28.3 per cent). Gallagher, op.cit., Appendices 1 and 2.

6 The Provisionals and the Rediscovery of Social Republicanism

In 1977 Jimmy Drumm, one of the group of older republicans who had played a central role in the emergence of the Provisionals in Belfast after August 1969, gave the annual address to the Wolfe Tone commemoration at Bodenstown. A traditionalist had been chosen to read out a withering critique of the main lines of Provisional strategy since 1970 which would publicly inaugurate a prolonged, contradictory and ultimately unresolved engagement with some of the central themes of social republicanism. Drumm complained of attacks on the Provisionals which accused them of 'having been devoid of political thinking, dependent entirely upon the bomb and the bullet'. At the core of the speech was a major reassessment of the 'armed struggle':

> We find that a successful war of liberation cannot be fought exclusively on the backs of the oppressed in the Six Counties, nor around the physical presence of the British army. Hatred and resentment of this army cannot sustain the war, and the isolation of socialist republicans around the armed struggle is dangerous and has produced at least in some circles, the reformist notion that 'Ulster' is the issue, which can somehow be resolved without the mobilisation of the working class in the 26 Counties. We need a positive tie-in with the mass of the Irish people who have little or no idea of the suffering in the North because of media censorship and the consolidation of conservatism throughout the country. We need to make a stand on economic issues and on the everyday struggles of people. The forging of the strong links between the Republican movement and the workers of Ireland and radical trade unionists will create an irre-

pressible mass movement and will ensure mass support for the
continuing armed struggle in the North.[1]

The speech was notable precisely because the 'reformist'
notion that 'Ulster is the issue' had been at the centre of
Provisional strategy since 1969. The Provisionals' major policy
statement, *Eire Nua* (1971), had, it is true, provided for a four-
province federal Ireland, and Ruairí Ó Bradaigh, president of
Provisional Sinn Féin, had assured Ulster Protestants that 'We
would never ask you to join the 26-County state – we are trying
to escape from it ourselves.'[2] But, as increasing northern disquiet with central aspects of *Eire Nua* would soon make clear, it
had never been more than a constitutional froth on an armed
struggle that had its own dynamics, and increasingly these
appeared to demand a significant strategic reappraisal.

The immediate pressure for change came as a result of the
truce between the Provisionals and the British army and RUC,
which had lasted for most of 1975. This had left the
Provisionals severely weakened, and militarily and politically
divided and demoralised. This was the second time the
Provisionals had entered into negotiations with the British government. In 1972 the first Secretary of State for Northern
Ireland, William Whitelaw, had arranged for six leading
Provisionals, including Gerry Adams, to be flown secretly to
England for negotiations.[3] These negotiations had come to
nothing and the associated truce had been brief, with no harm-
ful effects on the Provisionals' military capacity.

In 1975, however, the disruptive effect of the truce flowed in
large part from the analysis which the leadership group – still
largely Dublin-based – made of the British interest in negotiations. As one sympathetic observer has described it:

> The leadership then, and in particular Daithi O'Connaill [IRA
> Chief of Staff] believed that the British could be negotiated into
> a settlement or at least that the appearance of negotiations with
> the IRA would so destabilise the British position in the eyes of
> Northern Unionists, and indeed of established politicians North
> and South of the border, that they would have no option but to
> disengage.[4]

The disruption of British-sponsored reforms by the Ulster
Workers' Council strike was believed to have brought about a
fundamental reassessment of the link with Northern Ireland.

This notion was encouraged by the Northern Ireland Office negotiators, who needed a truce to create the requisite atmosphere for the release of internees. This was designed to allow the inauguration of a shift in security policy towards 'criminalisation' and away from those aspects of previous policy, like internment and reliance on the British army, which were seen as allowing the Provisionals to represent their activities as part of a legitimate national liberation struggle.[5] The coincidental effects of economic recession on industry in Northern Ireland were seen as evidence of an 'economic withdrawal'. Long after the collapse of the truce, it was still being argued that, 'The run-down of the Six Counties, commercially and industrially, has already begun, and this run-down is also taking place coincidentally with military withdrawal.'[6]

The wishful thinking involved in such predictions was forcefully repudiated in Drumm's speech:

> The British government is NOT [emphasis in original] withdrawing from the Six Counties and the substantial pull-out of businesses and the closing down of factories in 1975 and 1976 were due to world economic recession though mistakenly attributed to symptoms of withdrawal. Indeed the British government is committed to stabilising the Six Counties and is pouring in vast sums of money to improve the area and assure loyalists.[7]

Drumm had been involved, with his wife Maura, in the negotiations with the NIO and long remained convinced of the correctness of the strategy embodied in the truce.[8] The critique in his speech represented a reassessment, the core ideas of which came from Gerry Adams, in a series of contributions to *Republican News* under the pen-name 'Brownie', written in Long Kesh prison between 1975 and 1977.

Adams, who had joined the republican movement in 1964, had few of the reservations that led older republicans like Drumm and Joe Cahill to drop out of the movement. With other young IRA members like Joe McCann, he had been involved in housing and civil rights agitation which he later wrote about in positive terms:

> We were also enjoying the breakdown of republican isolation, the political exchanges and interchanges, the pooling of resources and experiences arising from the informal alliances which were being developed in the 'thick of the battle' between

the different elements of the civil rights movement. The traditional internalisation of republican activities and their restriction to a chosen few now seemed a thing of the past.[9]

The coming in from the cold of republicanism referred in
Adams's case to the emerging common ground – in analysis at
least – with the main ideologists of the student-based People's
Democracy organisation, who saw in the civil rights campaign a
way of hastening a crisis of the Northern Ireland state with a
potentially revolutionary outcome.[10]

For Adams, the fundamental reason for opposition to the
national leadership was the 'reformism' of its position on
Northern Ireland, not the concept of the National Liberation
Front or the commitment to socialism. Adams and other IRA
members in Ballymurphy had initially maintained a position of
distance from the developing schism after August 1969 and he
dissociated himself from the first major Provisional policy statement which denounced the Officials for their 'extreme socialism' and the NLF position.[11] Although he felt a degree of alienation from the more traditional elements in Belfast and in the
national leadership, such differences were soon far outweighed
by the common commitment to force a major crisis in the
northern state through aggressive military action. It was the
impasse of the Provisional military campaign which created the
conditions for Adams to reassert some of his 'lessons of 1968'.

The bankruptcy of the dominant military line was clearly
revealed in a defence of the Provisionals' campaign of commercial bombings – a central component of the military campaign since 1970 – written in 1976. It bluntly proclaimed that
its key purpose was to polarise political forces in Northern
Ireland and make British-sponsored reform impossible:

> It has disrupted parliamentary practice, helping to topple
> Stormont and polarised the electorate to the extent that the
> professional politicians are the victims of mutually incongruous
> manifestos. Therefore it has forced British direct rule into
> being and clarified that Westminster rule is imperialist: their
> army an army of occupation. The growth of reaction isn't to be
> frowned upon. We can inflate its importance and at our own
> leisure burst its credibility. As George Jackson, that great Black
> revolutionary, once said, 'What would help us, is to allow as
> many right-wing elements as possible to assume political
> power.'[12]

There was no mention of the Republic in a portrayal of strategy which was content to label itself as a 'Ghetto Peoples' War'. It proclaimed that the greatest achievement of the bombing campaign was within the Catholic ghettos themselves: 'Behind those bombers, is a massive structure based on streets and districts, whose existence is dependent upon the active support and mandate of the people.'[13] In fact, the article made clear that such support was limited to a minority in the ghettos, focussing only on those who actively assisted or identified with the 'armed struggle'. The degree of self-deception involved in this type of analysis – it also predicted imminent British withdrawal – was not shared by all leading Provisionals. In Long Kesh, a strain of leftist Provisionalism was emerging, with Adams at its centre. This displayed a much more realistic appreciation of the extent of popular identification with the 'armed struggle' and of British government intentions.

With some irony, conscious or unconscious, Adams chose an article on Mellows's *Jail Notes* to put forward a more realistic assessment of the limits of current Provisional strategy. Mellows had been a central figure in the ideological reorientation after 1962, and his reappearance in internal Provisional debates had to be treated delicately. Adams was careful to point out that the *Jail Notes* had been labelled 'Communist' by the anti-Treatyites, thus establishing at the beginning the lack of credibility of such charges. Mellows's message was 'the need to show an effective alternative to Brit/Free State institutions'. This was all the more necessary since the British government was seen as desiring, not withdrawal, but some internal accommodation between 'Orange and Green politicians' which could be foisted on a 'war-weary people'. The current resources of the Provisionals were realistically and critically assessed. The 'republican war machine' had survived 'despite attrition', but this was clearly insufficient as it countered only one facet of British involvement in Ireland: 'We need to counter the Brit economic, political, cultural, national and military fronts.' What was needed was a programme of 'active abstentionism' to win popular support for the Provisionals in the northern ghettoes and, just as important, to break the isolation of the 'anti-imperialist struggle' in Northern Ireland. Far from nearing its end, the building of a 'National Alternative' to 'Brit and Free State institutions' had not yet begun.[14]

In his prison contributions, Adams repeatedly stressed the need to avoid narrowing down the republican struggle to a military campaign in the north: 'We need to expand our struggle onto a 32 County basis. We are fighting for National Freedom but one major drawback appears to be that we are restricting ourselves a great deal to the North.'[15] Much of this approach demonstrated how extensively the *Ireland Today* analysis was capable of being appropriated by the Provisionals. This extended to the verbatim, but unacknowledged, reproduction of the analysis of the nature of imperialism and the characterisation of the south as a 'neo-colony' of Britain.[16] As the Officials moved to jettison the ideological legacy of Johnston and Coughlan, an important part of it was taken up by Adams and his supporters.

But the declaration of the need for an 'economic resistance' campaign encountered all the problems that had arisen a decade earlier. Adams sought to mobilise the masses in the Republic against their 'Vichy-type' government by exposing its various 'sell-out' policies, from foreign exploitation of mineral resources to the whole direction of post-1958 economic strategy 'which offered Irish resources and Irish labour for exploitation on a joint-partnership basis between Irish and American capital'.[17] The economic 'sell-out' was linked to the 'collaboration' of southern governments with the British government's campaign against the 'resistance struggle'.

Adams was prepared to admit that the national question was not at the top of the political agenda in the Republic:

> The overriding question is of course the National Question but there are many, many issues affecting people in the Free State in which we should be showing a lead – issues which are linked to the national question, and which can only be solved when it is solved, but issues which people do not relate as relevant to that issue.[18]

He instanced wages, equal pay for women, regressive taxation structures, capitulation to foreign mining companies and lack of resources in higher education. That these were all real issues was undeniable. The problem for the Provisionals was that there was no structural link between any of them and the 'national question', unlike the situation in Northern Ireland, where the deep-rooted structures of economic and occupational inequality between the Catholic and Protestant communities provided a material substratum for the reproduction of a communal nationalism of grievance. In the Republic, as the Officials had gradually perceived, any attempt to link agitation on economic and social issues to a nationalism bent on 'completing' the agenda of 1921 was doomed to popular rejection if it went beyond the passionate pieties of Fianna Fáil. By the mid-1970s the undoubted reserves of sympathy for northern Catholics and sentimental support for the ideal of a united Ireland were counteracted by a recoil from the seemingly endless violence in the North. Any organisation which sought to link economic or any other domestic issue to support for 'armed struggle' was doomed to remain forever on the margins in the Republic.[19]

Predictably, the resistance to these themes came from those for whom it raised the spectre of the earlier dispute with the Officials. At the Sinn Féin Árd Fheis in 1977, one Donegal delegate urged the movement not to become entangled with international socialism or communism: 'We are not engaged in a class struggle.'[20] At the time, Ruairí Ó Bradaigh disagreed: 'Whatever one liked to call it we were struggling against a corrupt system in which 70 per cent of the wealth was owned by 5 per cent of the people.' The Provisionals were committed, he claimed, to 'revolution across the board – to the Socialist Republic'.[21] In fact his conception of socialism, defined at the Árd Fheis as the redistribution of wealth, was one developed precisely to counteract the 'extremist' class-struggle ideas which he and others believed Goulding had attempted to introduce in the 1960s.

As Richard Davis has shown, *Eire Nua* had its origin in a programme of moderate socialism put forward in the first issue of the Provisional *An Phoblacht.* It was based on the philosophy of Comhar na gComharsan (Neighbours' Co-operation), traced by Ó Bradaigh and Seamus Ó Mongain to ideas developed by the IRA in the 1940s. In a situation of some similarity in so far as in both cases the 'philosophy' was a self-conscious attempt to distance the IRA from 'Communism', the emphasis was on 'Irish and Christian values'. In the 1940s there had been a discussion, clearly based on the papal encyclical *Quadragesimo Anno,* about 'distributive ownership', the duty of the state to protect a limited private property and the power of the community to appropriate the excess. As Davis sums it up:

In its specific ideas, Comhar na gComharsan did not stray very far from the ideas of the great popes. Emphasis was laid on the nationalisation of the monetary system through the commercial banks and the insurance companies ... It also followed the Douglas Credit movement popular in the Great Depression, which appealed to many wishing to change the economic system without upsetting the class balance. In their suggestion for nationalising key industries, mines, building land and fishing rights, the Provisionals fell well within Catholic guidelines which permitted government ownership of particular enterprises where such could be demonstrated to be in the public interest.[22]

The problem with *Eire Nua* for its critics arose precisely because its main purpose was to demonstrate that the Provisionals were not just reactionary militarists. Having accomplished this, it then assumed an increasingly formulaic existence. Critics of the Provisionals' lack of political development focused on the rank and file's lack of clarity about its purpose – was it, for instance, 'a programme for action or an election manifesto'?[23] Its concrete proposals for 'economic resistance' consisted of little more than a list of heterogeneous and often conflicting components: 'The elements of resistance are farming co-ops, producer and consumer co-ops, credit unions and trade unions.'[24] The problem was not, as Bishop and Mallie claim, that it was 'a document written by Southerners from a Southern perspective': its chief critics, particularly Adams, were concerned because the Provisionals had made so little political progress in the Republic.[25] It was precisely because the programme was written by people who were convinced that the 'war in the North' would be won relatively quickly that it had so little to say to those increasingly sure that the prospect was of a 'long war' in which political advance in the Republic would be of crucial importance.

Despite the major opportunity which the 'anti-national' coalition government of Fine Gael and the Labour Party was held to offer – 'the Coalition has failed to provide safety valves by which the instinctive Irish urge for freedom can be tapped and controlled by the government'[26] – there remained the major unspoken problem of the Provisionals' commitment to abstentionism in Dáil elections. Ruairí Ó Bradaigh told the 1977 Árd Fheis that Sinn Féin was the fourth largest political party in the Republic, basing this calculation on the number of

Sinn Féin seats in local authorities. Limits on progress were blamed on the 'establishment's' censorship of Sinn Féin views through the recently toughened ban on radio and television interviews with party members.[27] But for some of those listening to him, the obvious limit was abstentionism itself: after all, the policy was not applied to candidates for local government in the Republic, the one area where there was some evidence of limited electoral support. The issue of political advance in the Republic was all the more pressing because of the anticipation that the despised Officials, now Sinn Féin – The Workers' Party, might make significant progress, unconstrained by abstentionism. Thus one of the most vituperatively anti-Official commentators in *Republican News*, after dismissing them as a serious force in the North, admitted that the situation was different in the Republic:

> The situation in the South is different. For there is a possible place for their type of reformist policies in the South. They are trying to take over the spot previously held by the Labour Party before it openly sided with reaction. While rejecting the national liberation struggle the Sticks are taking up in a militant fashion, a struggle against wage restraint, against cuts in social expenditure, against misuse of natural resources and curbs on civil liberties. Given no other credible reformist party such a campaign could make an impact. It should come as no surprise if the Sticks were to grow in the South. This could be a sticky problem for republicans and socialists.[28]*

Although the problem was recognised, there was little evidence of a capacity to deal with it, beyond the assertion of the need for Sinn Féin in the Republic to take up all 'popular social and economic struggles ... within the revolutionary framework of the national struggle'.[29] The 'Sticks' might be a despised minority in the North, but their potential in the Republic demanded regular and intense denunciation: 'We need to continue to pick up the Sticks, chew them over, and spit them out into the gutter where they belong.'[30] But

---

* 'Stickies' or 'Sticks': a nickname for the Officials which grew out of early competition between the Officials and the Provisionals. In this case the issue was sales of the republican emblem, the 'Easter Lily', sold for display on the annual commemoration of the 1916 Rising. The Official version was attached by adhesive, the Provisional by a pin. Of the two resulting nicknames, 'Stickies' and 'Pinheads', only one has lasted.

although such tirades against the 'treacherous', 'pro-Brit' and 'Loyalist' Officials had a ready audience in northern ghettos, their effect in the Republic was severely limited. If the strength of traditionalism made it impossible to raise the issue of abstentionism, the radicals were reduced to exhortations, an increasingly ultra-left rhetoric and complaints about the need to break down 'partitionism' in the movement.

This latter problem was defined as 'the common Southern view that the "Black North" is somewhere apart and that the Brits are not a problem which directly affects the 26 Counties'.[31] This mentality, which was admitted to affect not only the broad mass of the population in the Republic but traditional republican supporters as well, could be broken down only by recognising that 'in many cases in the south the national question isn't of central importance' and that this dictated republican involvement in issues including unemployment, low wages, bad housing, high prices, that were of immediate significance.[32]

It was hoped that the merger in 1979 of *An Phoblacht*, the Dublin-produced and more traditionalist paper, and *Republican News*, under the editorship of Danny Morrison in Belfast, would give a major impetus to the radicalisation of the movement and its progress in the Republic. The first issue of the merged paper emphasised that the struggle was a 32-county one and that it would result in a very different 'Rising' from that in 1916:

> It will not occur some Easter morning. It will be the coalescence of sympathy and support in the south (which we shall have earned) with the Resistance of northern Republicans to British Imperialism and Loyalism.[33]

It focused on recent industrial unrest in the two Irish states and claimed that the 'labour situation' in the Republic had a great revolutionary potential. It was, however, admitted that the republican movement in the Republic had not demonstrated a capacity to work in these 'hitherto twilight areas', and responded to the obvious rank-and-file apathy by emphasising that coverage of 'working class struggles . . . doesn't mean we are going "sticky" '.[34] The problem remained that the only way to maintain a distinctive Provisional approach to social and economic issues was to emphasise constantly that there could be no 'real' answer to the problems of working-class existence

as long as partition remained, and that for all their significance
these issues were secondary in 'the revolution which consists
primarily of the armed struggle and resistance in the ungovernable north'.[35] So although by the end of the 1970s the
Provisionals' analysis and rhetoric had been radicalised, the
change entailed a variant of social republicanism even more
patently out of tune with key realities than the 1930s and 1960s
versions.

In a speech at Bodenstown in 1979, Gerry Adams gave an
assessment of the Provisionals' position after a decade of 'war'.
It was a view which mixed a sober assessment of the limits of
'armed struggle' with an essentially unrealistic view of how this
could be complemented by a southern strategy. He claimed
that the IRA was winning, but that this was insufficient, for
British withdrawal could lead to 'the establishment of a 32
county neo-colonial Free State'. This would be prevented only
by 'more than a military alternative to the establishment'. Once
again he emphasised the need for an agitational struggle in the
Republic, 'linking up republicans with other sections of the
working class'. But he acknowledged that, 'Our most glaring
weakness to date lies in our failure to develop revolutionary
politics and to build a strong political alternative to so-called
constitutional politics.'[36] The main obstacle to such a development was identified as lack of commitment and discipline, a
typically republican focus on will rather than circumstance.
That the problem was deeper than this would gradually
become apparent, and the question of the role of abstentionism would emerge. When it did, it was overshadowed by developments in the North which led to a major increase in the
Provisionals' political involvement.

'Active' Republicanism and Politics

One of Adams's major concerns about the situation of the
Provisionals in the post-truce period was their growing isolation
from the majority of people in the Catholic ghettos. The
demoralisation amongst republicans caused by the failure of
the truce and predictions of British withdrawal was complemented by a more widespread 'war-weariness', partly manifest
in the widespread support for the temporary upsurge of the
Peace Movement in 1976. Adams commented from Long Kesh:

The rate of attrition is increasing in Republican areas and the Brit news media is spreading stories to increase the confusion within the ghettos ... The Brit intends to isolate us from the people.[37]

His answer was a vaguely defined 'Active Republicanism' that took up all the issues of the 'people's struggle for survival'. At that time it was clear that the main priority was reinvigorating the republican hard core by putting more resources into the institutions which had emerged in the ghettos as a result of the prolonged violence and consequent communal involution. The 'war machine' needed to be surrounded by a popular infrastructure of 'very necessary things like housing committees, street committees, defence groups, advice centres, local policing, people's taxis etc.'[38]

Concern for the isolation of the IRA was exacerbated by the serious inroads being made by a modernised and reorganised RUC, now assuming a role of primacy over the army under a new security strategy. At the end of 1976, the head of the RUC could report that complete Provisional units had been eliminated in various parts of the North, and that charges against IRA members had more than doubled compared with 1975.[39] In 1977, the Labour Secretary of State for Northern Ireland, Roy Mason, was claiming that, 'The tide had turned against the terrorists.'[40] In fact, 1978 brought clear signs that the Provisionals had been able to regroup and reorganise, moving to augment the traditional geographically based structure of brigades and battalions with a cellular structure designed to be much less penetrable by the security forces. The British army's mislaid intelligence document *Northern Ireland: Future Terrorist Trends* (November 1978) commented admiringly that,

> there is a stratum of intelligent, astute and experienced terrorists who provide the backbone of the organisation ... our evidence of the calibre of rank-and-file terrorists does not support the view that they are merely mindless hooligans.

The report did note a political weakness – 'there is seldom much support even for traditional protest marches' – but downplayed its significance: 'By reorganising on cellular lines, PIRA has become much less dependent on public support than in the past and is less vulnerable to penetration by informers.'[41]

Adams publicly quoted the report, particularly the part which claimed that 'the campaign of violence is likely to continue while the British remain', as a 'projection of the inevitable and final defeat of British imperialism'.[42] Despite this, the Provisionals were profoundly disturbed by their apparent political weakness, even in the supposed heartlands of northern militancy.

Since the abolition in 1976 of 'political status' for people sentenced for terrorist offences, the Provisionals had put the issue of 'Prisoners of War' at the centre of attempts to build a popular 'anti-imperialist' alliance. Most IRA members convicted in the non-jury Diplock Courts after 1976 refused to wear ordinary prison clothes or to work as directed. When they were refused their own clothes they went 'on the blanket', and when the prison authorities attempted to pressurise them by refusing exercise and other facilities, they retaliated by adopting the 'dirty protest' – smearing their cells with excrement.[43] But by the end of 1979 the attempts of the Provisionals to mobilise support for the 360 'blanket men' in the H-Blocks at Long Kesh had been noticeably unsuccessful. Thus Anthony Cronin, a journalist with strong republican sympathies, noted of the position in the Republic:

> The fact is that response to the Provisionals' appeals on any issue whatsoever, H-Block included, is really dead in the south. Even if the old civil strife and massacre of the Catholics situation were to come about at last, the south would not respond.[44]

Gerry Foley, an American Trotskyist who had fervently supported the Officials in their militarist period and then transferred his loyalties to the Provisionals, was moved to admit:

> The limitations of the Provisionals' campaign had become evident. It was now seen by larger and larger sections of the ghetto population as getting nowhere, more and more out of control and a source of unnecessary hardship.[45]

At an internal Sinn Féin conference on the prisoners' issue similar points were made. Joe Cahill, head of the 'POW Department', admitted that, 'With a couple of notable exceptions, the main demonstrations on the H-Blocks issue have remained within the nationalist ghetto areas of the Six

Counties and have only mobilised republican supporters.' Little support had been developed in the Republic and Adams concluded that, 'The movement has to recognise that so far, in mobilising on the H-Blocks, it has failed to fully realise its potential'.[46] He blamed Sinn Féin's political exclusivism, which had insisted that it would only work in co-operation with groups and individuals who not only supported the prisoners but also the 'armed struggle'. Certainly the Provisionals' exclusivism had long been complained about by the various tiny 'anti-imperialist' groups like People's Democracy.

In the European elections in 1979 the former student activist and ex-MP for Mid-Ulster, Bernadette McAliskey (previously Devlin), stood as an 'anti-repression' candidate focusing on the H-Blocks issues. Sinn Féin boycotted the election and denounced McAliskey: 'An anti-repression ticket which will bring along to the polling booths those otherwise disillusioned with such procedures, or hostile to the EEC, is just what the Brussels bureaucrats desire.'[47] Although McAliskey obtained fewer than 40,000 votes, the result encouraged some to raise the issue of whether better use could not have been made of the European and Westminster elections in 1979 by running prisoners as candidates. In an interview, a member of the IRA Army Council would admit:

Perhaps we could have made more propaganda than we did . . . Certainly this question of standing candidates is one of continued dialogue within the movement. There is no principle involved in the question of whether or not to stand candidates.[48]

In fact, even the most militant supporters of 'active' republicanism shrank from the possibility of electoral rejection. It took the unwelcome initiative of the prisoners in starting a hunger strike for political status to force a reluctant leadership into electoral politics.[49]

The first wave of hunger strikes petered out before the end of 1980. A second, more determined wave led by Bobby Sands, the Provisionals' commanding officer in the H-Blocks, began in March 1981. As early as November 1980, the H-Block committees were turning out parades comparable in size to the great civil rights marches. The hunger strikers and their supporters, as Richard Kearney put it, 'articulated a tribal voice of

martyrdom, deeply embedded in the Gaelic, Catholic nationalist tradition'.[50] The death of the MP for Fermanagh-South
Tyrone (a strong republican sympathiser and semi-abstention-
ist) shortly after Sands went on the hunger strike created a
major opportunity. Again the Sinn Féin leadership was
extremely nervous about a prisoners' candidate, and was precipitated into the election by McAliskey's declaration of interest in running.

Sands's election was a major propaganda victory, soon to be
augmented by the election of two other hunger strikers in the
Republic's general election in June 1981 and, after Sands's
death, of his election agent, Owen Carron, as MP for the
Fermanagh-South Tyrone constituency.[51] The Provisionals'
relationship to the Catholic masses in the North was transformed by the hunger strikes and the resulting ten deaths. By
October 1981 they had to accept Thatcher's determination not
to concede political status, though they won substantial concessions on clothing and association. However they enjoyed a
major boost to their self-confidence and electoral fortunes,
revealed after their decision to contest the Northern Ireland
Assembly elections in 1982 and the Westminster election in
1983. In the first they received 10.1 per cent of the poll to the
SDLP's 18.8 per cent; in the second they cut even further into
the SDLP's support, with 13.4 per cent of the poll to the
SDLP's 17.9 per cent, and Adams was returned as MP for West
Belfast.

Sinn Féin's ambitions in Northern Ireland were encouraged
by the obvious disquiet which the 64,191 first preference votes
in the Assembly elections had caused in the Irish and British
governments. The Irish Prime Minister, Garret FitzGerald of
Fine Gael, gave an interview on BBC television in which he
spoke in anxious terms of the need for talks with the British
government to prevent 'destabilisation' in Northern Ireland.
The republican newspaper commented:

Any further advance by Sinn Féin, FitzGerald correctly con-
strues as a fatal blow to the SDLP. And Sinn Féin emerging as
the majority voice of Northern nationalists would obviously turn
traditional Dublin policy on its head.[52]

In March 1983 the Dublin government, under pressure from
the SDLP leadership, announced the establishment of the New

Ireland Forum, designed to produce a consensus among the 'democratic' parties on 'the manner in which lasting peace and stability can be achieved in a new Ireland through the democratic process'. Adams denounced it as a 'life-line for a party under threat from Sinn Féin'.[53] Increasingly, the SDLP would be portrayed as an effete, declining party of the Catholic middle class, facing imminent extinction due to its 'collaborationist' role. Although the dominant emphasis was placed on the 'revolutionary nationalism' of Sinn Féin, the 'class nature' of the struggle was also frequently referred to. Thus in the campaign for the 1983 Westminster election, it was claimed that,

> the class divisions between the SDLP and Sinn Féin are becoming clearly defined . . . as the nationalist middle class attempts to maintain its electoral sway and influence over the increasingly radicalised nationalist people, the bulk of whom are working class.[54]

The Catholic hierarchy was denounced for its support for the SDLP and its fear of 'the growing independent-mindedness of its flock'.[55] Such militant optimism was encouraged by the substantial increase in electoral support in the Westminster election. Ruairí Ó Bradaigh hailed the results as

> a turning point . . . the Sinn Féin vote increased from 64,000 to 103,000 and its share of the nationalist vote has increased from 35 to 42 per cent . . . In the 1985 local elections in the Six Counties Sinn Féin will finally overtake the SDLP and nationalist politics will undergo their most radical and significant change since 1918.[56]

It was now presumed in many quarters that the surge for Sinn Féin was irresistible. It was not to be; Adams and his forces were soon checked. Danny Morrison was heavily outpolled by the SDLP's reader John Hume in the European election of June 1984 (91,476 votes to 151,399). Hume fought a subtle campaign which effectively surrendered much nationalist territory to the Provisionals and sought instead to win moderate Catholic support away from other parties and thus swell his total. Even the normally cautious Adams had portrayed the election as part 'of the work of supplanting the SDLP as the party representing the nationalist people in the Six Counties . . . The smashing of the SDLP is an ongoing process.'[57] In the aftermath of the set-back, Adams consoled supporters with the claim that the vote was a 'principled, republican vote, as opposed to a nationalist or Catholic vote . . . It is ideologically sound.'[58] He also obliquely criticised the IRA: 'There is a number of people who while they voted for us in June 1983, may not have been able to tolerate some aspects of IRA operations . . . in which civilians were killed or injured.' He referred to his statement at the 1983 Árd Fheis, 'That revolutionary force must be controlled and disciplined so that it is clearly seen as a symbol of our people's resistance.'[59]

In fact, 1983 had seen the first of a string of 'fraternal' calls from the expanding Sinn Féin political organisation for a 'refinement' of IRA activity to minimise adverse electoral repercussions.[60] Although Adams publicly welcomed the set-back as 'an injection of reality', he still claimed that Sinn Féin had not hit an electoral ceiling in Northern Ireland: 'I think that if we work hard, if we pitch our campaign right, if republicans refine their tactics that we can win a majority of the nationalist electorate.'[61] The 'real battle between the SDLP and Sinn Féin', which he had predicted in the 1985 local government elections, while resulting in a substantial new Sinn Féin presence on Northern Ireland's local authorities (59 councillors out of a total of 566) still left the organisation with electoral support at 11.8 per cent, a substantial vote but indicating little progress in the struggle to supplant the SDLP.

Sinn Féin and the Anglo-Irish Agreement

Despite the evidence of a possible 'peaking' in Sinn Féin's electoral surge, the Thatcher government was soon to initiate a major shift in policy which would radically change the political context in which the Provisionals operated. After the failure of her Secretary of State for Northern Ireland, Humphrey Atkins, to secure an inter-party agreement on devolution, Margaret Thatcher had met the Irish Prime Minister, Fianna Fáil's Charles Haughey, for discussions in Dublin in December 1980. In the joint communiqué, Thatcher acknowledged Britain's 'unique relationship' with Ireland; she permitted the establishment of joint study groups to find ways of expressing this uniqueness in 'new institutional structures', and committed herself to future discussions on 'the totality of relationships

within these islands'. The Sinn Féin response came in a substantial analysis which emphasised that a major shift in British
policy was possible. Arguing that the main British interest in
partition was a strategic one, it accepted that this might now be
better defended by a shift away from reliance on the 'loyalist
veto':

> The policy shift involves, at the very minimum, acknowledging
> that an all-Ireland dimension is necessary to satisfy nationalist
> aspirations whilst maintaining the Union (at least for the time
> being) to satisfy Unionist aspirations . . . this shift could lead in
> the direction of a new constitutional – or as the summit com-
> muniqué put it (to avoid drawing too much Unionist fire) 'insti-
> tutional' arrangement between Britain and the Free State, even,
> at its maximum limit, meaning a 32 county, partitioned neo-
> colonial state.[62]

There were three possible variations on this 'dangerous
option': devolution plus an institutionalisation of the 'unique
relationship'; a condominium arrangement by which the
North would be jointly ruled by Britain and the Republic; and
a new 32-county confederal arrangement. All variants were
rejected as maintaining the 'Six County state' and not really
challenging British domination, but it was recognised that any
of them could have a powerful appeal to at least sections of the
Catholic population in Northern Ireland.

The deterioration in Anglo-Irish relations brought about by
the hunger strikes and Haughey's refusal to support Britain
during the Falklands War ensured that little more was heard of
such possibilities until Sinn Féin's electoral gains had resulted
in the setting up of the New Ireland Forum. The Forum
Report, when it was published, put forward three options: a
unitary Irish state, a federal Ireland and joint authority. Each
was brusquely dismissed by Thatcher when she met Garret
FitzGerald in November 1984. The subsequent developments
were perceptively summed up by Danny Morrison:

> At the Chequers London/Dublin summit in November 1984
> Thatcher made her infamous 'Out, Out, Out' reply. Dublin and
> the SDLP were shattered. Republicans were proved correct.
> However, there were allowances made in the comuniqué issued
> at the time for further inter-governmental developments, which
> went virtually unnoticed by republicans and most others.

Sometime afterwards (and probably as a delayed reaction to the October Brighton bomb), Thatcher realised the damage that her 'Out, Out, Out' remarks had done to the cause of 'constitutional nationalism'. Dublin also recruited intense political lobbying from the US Senate and Congress for a British change of heart.[63]

The Anglo-Irish Agreement signed by Thatcher and FitzGerald at Hillsborough in November 1985 was described by Adams as 'a coming-together of the various British strategies on an all-Ireland basis, with the Dublin government acting as the new guarantor of partition'.[64] It was also recognised that the creation of structures like the Inter-Governmental Conference and the permanent secretariat staffed by British and Irish civil servants and situated at Maryfield in the Belfast suburbs, were developments of major significance:

> Dublin has been granted a consultative role in Northern Ireland affairs far short of the least demand of the three Forum options – but a big step forward as far as Dublin and the SDLP are concerned, as it represents a significant recognition of them from Britain.[65]

The Sinn Féin leadership was seriously concerned about the various possible effects of the Agreement:

> It is an attempt to isolate and draw popular support away from the republican struggle while putting a diplomatic veneer on British rule, injecting a credibility into establishment 'nationalism' . . . and insulating the British from international criticism of their involvement in Irish affairs.[66]

An earlier consideration of the possible implication of such a major shift in British policy had warned that, 'The increasingly sophisticated approach of the enemy means that good "old-fashioned" nationalism and "pure" militarism will be an insufficient republican response.'[67] The previous tendencies to denounce the 'middle class' and collaborationist role of the SDLP might have been expected to intensify in the aftermath of the Agreement. In fact, Adams and his supporters would increasingly distance themselves from their previous 'ultra-leftism'. Thus in his book *The Politics of Irish Freedom*, Adams noted that the emergence of Sinn Féin 'may have unnecessarily brought out some of the class differences between ourselves and the SDLP leadership'. The differences, while real, should not be emphasised too much:

> It might have been better in this phase of the independence struggle if there could have been some kind of general unity, in which both parties would agree to disagree on social and economic issues and maximise pressure on points of agreement.[68]

Clearly, it was increasingly perceived that just as the Hillsborough Agreement was aimed at isolating and marginalising Sinn Féin, so some of the policy positions and rhetoric adopted by that organisation were achieving the same result.

Adams, who had earlier encouraged the movement to take up social and economic issues, was now anxious to stress the dangers of pushing such 'leftism' too far. He was particularly concerned with those in Sinn Féin who wanted the republican movement to style itself 'socialist republican':

> This must narrow the potential support-base of the republican movement and enable other movements to claim that they are 'republican' though they are not socialist; for example, Fianna Fáil or the SDLP. This carries the danger of letting these parties off the hook, for their leaders will be able to claim that they are the real republicans and that what the 'republicans' are offering is some foreign importation called socialism.[69]

The encouragement of a new radical note in Sinn Féin's repertoire in the early 1980s had led to the creation of trade-union and womens' departments and the cultivation of the left-wing fringe of the British Labour Party and a small number of sympathetic Labour MPs. Sinn Féin gained many new members as a result of the hunger strike mobilisation, most with no 'military' background, and some of the influx came from socialist sects like People's Democracy. The modernisation of the organisation's profile associated with this influx now appeared to have gone too far. In 1985, against the advice of the leadership, the Ard Fheis voted to support 'a woman's right to choose', hardly a vote-catcher in the Catholic ghettos. Adams, always careful to protect Sinn Féin from charges that it was a 'Marxist' organisation, was by 1986 seriously concerned that certain aspects of the organisation's public persona were dangerously extreme.[70]

The Politics of Illusion

Rather than launching attacks on the SDLP's class nature, Sinn Féin began to issue calls for talks to 'maximise not fracture nationalist unity'. Such calls had been made before 1985, but had sat incongruously with the bitter denunciations of the constitutional nationalists in the republican press. Unlike some of the 'greener elements' in the SDLP, who had periodically expressed an interest in talks,[71] Hume had refused on the basis that the real power in the republican movement lay with the IRA's Army Council. This position was maintained for as long as it seemed possible that the Hillsborough Agreement would seriously erode Sinn Féin's support base. However as some of the more extravagant hopes raised in the nationalist population by the Agreement were dissipated, new possibilities opened up for Sinn Féin.

Hume had always insisted that if the British 'faced down' Unionist opposition – 'lanced the Protestant boil' was his vivid phrase – Unionists would be forced to reassess their position and reach an accommodation with nationalist Ireland. He confidently predicted such a breakthrough before the end of 1986 and continued with this optimism in the early months of 1987:[72]

> The consequences of [the Agreement] for the Unionist community are that they have to consider the choice, either they continue to live apart, only now they are not being underpinned by a British government and they no longer have a veto on policy in Northern Ireland, or they decide to live together with us.[73]

However Unionist acquiescence in the Agreement was occasioned largely by the economic benefits of the Union: it did not presage any reassessment of relations with nationalist Ireland. Hume gradually came to realise during the course of 1987 that his earlier assessments had been over-sanguine. He also had to take into account the balance of forces within the nationalist community. The Westminster election in 1987 produced little evidence of a Sinn Féin electoral decline: the party won 11.4 per cent of the vote and Adams kept his West Belfast seat with an increased majority. By early 1988 Hume and some of his senior colleagues were involved in a series of discussions with Sinn Féin which went on from March to September and represented the only serious dialogue between physical force and constitutional nationalism since the onset of the present 'Troubles'.

The heart of the difference between the parties was the SDLP's contention that the Anglo-Irish Agreement demonstrated that,

> Britain has no interest of her own in remaining in Ireland, that she has no military or economic interests and that if Irish people reached agreement among themselves on, for example Irish unity, that Britain would facilitate it. Legislate for it and leave the Irish to govern themselves.[74]

Sinn Féin denied that Britain was neutral, but its list of interests that supposedly impelled Britain to maintain partition was not impressive; the key interests were strategic and economic.

Ironically, Danny Morrison had earlier accepted that, 'The occupation of the North is a net financial loss to, and a considerable drain on, British revenue.'[75] Now, although the British annual subvention to the North was admitted to be £1.6 billion, it was denied that this negated any British economic interest in Ireland. This however, turned out to be the defence of British investment and that of its 'multinational capitalist allies' from 'the potential or perceived threat posed by an independent Irish state'. Such preemptive ruling-class calculation was also supposed to determine Britain's other interest, which was strategic:

> Strategic interests are now the most important consideration in Britain's interference in Ireland. Quite apart from the very real, if somewhat exaggerated fear among the British establishment, that an Ireland freed from British influence could become a European 'Cuba', even the prospect of a neutral Ireland is regarded as a serious threat to British and NATO's strategic interests.[76]

As Paul Bew and I have argued at greater length elsewhere, the strategic interest of Ireland for Britain is much less than it was in the 1940s, when British thinking was dominated by the maritime losses of the Second World War, and it has also become clear that Irish governments are prepared to undertake to join NATO if the partition question is solved.[77] Even more significantly, there is evidence that Sinn Féin's leadership was itself less than convinced of these 'explanations'. Clearly, they imply that a British withdrawal will lead to a united Ireland in which radical forces will be in the ascendant: However Adams had earlier explained to a British audience the unlikelihood of such an eventuality:

> Certainly it is Sinn Féin's policy to see established in Ireland a democratic, socialist republic based upon the 1916 Proclamation. We would prefer that such a non-aligned nation would evolve fairly immediately from a British withdrawal . . . Regrettably our organisation, particularly in the 26 Counties is presently too small and lacking in influence to capitalise on the potential dividends accruing to the republican movement as the organisation which finally ended eight centuries of British interference in Ireland. Notwithstanding this state of play, one finds the 'Ireland another Cuba' scenario often being propounded by right-wingers as an excuse for maintaining partition.[78]

In the talks, Hume argued for an IRA ceasefire to facilitate a 'powerful response within Britain itself',[79] while Sinn Féin and the IRA leadership made it clear that this was out of the question. Despite this gulf, the talks ended with both sides claiming that the 'dialogue' would continue and Sinn Féin emphasising its view of their importance. While the talks were taking place, Adams issued a call for Fianna Fáil and other political parties in the Republic to join in a 'national consensus on Irish reunification', adopting a joint strategy to achieve it:

> Such a strategy must involve primarily a consensus of the clear national majority on Irish reunification as a policy objective and an international and diplomatic offensive to bring political pressure to bear on the British government to concede to the Irish people their national rights.[81]

Although he repeated the standard anathema against the Anglo-Irish Agreement – that its objective was 'the maintenance of partition' – there were signs that the Sinn Féin leadership saw very positive, if unintended, results flowing from some aspects of the Agreement.

Adams has referred more than once to the 'educational' nature of the Agreement:

> One of the shocks for loyalists in recent years has been the educational nature of Hillsborough. We have been saying to loyal-

ists for decades the British government will use and abuse them. There is no British loyalty. The British government have interests. When the British government want to dump them they will do so. Some loyalists have already started to take that on board.[82]

Thus, the disorienting effect of Hillsborough upon sections of Unionist opinion had been a positive one. Further, the Agreement had deepened the division between British and Unionist opinion: 'The British public watched loyalist opposition to what very many people see as a very mediocre treaty. Their response and behaviour alerted a lot of people to the fascist nature of loyalism.'[83]

Adams also discerned signs that useful changes were emerging in constitutional nationalism. Hume, convinced that the failure of the Unionists to dislodge the Agreement demonstrated a fundamental shift in the balance of forces, argued that the next stage was for the Unionist leadership to 'sort out' its relationship with Dublin through an all-Ireland constitutional conference. Although one of the stated objectives of the Hillsborough Agreement was the creation of devolved institutions of government in Northern Ireland, Adams was pleased to note that Sinn Féin's bitter opposition to 'diversions like internal devolutionary Stormont arrangements' was increasingly mirrored in the SDLP.[84]

Also important was the return of Fianna Fáil to power in the Republic's general election in 1987. Charles Haughey had criticised the Hillsborough Agreement on the predictable nationalist grounds that the 'majority consent' clause in the Agreement was an acceptance in principle of the northern Unionist majority's right to refuse to join a united Ireland. It was a renunciation of the claim to unity embodied in the Irish constitution.[85] This position, while initially unpopular with public opinion, allowed Fianna Fáil to define itself as 'the lone party with the nationalist forces'.[86] Once in office, however, Haughey gave a guarded commitment to working within the Agreement to extract reforms for northern nationalists while continuing to reiterate that the only way forward was an all-party conference to discuss a possible federal Ireland. Sinn Féin would be invited to such a conference if IRA violence ceased.[87] The Anglo-Irish Agreement, which had been seen as a measure to marginalise and isolate Sinn Féin had, in less than three years, come to produce radically different results. Most crucially, it had shifted the ideological balance in nationalist Ireland in a direction which Sinn Féin could only welcome.

The SDLP's case was that an IRA ceasefire would allow a united approach by all the nationalist parties in Ireland to the British government with a 'peaceful and comprehensive approach to achieving self-determination in Ireland'.[88] Sinn Féin had always poured scorn on the SDLP's desire to attain unity with the consent of Unionists, on the not unrealistic assumption that consent was unlikely to be forthcoming. The 1988 talks did little to persuade them of the redundancy of the 'armed struggle', and had they been persuaded there is little evidence that the IRA would have listened to them. It is unlikely that Adams and his colleagues failed to be impressed by Hume's very concrete vision of fundamental constitutional change. Such optimism, baseless though it may have seemed to more dispassionate observers, was none the less an increasing ideological reality. It brought Sinn Féin dramatically in from the cold, as the SDLP declared that, 'Politically the positions of the SDLP and Sinn Féin are not unduly removed from one another and are bridgeable.'[89]

In response, Sinn Féin leaders explained to their activists the errors of past 'ultra-leftism'. At a conference of party activists held during the talks with the SDLP, Tom Hartley, Sinn Féin general secretary, explained the need for a 'more structured and political way' of relating to the SDLP:

> Since the beginning of its electoral strategy, Sinn Féin has been in confrontation with the SDLP . . . As a party we have tended to see the SDLP as collaborators. Because of this we have a blinkered view of the SDLP. The Sinn Féin view has always allowed for a well defined ideological separation to take place. The SDLP have now emerged as our class enemy. As a result we have found it more difficult to bring broader sections of the nationalist population into struggle. We are now thrust into a full headlong clash with the SDLP which restricts our development into wider areas of the nationalist community.[90]

Already the call by some IRA prisoners for the 'upgrading of the socialist content of the party'[91] had been sidelined. As Danny Morrison explained, 'Sinn Féin, as its leadership maintains, is not a Marxist organisation, and indeed many of its members and leaders, including Gerry Adams and Martin

McGuinness are committed Catholics.'[92] In 1986 Adams had disabused a journalist who had claimed that Sinn Féin asked people to vote for socialist and republican policies:

> I don't think socialism is on the agenda at all at this stage except for political activists of the left. What's on the agenda now is an end to partition. You won't even get near socialism until you have national independence.[93]

This was in stark contrast to the positions taken up in the early phase of the 'long war' strategy. In an earlier critique of the movement's lack of political development, Adams had castigated those who thought the armed struggle by itself could establish a 'Democratic Socialist Republic'. The best conditions for a British withdrawal would be created by the IRA in alliance with a radical popular movement 'capable of articulating not only the republican movement's position but also of being representative of all those with the commitment to a socialist republic'.[94]

In 1986 the Sinn Féin Árd Fheis voted to remove the ban on attendance in the Republic's parliament from the organisation's constitution. A minority of traditionalists led by Ó Bradaigh and O'Connaill walked out and created a new organisation, Republican Sinn Féin. In his presidential address, Adams upbraided those who identified politics with 'constitutionalism' and the 'Stickies' as having 'little concept of the class nature of the struggle'.[95] Again he reiterated that the most important task was to develop an all-Ireland political struggle: 'While consolidating our base in the Six Counties, we must develop a popular struggle in the 26 Counties to complement the struggle in the Six County area.' Sinn Féin was still an isolated organisation, particularly in the Republic, where it was 'a party apart from the people, proud of our past but with little involvement in the present and only dreams for the future'.[96] The way out of isolation was by

> approaching people at the level they understand. This is the sad and unfortunate reality of the dilemma facing us . . . This means Sinn Féin getting among people in the basic ways which people accept.[97]

The implication was in many ways similar to the social republicanism of the 1960s – 'projects of economic, social or cultural resistance'.[98] But this time there was to be no down-playing of 'our republican gut': 'While developing the struggle in the 26 Counties we must never lose sight of our national objectives.' Strong support for the 'armed struggle' would be maintained and delegates doubtful of the new direction may have been encouraged by a previous decision of the General Army Convention – the first for sixteen years – to support the ending of abstention from the Dáil.[99]

Adams warned delegates not to expect a breakthrough in the next election – the election after that would be the first major test of Sinn Féin's ability to win major support.[100] But even he may have been shocked by Sinn Féin's miserable performance in the 1987 general election for the Dáil, when it got a mere 1.9 per cent of the poll. An article in Sinn Féin's journal *Iris* noted that,

> For all complaints about Section 31 [the legislative ban on Sinn Féin appearing on radio or TV in the Republic], Gardai harassment, etc., most of them [Sinn Féin members] knew it was a fairly accurate reflection of how ordinary people viewed Sinn Féin.

Although anticipating that the new Fianna Fáil government would introduce major public expenditure cuts, creating the conditions for a 'modest swing to the left', it admitted that this would most likely benefit the Workers' Party, as Sinn Féin – The Workers' Party had become, and the Labour Party. It would take a long time for Sinn Féin to shake off the 'burden of history . . . Southern workers see Sinn Féin as a party that avoided domestic class issues by concentrating on the national question' and this could only be compensated for by 'the long and sometimes painfully slow effort of involving itself in working-class and community struggles'.[101]

Adams, perhaps too influenced by the irruption of Sinn Féin in Northern elections, was dangerously exposed in the adoption of this southern strategy. His grasp of southern politics was less than sure. His hopes for the expansion of the Sinn Féin vote were expressed in terms of winning working-class support from the Workers' Party and the Labour Party on the basis that they are both 'reformist', and the former 'pro-Unionist' as well. This implies a heavy emphasis on the 'revolutionary' nationalism of Sinn Féin, the raising of just that syndrome of issues for which he also recognises the mass of the working class in the Republic is not 'ready'.[102]

In fact, the major party from which Sinn Féin might hope to take support is Fianna Fáil. As Peter Mair puts it:

> The increased profile of Sinn Féin, both North and South, inevitably stimulates a more militant position among those voters who would welcome unity almost regardless of the cost . . . history and tradition suggest that these are more likely to be inclined towards Fianna Fáil.[103]

Mair's important analysis of surveys of popular attitudes to Northern Ireland in the Irish Republic registers the continued existence of a 'sea of territorial nationalist commitment'. The proportion of survey respondents approving of Irish unity was 74 per cent in the year the Forum reported.[104] Within this sea, Adams would be encouraged by the increase in levels of sympathy for the IRA. Thus, those reporting actual approval for the IRA rose from 2 per cent in 1978 to 5 per cent in 1984 – just slightly above Sinn Féin's share of the poll in the 1984 European election.[105] More significant was the group of respondents who indicated an admiration for the motives or ideals of the IRA, while disapproving of their methods; this rose from 32 in 1978 to 41 per cent in 1980, falling to 39 per cent in 1984. The long years of Fianna Fáil control of the state had produced a calcified irredentist political culture which increasingly formed the main basis of Sinn Féin aspirations in the Republic. As Adams puts it, quoting a *bête noire* of Sinn Féin:

> In all the different walks of Irish life there is a grudging respect for the concept of republicanism. As Conor Cruise O'Brien has pointed out, republicanism is in a sense the conscience of the Irish people. There is a feeling that if the rising of 1916 was . . . right, then the resistance in 1969 was right and in 1986 is right as well. There is a tolerance and an ambivalence because in the back of people's minds is the notion that there is some logic and rectitude to what republicans are saying.[106]

As it became increasingly clear that Sinn Féin's appeal on economic and social issues was rebuffed by some sections of the working class because of its association with northern violence, the only hope of the Adams strategy lay in an appeal to the undoubtedly large reservoirs of nationalist sentiment in the southern electorate. Sinn Féin's problem was that, except in a few border constituencies in a time of major crisis in the North, southern nationalism is what O'Brien has called a 'low-intensity aspiration'. Thus in 1980 only 29 per cent found paying more taxes an acceptable price for unity while 63 per cent thought this unacceptable. As Mair sums up his review, 'Support for the aspiration for unity is quite pervasive . . . there is little support for anything beyond this.'[107]

Such national sentiment was a shaky basis for a project of southern expansion, yet Adams was increasingly reduced to this with his repeated calls for a broad 'anti-imperialist' alliance to include the SDLP and Fianna Fáil, a bathetic reprise of the 1930s, when O'Donnell and his supporters sought such an alliance to prove to the masses the 'compromising' nature of middle-class leadership of the 'national struggle'. The dominant position in the Republican Congress was that the struggle for the Republic would have to be transformed into a class struggle to be successful. In the late 1970s and early 1980s this approach was temporarily influential in the Provisional leadership, but the apparent opportunities offered by developments since Hillsborough produced a significant shift in emphasis.

By the end of 1988 Adams had returned to the position of Sinn Féin in 1919 – one subsequently bitterly criticised by left republicans like O'Donnell. The issue was now declared to be self-determination, not the social content of 'freedom': 'The choice of the type of society chosen in that context is a matter for an Irish nation freed from outside interference.'[108] The emphasis is no longer on a 'Scenario for a Socialist Republic' but rather on building a new mass movement on an all-Ireland basis, 'open to everyone committed to the principle and objective of Irish self-determination'.[109]

This movement, which would include non-republicans and non-socialists, could, Adams suggested, be built around a 'Freedom Charter' similar to that of the ANC.[110] The purpose of such a movement would be to expose the merely 'verbal nationalism' of the main constitutional nationalist parties, the SDLP and Fianna Fáil:

> Since at this stage the majority of nationalists look to constitutional nationalism for their political leadership, this requires placing pressure on constitutional politicians to take up and

defend the interests of the people they claim to represent . . .
either they get involved for fear of being discredited with their
own base, in which case there will be a dynamic which will bring
wider sections of the people into the struggle, or they will
refuse, in which case they will be exposed.[111]

This new strategic emphasis is very clearly influenced by the
Sinn Féin leadership's positive evaluation of the talks with the
SDLP. As Richard McAuley, a key Sinn Féin propagandist, told
the delegates to the 1989 Árd Fheis, 'The talks with Hume were
extremely important and beneficial.'[112] Adams had earlier
specified their importance in terms of narrowing the British
state's options in Northern Ireland:

It was a welcome sign, perhaps, that the SDLP recently said that
they have no ideological adherence to devolution. The SDLP
are a very important part of the equation in the Six Counties.
The British need to have a party or an element which is nationalist or at least non-Unionist.[113]

The 'verbal commitment' given by the SDLP leadership during
the talks to the republican view – 'An internal Six County settlement is no solution and that the real question is how do we
end the British presence in Ireland' – was seen as a major shift
favouring Sinn Féin and representing a 'marker against which
their activity can be judged . . . Future involvement by the
SDLP in a British Six County arrangement would be examined
against the above.'[114]

The failure of the Anglo-Irish Agreement significantly to
erode electoral support for Sinn Féin, the unlikelihood of any
internal accommodation between constitutional nationalism
and Unionism and the increasingly all-Ireland flavour of the
Fianna Fáil-SDLP discussions of the future development of the
Agreement all encouraged the Sinn Féin leadership in its
hopes of a quicker resolution of the conflict than had been
envisaged at the beginning of the 1980s. A central problem
that emerged in this context was the IRA's 'armed struggle'.

The Armalite versus the Ballot Box

In 1986 an Army Council statement claimed that the movement 'had overcome many of the genuine fears that increased

political activity would lead to a downgrading of armed struggle'.[115] The process had not been conflict-free and 1985 saw the court martial and expulsion from the IRA of Ivor Bell, a former commander of the Belfast brigade and Chief of Staff, who had opposed the diversion of funds into political development.[116] Brendan O'Brien claims that the pre-emptive decision of the Army Convention to support the ending of abstentionism for Dáil elections was only bought at the price of a deal with traditionalists which saw both the promotion of militarists to the Army Council and a decision to allow local units more freedom of action, the so-called 'local commander prerogative'.[117] It is certainly the case that while Adams would assert that, 'There is now a realisation in republican circles that armed struggle on its own is inadequate and that non-armed forms of political struggle are at least as important,'[118] the 'Long War' strategy could not resolve the increasingly obvious contradictions between politics and force.

Adams may by 1986 have come to the conclusion that the military campaign had reached a stalemate,[119] but this was by no means the predominant view in the IRA's leadership. The organisation's armoury was massively augmented in 1985-86 by four shipments of *matériel* from Libya amounting to more than one hundred tons of arms and explosives, including RPG-7 rocket-launchers, SAM-7 surface-to-air missiles, heavy machine-guns and semtex, the Czech-made plastic explosive.[120] The Libyan weapons had the immediate effect of propelling the IRA Army Council back to the militarist vistas of the early 1970s. A decision qualitatively to intensify the 'war' in Northern Ireland, Britain and abroad was made in 1986. In July the IRA extended its list of 'legitimate targets' to include civil servants, building contractors, caterers and British Telecom employees in so far as any of these did work for the security forces.[121] Semtex, which is both odourless and very powerful, allowed the IRA significantly to increase its use of booby-trap devices attached to the underside of vehicles used by members of the security forces, the infamous 'up-and-unders'. But the intensification of military activities proved to have very ambiguous results. 'Spectaculars' like the killing of Lord Justice Gibson and his wife by a bomb in April 1987 and the Ballygawley landmine which destroyed a bus and killed eight soldiers in August 1988 encouraged those who still hankered after a military victory. In September 1988 a senior republican claimed, 'This is the final phase. The next eighteen months to two years will be critical because the IRA has the resources and will then know if it has the capacity to end it.'[122] Although this was read at the time as a clear indication of a militarisation of republicanism, it did not in fact portray the intensification of violence as inevitably destined to succeed.

Smith has noted that, from a military point of view, the 'Long War' was in fact an admission of weakness. This was because, while a much smaller IRA waging a more selective campaign could be more easily sustained than the intensive, large-scale assaults of the early 1970s, it was much less of a military threat to the British state.[123] At the same time the reduction in size of the IRA made it easier for the security forces to concentrate resources against known activists and this led in 1987 and 1988 to significant IRA losses. The SAS wiped out an eight-man IRA unit which was in the process of attacking the RUC station in Loughgall, County Armagh, in May 1987. This was the IRA's largest single loss of members since the formation of the Provisionals and a major blow to its East Tyrone brigade, until then one of its most effective units.[124] The same brigade would suffer another devastating blow in August 1988 when another three leading members were killed in an SAS ambush as they attempted to kill a lorry-driver who was a part-time member of the UDR.[125] In March 1988 three of the IRA's most experienced operatives had been shot dead by the SAS in Gibraltar. Unarmed at the time, it was alleged that they were preparing a major bomb attack on a British army band as a spectacular indicator of the intensification of the armed struggle.[126]

The IRA 'New Year Statement' in January 1989 noted that the previous twelve months 'have been a particularly difficult time for republicans when the deaths of volunteers were a regular occurrence and when a high number of civilians met their deaths in tragic circumstances at our hands'.[127] Later in the month the IRA announced the disbanding of the West Fermanagh brigade after it killed a former RUC man in Donegal.[128] This was the unit which had detonated a bomb at the Remembrance Day ceremony in Enniskillen on 8 November 1987, killing eleven people and injuring 63 others. Although Adams would admit that Enniskillen was a major setback – 'Our plans for expansion will have been dealt a body-blow'[129] – Enniskillen was a direct result of the 1986 decisions to intensify the 'war' and allow local units more autonomy. In

Fermanagh this meant letting loose elements whose republicanism was strongly marked by a Catholic 'defenderism' with its roots in the sectarian animosities of the seventeenth and eighteenth centuries. In addition to sectarianism, the intensification of IRA activities in 1987 and 1988 was also characterised by a large number of what it referred to as 'civilian' casualties. A 'spokesperson' for the IRA GHQ staff admitted that these deaths

> dented the confidence of some of our supporters. They have given our critics the opportunity to raise once again the proposition that the armed struggle is contradictory to and undermining the political struggle ... we realise that we have a responsibility to correct the problem and refine our activities so that they do not hinder but complement the effort to build a broad-based front against imperialism.[130]

But refinement proved difficult and in March the IRA killed three Protestant men in the village of Coagh, County Tyrone, claiming that they were either paramilitaries or members of the security forces. It subsequently transpired that all the men were civilians and Sinn Féin issued a statement denying any sectarian intent in the attack, but adding, 'All this only further serves to emphasise the need for the IRA to constantly examine its tactics and strategy in armed struggle.'[131] In his presidential address to the Sinn Féin Árd Fheis in January 1989 Adams defended the armed struggle as a 'necessary and morally correct form of resistance in the Six Counties' and claimed that it could 'advance the overall struggle to the advantage of those in whose interest it is waged'. His criticism was soft-toned and understated:

> IRA mistakes are welcomed by the British state ... It seeks to demoralise and confuse the wider nationalist support base which does not have the same insight and understanding as the republican base which remains solid.

He appealed to the IRA to 'be careful and careful again'.[132]

The contradictions of republican strategy were clearly evident at the Árd Fheis. The main discussion centred on the resolution proposed by Tom Hartley, a close confidant of Adams and a key strategist in the movement. It committed the organisation to building an all-Ireland 'anti-imperialist mass movement' based on a broad range of forces. The debate on the resolution showed how far Sinn Féin still had to go in breaking out of the republican ghetto in the Republic. Martin McGuinness hoped that the debate would encourage republicans to engage in discussion with other people: 'We are not the only anti-imperialists in Ireland . . . we must allow everyone who thinks as we do on the national question the opportunity to take part in this struggle.'[133] Although some of the remnants of the Provisionals' leftist phase decried the resolution on the grounds that it would dilute the 'socialist stand of Sinn Féin' by aligning the party with Fianna Fáil,[134] the real problem for a leadership which had – except during appearances before Labour Party audiences in Britain – abandoned notions of class struggle, was the armed struggle's deterrent effects on potential political allies in the Republic.

Another of Adams's allies, Mitchell McLaughlin, in an article marking twenty years of Provisionalism, pointed out that Fianna Fáil and other parties in the Republic had received their mandate,

> partially if not primarily because they have placed on record their support for national independence. This mandate must now be applied in a practical campaign with the minimum objective of a negotiated British withdrawal.[135]

Adams in his booklet *A Pathway to Peace*, published in March 1989, set out the most developed justification of the broad-front strategy. The task was to appeal to the anti-imperialist impulses of the southern masses against their 'collaborationist' political elite. Haughey's decisions to work with the Anglo–Irish Agreement and allow the extradition of an IRA man to the authorities in the North were portrayed as clear evidence that the Republic was a 'neo-colony, dependent on and answerable to foreign capital'.[136]

Adams had claimed at the Árd Fheis that the European elections would 'give us the opportunity to strengthen our struggle nationally and to put our alternative to the EEC and challenge the further dilution of our sovereignty in 1992'.[137] The results were a bitter disappointment. In the Republic there was a significant swing to the left and the Workers' Party's Proinsias de Rossa, much loathed by Adams and his supporters, topped the poll in Dublin, while the Sinn Féin vote nationally collapsed by

more than half to 2.3 per cent.[138] The previous month's results
in the Republic's general election had been similarly poor for
Sinn Féin, whose vote declined to 1.2 per cent, whilst both the
Workers' Party and Labour gained substantially in votes and
seats.[139]

Readers of the letters page of *An Phoblacht/Republican News*
should not have been surprised. In April the journalist Fintan
O'Toole had written a bitterly critical article in the *Irish Times*
after an IRA 'mistake' led to the death of a young girl in
Warrenpoint, County Down. This had produced a disparaging
response in the republican paper which provoked a letter from
a 'Dublin republican' who argued that Sinn Féin's marginalisation in the south was directly due to the representativeness of
O'Toole's views:

> Whether we like it or not, we must acknowledge that O'Toole's
> views are shared by most of the leadership of the working class in
> the 26 Counties. Outside the republican ghetto, opinions as to
> the ultimate objectives of the republican movement are many
> and varied. In the 26 Counties it is still commonplace to hear the
> republican movement referred to as 'Catholic fascists', as a
> Hibernian version of Pol Pot or, at best, as 'green nationalists'.[140]

Gerry Adams appeared to concur with this analysis in his
address to the Wolfe Tone commemoration at Bodenstown in
June when he referred to the election results in the Republic.
He admitted Sinn Féin's continued failure to persuade 'any
additional, sizeable section of the electorate of our relevancy'
and added:

> The desire for change among some voters passed us by. Of
> course we can truthfully protest that our small party was
> stretched to the limit in electoral contests through Ireland, and
> we can point to the legacy of elitism and bad organisation that
> we inherited three years ago. None of these explanations are
> good enough outside our own ranks.[141]

He attempted to brighten the electoral vista by referring to the
'excellent' results in the northern local government elections
and pointed out that Sinn Féin was the second largest party in
Belfast. In fact, the party's performance in the North was also
giving cause for concern. It was true that its share of the vote

declined only marginally in comparison with 1985, from 11.8 to 11.2 per cent,[142] but, as Mitchel McLaughlin pointed out, this only happened because of a substantial increase in loyalist abstentionism which particularly hit the DUP.[143] There was a 6,500 drop in the Sinn Féin vote and it lost sixteen of its council seats, many of them to the SDLP, whose vote increased by 3.2 per cent to 21 per cent.[144] McLaughlin pointed out that many of the lost seats reflected the fact that Sinn Féin lost less committed voters because of IRA 'mistakes': 'IRA operations that went wrong did have an effect because in a sense Sinn Féin is held accountable at a local level for all aspects of republican strategy.'[145]

Thus although an increase in support in West Belfast demonstrated the reality of hard-core support, the election showed that the party had little capacity to erode the SDLP's dominant position. After an analysis of survey evidence, two political scientists concluded that, 'The gap between Sinn Féin and the SDLP reflects two largely different electorates – only to a limited extent are they fishing for votes in the same pond.'[146] Most Sinn Féin voters were drawn from the manual and semi-skilled working class and the unemployed. Sinn Féin was also disproportionately strong among the young; about half its voters were under 34, compared to a third of the SDLP's and it was particularly over-represented in the 18-24 age group. Such evidence seemed to support the image of the party encouraged by the leadership in the early 1980s as the vanguard of a young and impatient Catholic working class. It did not encourage much confidence in the success of Adams's increasing commitment from 1986 to develop a broader 'anti-imperialist alliance'. The European election result in Northern Ireland was further confirmation of the party's weakness, with its vote slumping to 48,918: 9.2 per cent compared to 13.3 per cent in 1984. Adams's explanation that it was 'not an election that greatly interested our supporters' was particularly limp.[147]

The difficulty of building broader alliances as long as IRA violence continued was obvious. The northern editor of the *Irish Times* had commented on an earlier call by Adams for a 'national consensus' that, 'The logic of his demand for a broad nationalist front, including most of the political parties in the Republic, is the abandonment of violence by the IRA.'[148] It has been argued that a key development in republican attitudes to the role of armed struggle was the growth of Sinn Féin's local government presence in the 1980s.[149] It is certainly the case that some Sinn Féin councillors were well aware of the contradictions created by the IRA's activities. Adams had become a sponsor of Obair, a campaign for employment in West Belfast which produced an analysis of the local economy and its major problems of unemployment and poverty. Obair provided a critique of the limits of current government policies with a set of proposals for state-funded job creation in the area.[150] At a meeting of Sinn Féin party activists Martin O'Muilleoir, a councillor from the Upper Falls, pointed to the problem by arguing that many people 'believe we can't call for jobs to be created while the IRA campaign continues'.[151]

There was, however, little evidence that such a critique would do more than cause the IRA to add a convoluted anticapitalist rhetoric to its attacks on 'economic targets'. Thus after the bombing of the site in Belfast where the large Castle Court shopping mall was in the final stages of construction, an IRA statement denied that it was opposed to the creation of jobs. While making clear that the purpose of the bombing was an attack on 'a symbol of bogus normality', it disparaged its job-creating effects:

> In reality it is an employment sham which allows major firms such as Debenhams to accrue massive profits with minimum investment, while the task of building a real economic base in the most deprived area such as North and West Belfast is ignored.[152]

How the armed struggle would assist job creation in these areas was precisely the question raised by O'Muilleoir, but there was little sign that the leadership was prepared to contemplate more than an attempt to 'refine' a campaign of violence which was still seen as the 'cutting edge' of republicanism. As Adams explained to those readers of *Playboy* who were interested in such things, the British 'will leave only when they are forced to leave'.[153]

Even those Irish and British politicians most supportive of the idea of a broad nationalist front were sternly rebuffed when they made an IRA ceasefire a condition. At a meeting in Dublin in May 1989 organised by 'Trade Unionists for Irish Unity', Clare Short, the British Labour MP who chaired the British

'Time to Go' campaign, proclaimed, 'Our job is to work for the decolonisation of Ireland. For those who denounce violence and terrorism, who say that it is holding back political progress, as I do, you have to show another way.' Emmet Stagg, the Irish Labour Party TD whose brother had died on hunger strike as an IRA prisoner in England in 1976, also took part in the meeting. Speaking, *An Phoblacht* claimed, with the full support of his party, Stagg called for a British declaration of interest in Irish reunification as part of progress towards an ultimate declaration of intent to withdraw. He responded directly to Adams's call for a broad front: 'A national coalition pursuing the road to reunification, as urged by Gerry Adams, would be a tremendous boost, but at a price – the renunciation of support for armed struggle.'[154] A leader in *An Phoblacht* rejected Stagg's precondition:

> Democrats can have principled opposition to the tactic of armed struggle and still work for British withdrawal. If they are convinced it can be achieved without armed struggle they are duty-bound to build that movement and to show the alternative way as Clare Short stated last week.[155]

But it was clear that the IRA continued to be unconvinced by arguments for an unarmed strategy. In an interview as the twentieth anniversary of the deployment of British troops approached, 'spokespersons' for the GHQ Staff and Northern Command made it clear that violence was still the core of republican strategy:

> The IRA strategy is very clear. At some point in the future, due to the pressure of the continuing and sustained armed struggle, the will of the British government to remain in this country will be broken . . . we can state confidently today that there will be no ceasefire until Britain declares its intention to withdraw.[156]

However it was also clear that Adams and others feared the real possibilities of political isolation which such fundamentalism brought with it. Sinn Féin was very worried about the effect of the ban on the broadcasting of direct statements by representatives of Sinn Féin, Republican Sinn Féin and the UDA introduced by Douglas Hurd in October 1988 as a response to the Ballygawley bus bombing. The effect of the Anglo–Irish Agreement in what was seen as tying the Republic into the

British 'counter-insurgency' strategy and war-weariness in the nationalist community were also noted. Adams told the faithful that:

> Britain's carrot and stick strategy is now in top gear with the full co-operation of the Dublin government. The British believe they now have the ability to crush nationalist and republican dissent and they are obviously trying to use the long twenty years of struggle against us. The British have created for themselves an image of respectability in their occupation of Ireland.[157]

The evident contradictions in the 'armalite and ballot box' strategy, together with the failure to displace the SDLP and political marginalisation in the Republic, had begun to generate a debate within republicanism. John Hume had proclaimed the existence of this debate in 1988. A journalist interviewing Peter Brooke in November 1989 on his first hundred days as Secretary of State for Northern Ireland had provided the opportunity for what was clearly an intervention in that debate:

> Interviewer: Not so long ago a very senior republican described to me that in the present state of play there were yourselves and themselves, basically it was a Mexican stand-off position. Can you ever see the day when . . . the British government can sit down and talk to Sinn Féin?
>
> Brooke: . . . The first factor is that I would recognise that in terms of the late twentieth-century terrorist, organised as well as the Provisional IRA have become, that it is difficult to envisage a military defeat of such a force . . . though the security forces can exercise a policy of containment to enable, broadly speaking, normal life to go on. So in that sense it would require a decision on the part of the terrorists that the game had ceased to be worth the candle, that considering the lifestyle they have to adopt, that the return which they were searching from their activities did not justify the costs it was imposing in personal terms on those who were engaged in their activities. There has to be a possibility that at some stage that that debate might start within the terrorist community and that moment might come.[159]

The fact that Brooke also said that creating jobs in areas like West Belfast would not in itself 'cause terrorism to falter', and neither would the return of acceptable institutions of devolved government, helped to make this a speech which grabbed republican attention. His use of the Cyprus analogy when asked if he would ever consider speaking to Gerry Adams and Danny Morrison was sure to appeal:

> Let me remind you of the move towards independence in Cyprus and a British minister stood up in the House of Commons and used the word 'never' in a way which within two years there had been a retreat from that word.

The response was one of guarded and suspicious interest. While the 'startling' admission of there being no military solution was welcomed, it was also pointed out that it was not new, as Reginald Maudling had recognised as early as 1971 that the British state could only hope to reduce IRA violence to an 'acceptable level'. The SDLP was scorned for its more enthusiastic response – Seamus Mallon had described Brooke's interview as a 'quantum leap'. John Hume was denounced for his suggestions that the IRA should give up violence and that the way to Irish self-determination lay in two separate referenda in the Republic and Northern Ireland:

> Behind the rhetoric Hume's plan is for the SDLP and the Unionists to agree on some devolution scheme for the North and have it endorsed by the South's electorate. Given the censorship on both sides of the border, Sinn Féin's views on self-determination would not even get an airing.[160]

Hume was also blamed for encouraging media speculation of internal divisions between 'hawks and doves'. Brooke's interview was supposedly based on this analysis. The paper declared that, 'Such a debate is a figment of Mr Hume's imagination.'[161] At a Sinn Féin press briefing on the Brooke interview, Martin McGuinness was categorical:

> The question is, is there a group of people within the republican movement or within Sinn Féin who believe that the freedom of Ireland can be won only through political involvement in constitutional politics or in elections. I have heard absolutely no discussion from any group or person within Sinn Féin along those lines – so it's total and absolute nonsense.[162]

As we have seen, the question of a ceasefire had been implicitly raised during at least one internal party conference, so

McGuinness's denial was not strictly accurate. Although a debate was certainly taking place, it was not of the sort depicted in the media. There is little evidence to suggest that there was support for a ceasefire to allow Sinn Féin into talks with the British. If anything, the Brooke interview seems to have suggested that the continuation of a perhaps more 'defendable' armed struggle would play a key role in persuading the British to negotiate. As McGuinness put it at the relaunch of 'A Scenario for Peace':

> While republicans remain dedicated to their current strategy, the British government is becoming weary and tired of the Irish problem. There may well be debate going on within the Establishment in England regarding Britain's future role in the Six Counties.[163]

As republicans entered a new decade, force appeared to have been revived as the key determinent of the struggle with Britain.

Notes

1. *Republican News*, 18 June 1977. Drumm's speech was written by Adams and Danny Morrison; see Gerry Adams, *Before the Dawn, An Autobiography*, London 1996, p.264

2. *Eire Nua: The Economic and Social Thought of Sinn Féin*, Dublin 1971. The quote from Ó Bradaigh is in Christine N. Elias, 'Know your Eire Nua: The New Ulster', *Republican News*, 25 June 1973.

3. Paul Bew and Henry Patterson, *The British State and the Ulster Crisis*, London 1985, p.50.

4. Vincent Browne, 'The Provos Settle Down for a 20 Year War', *Magill*, August 1982.

5. For a more detailed analysis of the truce, see Bew and Patterson, op.cit., pp.78-88.

6. Patricia Davidson, 'British Withdrawal: The Economic Case', *Republican News*, 29 May 1976.

7. Ibid., 18 June 1973.

8. Interview with Jimmy Drumm.

9. Gerry Adams, 'A Republican in the Civil Rights Campaign' in M. Farrell (ed.), *Twenty Years On*, Dingle 1988, p.47.

10. Paul Arthur, *The People's Democracy*, Belfast 1974, and for conflicting assessments of the PD and 1968, see Ronald Fraser, *1968*, London 1988.

11. Adams, *Before the Dawn*, p.129 and interview with Gerry Adams.

12. Peter Arnlis, 'The Nature of Strategy, Politics, Revolution and British Withdrawal', *Republican News*, 27 March 1976.

13. Ibid.

14. 'Brownie', 'The Republic: A Reality', *Republican News*, 29 November 1975.
15. 'Brownie', 'Agitate, Educate, Liberate', ibid., 22 May 1976.
16. See, 'The North – Key to English Influence in Ireland', ibid., 23 September 1974, which copies the *Ireland Today* analysis almost word for word.
17. 'Why Died the Sons of Roisin Dubh? Was it Greed?' *Republican News*, 10 January 1976.
18. 'Brownie', 'Agitate, Educate, Liberate'.
19. See Peter Mair, 'The Irish Republic and the Anglo-Irish Agreement' in Paul Teague (ed.), *Beyond the Rhetoric*, London 1988.
20. *Republican News*, 29 October 1977.
21. Ibid.
22. Richard Davis, *Political Propaganda and the Ulster Troubles: A Mirror Image of Antagonism 1968-82*, unpublished manuscript, University of Tasmania, 1983, pp.214-5.
23. 'Thoughts on Eire Nua', *Republican News*, 5 November 1977.
24. Ibid.
25. Bishop and Mallie, op.cit., p.262.
26. 'Brownie', 'Agitate, Educate, Liberate'.
27. *Republican News*, 29 October 1977.
28. Peter Dowling, 'Stickies in Trouble', ibid., 26 February 1977.
29. Ibid.
30. 'Now it's Official – Stickies Accept Orange Rule', ibid., 9 April 1977.
31. 'Success Opens up New Challenges: 1978 Review', *An Phoblacht/Republican News* (*AP/RN*), 27 January 1979.
32. 'Struggle on All Fronts', ibid., 10 February 1979.
33. 'Out of the Ashes', ibid., January 1979.
34. 'Struggle on All Fronts'.
35. 'Out of the Ashes'.
36. 'Not Just a Brits Out Movement', a speech at Bodenstown, June 1979, reprinted in Gerry Adams, *Signposts to Independence and Socialism*, Dublin 1988, pp.23-7.
37. 'Active Republicanism', *Republican News*, 1 May 1976.
38. 'The National Alternative', ibid., 3 April 1976.
39. Bew and Patterson, op.cit., p.93.
40. Ibid.
41. The Glover Report is reproduced in full as an appendix to Seán Cronin, *Irish Nationalism: A History of its Roots and Ideology*, Dublin 1980.
42. *AP/RN*, 19 May 1979
43. For a detailed analysis of the issues, see Liam Clarke, *Broadening the Battlefield*, Dublin 1987.
44. *Magill*, May 1979.
45. 'Bernadette and the Politics of H-Blocks' in *Callaghan's Irish Quarterly*, Vol. 1, No. 1, p.14.
46. 'Sinn Féin Prisoners Conference', *AP/RN*, 29 September 1979.
47. 'A Tragedy not a Farce', ibid., 2 June 1979.
48. IRA interview, ibid., 11 August 1979.
49. Interview with Jimmy Drumm.
50. *Myth and Motherland*, Field Day pamphlet no. 5, Derry 1984, p.12.

51. See Clarke, op.cit.
52. *AP/RN*, 3 February 1983.
53. Ibid., 17 March 1983.
54. Ibid., 5 May 1983.
55. Ibid.
56. 'Establishment Poll-axed by Sinn Féin Vote', ibid., 16 June 1983.
57. 'Sinn Féin EEC Challenge', ibid., 3 May 1984.
58. 'Steady Progress and an Injection of Reality', ibid., 21 June 1984.
59. Ibid.
60. See *Magill*, July 1983, where Adams called for a refinement of IRA activity while a member of the IRA Army Council called for an escalation.
61. *AP/RN*, 21 June 1984.
62. Peter Dowling, 'Dublin Summit Opens Dangerous Option', *AP/RN*, 17 January 1981.
63. Danny Morrison, *The Hillsborough Agreement*, Dublin 1986, pp.8-9.
64. Gerry Adams, *The Politics of Irish Freedom*, Dingle 1986, p.105.
65. Morrison, op.cit., p.9.
66. Adams, op.cit., p.105.
67. *AP/RN*, 17 January 1981.
68. Adams, op.cit., p.154.
69. Gerry Adams, 'A Bus Ride to Independence and Socialism', speech given to Sinn Féin Internal Conference 1986, reprinted in *Signposts to Independence and Socialism*, p.13.
70. See his 1979 interview: 'There is no Marxist influence within Sinn Féin. I know of no one in Sinn Féin who is a Marxist or who would be influenced by Marxism.' *Hibernia*, 25 October 1979.
71. In the autumn of 1980 Seamus Mallon and John McEvoy of the SDLP had met Morrison and Joe Austin of Sinn Féin for a series of talks. In October 1984 a lack of response from Britain to the Forum Report prompted a prominent SDLP councillor in Belfast, Brian Feeney, to suggest co-operation with Sinn Féin in councils to make Northern Ireland ungovernable. *AP/RN*, 11 October 1984.
72. *Observer*, 27 April 1986.
73. *Guardian*, 30 March 1987.
74. The Sinn Féin and SDLP documents were reproduced in the *Irish Times*, 19 September 1988.
75. *AP/RN*, 5 April 1984.
76. Quotes from Sinn Féin document 'A Strategy for Peace' sent to the SDLP in March 1988, reproduced in full in the *Irish Times*, 7 September 1988.
77. Bew and Patterson, op.cit., pp.140-2.
78. *Guardian*, 9 March 1987.
79. *Irish Times*, 19 September 1988.
80. Ibid., 6 September 1988.
81. *Irish Times*, 13 June 1988.
82. *Magill*, August 1988.
83. Ibid.
84. See Fergus Pyle's interview with Adams in the *Irish Times*, 19 July 1988, and *Magill*, August 1988.
85. Mair, op.cit., p.100.

86. Ibid., p.101.
87. See his speech at Harvard, *Irish Times*, 23 April 1988.
88. *Irish Times*, 19 September 1988.
89. Ibid.
90. *Irish News*, 21 June 1988.
91. *An Reabhloid*, Journal of People's Democracy, Vol. 1, No. 2, Autumn 1988, p.12 – A. McIntyre and M. McMullen.
92. *Borderline*, Vol. 1, No. 3, Autumn 1986.
93. 'What's on the agenda now is an end to partition' – Adams interview with Fergus Pyle, *Irish Times*, 19 July 1988.
94. 'Scenario for a Socialist Republic', *AP/RN*, April 1980, reprinted in *Signposts to Independence and Socialism*, pp.28-31.
95. Gerry Adam's address, reprinted in *The Politics of Revolution: Main Speeches on 1986 Sinn Féin Árd Fheis*, Dublin 1986, p.11.
96. Ibid., p.8.
97. Ibid., pp.12-3.
98. Ibid.
99. Clarke, op.cit.
100. Adams, *The Politics of Revolution*, p.13.
101. John Ward, 'What is to be Done? The Struggle in the 26 Counties', *Iris: The Republican Magazine*, October 1987.
102. Interview with Gerry Adams.
103. Mair, op.cit., p.94.
104. Ibid., p.90.
105. Ibid.
106. Gerry Adams, *The Politics of Irish Freedom*, Dingle 1986, p.157.
107. Mair, op.cit., p.92.
108. Gerry Adams, *A Pathway to Peace*, Cork and Dublin 1989, p.8.
109. Ibid., p.77
110. Ibid., pp.80-1.
111. Ibid., p.62.
112. Robin Wilson, 'Civilian Unrest', *Fortnight*, March 1989.
113. 'Peace, War and Understanding', interview with Adams, *Magill*, August 1988.
114. Gerry Adams, *A Pathway to Peace*, pp.74-5.
115. M.L.R. Smith, *Fighting for Ireland: The Military Strategy of the Irish Republican Movement*, London and New York 1995, p.169.
116. Brendan O'Brien, *The Long War: The IRA and Sinn Féin from Armed Struggle to Peace Talks*, Dublin 1993, pp.129-70.
117. Ibid., p.130
118. Gerry Adams, *The Politics of Irish Freedom*, p.64.
119. Eamonn Mallie and David McKittrick, *The Fight for Peace: The Secret Story Behind the Irish Peace Process*, London 1996, p.72.
120. Ibid., pp.44-7.
121. Paul Bew and Gordon Gillespie, *Northern Ireland: A Chronology of the Troubles 1968-1992*, Dublin 1993, p.207.
122. Eamonn Mallie, 'Provo Resurgence', *Fortnight*, September 1988.
123. Smith, op.cit., p.188.
124. Bew and Gillespie, op.cit., p.205.
125. Jack Holland and Susan Phoenix, *Policing the Shadows: The Secret War*

against Terrorism in Northern Ireland, London 1996, pp.162-4.
126. O'Brien, op.cit., p.151.
127. *AP/RN*, 5 January 1989.
128. Ibid., 26 January 1989.
129. Mallie and McKittrick, op.cit., p.59.
130. *AP/RN*, 26 January 1989.
131. Ibid., 9 March 1989.
132. Ibid., 2 February 1989.
133. Ibid.
134. See the speech by Johnny White in ibid.
135. 'Twenty Years On', ibid., 5 January 1989.
136. See the review of *Pathway to Peace* in ibid., 6 April 1989 and the attack on 'Haughey's Treachery' in ibid., 13 April 1989.
137. Ibid., 2 February 1989.
138. Michael Holmes, 'The 1989 Election to the European Parliament in the Republic of Ireland', *Irish Political Studies*, Vol. 5, 1990, p.88.
139. Sinn Féin got 20,003 first preference votes (1. 2 per cent) and no seats; the Irish Labour Party 156,989 votes (9.5 per cent, an increase of 3 per cent) and fifteen seats; the Workers' Party 82,263 votes (5 per cent, an increase of 1.2 per cent) and seven seats. Pat Neville, 'The 1989 General Election in the Republic of Ireland', *Irish Political Studies*, Vol. 5, 1990, p.73.
140. *AP/RN*, 18 May 1989.
141. Ibid., 25 June 1989.
142. Colin Knox, 'The 1989 Local Elections in Northern Ireland', *Irish Political Studies*, Vol. 5, 1990, p.82.
143. Interview with Martin McGuinness, *AP/RN*, 25 June 1989.
144. Knox, op.cit.
145. *AP/RN*, 25 June 1989.
146. Cynthia Irvine and Eddie Moxon-Browne, 'Not Many Floating Voters Here', *Fortnight*, May 1989.
147. *AP/RN*, 25 June 1989.
148. 'Adams Calls on Southern Parties', *Irish Times*, 13 June 1989.
149. Kevin Bean, *The New Departure: Recent Developments in Irish Republican Ideology and Strategy*, Liverpool 1994, p.8
150. Bill Rolston and Mike Tomlinson, *Unemployment in West Belfast: The Obair Report*, Belfast 1988.
151. *Irish Times*, 27 June 1988.
152. *AP/RN*, 8 June 1989.
153. Quoted in the *Irish Times*, 24 February 1989.
154. *AP/RN*, 4 May 1989.
155. Ibid.
156. Ibid., 17 August 1989.
157. Ibid., 29 June 1989.
158. Ibid., 16 November 1989.
159. Ibid.
160. Ibid.
161. Ibid.
162. Mallie and McKittrick, op.cit., p.101.
163. *AP/RN*, 23 December 1989.

7 The Tactical Use of Armed Struggle, 1990–1996

The IRA's announcement of a 'complete cessation of military operations' on 31 August 1994 has inevitably coloured most subsequent writing about the republican movement in the early 1990s. There has been a strong tendency in Irish nationalist accounts to construct a teleology of the peace process, reaching back to the 1980s, in which dialogue between warweary republican leaders and far-seeing constitutional nationalist politicians, particularly John Hume, inexorably brought the doubters and traditionalists towards acceptance of the need for a 'Totally Unarmed Strategy'.[1] For Unionists and some of their most articulate representatives, like Dr Conor Cruise O'Brien, the peace process was a sham, the fundamental purpose of which was to destabilise the Union whilst the apparatus of the IRA was kept intact to be used if the unarmed strategy faltered.[2] This chapter will argue that, while there were certainly some republicans who believed that the armed struggle had become an obstacle to further progress, and the peace process was not in that sense a sham, it was, however, a much more ambiguous and contradictory strategy than many of its uncritical supporters would allow.

Armed Struggle and British Neutrality

In November 1990 Peter Brooke made an important speech in his Westminster constituency on the nature of the British presence in Northern Ireland. He distinguished four aspects of this presence: British troops, the machinery of Direct Rule headed by himself as Secretary of State, the annual financial subvention and, lastly, what he referred to as the

> paramount reality that the heart and core of the British presence is not the British army or the British ministers but the reality of nearly a million people living in a part of the island of Ireland who are, and who certainly regard themselves as, British.[3]

Partition, he claimed, was 'an acknowledgement of reality not an assertion of national self-interest'. He concluded with a sentence which was to intensify republican interest in a possible shift in British policy: 'The British government has no selfish strategic or economic interest in Northern Ireland, our role is to help, enable and encourage.'

Sinn Féin's response to Brooke's speech accepted at least some of the terms of the argument on the British presence. There was no attempt to argue that Britain had either a strategic or economic interest. That, however, did not mean acceptance of Hume's argument that Britain was neutral, for Brooke still gave a 'veto' to the Unionists: 'The argument that the consent of this national minority is necessary before constitutional change can occur is a nonsense.'[4] While the response was critical, it clearly saw the speech as having major significance:

> If Britain is neutral then they are open to persuasion that they should shift the massive resources and energy presently put into maintaining partition and attempting to find partitionist solutions and direct them instead towards some alternative arrangements.

Britain, in other words, should join the ranks of those trying to persuade the Unionist community that its future lay in a united Ireland. Adams was well aware that there was an important strand of constitutional nationalist opinion in favour of a joint approach with Sinn Féin to pressurise the British into this course of action. Martin Mansergh, a key adviser on Northern Ireland policy to successive Fianna Fáil leaders, dates the beginning of the peace process to the 'psychological turning point' of the Ennikillen bombing when, in November 1987, Father Alex Reid, a Redemptorist priest from the Clonard monastery off the Falls Road, put forward a written proposal for dialogue between the SDLP and Sinn Féin.[5]

Reid had earlier arranged a meeting between Adams and the Catholic primate of Ireland, Cardinal Tomás Ó Fiaich. The cardinal was well regarded by republicans for his championing of a Fianna Fáil-type anti-partitionism and also for his support for the Sinn Féin position during the Hunger Strikes. Although in the 1970s Ó Fiaich had supported the idea of a British declaration of intent to withdraw as 'the only thing that will get things moving',[6] by the mid-1980s he was in favour of a more modulated approach:

> Probably the only hope of getting the IRA to desist from the campaign of violence is to try to sell the idea to them ... that a united Ireland is attainable – but by peaceful methods and by gradual advance towards it.[7]

In 1989 he called publicly for a statement by Britain that it would not stay in Northern Ireland indefinitely.[8]

The notion that a public declaration by Britain of its intention eventually to withdraw from Ireland would have a positive catalytic effect on Unionists, causing them to rethink their attitude to Irish nationalists, was a long-standing component of Fianna Fáil thinking on the North. The upsurge of violence after 1969 had produced a lurch to a simpler position of 'declaration of intent to withdraw' but, as Ó Fiaich pointed out, the continuation of IRA violence had reduced sympathy for northern Catholics in the Republic and the shift towards the older and more measured position was a product of this.[9]

Ironically, the conception of British interest and Irish strategy which underlay the peace process was first clearly developed in the early 1960s by Seán Lemass, long reviled by republicans for his 'pro-British' free trade agreement of 1965. Lemass had believed that in a post-war context of decolonisation symbolised by Harold Macmillan's 'Winds Of Change' speech, the British political elite would be willing to reconsider its support for the 'colonialist' partition settlement. As part of that process he had attempted – unsuccessfully – to enlist the support of President Kennedy to encourage the British to make a declaration of support for an eventually united island. Lemass was clear that unity could not be imposed on the Unionists, but he did believe that such a British declaration would, over time, encourage a shift in their attitudes.[10]

It was John Hume who, in his interpretation of the Anglo-

Irish Agreement, portrayed it in a similar way to Lemass's view of the 'Winds of Change' speech as indicating a break from active support for partition. Until Brooke's speech republicans had been disdainful of Hume's analysis. When Hume contributed an article to the *Independent on Sunday* arguing that the 1992 European Single Market, with its undermining of the nation state and outdated conceptions of sovereignty, made traditional forms of nationalism redundant, the important 'Hilda MacThomas' column in *An Phoblacht/Republican News* gave a trenchant rejoinder. A new and expanded Europe, it argued, was seeing the intensification of national struggles and neither membership of the European Community nor Article One of the Anglo-Irish Agreement had in reality established British neutrality. Rather, Brooke's announcement in January 1990 that he believed that there was a sufficient basis for the establishment of all-party talks was seen as yet another attempt to stabilise the North through some form of devolution together with an institutionalised Irish dimension.[11]

At a major internal Sinn Féin conference in the North held in March 1990, Tom Hartley and Adams had both emphasised that the British strategy was that of stabilising the North and defeating the republicans in collusion with the leadership of the SDLP, the churches and the Dublin government. Revealingly, the emphasis of the leadership's speeches to the conference was on the need to build and strengthen the republican struggle for June 1992 and the arrival of a new British government. Little was expected from London as long as Thatcher was in power. In the interim there was no disguising the party's failure to expand beyond its ghetto roots. Mitchel McLaughlin enthused over the effect 'a vibrant republican struggle with clear popular involvement would have on international public opinion', and cited 'examples of mass action' like the civil rights campaign, the anti-internment campaign and the H-Block campaign. The party's present position was, he argued, far removed from these high points. It was locked into a sub-culture through a 'fixed calendar of commemorations, anniversaries and protests'. Although the broad-front strategy had been adopted more than two years earlier, the organisation had failed to involve itself fully in building a mass movement against imperialism.[12] Hartley noted a 'constriction' of the party and its failure to break out of a narrow band of political activity centred on elections and its public representatives

– something all the more damaging given the effects of the media ban in Northern Ireland. The perspective, if not depressing, was clearly one of long-term development.[13]

There was concern that the SDLP would, with Dublin's support, be drawn into all-party talks leading to what Sinn Féin referred to as a 'return to Stormont',[14] but it obviously feared that the SDLP might be able to win the support of a significant sector of the nationalist electorate. In a two-part analysis of the history of the SDLP, 'Hilda MacThomas', after making disparaging remarks about it being 'middle-class, middle-aged and middle of the road' and mentioning a graffito in Hume's constituency referring to the 'Stoop-Down-Low-Party', had to admit that, 'In spite of the fact that the SDLP represents clearly the interests of the nationalist middle class, it receives most of its votes from working-class areas.' It was recognised that middle-class Catholics did have 'a stake in the Six County state and would be content with a share of power'. The worrying fact was that this middle-class interest had been able to establish leadership over many working-class nationalists through 'Humespeak', in other words the successful portrayal of the Anglo-Irish Agreement as a major victory for nationalists. Thus while 'MacThomas' argued that, like Sunningdale, the Agreement was essentially about 'copper-fastening' partition, he also admitted that,

> The framework it set up was very different: the symbolic location of the intergovernmental secretariat in Maryfield, near Belfast, was one of the SDLP's insistent demands. As symbols go, it worked remarkably. Its termination, relocation, or even temporary closure have become the Unionists' main demand.

The work of the inter-governmental conference and the secretariat, the institutions through which the Irish government could seek an input into the governance of Northern Ireland, 'suited the SDLP like a glove' and allowed it to claim that the Agreement marked a watershed which showed that constitutionalism rather than violence was the way to achieve unity. Hume, it was alleged, had started a 'pincer movement on Sinn Féin' based on a proposed gradualist approach to Irish unity: firstly, equality of treatment for both communities in Northern Ireland, secondly, agreement on power-sharing and then unity: 'The fact that stage one had defied all reformist attempts for nearly twenty years did not matter, the words "Irish Unity" were the message to nationalist voters.'[15]

Peter Brooke's failure, in July 1990, to secure agreement from the SDLP and the Dublin government for his proposal that there would have to be substantial progress on talks on the internal government of Northern Ireland before moving on to north-south discussions involving Dublin, heartened republicans, and there was a premature declaration that the Brooke initiative was dead. 'Hume's stages theory lies in tatters,' 'MacThomas' claimed, and said of his claim of British neutrality: 'Surely if that were so Peter Brooke would not have sided with Unionists in his "talks about talks" initiative?'[16]

In fact, by the time of his speech on the British presence Brooke had already made it clear that he would continue to press the parties to agree to a talks format and that 1991 would see the beginning of substantive talks. This commitment was a major factor in determining republicans' response to the speech, as it seemed to underline the continuation of a major British commitment to stabilising partition on the basis of an accommodation with constitutional nationalism. At the same time Brooke's speeches indicated that perhaps a section of the 'British establishment' was tiring of its Northern Irish commitment, and this idea was no doubt encouraged by the secret line of communication with the British government which was re-established with Brooke's sanction in October 1990.[17] However any thinking in favour of withdrawal from Northern Ireland was seen by republicans as but one tendency, and 'stand pat' and even pro-Union elements were still believed to be entrenched within the British state.

For this reason violence continued to be seen as directly functional in pushing the British political elite towards a commitment to withdrawal. The early 1990s saw a new emphasis on IRA attacks on 'establishment' targets in England. The IRA bombed the Carlton Club in June 1990, claiming a blow 'at the heart of Tory rule', and in July the Stock Exchange was bombed.[18] Ian Gow, MP, a close friend and in the early 1980s adviser to Thatcher on Irish affairs, was murdered with a car-bomb in July 1990, and in August there were failed attempts to kill Lord Armstrong, who, as Cabinet Secretary, had been an architect of the Anglo-Irish Agreement, and General Sir Anthony Farrar-Hockley, a former Commander of Land Forces in Northern Ireland.[19] Senior republicans explained to the editor of *Fortnight*, the North's current affairs journal, that as opinion polls in Britain had consistently shown majorities for withdrawal, it was the 'British establishment' that needed to be shifted:

> Republicans feel that British politicians and the British establishment aren't, on a long-term basis, going to be prepared to put up with the severe hardships and restrictions which are being imposed on them as a result of being under constant threat of IRA attack.

It was claimed that when Thatcher retired, a new breed of Conservatives, faced with the continuing IRA threat to their lifestyles, would take the inevitable decision to withdraw.[20]

The same issue of *Fortnight* contained a round-table discussion of republican strategy by academics and journalists. Entitled 'The IRA Goes Back to Basics', the predominant tone was one of bleak pessimism. Thus the journalist who was later to write a book tracing the origins of the 'Irish peace process' back to the mid-1980s, was then oblivious to such a benign tendency:

> Robin Wilson: So is the general assessment then that if we were sitting here in five years' time the IRA campaign would be ticking along at much the current rate, that Sinn Féin would be much as they are, possibly a bit lower, and that if there had been any change it would be in a shift in focus towards other theatres?
>
> David McKittrick: My belief is that we're going out of a political period now. There'll always be Sinn Féin as a political adjunct. It doesn't seem to have any scope for advancement . . . You're now into a military period where it goes to the Continent, goes to Britain and tries to create enough havoc there to blow Britain out of Ireland.[21]

If, as *An Phoblacht* claimed, the republican movement was 'planning for peace in the '90s',[22] it was also made clear that this was still conceived as peace created by victory and that politics and armed struggle would both be essential tactics in the achievement of that victory.

Although republicans regularly denounced Brooke's attempt to establish a talks process involving the Northern parties and Dublin as a waste of time and a diversion from the 'real' issue of national self-determination, there was also a fear that he might just succeed. In his presidential address to the 1991 Árd Fheis, Adams, although welcoming Brooke's speeches as possible indicators of debate in government circles, denounced what he claimed still appeared to be the main aim of British policy, 'a locally elected partitionist administration in the Six Counties as envisaged in the Hillsborough Treaty'. His fear was that such a settlement, if it was underpinned by Dublin, 'will almost certainly strengthen the Union and insulate the British government once again from any criticism for its role in Ireland'.[23] Although Adams claimed this was unlikely, it was clearly still seen as a definite possiblity leading to Sinn Féin's isolation and the introduction of internment on both sides of the border.

Yet there was a marked reluctance to give up on a more optimistic interpretation of Brooke's speech as heralding a possible shift in government policy:

> Maybe, some political analysts will speculate, maybe these [strategies to cement partition] aren't the factors governing British strategy? Fair enough, it is up to Mr Brooke to clarify the situation.[24]

The final paragraphs of Adams's speech raised the possibility that John Major's replacement of Mrs Thatcher could create a real opportunity for a change of British strategy. Adams referred to his letter to the new Prime Minister which had informed Major that, freed from Mrs Thatcher's 'imperialist' baggage, he was in a 'unique position to initiate change'. A few days after the Árd Fheis the IRA fired a mortar into the garden of Number 10 Downing Street as Major was presiding over a Cabinet meeting.[25]

Some leading republicans still held to the belief that, even if an internal debate on Irish policy had begun at the very highest level in Britain, the force of nationalist argument would only have effect if backed up by the continuing 'argument of force'. At Sinn Féin's annual Six County conference, Martin McGuinness, after providing an elitist 'historical' justification for violence – 'Pearse and Connolly used armed struggle to further their aims and objectives' – went on to give the core functional justification: 'If there were no military struggle, then the nationalist community would be trampled on and walked over and the SDLP would become as irrelevant as the Nationalist

Party under Stormont.'[26] John Hume's contention that a cease-fire would actually strengthen nationalist bargaining power with Britain evidently still lacked the support of certain key individuals. Another republican strategist, Jim Gibney, declared that a ceasefire would come only when 'the British government accepts that its role in Ireland is over and that it will withdraw its forces from this country within the lifetime of a British parliament'.[27]

Brendan O'Brien, an Irish television reporter with extensive republican contacts, has claimed that in 1991 there was a serious debate in the IRA's Army Council over how to respond to Brooke's speeches and that, eventually, a decision was reached that, in certain circumstances, there could be a ceasefire before a British declaration of intent to withdraw. Ultimately, the 'hard-liners' found themselves in a minority and, in a 'highly significant shift', it was decided that, instead of a declaration of intent to withdraw, the British should adopt the role of 'persuaders' for Irish unity: 'A broadly held consensus grew within the leadership that Britain was no longer in Northern Ireland pursuing interests of her own and, further that Britain wanted out.'[28]

This appears to be an exaggeration of the extent of change. There is evidence that some republican strategists believed that a current in favour of withdrawal did exist in London, but this was within an 'establishment' which also contained counter-tendencies based on a conservative defence of the status quo and even strong support for the Union. Adams made it clear, in an interview with Brian Rowan in 1995, that he never accepted the notion of British 'neutrality' or of a dominant disposition to withdraw:

Adams said that he believed that the British establishment wanted a settlement but it was not a monolith: while he was certain that there were elements within it that wanted to end the Union, there were others who wanted to maintain it: 'My one sentence description of the British establishment position is that they have no bottom line. They can be moved as far as the political influence or power that can be harnessed for a democratic solution; they will move as far as we can push them.'[29]

Even those most convinced of the existence of a current favouring withdrawal would have had problems persuading their more traditionalist comrades given the continued efforts made by Brooke in 1991 to establish all-party talks on the basis of what had become known as 'the three sets of relations'. (This was the terminology of John Hume imported into NIO pronouncements referring to internal Northern Ireland structures of government, possible north-south structures and the London-Dublin relationship.) Republicans acknowledged that if such talks got off the ground, since Sinn Féin would be excluded, they would benefit the SDLP.[30] Although supposedly doomed to failure, such talks were also held to be bad news for republicans because they 'would serve to distract international opinion away from British responsiblity for the ongoing conflict in the North'.[31] The talks were seen as a 'holding operation',[32] but dangerous for all that.

As Britain moved towards a general election in 1992, any revisionists in the republican leadership also had to weather increasingly warm pro-Union speeches from leading members of the government. At the Conservative Party conference in Blackpool in October 1991 Brooke declared, 'We will stand by Ulster through thick and thin,' and the Foreign Secretary, Douglas Hurd, depicted the Irish government as

> not a rival for sovereignty but a partner in ending political violence. The discussion now focuses not on the border or the unification of Ireland but on how Northern Ireland can run its affairs within the United Kingdom.[33]

Exception was also taken to an interview which Brooke had given to the *Irish Times* in September 1991 in which he had said that Articles 2 and 3 of the Irish Constitution were 'unhelpful' and 'overtly at variance with Article One of the Hillsborough Agreement', dismissing any idea of developing the Anglo-Irish Agreement.[34]

Brooke, who has subsequently claimed to have been an avid reader of *An Phoblacht*,[35] may have been impressed by the assiduity with which some republican strategists followed his spoken and written word. Thus doubts about his hankerings after a shift of direction were also caused by an interview with an academic in which he specifically denied that Britain was 'politically neutral on Northern Ireland'. Brooke distanced himself from Hume's reading of Article 1(c) of the Anglo-Irish Agreeement as indicating 'neutrality'. The position was the same as in 1920 and Hume 'would have a fairly large task if he was seeking to move the Conservative Party to change this position'.[36]

But those inclined to a belief in the need to move from a simple British withdrawal position were shored up by two developments in 1991. Of these, the most important was evidence that the British were interested in maintaining and amplifying the renewed secret contacts. In April 1991 the British government representative gave advance notice to Martin McGuinness that the loyalist paramilitaries were about to announce a ceasefire for the duration of the inter-party talks. June saw the appointment of a new British representative who produced a letter from Brooke verifying his status. The channel was used by the British to check rumours that the IRA's traditional three-day 'suspension of operations' at Christmas might be extended in 1991 and to discover whether republicans thought it might be useful to use the Derry home of a retired civil servant for meetings.[37]

The possiblity of a change of government in 1992 was also the basis for guarded optimism. Adams, while condemning the 'disgraceful' record of past Labour governments, welcomed the 1988 policy document, 'Towards a United Ireland. Reform and Harmonisation', for its attempt to set out measures of north-south integration over which there would be no Unionist veto.[38] When Sinn Féin launched its revised policy document, 'Towards a Lasting Peace in Ireland', in February 1992, Jim Gibney appealed to Neil Kinnock, if Labour won, to 'honour the letter and spirit of your policy on Ireland. We are willing to help you reunite our country.'[39]

The second and more decisive factor was John Hume's approach to Gerry Adams in October 1991 with a draft joint declaration which he proposed should be signed by the Irish and British governments. This proposed that the British government declare that it had no longer

> any selfish, strategic, political or economic interest in Northern Ireland and that their sole interest is to see peace, stability and reconciliation established by agreement among the people who inhabit the island. The British government acknowledge that it is the wish of the people of Britain to see the people of Ireland live together in unity and harmony.[40]

The draft contained the Irish government's acceptance of Hume's reformulation of the 'people of Ireland's' right to self-determination which had to be achieved with 'the agreement and consent of the people of Northern Ireland'. This 'very subtle concept'[41] was, by itself, flawed from the republican point of view because it gave Unionists, as a majority of the people in the North, a 'veto' on Irish self-determination.

What attracted republicans to the draft was the reference to the two governments using 'all their influence and resources ... to foster agreement and reconciliation and to promote intensive co-operation at all levels'.[42] This was a toned down reference to the demand, reiterated by republicans since Brooke's first speech, that Britain bend itself to 'persuading' Unionists that their future lay in unity with the rest of the island. Combined with the clear declaration of the British government of its absolute lack of any remaining interest in staying in Ireland, apart from helping the process of 32 County 'reconciliation', this was exhilarating stuff for the republican leadership.

When Adams was presented with the document by Hume, he also knew that Hume's orignal draft had been modified after discussions with the Taoiseach, Charles Haughey, and his key advisers on the North. Martin Mansergh, Haughey's personal adviser on Northern Ireland, had, at Haughey's request, engaged in secret exploratory talks with Adams and other leading republicans on two occasions in 1988, but had ended the contacts because he was convinced that there was no chance of an IRA ceasefire.[43]

The prospect of a direct alliance with Haughey and Hume, even if the terms of the proposed declaration were not entirely to republicans' liking, was catalytic in its effects on republican strategists. It removed the herculean task of trying to build a broad-based 'anti-imperialist broad front' in the Republic. After all, the purpose of such a front was to pressurise 'collaborationist' governments in Dublin to take a harder nationalist line with Britain. Thus although the rank and file of the movement was still being urged to build a 'republican labour party' in the south as the core of the broad front,[44] the very fact that, as *An Phoblacht* admitted, Sinn Féin 'found itself in an isolated and marginalised position in the 26 Counties',[45] made the possibility of an alliance with Haughey all the more entrancing.

At the same time there remained the problem of IRA violence. While this may still have been defined as 'functional' in

terms of pushing the 'British establishment' towards disengagement, it precluded an open common front with Hume
and Haughey. 1991 had seen an intensification of IRA activities
in Northern Ireland, and that year the IRA planted more
incendiary devices in commercial premises than it had in the
previous nine years, as well as launching some massive car-
bomb attacks in Belfast.[46] 1992 opened with the killing of eight
Protestant building workers whose van was destroyed by an IRA
bomb at Teebane Cross in County Tyrone as they returned
from working on a security base. The 'War News' feature of *An
Phoblacht* which reported the deaths of these so-called 'collabo-
rators' was also full of exultant coverage of further car-bombs
in Belfast.[47]

Although the fact that Sinn Féin had won two council by-
elections in Tyrone and North Belfast in 1991 was used to keep
up party spirits, there was no doubting that, outside its hard-
core support, Sinn Féin was suffering from the intensification
of the IRA's campaign. Loyalist violence had increased dramatically in 1991 and the year had seen more civilian deaths in
Northern Ireland than in any year since 1976.[48] Shocking
events, like the Ulster Freedom Fighters' killing of five
Catholics in a bookmakers' shop on the Ormeau Road as a
response to the Teebane Cross murders, could solidify communal defensivness behind the republican movement in some
areas. In others, however, it consolidated support for the SDLP.

Sinn Féin lost ground to the SDLP in the Westminster election in April 1992. Its proportion of the vote dropped by 1.4
per cent compared with 1987, reducing it to 78,291 votes, 10
per cent of the total. The SDLP won 23.5 per cent of the total
vote, an improvement of 2.4 per cent on 1987, with 184,445
votes. Adams's vote in West Belfast held up, but he lost the seat
to Joe Hendron of the SDLP because of tactical voting by
almost 3,000 Protestants from the Shankill. Although Sinn Féin
support held up in three of the four Belfast constituencies, it
fell in North Belfast and in six of the nine other constituencies
which it contested.[49]

For one commentator, the result showed that the republican
movement had had its agenda transcended by the 'new world
order', a world of 'post-nationalism' in which local politicians
faced by the 'end of history' would at last make a settlement:
'The Provos are seen as essentially finished; the politicians as
slowly waking up to the fact that they have no choice but to co-

operate in the new world order.'[50] Rather more plausible was
Wilford's judgement:

> For the architects of the political strategy in the republican
> movement the loss of West Belfast was a heavy blow. There is no
> question that the politicos in the movement will cede to those
> more intent on the continuing or indeed the escalating use of
> violence.[51]

This counterposing of 'politicos' and militarists – a commonplace in analyses of the 'peace process' – misread the recali-
bration of the 'Armalite and ballot-box' strategy which took
place at the beginning of the 1990s. Even a cursory investigation of the words and deeds of republicans in the period punc-
tures the balloon of 'politicos' and 'strategies for peace'.

Here it is necessary to examine the intellectual basis for
claims about republican 'new realism', the revised strategy document, 'Towards a Lasting Peace in Ireland' presented to the
1992 Árd Fheis after a year's work by leading republican strategists. One of these, Mitchel McLaughlin, outlined why the
review had been necessary in terms of the inadequacies of the
1987 'Scenario for Peace' document. These were, firstly, that it
had not produced 'a coherent statement on how a British withdrawal would be timetabled and accomplished'.[52] This meant,
he went on, that there was no discussion of a possible 'power
vacuum' after British withdrawal and the disbanding of the
RUC. This was the basis for the 'nightmare scenario' of a
Protestant backlash. Here there was certainly a shift from the
traditional nationalist idea that Protestants, bereft of British
support, would quickly come to heel. The second major inadequacy was the lack of discussion of the social and economic
implications of British withdrawal. Here again there was a shift
in the analysis. Hitherto the republican sub-culture's economic
'analysis' was gained from articles in *An Phoblacht* which condemned Northern Ireland as an 'economic slum' artificially
propped up by an annual British subvention. Now it appeared
to have dawned on some of the republican leadership that that
subvention might be necessary for some considerable time and
that, as the Economists' Report to the New Ireland Forum had
pointed out, when the British went they were most unlikely to
leave their subvention behind.[53] At the core of the rethinking,
therefore, lay the role that Britain could be pushed to play in

what, at least by the republican leadership, was increasingly seen as quite a lengthy and complex process of withdrawal.

A New Fluidity

There were increasing signs of what Adams referred to as 'new realism' in 1992.[54] In his Árd Fheis address he had restated Sinn Féin's position on armed struggle: 'We believe that Irish people have the right to use armed struggle in the context of seeking Irish independence and in the conditions of British occupation in the Six Counties.' However in an interview with the *Irish Times*'s political correspondent, he set out to establish his distance from the IRA:

> Personally, two or three years ago I would have seen it necessary to state publicly that, yes, there was the right of the IRA to engage in armed struggle and perhaps even at times that armed struggle was a necessary ingredient in the struggle. I don't feel the need to do that now.[55]

The decision of Dublin Corporation to ban Sinn Féin from using the Mansion House for its Árd Fheis, banishing it to a community hall on the outskirts of Dublin, clearly rankled with Adams. He blamed the decision on the 'ongoing agony and intensity of events in the Six Counties' which was undermining his attempt to build the organisation in the Republic and admitted that this was a 'source of considerable personal frustration'.[56]

A blunter expression of Provisional revisionism was provided by Sinn Féin's press officer, Richard McAuley, in an interview with an American left-wing publication:

> We're not going to realise our full potential as long as the war is going on in the North and as long as Sinn Féin is presented the way it is with regard to armed struggle and violence. I think that is a reality that perhaps we weren't conscious or aware of back in the early 80s when we first got involved in electoral politics.[57]

Although such iconoclasm was kept out of the pages of *An Phoblacht*, even that journal began tentatively to raise the question of a possible shift in Britain's position on Northern Ireland, and in two pieces 'Hilda MacThomas' wrote of a possible 'new fluidity' in the position of 'elements of the British and Irish establishment'.[58] Although pointing out that the failure of the Anglo-Irish Agreement to marginalise Sinn Féin and the continuing military capacity of the IRA had led some figures in the security forces and the media to support the reintroduction of internment, the articles focused instead on those voices in the British media which supported the idea of a reassessment of policy involving direct talks with Sinn Féin. The figures concerned were hardly representative of the 'British establishment'[59] and were probably proxies for what really convinced some in the republican leadership of a possible change of direction: the continuing secret contacts with the British state.

It was, however, still thought crucial to maintain pressure through the IRA's campaign. The day after the British general election two bombs killed three people and caused £800 million worth of damage at the Baltic Exchange in London.[60] Attacks in London would continue throughout the year and be complemented in Northern Ireland by a series of car-bomb attacks which devastated the centres of predominantly Protestant towns.[61]

A speech by Jim Gibney to the annual Wolfe Tone commemoration was seen by some to indicate a potential willingness to call a ceasefire.[62] Gibney raised the question of whether the republican movement was enveloped in a bunker mentality

> deafened by the deadly sound of their own gunfire . . . trapped inside a complex web of struggle from which they can't or won't emerge . . . incapable of recognising that there is a different world to the one that existed in mid-60s or that they ignore the more recent changes sweeping across the globe?

The answer, predictably, was that the republican movement had moved on from 'simplistic slogans' to a 'realistic programme for peace in our time'. This realism involved, amongst other things, that, 'We know and accept that this is not 1921 and that at this stage we don't represent a government in waiting.' More startling for many observers was his statement that, 'We know and accept that the British government's departure must be preceded by a sustained period of peace and will arise out of negotiations.'[63]

This was certainly a new idea for the Provisionals. Before this the only sign of flexiblity had been a statement by Adams in November 1991 that there would be an interim period between 'the ending of the Union and the building of a new society. Uniting the country would be easier than uniting the people. That could take up to a generation.'[64] However this signified merely a willingness to reconsider the idea of a federal Ireland. What Gibney seemed to indicate was a willingness to consider a ceasefire in return for less than than the traditional demand for a declaration of intent to withdraw in the lifetime of one British parliament.

What republicans wanted was set out clearly in their response to the proposed Joint Declaration drafted by John Hume and the Dublin government. Delivered in February 1992, it accepted Hume's reworking of the doctrine of Irish self-determination to include that its exercise had to have the agreement and consent of the people of Northern Ireland. It was, however, made clear that this was to be balanced by a British commitment to the principle that, 'The Irish people have the right collectively to self-determination and that the exercise of that right could take the form of agreed independent structures for the island as a whole.' The British government was to commit itself to the achievement of unity within an agreed period. Central to what republicans clearly saw as 'new realism' on their part was a British commitment to 'use all its influence and energy to win the consent of a majority in Northern Ireland for these measures'.[65]

This 'realism' did not impress Hume and Dublin, where Charles Haughey had been forced to resign following the re-emergence of allegations of his involvement in illegal tapping of journalists' telephones in the early 1980s. His successor, Albert Reynolds, approached the declaration with a businessman's pragmatism and little of Haughey's ideological traditionalism. The republican draft was seen as making an impossible demand on London to commit itself to unity without the consent of a majority in the North. Further discussion produced a new Sinn Féin draft which was subseqently the basis for what became known as the 'Hume-Adams' document. Mallie and McKittrick claim that the June draft represented a shift from the original republican position: 'The principle of consent was now given much more emphasis, with the British asked to commit themselves not to unity but to self-determination.'[66] Yet it was clear that republicans wanted a British commitment

to 'collective', i.e. 32 County, self-determination within a specified time period and the underlying assumption was that the
British state could actively engineer sufficient Protestant consent for this to happen.

Republican pronouncements began to take on a tone of
optimism that reflected the continuing secret contacts with
Hume and the British and Irish governments. Thus although
the new Secretary of State, Sir Patrick Mayhew, had relaunched
the talks process, republicans were less concerned about such
a process leading to an agreement which would marginalise
them. This was in part because of the leak, in May 1992, of the
SDLP's proposal for a 'Northern Ireland Executive
Commission' which would have had three members directly
elected and three nominated by the British government, the
Irish government and the European Commission respectively.
Although republican scorn was publicly poured on the commission idea, it did serve to make it clear that, given Hume's
refusal to budge from the proposal, the talks were unlikely to
get anywhere.[66] Although Adams denounced the 'secretive and
undemocratic nature' of the talks, detailed information on
their progress was being regularly given to republicans by the
British government representative. This would have shored up
the belief that there was little chance of success.[67]

The talks process was brought to an end in November 1992,
and a month later Mayhew made a significant speech at the
University of Ulster in Coleraine which Adams claimed as evidence of the 'continued centrality of the republican struggle'.[68] Mayhew had used the speech to indicate British openness to the republican world-view as long as it was expressed
non-violently. Unionists were outraged by his statement that,

> You will not find me seeking to argue that Britain's role in this
> island had only ever been associated with what has been uplift-
> ing. On the contrary, there is much in the long and tragic his-
> tory of Ireland for deep regret and the British government
> shares in that regret to the full.[69]

The speech did, however, indicate that at least a section of the
British political elite was willing to attempt to entice republicans into negotiations.

Whatever new signs of republican flexibility had impressed
some on the British side, there was little evidence of a shift in

the republican movement's insistence that it be included in talks without an IRA ceasefire. Thus Mitchel McLaughlin, often seen as the most 'realistic' and conciliatory member of the republican leadership, could publicly declare that, 'We cannot and should not even try to coerce the Protestant people into a united Ireland,'[70] and still claim that the logic of 'conflict resolution situations' in South Africa, the Middle East and the former Yugoslavia demanded immediate 'inclusive dialogue' in Ireland.

The intensification of the 'back-channel' contacts between republicans and the British representative in the first few months of 1993 was accompanied by the continuation of the IRA's campaign on the British mainland.[71] Between the Baltic Exchange attack and October 1993 there would be more than 50 bomb attacks in England, including the bombing of a Warrington shopping centre on 20 March, in which two children were killed, and the NatWest Tower explosion in the City of London which killed one person and caused over £1 billion worth of damage on 14 April 1993.[72]

Martin Mansergh has referred to the 'myth that the Bishopsgate bomb in April 1993 had in some way moved the British'.[73] The myth certainly seems to have been believed at the time by some in the republican leadership. In a letter sent by the IRA to foreign-owned financial institutions in the City of London in the aftermath of the bombing, it was claimed that the IRA was committed to exploring 'any realistic peace process'. However its conception of that process and of the role of force in bringing it about carried strong echoes of the 1970s:

> The British have the power but not yet the inclination to bring the conflict to an end. We in the IRA point out that peace will only ensue when the causes of the conflict are removed. This can only be achieved through inclusive negotiations leading to a democratic settlement which recognises the fundamental and immutable right of the Irish people to national self-determination.[74]

The 'back-channel' contacts made it clear that an end to violence was necessary. The British representative had told Martin McGuinness in February 1993 that secret talks between British officials and a republican delegation could take place on the basis of a private 'no violence understanding' and that the

British believed that they could convince the republicans in two to three weeks of talks that armed struggle was no longer necessary.[75] Yet republicans would have received little encouragement from the nine-paragraph document sent to them on 19 March 1993 setting out the British government's approach to any dialogue. It emphasised that,

> any dialogue could only follow a halt to violent activity. It is understood that in the first instance this would have to be unannounced. If violence had genuinely been brought to an end, whether or not that fact had been announced, then progressive entry into dialogue could take place.

Once a halt to violence became public, the government would have to defend its entry into discussions by pointing out that it had received an assurance that 'organised violence had been brought to an end'.[76]

Even more difficult for republicans to swallow was the declaration that,

> The British government does not have, and will not adopt, any prior objective of 'ending partition'. The British government cannot enter a talks process, or expect others to do so, with the purpose of acheiving a pre-determined outcome, whether the 'ending of partition' or anything else. It has accepted that the eventual outcome of such a process could be a united Ireland, but this can only be on the basis of the consent of the people of Northern Ireland.[77]

If republicans were not impressed, they did at least have the compensation of the clear evidence of the British government representative's enthusiasm for inclusive talks. Even the Warrington bomb does not appear to have dampened this enthusiasm in the attempt to sell a new British commitment to 'inclusive dialogue':

> Mayhew had tried marginalisation, defeating the IRA etc. That's gone. Coleraine speech was a significant move. Mayhew is now determined. He wants Sinn Féin to play a part not because he likes Sinn Féin but because it cannot work without them. Any settlement not involving all of the people North and South won't work. A North/South settlement that won't frighten Unionists. The final solution is union. It is going to happen anyway. The historical train-Europe-determines that. We are com-

mitted to Europe. Unionists will have to change. This island will
be as one.[78]

If the British representative had been reading *An Phoblacht* in
the assiduous way that Peter Brooke claimed he did when
Secretary of State,[79] he might have realised that this vision of
Europe as a fundamental force for undermining borders was
regularly scoffed at as part of naïve 'Humespeak'. Thus in an
analysis of the implications of the Maastricht Treaty on
European Union, the theory 'particularly associated with the
political analysis of John Hume' that Maastricht would lead to
the disappearance of the economic and political border
between North and South, was rejected as 'fatally flawed': 'The
Hume theory does not face up to the basic source of the problem i.e. the conflicting claims to sovereignty between the Irish
and the British.'[80]

Thus when the IRA agreed to an undeclared two-week ceasefire, the accompanying document setting out the Sinn Féin
response to the nine-paragraph British document showed a
clear rejection of the British position that the talks process
could not have a pre-determined outcome:

> British sovereignty over the Six Counties ... is the inherent
> cause of political instability and conflict. This must be
> addressed within the democratic context of the exercise of the
> right of national self-determination if the cause of instability
> and conflict is to be removed. We seek to assist the establish-
> ment of a process which, with due regard for the real difficulties
> involved, culminates in the exercise of that right and the end to
> your jurisdiction.[81]

The British government claim that it had no 'blueprint' was
repudiated on the basis that it was 'contradicted by your commitment to uphold the Unionist veto'.[82] The recognition of
'the concerns and the perceived concerns of the Unionist population' was confined to those about 'their position in an Irish
national democracy'. Unionist concerns that arose from the
desire to maintain their citizenship of the United Kingdom
were not recognised. Martin McGuinness defined those concerns not as democracy but as 'fascism'.[83] For Sinn Féin, the
peace process was one that could only end in Irish unity and its
document made it clear that the stated British position was
sorely lacking from this perspective: 'It is our view that the

British government should play a crucial and constructive role in persuading the Unionist community to reach an accommodation with the rest of the Irish people.'[84]

The idea that two to three weeks of dialogue would convince the republicans of the redundancy of armed struggle was, given the profound gap between the two positions, fanciful, but the IRA's activities ensured it was never tested. The British had made it clear that 'events on the ground' were crucial if the process was to go anywhere.[85] This coded reference to the Bishopsgate bomb was subsequently elaborated upon when British representatives told McGuinness that Mayhew, who in March was said to be a 'determined' supporter of dialogue with Sinn Féin, 'wanted now to revert to his more comfortable position i.e. "These bad boys must obey our rules and then we would consider what action we'll take." '[86] Mayhew was apparently overruled by Major and the Cabinet Secretary, but at a subsequent meeting attended by John Major, the Foreign Secretary Douglas Hurd, Mayhew and Sir John Chilcott, permanent secretary of the Northern Ireland Office, on 17 May, Major raised clear doubts about the sincerity of the republicans and instructed officials to draw up a new negotiating position which would have demanded a longer cessation.

Although there was still clear interest at the highest level of the British state in drawing republicans into politics, the optimism of the early part of the year had clearly dissipated. However the IRA, which had been restraining itself in order to maximise Sinn Féin votes in the Northern Ireland local government elections on 19 May, returned to business as usual with potentially disastrous effects on the 'back-channel'. Two massive car-bombs devastated the Belfast district where the Ulster Unionist Party had its headquarters and the centre of Portadown in County Armagh. Shortly afterwards bombs destroyed an hotel in south Belfast and the town-centre of Magherafelt, County Londonderry.[87] A message from the British government informed Sinn Féin that work on the drafting of a possible 'logistics' for negotiations had been stopped because of the violence, that it could be restarted, but all would depend on 'events on the ground'.[88]

The evidence from the 'back-channel' thus does nothing to support the idea that IRA bombs could strengthen the hand of those at the heart of the British government who republican strategists believed wanted a radical shift of strategy. The City bomb seems to have heavily reinforced John Major's doubts about the conviction of the Irish Taosieach, Albert Reynolds, that Adams had the desire and the ability to lead the republican movement into democratic politics. It was this, rather than Major's dependence on the support of the Ulster Unionists for the House of Commons vote on the Maastricht Treaty in July, which both effectively closed the 'back-channel' and caused much of the conflict between London and Dublin in the negotiation of the joint declaration.

From a republican point of view, conflict with the British over terms for Sinn Féin's inclusion in the peace process was to be expected. Republicans were buoyed up by the knowledge that, through Hume, they had entered into a serious engagement with what, in public, they still denounced as the corrupt 'Free State Establishment'. The achievement here was breathtaking. There had been discussions between Martin Mansergh, acting as Reynolds's representative, and republicans, as well as Hume's continuing meetings with Adams, both attempting to make 'Hume-Adams' more attractive to London. The ultimate response of the Army Council in April 1993 was to treat 'Hume-Adams' as non-negotiable on the three key points of a 'collective', i.e. 32 County, right to self-determination, a specific time frame for the attainment of self-determination and a commitment of the British government to act as persuaders.[89] Reynolds, who had written to Adams holding out the prospect of unity 'in a generation', defined as between fifteen and 40 years, was told that this was fine as long as the British would either publicly or in a private agreement underwritten by some international guarantor commit themselves to a definite timeframe for withdrawal.[90] Ultimately, it was the unamended document that was given to the British in June 1993. The republican objective then became that of maintaining pan-Irish unity around 'Hume-Adams'.

Republicans were encouraged by private talks which Adams had with one of the architects of the Anglo-Irish Agreement, the former Department of Foreign Affairs official, Michael Lillis. Now an executive with Guinness Peat Aviation, Lillis had argued in an article in the *Irish Times* that the Irish government should use the Agreement to push for radical reform of the Northern Ireland state towards something akin to joint authority: 'A drastic scenario of new structures which would come into effect immediately the violence clearly ended.'[91] Lillis subse-

quently claimed, on the basis of his talks with Adams, that
although Adams believed that violence had produced 'useful
political effects' and 'whatever progress they were prepared to
see [sic] in the attitude of Britain', that he had now moved to
a position much closer to John Hume's, 'That this is a divided
community which requires a more complex response than simply the imposition of one nationality over another.'[92] As has
been argued above, there is no evidence that Adams or any
other republican leader accepted Hume's idea that Britain was
neutral. Republican 'new realism' did have a more complex
attitude to community division in the sense that it thought that
the traditionalist idea of a rapid British withdrawal leading to
Unionist resigned acceptance of unity was far-fetched. But it
certainly believed that Unionism, as a 'supremacist' ideology
which wanted to frustrate nationalist objectives, did have to be
vanquished and that this might entail substantial British help.

From 10 April 1993, when the Hume-Adams dialogue first
became public knowledge, Sinn Féin set out to define the
peace process as one driven by hard-won nationalist consensus
and constantly blocked by British unwillingness to break the
'Unionist veto'. When Dick Spring, Irish Labour Party Leader
and Foreign Minister, and Patrick Mayhew had what one Irish
politician described as 'the most acrimonious meeting of the
Anglo-Irish Conference since 1985' after an interview in the
Guardian in which Spring had suggested that the two governments might have to come to an agreement and put it to the
northern electorate over the heads of the politicians, Adams
claimed that Mayhew's annoyance depicted the reality of
British policy. It was time for the Irish government to 'face
Mayhew down' and pursue an 'Irish agenda'.[93]

Spring had referred in the interview to a leaked British
Labour Party discussion document which favoured joint sovereignty as 'interesting', and *An Phoblacht* noted that, 'while
falling short of Irish national self-determination, they [the joint
joint sovereignty proposals] are a contribution to moving the
argument on'.[94] In a subsequent interview Adams said republicans might be prepared to accept joint sovereignty as 'part of
the process towards the end of partition'.[95] Joint sovereignty
had been at the core of the Irish government's strategy in the
negotiations which led to the Anglo-Irish Agreement, and it
clearly signified an intermediate objective on which republicans could attempt to build a consensus with the Irish state.

However the earlier attempts of Reynolds and Hume to persuade the IRA Army Council to amend 'Hume-Adams' to make it less likely to be rejected by the British suggested that Sinn Féin might ultimately have to pay a price for the maintenance of the common front with the Irish government. IRA violence also made it appear that Reynolds would have to set aside any pan-nationalist consensus and return to the inter-governmental approach of the 1980s. After the IRA bombing of a fish shop on the Shankill Road, which killed ten people in October 1993, republicans clearly feared the conservative disposition of the 'southern establishment' would reassert itself under British pressure.

By then the 'back-channel' had been effectively closed down and republicans were increasingly fixated on the suppposed 'Unionist agenda' being followed by London.[96] Dick Spring was denounced for his 'cowardice' in asking for the postponement of the next Intergovernmental Conference meeting out of respect for the Shankill dead.[97] Even more resented was Spring's subsequent speech in a special Dáil debate on the North in which he appeared to reinforce the consent principle by extending it from a majority in Northern Ireland to the right of Unionists to withhold their consent to constitutional change. As Mitchel McLaughlin put it in a speech in Scotland, 'Common sense tells us that the peace process in Ireland will only succeed if Unionists are not allowed to impede the search for agreement.'[98]

From the point of view of a republican leadership fearful of Dublin's capitulation to London's 'Unionist agenda', the nadir was reached with the joint statement which Major and Reynolds made at an EU summit in Brussels on 29 October which appeared to bury 'Hume-Adams'. Adams temporarily reverted to the language of the 1980s, appealing to the nationalist sentiment of the people of the Republic to come out against a policy 'which surrenders Irish national interest to the narrow interest of a British Tory government'. Reynolds needed to realise that 'the seriousness of the situation demands urgent action' and in particular a move away from Spring's apparent endorsement of the 'Unionist veto': 'The sense of abandonment is acute . . . [it] was palpable within the nationalist areas of the Six Counties following the launch of Dick Spring's six points.'[99]

On the eve of the joint declaration by the two prime minis-

ters, 'Hilda MacThomas' made it clear that the Downing Street
Declaration would be judged by how far its principles were
consonant with those in 'Hume-Adams'. Whether the joint declaration would contribute to the creation of a peace process
was said to depend on the answer to three questions:

> Do Unionists retain a veto on constitutional change? Do the
> British recognise that they have a major role to play in persuad-
> ing Unionists otherwise? If they do, what practical steps do they
> say they will take to effect change?[100]

It was thus inevitable that republicans registered almost instant
unhappiness, with Mitchel McLaughlin claiming that, 'The
general reaction among many nationalists is one of disappointment.'[101] Yet as a leader in *An Phoblacht* put it, there were
'points to ponder' in the declaration and it was a 'time for serious consideration of this declaration'. This was despite Major's
speech in the House of Commons which appeared to support
the attitude of the Ulster Unionist Party leader, James
Molyneaux, who declared that the declaration was not a 'sell-
out' of Unionists. As the editorial pointed out:

> John Major said that there was no suggestion in it that the
> British government should join the ranks of the persuaders of
> Unionists, that it did not recognise the right of the Irish people
> as whole to national self-determination and that there was no
> timetable for constitutional change. He also said that the con-
> stitutional guarantee of the position of the Six Counties in the
> United Kingdom was 'rock solid'.[102]

The British government's 'confrontational approach' was
lamented as Douglas Hurd demanded an end to prevarication
and other ministers stated that there could be no amnesty for
IRA prisoners. Significantly for the subsequent history of the
peace process, it was also made clear that the IRA's handing
over of arms and explosives would figure high on the agenda of
the 'exploratory talks' that would take place three months after
a ceasefire. Yet Adams insisted that the declaration did represent important movement on the part of the British, who had
for the first time recognised, if in a 'heavily qualified' manner,
the right of the Irish people as a whole to self-determination.[103]
That the republican elite favoured a process of asking that the
declaration be 'clarified', rather than the outright rejection

demanded by many in the rank and file and by nationalist fundamentalists like Bernadette McAliskey, reflected the crucial importance of maintaining the alliance with Hume and Reynolds.[104]

The pan-nationalist alliance did produce important propaganda coups for Sinn Féin, first with the lifting of the Republic's broadcasting ban in January 1994 and then with Reynolds's successful lobbying of the White House, against strong British opposition, to grant Adams a visa to enter the USA later the same month.[105] Yet, as Sinn Féin launched a Peace Commission to hold public hearings on 'how to establish a lasting peace in Ireland',[106] Anthony McIntyre, an ex-prisoner and important critical voice within Sinn Féin, declared that the declaration was 'not worth the paper':

> The declaration was a development in so far as it marked a shifted in the discourse about the North of Ireland. It acquired a nationalist shadow. The substance, however, remains very much Unionist. The veto of Unionism is to stay firmly in position. Once that is established, all that is novel in the declaration – such as references to 'self-determination' – becomes secondary or irrelevant. It was the type of change that allowed everything to remain the same.[107]

Many of the submissions to the Peace Commission took a similarly critical attitude, with some of the most militant expressions of traditional nationalism coming from non-Sinn Féiners.[108] Yet there were signs that the republican leadership was using the demand for clarification to focus increasingly on potential radical shifts in the governance of the North and north-south institutions as a substitute for a British declaration in favour of unity. Thus in his address to the Sinn Féin Árd Fheis, Adams said that the clarifications related 'fundamentally' to the position of northern nationalists:

> What guarantees are there or will there be that there will be no return to bigoted Orange supremacy in northern nationalist communities pending final British disengagement? What about security issues . . . parity of esteem for nationalists in all areas?[109]

Part of the reason for the shift was undoubtedly due to the price which Dublin and Washington demanded for supporting the pan-nationalist alliance.[110] In a critical analysis of republicans' 'peace strategy', Anthony McIntyre traced its origins to an attempt to escape the British state's 'marginalisation squeeze' after the Anglo-Irish Agreement. The republican attempt to 'discursively seize' the moral high ground by adopting the language of the peace process exposed the movement to the unintended consequence of greater public pressure to bring to an end the armed struggle. Thus he concluded,

> After many months of 'clarification seeking' and internal and public debate, republicans gave the appearance of rejecting the Downing Street Declaration at their Letterkenny conference in the summer of 1994. But given that the IRA ceasefire was announced shortly after the conference, it appears that republicans have in fact accepted the declaration under the very guise of having rejected it. Dublin and London have both made it clear that any future negotiations will have to take place within the partitionist parameters stipulated within the Declaration.[111]

In fact, Reynolds had responded to a message from Sinn Féin in March saying that they could not accept the declaration as it stood by informing them that, 'They don't have to buy it provided they end the campaign of violence.'[112] While McIntyre was clearly correct to point out the inevitable pressures to compromise on traditional republican objectives brought about by the alliance with the hitherto execrated 'establishment', he omitted the incentives that republicans were offered by the Irish government's proposals for 'interim structures' as part of the Joint Frameworks Documents on which both governments had been working.

Some indication of what might be on offer had been revealed in November 1993, when Emily O'Reilly published the details of a leaked Irish position paper in the *Irish Press*. Drafted by the Department of Foreign Affairs, it called on the British government to acknowledge 'the full legitimacy and value of the goal of Irish unity by agreement' in return for change to Articles Two and Three of the Irish constitution. It also proposed new north-south administrative bodies with executive powers.[113] After the Downing Street Declaration Reynolds continued to whet republican appetites with hints of what a united nationalist position could press for in the event of a ceasefire. At the Oxford Union in May he set out his government's approach to the discussions with Britain on the

Frameworks Documents. The principle of consent, he argued, must apply equally to all constitutional arrangements, and this had implications for the Government of Ireland Act. This and the reference to northern nationalists' 'nightmare' under Stormont brought praise from Adams.[114] June produced another Reynolds speech declaring that cross-border institutions with executive powers would be a quid pro quo for any change to Articles Two and Three.[115]

An Irish version of the Frameworks Documents with a strong institutionalised Irish dimension was part of the 'dynamic' which republicans were demanding. So was the increasing role played by the Clinton administration in the process. Republicans were impressed by what they perceived as the leverage of a more ruthlessly pragmatic and business-oriented Irish-American lobbying operation.[116] The British decision eventually to provide the 'clarification' for which republicans had been asking was, in part at least, put down to US pressure.[117] When the leadership explained the thinking behind the ceasefire decision to the IRA membership in the 'Tactical Use of Armed Struggle' document in the summer of 1994, two of the six factors mentioned as influencing the decision were 'a very powerful Irish-American lobby not in hock to any particular party in Ireland or Britain' and the fact that, 'Clinton is perhaps the first US president in decades to be substantially influenced by that lobby.'[118]

The American factor assumed particular importance precisely because republican strategists had increasingly despaired of movement by Major, who was seen as too preoccupied by his weakening position in the House of Commons, a factor that republicans believed increased Unionist leverage. In his Árd Fheis speech Adams had portrayed the joint declaration as marking 'a stage in the slow and painful process of England's disengagement from her first and last colony'.[119] Another republican analyst took up Martin McGuinness's claim in an Ulster Television programme that the British were embarking on a process of disengagement, and backed this up by using the arguments of Robert McCartney, the Unionist lawyer, who depicted the joint declaration as part of a long-term British strategy to phase withdrawal in such a way as to avoid destabilising Ireland and parts of Britain.[120]

Within a month, however, *An Phoblacht* was referring to a peace process in crisis, and the Conservatives' heavy losses in the local elections in Britain provoked 'Hilda MacThomas' to claim that 'Major's slow death' had 'enormous' implications for the 'Irish peace process': 'He is not likely to be the prime minister who will initiate a bold move towards a lasting peace in Ireland.'[121] This air of pessimism was partially dissipated by the British decision to give clarification and it allowed the republican leadership to argue that, despite Major's dependence on the Unionists, the pan-nationalist alliance could, with US support, push a weak and vacillating British government in the direction towards which it fundamentallly wanted to move, but this was prevented by short-term parliamentary arithmetic. However any serious reflection on the conditions identified in the 'TUAS' document as justifying a ceasefire could not but be impressed by the shakiness of republican assumptions. For while Britain was continuing to be asked to make a most radical shift in policy, the forces identified as being able to bring it about were characterised by their provisional and short-term nature.

A 'High Risk' Strategy

The IRA's decision to announce a 'complete cessation' of military activities on 31 August 1994 came as a surpise to many and, as Garret FitzGerald noted, 'The assessments of the very many journalists and politicians who have contributed their views have been all over the place.'[122] Although the Sinn Féin leadership celebrated with champagne and carnations outside Connolly House, the organisation's headquarters in West Belfast, the cessation and the radical terms in which it was expressed – a complete cessation rather than a time-limited ceasefire – produced much heart-searching in the republican movement.

Danny Morrison later recalled the response in Long Kesh, where he was serving a sentence for false imprisonment: 'I think people were mature enough to understand developments even though the announcement of the cessation came as a severe shock and ran contrary to all our instincts.'[123] As Anthony McIntyre remarked, 'The ceasefire has come, and the British have not gone. Such a strategic shift seemed unthinkable a few years ago.'[124] Indeed, for one journalistic observer the real victor of the cessation was the SDLP:

> Unless Sinn Féin has struck a secret deal with the British gov-
> ernment – a possibility discounted in London, Dublin,
> Washington and West Belfast – the IRA ended its campaign
> without achieving its aims. It also accepted constitutional
> nationalism as the way forward.[125]

In fact, some leading republicans had privately claimed that
they had received a signal that the British would withdraw
within ten years and that a deal to this end had been struck
between Reynolds and Major.[126] Martin McGuinness was also to
claim that in the 'back-channel' talks in 1993 he was told that
the British were planning on a disengagement from Ireland.[127]
It is possible that the notion of a secret deal was used to sell the
cessation to the many sceptics in the IRA. Those who maintain
the idea that there was a secret deal still have to explain why
such a commitment by the British would have been acceptable
given that a similar one in the 1970s was seen to have been
duplicitous and leading to the disastrous ceasefire of 1975.
More fundamentally, however, this talk of a secret deal is belied
by the stress in the TUAS document that a central aim of the
pan-nationalist alliance made possible by a cessation would be
to 'expose the British government and the Unionists as the
intransigent parties' and 'to assist the development of whatever
potential exists in Britain to create a mood/climate/
party/movement for peace'.[128] The TUAS strategy assumed
that its fundamental purpose was to 'open up another front'
and to 'double the pressure on the British'.[129] Adams stated his
own position in a book published in 1995:

> It is my view that the British do not, at this time plan to leave
> Ireland. I start from this premiss. However, they have moved
> considerably and the core issues of their involvement in Irish
> affairs are being exposed. If these issues are addressed properly,
> the argument for their involvement and for their present policy
> is very hard for them to defend, especially in the international
> arena and particularly in the current climate. I believe that the
> British can be persuaded to leave Ireland, but they will do so
> only as a last option and when all other options have failed.[130]

For Adams, the first priority was to provide evidence of the
immediate benefits the TUAS strategy would have on strengthening the pan-nationalist alliance in Ireland and increasing
republican leverage in the United States. Within a week he was

to meet and publicly shake hands with Albert Reynolds, and later in September he was granted another visa to visit the USA where, for the first time, a Sinn Féin delegation met senior US government officials.[131] Adams claimed that the obtaining of a visa, against strong British lobbying of the Clinton administration, was

> of enormous symbolic and political importance. It illustrated that international interest and concern can play an important and constructive part in the development of a viable peace process.[132]

Yet this begged the question of just how far a Clinton administration would press Major to accommodate republicans, and Washington's stated commitment to be 'even-handed' was a sign that Adams should not expect too much.

The statement from the Combined Loyalist Military Command on 13 October 1994 declaring a ceasefire increased the doubts of many republicans about their own leadership's peace strategy. It claimed that the decision had been made after the loyalist leadership had received 'confirmation and guarantees in relation to Northern Ireland's constitutional position within the United Kingdom'.[133] One republican commentator noted the effect on the grassroots of 'a cacophony of cries that the Union is safe. Many republicans on the ground are asking questions of the leadership pertaining to the direction their struggle is now taking.'[134]

Even more destabilising to the cessation was the unexpected resignation of Albert Reynolds as Taoiseach on 17 November 1994 after Dick Spring and other Labour ministers resigned from his government over his decision to go ahead with appointing as President of the Supreme Court a man who as Attorney General had been involved in delaying the extradition to Northern Ireland of a paedophile priest. The formation of a new coalition government led by John Bruton of Fine Gael, and including the Irish Labour Party and Democratic Left, led by Proinsias de Rossa, was more than a temporary hiccup in the peace process. The TUAS document had referred to the Reynolds government as, from a nationalist point of view, 'the strongest government in 25 years or more' and had attached particular importance to the Taoiseach himself: 'Reynolds has no historical baggage to hinder him and knows how popular such a consensus would be amongst the grassroots.'[135]

Republicans saw Bruton as the leader of a 'West British' party and as dangerously open to Unionist arguments. Proinsias de Rossa's presence in the government was, if anything, even more depressing for republicans. The party of which he was president had emerged in 1992 out of the terminal convulsions of the Workers' Party, the name adopted by Sinn Féin – The Workers' Party in 1982. The Workers' Party's first TD was elected in 1981, and by the 1987 general election over a decade's work as a hard-left scourge of the Irish Labour Party had produced a real but limited increase in support: four TDs were elected with 3.8 per cent of the national vote compared to the Irish Labour Party's twelve TDs and 6.4 per cent of the vote. Electoral progress accelerated in the final years of the decade with increases of support in the Dáil and European elections of 1989: 5 per cent of the vote and seven TDs and 7.5 per cent of the vote and one MEP respectively. De Rossa, who had become the party's president in 1989, had topped the poll in the Dublin Euro constituency with nearly 16 per cent of the votes cast.[136]

His campaign strategy had been heavily influenced by Eoghan Harris, the intellectual author of Sinn Féin – The Workers' Party's decisive rupture with the republican tradition. Ironically, it would be Harris who would be a major stimulus to the profound internal crisis which wracked the party for two years from 1990 and out of which Democratic Left emerged. Deeply impressed by Gorbachev's radical approach to the reform of the USSR and by the modernisers in both the Italian Communist Party and the British Labour Party, he had begun, as early as 1988, to argue for a decisive shift away from the statist model of socialism that still dominated the intellectual horizons of many in the Workers' Party. His was the dominant influence on de Rossa's first presidential address to the party's 1989 Árd Fheis. This had shocked more than the Marxist-Leninist traditionalists like Sean Garland, the party's general secretary. It argued strongly for an acceptance of the market economy and the profit motive, criticised the 'dogmas' of traditional socialist economics, attacked welfare dependency and argued that enterprise and hard work should be rewarded. This was 'Blairism' ahead of its time and, written before the fall of the Berlin Wall, demonstrated Harris's acute sensitivity to those epochal changes that radically transform the basic contours and language of politics – he was later to bring this same talent to Mary Robinson's successful campaign for the presidency of Ireland.

However he failed in his attempt to get the party leadership to accord a similar status to his manuscript, 'The Necessity of Social Democracy', to that accorded to *The Irish Industrial Revolution*.[137] Delays in publication and the demotion of his long-time friend and ally, Eamonn Smullen, for supporting publication, led to Harris's resignation from the party in 1990. But by highlighting the profound inadequacy of the party's existing ideology, strategy and organisation for dealing with even a limited amount of electoral success, Harris accelerated a growing conflict between the traditional party leadership of full-time functionaries and the new power centre of the party's TDs and most of its local councillors and aspirant public representatives. The latter were increasingly impatient with the Marxist language and the notions of the 'vanguard' and 'democratic centralism' which key traditionalists like Garland and Des O'Hagan regarded as the only means of controlling 'parliamentary cretinism' and mere 'reformism'.[138] The collapse of the East European regimes and the decomposition of the USSR deepened the division by serving further to discredit the traditionalists in the eyes of the parliamentary group.

This was the context in which it appears that the hitherto largely moribund Official IRA was reinvigorated as part of the struggle for control of the party. It was seen as a means of mobilising a base for the traditionalists whose support was significantly greater in the North than in the Republic. The unintended effects of this, media speculation about the IRA's role in the party and embarrassing court appearances of members, pushed the conflict to the point of no return by the end of 1991. When de Rossa's attempt to have a special Árd Fheis reconstitute the party failed, six of the seven TDs and most of the southern membership set up a new organisation in March 1992. But whatever its differences with the Workers' Party, Democratic Left retained the former's visceral anti-republicanism.

A government with this large 'Blue-Shirt/Stickie' component represented a potentially major unravelling of the TUAS strategy. Thus the appointment of Sean Donlon, the former Irish Ambassador to Washington seen by republicans as an architect of the Anglo-Irish Agreement, as special adviser on Northern Ireland to the new government was a particular cause for concern. Donlon, who had worked to combat republican fund-raising efforts in the United States, was denounced on the basis that, 'He sees Irish interests as being best served by prostrating Irish foreign policy before the interests of British imperialism.'[139]

Despite this, and a very gradualist, not to say minimalist, British response to the cessation, the republican leadership entered 1995 with a clear intention to accentuate the positive. Thus Martin McGuinness declared that 1995 'can be the year of resolution of the conflict in Ireland'.[140] British government 'intransigence' and 'lack of generosity' were defined as key problems, but put down to the short-term pressures of the parliamentary arithmetic at Westminster on top of unpreparedness for the radical nature of the IRA cessation.

It was certainly the case that RUC and British intelligence had expected only a time-limited ceasefire,[141] and also that Major's small and dwindling majority in the House of Commons increased the leverage of Ulster Unionists and that of the right in the Cabinet and on the Tory backbenches. There was, nevertheless, a degree of myopia in the republican perspective. Major's initial demand that the IRA publicly declare the cessation 'permanent', and the subsequent British determination that the question of the decommissioning of IRA weapons be addressed before Sinn Féin's inclusion in all-party talks, reflected more than just parliamentary arithmetic.

There remained a profound gulf between British and republican views on a realistic pace of development for the peace process and what was likely to result from negotiations when they finally got under way. There is some evidence that the British saw a process lasting up to two years before it would be possible to start all-party negotiations on a settlement.[142] The gap between the British and the republicans remained what it had been at the time of the 'back-channel' negotiations, the question of Unionist consent. This was revealed clearly in a critique by 'Hilda MacThomas' of Britain's approach to the peace process:

'Consent' for republicans means the right of Unionists to secure their place, their political representation, their religious, national and cultural rights in any transitional or final arrangement which all the people of Ireland have arrived at free from outside interference.[143]

Interestingly, the article claimed that the 1920 Government of Ireland Act implicitly recognised this all-Ireland approach but that the British then disregarded it for fear of the strategic implications of a united sovereign Ireland on their doorstep. Now, however, it was claimed that in a post-Cold War world the strategic context had changed radically and that, as the North was no longer the economic asset it was at the beginning of the century, the British state had no strategic interest in maintaining the status quo. Prevarication on the issue of decommissioning was therefore a product of Major being driven by short-term considerations of political survival. It was accepted, by implication, that a British government with a secure majority would, if necessary, be in a position to push forward with the peace process over the heads of the Unionists. For republicans there was nothing undemocratic about this, as such a development would only serve to help free Protestants from their subservience to an ultimately unsustainable Unionist ideology.

It is nevertheless undeniable that there was a growing sophistication in republican discussion of the role of Unionists in the peace process. Thus at Sinn Féin Árd Fheis in February 1995 a number of key speeches by the leadership were given over to the need for reconciliation with the Unionist community. Tom Hartley disputed the traditional republican view that, 'If you want to dislodge northern Protestants from their political ties with the London government then you must first move that government.' This was, 'theoretically' correct, but, 'Politically it may be a cul-de-sac as it suggests that republicans don't need to do anything until the British move.' Such a view, he argued, made Protestants 'a non-people robbed of their power to be a crucial component in the search for a just and lasting settlement on the island'. Republicans had to use 'the language of invitation' in their approach to Protestants: 'In our vision of a united and independent Ireland there must be a place for those who consider themselves British and those who wish to stay British.'[144]

In a useful analysis of shifts in republican ideology and strategy since the late 1980s, Kevin Bean has argued that change in this area has been portentous:

The most significant recent developments in the ideology and politics of republicanism have been explicitly pluralist attempts to empathise with, and explore the identity and real fears of the

Unionist population. Although elements of coercion are often implied in phrases such as 'persuasion' and 'facing down the Unionist leadership', concepts of dialogue, agreement and consent are more and more frequently used by republicans.[145]

Yet, as is shown by Bean's analysis of the position adopted by Mitchel McLaughlin, the republican leader most sympathetic to a 'vibrant discourse' with Protestants, the purpose of dialogue is to help Protestants negotiate what republicans defined as a crisis of identity produced by an increasing awareness that the British government was not a reliable ally.[146] Gerry Adams and some close associates had been involved in secret discussions with Presbyterian ministers from September 1990. One of the minsters concerned noted that, although for the first year and a half they met a general defence of the armed struggle, 'In spring 1992 we noticed Sinn Féin were prepared to make peace.'[147] This was precisely the time when the Hume-Adams document, with its central notion of Britain acting as a 'persuader' for unity, was being elaborated. Sinn Féin may well have been preparing for peace, but it was a peace that was seen, by republicans, necessarily to involve only respect for the individual and communal rights of Protestants. There was little evidence that they were prepared to accommodate significantly Unionism as a political identity.

Bean argued, just after the cessation, that the republican movement's thinking was 'poised between two visions of the future'. One of these was the traditional view that Britain was the key to the situation and in its modernised form adopted the notion of Britain as 'persuader'. The other proposed consent and 'dialogue between nationalists and Unionists resulting in an historic compromise and rapprochement as a means to end the conflict'.[148] Hartley's Árd Fheis speech is, perhaps, suggestive of the latter approach. Hartley showed a courageous willingness to put his Árd Fheis sentiments into practise when, in April 1995, he attended a Dublin ceremony of remembrance for all Irishmen who had died in the two world wars.[149] However this ecumenical gesture was not well received in republican ranks and appears to have damaged his standing in the movement. Pat McGeown, erstwhile hunger-striker and leader of the Sinn Féin group on Belfast City Council, was another prominent republican who made a genuine effort to engage with Unionists, particularly those like Billy Hutchinson of the Progressive Unionist Party, who helped broker the loyalist ceasefire.[150]

Yet, even at its most flexible and generous, republicans' search for an historic compromise had severe limits. The accommodating language could not disguise the fact that Protestants were being cordially invited to participate in a journey to a destination which they had repeatedly made clear they had no wish to reach. Republican generosity was based on the assumption that the 'tide of history' was flowing in an all-Ireland direction and that northern Protestants would ultimately be forsaken by the British. The purpose of dialogue was to explain to Unionists that when the inevitable occurred, they had nothing to fear. As a republican journal explained:

> We covenant that we will insist on full recognition of the Protestant identity in the new Ireland. The right of those in Ireland who wish to retain a British passport must be guaranteed.[151]

The republican proposal that the British citizenship of Northern Ireland Protestants be reduced to the same level as that of certain Hong Kong Chinese after the handover to Communist China showed just how out of touch Sinn Féin was with the reality of Unionists' aspirations. Sinn Féin's participation in the Forum for Peace and Reconciliation set up by Albert Reynolds to 'examine ways in which lasting peace, stablity and reconciliation can be established by agreement among all the people of Ireland' served to highlight Sinn Féin's continued refusal to accept the consent principle embodied in the Downing Street Declaration and accepted by all the other parties participating in the Forum. Unionist consent was defined as necessary for the working out of an 'agreed Ireland' but not as a precursor of the exercise of self-determination itself – then it became the 'Unionist veto'. At the Forum Sinn Féin called for Britain's 'constructive disengagement' as a pre-requisite for the opening up of Unionist community to dialogue with republicans.[152]

It was this demand for 'constructive disengagement' which meant that when the two governments produced the long-awaited Joint Frameworks Documents on 22 February 1995, the republican leadership's response was enthusiastic. The provision for a north-south body with executive, harmonising and consultative functions with a 'dynamic remit' allowing the progressive extension of its functions was portrayed by Adams as 'explicit acknowledgment of the failure of partition and of British rule in Ireland'. He focused on the documents' all-Ireland character: 'It deals with the general notion of one-island social, economic and political structures.'[153] A leader in *An Phoblacht* was exultant over what it claimed the documents revealed about core British strategy:

> The Union is not safe. For over twenty years now, the British have been trying to bypass the Unionists and go to Dublin for support in bringing about a settlement in the Six Counties. Short-term considerations such as political survival and the fear of a worsening 'security situation' are probably now the only obstacles to Britain disengaging from Ireland.[154]

Mitchel McLaughlin expressed the high-point of republican optimism about the Frameworks Documents when he told an audience at the University of North London that,

> John Major, by the very act of publishing the Framework Document [sic] in the teeth of opposition from right-wing Conservatives and the Unionist leaderships, has demonstrated that his government is not totally hostage to the mathematics of Westminster.[155]

Yet such optimism remained hostage to the continued British insistence that there be substantive progress on the decommissioning issue before talks could start. Initially there is evidence that it was hoped that this British position would not be maintained against pressure from nationalist Ireland and the United States. It was also believed that the RUC Chief Constable had advised that it was impractical.[156] It was certainly the case that the British line was not consistent. On 16 January 1995, for example, after a meeting between a Sinn Féin deputation and NIO officials, Michael Ancram, the NIO Minister, said that the decommissioning of weapons was not a precondition for Sinn Féin's entry into substantive talks.[157]

Various Irish politicians, including Garret FitzGerald and Albert Reynolds, criticised the British for allegedly introducing decommissioning as a precondition after the ceasefire when, they claimed, it had not been mentioned in pre-cessation negotiations, and it was relatively easy for defenders of the British position to find evidence to the contrary. Thus in a radio inter-

view interview on 10 October 1993 Sir Patrick Mayhew said that
the IRA would have to make available its guns and explosives to
show that its use of violence was over, and in an *Irish News* interview on 8 January 1994 Gerry Adams criticised Mayhew for stating after the Downing Street Declaration that talks between
Sinn Féin and the government would concern the decommissioning of arms.[158] However it has been argued, with some
plausibility, that republicans tended to dismiss such statements
as 'part of the public posturing and semantics which constitute
much of the thrust and parry of political discourse at public
level',[159] and that the 'real' attitude was that conveyed in the
'back-channel' where decommissioning was not raised as a precondition for admittance to all-party talks.

When, on 7 March 1995 in Washington, Mayhew set out a
three-point plan for decommissioning, including what became
known as 'Washington Three', he called for 'the actual decommissioning of some arms as a tangible confidence-building
measure', the republican response was a muted one.[160] Within
days any doubts about the direction of the TUAS strategy which
were raised by 'Washington Three' were temporarily sub-
merged by Adams's media coup when the White House agreed
to invite him to the President's St Patrick's Day reception and
also to allow Sinn Féin to raise funds in the United States. For
articulate defenders of the leadership's strategy like Mitchel
McLaughlin, such dramatic media events were a sure sign that
the TUAS strategy, although admitted to be a 'high risk' one,
had transformed the situation:

> Sinn Féin now, through our president Gerry Adams, has had
> direct access to the corridors of power in Washington. We see
> the international community including the European
> Community mobilising. We see Sinn Féin now at the centre of
> political debate in Ireland, and the republican analysis being
> promulgated on a consistent basis.[161]

Yet the purpose of such international and all-Ireland public
relations breakthroughs was to place irresistible pressure on
the British government to accommodate Sinn Féin, and in
terms of that substantive outcome there was little sign of
progress in the first year of the cessation. McLaughlin, while
castigating the British for lack of response, provided an almost
apologetic explanation: 'It's quite obvious that they didn't

expect the decision and had no strategy.' This had allowed 'short-term' considerations to dominate their response but now, he claimed, with Major having overcome the challenge to his leadership of the Conservative Party, 'The British government are now recognising that they have quite significantly damaged the Irish peace process.'[162]

By the time of these comments, on the first anniversary of the ceasefire, there were signs of a much more pessimistic mood amongst many republicans. The British, it was claimed, were duplicitously using the peace process to achieve that which they had failed to do militarily: the defeat of republicanism. Although such a response would have been an almost instinctive one amongst the republican grassroots, it was articulated as early as April by Albert Reynolds in an interview with the *Observer* in which he claimed that there was an element in the British establishment that wanted to defeat the IRA.[163] At the Wolfe Tone commemoration in June, Martin McGuinness depicted the British as

> still at war with Irish republicans. They are engaged in psychological and diplomatic offensive which has as its primary aim the removal of Irish republicans from the centre of the peace process.[164]

By the time of a special Sinn Féin Internal Conference on the peace process on 30 September the mood was dark but not particularly bellicose. There were over 700 delegates, and of the 60 who spoke only six indicated outright opposition to the leadership's strategy. However the opinion of one speaker that, 'The British strategy is to break the nationalist consensus and split the republican movement,' was echoed repeatedly throughout the day. As *An Phoblacht* put it, 'The vast majority of delegates expressed trust, if not in the future of the peace process, at least in the Sinn Féin leadership and its handling of a difficult situation.'[165] With reports that some republicans were leaving the movement because of disagreement with the peace strategy and the emergence of others with a rallying cry of 'back to war',[166] the main leadership speaker emphasised that the peace process was not some temporary tactic but 'the kernel of Sinn Féin's political programme'. At the same time he expressed the fear that the peace process 'might not be fully rooted in Sinn Féin's consciousness'.[167] Anthony McIntyre,

who had given one of the speeches most critical of the peace
strategy, subsequently noted that, although there was no major
demand for a resumption of violence, 'The cumulative effect of
British stalling tactics has led to the development of a particular mind-set that the peace process is doomed to failure.'[168]

Two developments which impinged negatively on the core
calculations of the TUAS strategy and one external factor
destroyed the cessation. Republican suspicions of John Bruton,
which had been somewhat allayed by his successful conclusion
of the negotiations on the Joint Frameworks Documents, were
rekindled when he publicly supported 'Washington Three'.[169]
In July *An Phoblacht* claimed that the British were suggesting
'off the record' that an international commission on decommissioning might resolve the issue. The republican response
was that it was a non-starter if 'it is merely a device to process
the British government's precondition'.[170] When in September
it appeared that Bruton was prepared to issue a joint communiqué with Major setting up such a commission, Sinn Féin pressure, based on warnings that it would mean an end to the ceasefire, got the summit called off.[171] However subsequent pressure
from the White House for significant progress towards talks by
the time of Clinton's visit to Ireland in November showed that
Adams's US strategy would have costs as well as benefits for
republicans.

Although the White House had studiously avoided supporting the British position on decommissioning, and republicans
would make much of some US-based support for their position,
there was in fact a substantial difference between the White
House, which supported what became known as the 'twin-
track' approach of preparatory talks in tandem with an international commission to address the decommissioning issue,
and Sinn Féin, which saw this as yet more British prevarication.[172] When, just two days before Clinton's scheduled arrival
in Belfast, the British and Irish governments launched the twin-
track strategy – a target date of all-party talks by the end of
February 1996 and an international body headed by former US
Senator George Mitchell to provide an independent assessment of the decommissioning issue – the TUAS strategy had
the unintended and undesired effect of forcing republicans to
accept a process about which they had profound doubts.

For although it seemed probable that the Mitchell
Commission would remove 'Washington Three' from the

agenda, it was most unlikely that it would accept the IRA's position that, 'There is absolutely no question of any IRA decommissioning at all, either through the back door or the front door.'[173] When the Commission's report was published on 24 January 1996, it did indeed reject 'Washington Three' as not achievable, but instead suggested a process involving some decommissioning during the talks process. It combined this with a set of six principles of democracy and non-violence which all parties to talks would have to endorse. Ed Moloney, the Belfast journalist with the best grasp of republican thinking, noted that while the report was much praised by nationalist Ireland because of its rejection of 'Washington Three', 'It went down like the proverbial lead balloon with grassroots republicans.'[174]

Just two weeks earlier Mitchel McLaughlin had described the idea of decommissioning during talks as 'Washington Three by instalments'. Moloney pointed out that since the start of the peace process, and particularly since IRA weapons became an issue, republican leaders had assured their followers that no guns would be given up until after a final settlement: 'Translated into West Belfast-ese, that meant either there would never be decommissioning or it would happen only when the British had left Ireland.'[175] One of the six principles was to oppose 'punishment' beatings and killings, and amongst related 'confidence-building measures' was 'the early termination of paramilitary activities, including surveillance and targeting'. The termination of activities like these would have effectively decommissioned the IRA. The logic of the TUAS strategy might ultimately lead to the dismantling of the IRA, but it could only be sold within the movement on the basis of the prospect of relatively rapid political and constitutional change while the IRA continued to function at a certain level. As Gerry Kelly, one of the republicans believed to have been most sceptical of the cessation decision, told a republican audience, 'The IRA did not make this announcement [of the cessation] because they became born-again pacifists overnight.'[176] Indeed, within two months of the cessation the IRA had killed a post office worker in Newry during a robbery.[177] Although this murder was claimed to be 'unsanctioned' by the leadership, the organisation continued to impose a brutal 'policing' regime against petty thieves, joy-riders and alleged drug-dealers in working-class Catholic communities. Operating under the

nom de guerre of 'Direct Action Against Drugs', it had by the end
of 1995 killed six alleged drug-dealers and, despite a public
plea against 'punishment' beatings by Clinton during his visit
to Belfast, the level of attacks increased during the delibera-
tions of the Mitchell Commission.

The new wave of violence reflected a shifting balance in the
movement in favour of those who had never had much – or any
– faith in the TUAS strategy. However if the Mitchell Report
was likely to have made a return to violence inevitable, the
exact timing may well have been determined by a factor external to the TUAS strategy – a rising level of communal tension
in Northern Ireland. Public republican reaction to the report
was focused not on the decommissioning proposals but instead
on John Major's qualified acceptance of the report, particularly
his decision to support the idea of elections as an alternative to
decommissioning as a way for Sinn Féin to gain entry to all-
party talks.

A commentator as sympathetic to Adams's strategy as Mary
Holland could note that if 'Washington Three' was to be
dropped, 'There would have to be some quid pro quo to make
this very distasteful medicine palatable to the Unionists,' and
that 'simple rejection of an elected assembly is not an adequate reaction'.[178] Yet the response from Sinn Féin and, it
needs to be added, just as vehemently from John Hume, was
that Major had 'binned the report' and was working to a
totally Unionist agenda. The key determinant of the nationalist response was that the idea of an elected body as a way
around the decommissioning issue had come from David
Trimble, the new leader of the Ulster Unionist Party. Trimble
had, as the local MP, been involved in the negotiations that
tried to deal with the 'Siege of Drumcree' in July 1995 when
the RUC prevented Orangemen from marching along the
nationalist Garvaghy Road in Portadown. The stand-off esca-
lated into a sometimes violent confrontation between 1,000
RUC men and 10,000 Orangemen. Although a deal was eventually brokered, Trimble and the DUP leader, Ian Paisley, were
seen by many nationalists to have presented it as an Orange
victory. Trimble's reputation, which had already been one of
an articulate and formidable hard-liner, suffered even more
because of Drumcree and his winning of the leadership over
rivals who were perceived as more conciliatory towards nationalist Ireland did not help those in the republican leadership

who had been talking of the need to accommodate Protestants.

It was also the case that a key part of the republican leadership's vision of the sort of 'interim structures' which would grow out of the Frameworks Documents was that they would be based on 'parity of esteem' for nationalists within Northern Ireland. Part of the strategy for keeping militants occupied in the absence of the action and 'drama' of the armed struggle was a return to 1960s-type 'street politics' and a strategy of 'reclaiming' public buildings and spaces for nationalists whilst denying 'supremacist' manifestations of Orangeism to pass uncontested through what was defined as nationalist territory. 1995 saw the birth of 'Concerned Residents' Associations' in various parts of north and south Belfast to contest Orange parades. Insensitive and at times brutal policing of these associations' protests had by the end of the year done much to feed into grassroots republican feelings of frustration with the pace of change. It was this underlying tendency to communal polarisation in areas where republicanism was strong that created the conditions in which those opposed to the TUAS strategy could, temporarily at least, move into the ascendant. On 9 February 1996 an IRA bomb devastated Canary Wharf in London's Docklands, killing two people and causing more than £85 million worth of damage. Although Adams and other leading republicans would claim that their 'peace strategy' remained intact, the explosion raised major questions about the direction and future of the republican movement.

Notes

1. This is the title of one of the chapters in what is undoubtedly the classic example of this approach: Eamonn Mallie and David McKittrick, *The Fight for Peace: The Secret Story Behind the Irish Peace Process*, London 1996. They claim that TUAS, the title of a confidential strategy paper circulated in the republican movement in the summer of 1994, stood for 'Totally unarmed strategy'. It has subsequently transpired that it in fact referred to 'Tactical use of armed struggle': see Paul Bew and Gordon Gillespie, *The Northern Ireland Peace Process 1993-1996: A Chronology*, London 1996, p.97.
2. 'The IRA has accorded a complete cessation of military operations but it has refused to define that cessation as permanent . . . In the circumstances, to equate the present ceasefire with peace is irresponsible . . .

The private army of whose pacifist intentions the Irish government is apparently convinced is still in being, heavily armed and organised within our territory, in defiance of our laws. It disposes of approximately one hundred tons of arms, ammunition and explosives.' *Irish Independent*, 10 September 1994.

3. The speech was quoted in full in *An Phoblacht/Republican News* (*AP/RN*), 22 November 1990.

4. See Sinn Féin response in ibid.

5. 'Secrecy on the Path to Peace', *Sunday Tribune*, 5 May 1996.

6. Paul Bew and Gordon Gillespie, *Northern Ireland: A Chronology of the Troubles 1968–1993*, Dublin 1993, p.125.

7. Cardinal Ó Fiaich: unpublished interview with Eamonn Mallie in 1986, quoted in Mallie and McKittrick, op.cit., p.76.

8. *AP/RN*, 7 December 1989.

9. Interview with Cardinal Ó Fiaich in Mallie and McKittrick, op.cit.

10. See Henry Patterson, 'Seán Lemass and Ulster 1959-1966', in *Journal of Contemporary History*, forthcoming.

11. Apart from the editorials, the 'Hilda MacThomas' column provided the most serious expression of the thinking of the republican collective leadership. Although written by one individual, it was done on the basis of prior discussions amongst key figures. Information from Anthony McIntyre. 'Hume Plays the Strasbourg Card', *AP/RN*, 24 May 1990.

12. 'Confronting British Power in the 1990s', ibid., 5 April 1990.

13. 'Where Sinn Féin Stands Today', ibid., 5 April 1990.

14. See Adams's presidential address to the Árd Fheis: 'Do they [the SDLP] wish merely to be place-seekers and time-servers, Castle Catholics in a discredited British colony?' ibid., 8 February 1990.

15. 'The SDLP', ibid., 17 May 1990.

16. 'Hilda MacThomas', 'Planning the Next Move', ibid., 8 November 1990.

17. See *Setting the Record Straight: A Record of Communications between Sinn Féin and the British Government October 1990-November 1993*, Belfast 1994. According to this Sinn Féin account after the first meeting between Martin McGuinness and the British government representative in October 1990, an advance copy of Brooke's speech was given to Sinn Féin.

18. Bew and Gillespie, *Northern Ireland: A Chronology of the Troubles*, p.236.

19. Ibid., p.237.

20. Robin Wilson, 'The Argument of Force', *Fortnight*, September 1990.

21. 'Assessing the Current Sitution', ibid.

22. 'Plans for Peace in the 1990s', *AP/RN*, 29 March 1990.

23. Ibid., 7 February 1991.

24. Ibid.

25. Bew and Gillespie, *Northern Ireland: A Chronology of the Troubles*, p.243.

26. *AP/RN*, 25 April 1991.

27. 'Sinn Féin Speaker Wins Trinity Debate', ibid., 31 January 1991.

28. Brendan O'Brien, *The Long War: The IRA and Sinn Féin from Armed Struggle to Peace Talks*, Dublin 1995, pp.222-3.

29. Brian Rowan, *Behind the Lines: The Story of the IRA and Loyalist Ceasefire*, Belfast 1995, pp.48-9.

30. 'Hilda MacThomas', 'British Ultimatum Whips Parties into Line', *AP/RN*, 23 May 1991.

31. Gerry Adams addressing Six Counties Internal Conference, ibid., 23 May 1991.
32. Ibid.
33. 'Hilda MacThomas', 'A Very Unionist Agenda', ibid, 17 October 1991.
34. Ibid.
35. Mallie and McKittrick, op.cit., p.104.
36. 'Hilda MacThomas' on Brooke interview in Padraig O'Malley, *Northern Ireland: Questions of Nuance* in *AP/RN*, 25 July 1991.
37. *Setting the Record Straight*, pp.17-8.
38. 'We are committed to a real peace process' – interview with Gerry Adams, *AP/RN*, 12 September 1991.
39. 'Peace Plan Endorsed', ibid., 27 February 1992.
40. The text of Hume's draft, 'A Strategy for Peace and Justice in Ireland', is reprinted in Mallie and McKittrick, op.cit., pp.118-9, along with the successive redrafts made in consultation with Dublin, pp.371-84.
41. Ibid., p.120.
42. From second draft, October 1991 in ibid., pp.371-2.
43. Ibid., p.89.
44. Report of Sinn Féin's National Internal Conference, *AP/RN*, 23 May 1991.
45. Ibid.
46. Henry Patterson, 'The Republican Tradition' in Jurgen Elvert (ed.), *Northern Ireland – Past and Present*, Stuttgart 1994, p.418.
47. 'IRA Blasts Belfast City Centre', *AP/RN*, 9 January 1992.
48. Adrian Guelke, 'Throw up the Pieces and See How They Fall', *Fortnight*, February 1992.
49. Rick Wilford, 'The 1992 Westminster Election in Northern Ireland', *Irish Political Studies*, Vol.7, 1992, pp.108-9.
50. Tom Kelly, 'All Over Bar the Talking?', *Fortnight*, May 1992.
51. Wilford, op.cit.
52. Rowan, op.cit.
53. For a good example of republican economic analysis, see 'Economic Slum Behind the Façade', *AP/RN*, 9 January 1992. This used the Thatcherite argument that the sickness of the North's economy was shown by (a) the subvention and (b) the fact that 40 per cent of the workforce was in the public sector.
54. See his presidential address to the Árd Fheis, *AP/RN*, 27 February 1992.
55. Interview with Mark Brennock, *Irish Times*, 18 February 1992.
56. Ibid.
57. Quoted in leader in *Fortnight*, September 1992.
58. See 'A New Fluidity', *AP/RN*, 23 January 1992 and 'Not If But When', ibid., 30 January 1992.
59. The 'evidence' included two Irish expatriates; Neil Lyndon writing in the *Spectator*, misdescribed as 'the British magazine of liberal tendency', and Ronan Bennett, just emerging as Sinn Féin's most able apologist in the British media. Another 'representative' figure was Neal Ascherson, who had written a piece for the *Independent on Sunday* entitled 'Troops Out, if Nationalists Lower Their Sights'. *AP/RN*, 23 January 1992.
60. Bew and Gillespie, op.cit., *Northern Ireland: A Chronology of the Troubles*, p.261.

61. Ibid., pp.258 and 274-5.
62. Ibid., p.266.
63. 'It is our Job to Develop the Struggle for Freedom', *AP/RN*, 25 June 1992.
64. David Shanks, 'Adams Joins in Condemnation of Killing', *Irish Times*, 15 November 1991.
65. Document sent to John Hume and Dublin government by the republican movement in February 1992, Mallie and McKittrick, op.cit., pp.373-4.
66. 'Hilda MacThomas', 'Agenda Stays Hidden in Secret Talks', *AP/RN*, 21 May 1992.
67. In October 1992 Sinn Féin was informed by the British that due to lack of progress in the Stormont talks the British and Irish governments were considering imposing a solution: *Setting the Record Straight*, p.20.
68. 'There Can be Peace in 93', *AP/RN*, 31 December 1992. An advance copy of the Coleraine speech was sent to Sinn Féin.
69. Quoted by Martin McGuinness in a speech to the 1993 Árd Fheis; this is reprinted in *Setting the Record Straight*, p.24.
70. 'Ceasefire Should not be a Precondition for Talks', *AP/RN*, 19 September 1992.
71. Report of meeting with British government representative, 12 January 1993, *Setting the Record Straight*, p.22.
72. Interview with a representative of the General Headquarters Staff of IRA, *AP/RN*, 14 October 1993.
73. 'Secrecy on the Path to Peace', *Sunday Tribune*, 5 May 1996.
74. 'More City Attacks Inevitable Unless British Policy Changes', *AP/RN*, 8 July 1993.
75. Reports of meetings with British government representative, 24 and 26 February 1993, *Setting the Record Straight*, p.25.
76. Nine-paragraph document sent by British government to Sinn Féin, 19 March 1993, *Setting the Record Straight*, p.26.
77. Ibid.
78. Report of meeting with British government representative, 23 March 1993, *Setting the Record Straight*, p.28.
79. Mallie and McKittrick, op.cit., p.104.
80. 'Maastricht – the End of Partition in Sight?', *AP/RN*, 11 June 1992.
81. 'Sinn Féin's Basis for Entering into Dialogue', *Setting the Record Straight*, pp.32-3.
82. Ibid.
83. 'We Will Have Peace', *AP/RN*, 18 November 1993.
84. 'Sinn Féin's Basis for Entering into Dialogue'.
85. Message sent by British government to Sinn Féin, 5 May 1993, *Setting the Record Straight*, p.30.
86. Report of meeting with British government representative, 15 May 1993, *Setting the Record Straight*, p.34.
87. Bew and Gillespie, *Northern Ireland: A Chronology of the Troubles*, p.300.
88. Message from British government to Sinn Féin in response to 10 May, 3 June 1993, *Setting the Record Straight*, p.35.
89. Mallie and McKittrick, op.cit., pp.173-4.
90. Ibid., pp.174-7.
91. See editorial on Lillis article, *AP/RN*, 7 January 1993.
92. Mallie and McKittrick, op.cit., p.170.

93. 'Time for an Irish Initiative', *AP/RN*, 15 July 1993.
94. Ibid.
95. *Sunday Tribune*, 4 July 1993.
96. 'Irish Initiative is Only Plan for Peace', *AP/RN*, 28 October 1993.
97. Ibid.
98. 'Unionists Must Not be Used to Veto Change', ibid., 4 November 1993. Spring's adviser Fergus Finlay explained to Mallie and McKittrick that the purpose of speech was to prevent a downward spiral of violence. Three days after the speech the Ulster Freedom Fighters murdered seven people in the Rising Sun bar in Greysteel, County Londonderry. For Finlay, the core purpose of the speech was to indicate, 'that it was still open to the Provos to come into politics despite Shankill'. Mallie and McKittrick, op.cit., p.207.
99. 'An Appeal to the People of the 26 Counties', *AP/RN*, 11 November 1993.
100. 'British Hold Veto to Peace', ibid., 16 December 1993.
101. 'Disappointment Among Nationalists over Declaration', ibid., 16 December 1993.
102. 'Points to Ponder', ibid., 16 December 1993.
103. 'National Self-determination is the Key', ibid., 6 January 1994.
104. Hume wrote to Adams and the Army Council of the IRA arguing for a ceasefire on the basis that there was no difference of substance between the Downing Street Declaration and 'Hume-Adams', Mallie and McKittrick, op.cit., pp.274-5.
105. Conor O'Clery, *The Greening of the White House*, Dublin 1996, pp.89-107.
106. *AP/RN*, 3 February 1994.
107. Anthony McIntyre, 'Not Worth the Paper', *Fortnight*, February 1994.
108. For example: Jim Fleming, a member of Fianna Fáil, 'The declaration was of no value. Its two flaws were that it did not refer to the Unionist veto or to the British presence which is the main problem in Ireland.' Des Bonass of the Amalgamted Transport and General Workers' Union: 'Northern nationalists are still "under the thumb". Republicans must continue their campaign for a simultaneous ceasefire by the IRA, British forces and loyalist death squads,' *AP/RN*, 10 February 1994.
109. Ibid., 3 March 1994.
110. Sean Duignan, government press secretary in Dublin at the time, recorded the calculations of the Irish Prime Minister, Albert Reynolds: 'The Adams visa will advance the peace. Sinn Féin will pay a price for going to Capitol Hill. A lot of powerful people went out on a limb for Adams. If he doesn't deliver, they'll have him back in the house with shutters [Sinn Féin headquarters in Belfast] so fast his feet won't touch the ground. We're slowly putting the squeeze on them, pulling them in, cutting of their line of retreat.' 31 January 1994, Sean Duignan, *One Spin on the Merry-Go-Round*, Dublin n.d., pp.139-40.
111. Anthony McIntyre, 'Modern Irish Republicanism: The Product of British State Strategies', *Irish Political Studies*, Vol.10, 1995, pp.115-6.
112. Duignan, op.cit., p.141.
113. Ibid., p.121.
114. 'Hilda MacThomas', 'British Drag their Feet', *AP/RN*, 2 June 1994.
115. Bew and Gillespie, *The Northern Ireland Peace Process*, p.56.

116. The most comprehensive account of the group and its relation with Clinton is in O'Clery, op.cit.
117. 'The visit of Patrick Mayhew to the US where he came under strong pressure to give clarification was significant,' Neil Forde, 'The Background to Clarification', *AP/RN*, 26 May 1994.
118. The TUAS document is reproduced in Mallie and McKittrick, op.cit., Appendix 3, pp.381-4.
119. *AP/RN*, 3 March 1994.
120. 'Susini' (Anthony McIntyre), 'Why Unionists Will Talk', ibid., 14 April 1994.
121. 'Major's Slow Death Affects the Irish Peace Process', ibid., 12 May 1994.
122. Garret FitzGerald, 'Still Making History', *Fortnight*, October 1994.
123. 'It Was the IRA Broke the Logjam', interview with Danny Morrison, *AP/RN*, 15 June 1995.
124. Anthony McIntyre, 'Waking Up to Reality', *Fortnight*, October 1994.
125. Suzanne Breen, 'Deja Vu All Over Again', ibid., October 1994.
126. Bew and Gillespie, *The Northern Ireland Peace Process*, p.162.
127. Anthony McIntyre, 'Can a Safe Union be a Safe Peace?', *Parliamentary Brief*, Vol.3 No.2, November 1994.
128. Mallie and McKittrick, op.cit., p.382.
129. Ibid., p.383.
130. Gerry Adams, *Free Ireland: Towards a Lasting Peace*, Dingle 1995, p.188.
131. Bew and Gillespie, *The Northern Ireland Peace Process*, pp.68-71.
132. Adams, op.cit., p.239.
133. Bew and Gillespie, *The Northern Ireland Peace Process*, p.71.
134. Anthony McIntyre, 'Can a Safe Union be a Safe Peace?'
135. Mallie and McKittrick, op.cit., p.383.
136. Results of the February 1987 general election from Niamh Hardiman, *Pay, Politics and Economic Performance in Ireland 1970-87*, Oxford 1988, p.237.
137. Eoghan Harris, 'The Necessity of Social Democracy', manuscript given to the editor of *Making Sense* (Workers' Party journal) in December 1989.
138. Richard Dunphy and Stephen Hopkins, 'The Organisational and Political Evolution of the Workers' Party of Ireland', *Journal of Communist Studies*, Vol.8 No.3, 1992.
139. *AP/RN*, 5 January 1995.
140. Ibid.
141. Mallie and McKittrick, op.cit., p.328.
142. Ibid., p.338. They quote a 'senior British source' soon after the cessation: 'Bringing all concerned to the table for full negotiations on a political settlement will take, at our first rough guess, two years.' A republican had picked up similar ideas, although interpreting them from a predictably suspicious perspective: 'In the latter half of 1994 credible press reports based on Whitehall briefings were strongly suggesting that it was the intention of the British government not to facilitate all-party talks until a period of two years had elapsed.' Anthony McIntyre, 'An Anniversary Going Nowhere', *Parliamentary Brief*, Vol.3 No.9, Summer 1995.
143. 'Britain's Selfish Interest', *AP/RN*, 9 February 1995.

144. Ibid., 2 March 1995.
145. Kevin Bean, *The New Departure: Recent Developments in Irish Republican Ideology and Strategy*, Liverpool 1994, p.18.
146. Ibid., p.20.
147. The Reverend Ken Newell of Fitzroy Presbyterian church in south Belfast, in Mallie and McKittrick, op.cit., pp. 136-7.
148. Bean, op.cit., p.21.
149. Bew and Gillespie, *The Northern Ireland Peace Process*, p.98.
150. McGeown died at the age of 40 as a result of damage caused to his health by 42 days without food during the 1981 Hunger Strike. David Sharrock, 'Child of the Troubles who Grew into Politics', *Guardian*, 3 October 1996.
151. *Starry Plough*, Autumn 1994, quoted in Jon Tonge, 'The Political Agenda of Sinn Féin: Change without Change?' in Jeffrey Stanyer and Gerry Stoker (eds), *Contemporary Political Studies*, Vol.2, Exeter, 1997, p.759.
152. Ibid., p.758.
153. *AP/RN*, 23 February 1995.
154. 'Facing the Challenge', ibid., 23 February 1995.
155. Bew and Gillespie, *The Northern Ireland Peace Process*, pp.89-90.
156. See 'Hilda MacThomas', 'British Squandering the Chance of Peace': 'Today the Dublin government, the RUC and Garda chiefs, and many political parties agree that the issue of arms should not be pushed forward as an obstacle to the peace process. One suspects that even John Major does not believe that this should happen.' *AP/RN*, 12 January 1995.
157. Bew and Gillespie, *The Northern Ireland Peace Process*, p.81.
158. Paul Bew and Gordon Gillespie, 'Timetable of a British Message', *Parliamentary Brief*, Vol.3 No.9, Summer 1995.
159. Anthony McIntyre, 'An Anniversary Going Nowhere', ibid.
160. Bew and Gillespie, *The Northern Ireland Peace Process*, p.90.
161. 'Republican Struggle Has Set the Agenda', interview with Mitchel McLaughlin, *AP/RN*, 31 August 1995.
162. Ibid.
163. Ibid., 27 April 1995.
164. Ibid., 22 June 1995.
165. 'Anger At Lack Of Progess', ibid., 5 October 1995.
166. Anthony McIntyre, speech to Sinn Féin Internal Conference at RDS, Dublin, 30 September 1995. Copy in Linen Hall Library, Belfast.
167. 'Anger At Lack Of Progress'.
168. Antony McIntyre, 'Gerry Adams, Keeping The Mutterers At Bay', *Parliamentary Brief*, Vol.4 No.2, November 1995.
169. On 14 March 1995, speaking at Dublin Airport, John Bruton said that some method would have to be devised whereby arms could be decommissioned before political talks in Northern Ireland could proceed. Bew and Gillespie, *The Northern Ireland Peace Process*, p.91.
170. *AP/RN*, 27 July 1995.
171. Bew and Gillespie, *The Northern Ireland Peace Process*, p.118.
172. Thus Nancy Soderberg of the National Security Council: 'The twin-track was originally rejected by Sinn Féin, and we felt we had a role in trying to get them back on track ... their rejection of it cost a couple of

months in the process,' quoted in O'Clery, op.cit., p.226.

173. A senior IRA spokesman on 1 September 1995, quoted in Bew and Gillespie, *The Northern Ireland Peace Process*, p.117.
174. Ed Moloney, 'Shattered', *Sunday Tribune*, 11 February 1996.
175. Ed Moloney, 'Adams Faces Final Retreat From Republican Ideals', *Sunday Tribune*, 28 January 1996.
176. Gerry Kelly giving the Bobby Sands Memorial Lecture, *AP/RN*, 18 May 1995.
177. Bew and Gillespie, *The Northern Ireland Peace Process*, p.76.
178. 'Sinn Féin Stand Is Challenged As Well As London's', *Irish Times*, 25 January 1996.

Conclusion

For one Belfast journalist who was consistently sceptical about the gains the peace process would bring the republican movement, Canary Wharf marked the 'complete failure, thus far, of the Sinn Féin leadership . . . In terms of traditional republican goals, or even cosmetic changes to the Northern state, [Adams] was unable to deliver.'[1] She quoted from Anthony McIntyre's speech at Sinn Féin's Internal Conference on the peace process in which he had criticised the leadership's strategy as having 'good ringcraft but no punching power'. The core of McIntyre's argument was that the TUAS strategy would not deliver a British declaration of intent to withdraw. Republicans, he pointed out, were demanding entry to talks which would be based on the principles set out in the Downing Street Declaration, and particularly that there had to be majority consent in the North for any final settlement. This compromised the principle of national self-determination by 'fracturing the concept'. It could at best produce 'an internal solution with the externality of an Irish dimension grafted on . . . It is unity by consent, which is a partitionist fudge'.[2]

Although there were some in the republican movement who shared McIntyre's pessimism about what the TUAS strategy could deliver,[3] his critique of the leadership's position was weakened by its lack of any viable alternative strategy. He made clear his own refusal to support the 'back to war' position of those, he derisively noted, who could only think in terms of 'blattering on for another twenty years'.[4] This rejection of a return to armed struggle was one indicator of the liberating effects of the peace process in the republican heartlands. For when talk of a possible ceasefire had surfaced in the early

1990s, McIntyre had written a sustained critique of those who supported it on the basis of the idea that there was a military stalemate: 'Stalemate seems to suggest a form of draw, a position from which there is no way out. It is much too static a term.' Armed struggle, he argued, was a protracted war of attrition, and he quoted a senior British security source who informed a journalist that the IRA could keep going for years, 'provided they have the bottle to stand up to a rate of attrition'.[5] But it was precisely this prospect of continuing armed struggle in conditions that the republican leadership believed to be military stalemate with which the TUAS strategy attempted to break. It did this by openly declaring that, 'Republicans at this time and on their own do not have the strength to achieve the end goal.'[6]

'Sacrifice Simply for a Better Seat at the Table'

McIntyre's exasperation reflected the existential angst of those republicans who had inflicted much and suffered much in return and who found the 'new realism' of the republican leadership a bitter pill:

> We went to jail, our people hunger striked, we suffered in protest, we died, and we killed an awful, awful lot of people in the process – we killed British soldiers, we killed an awful lot of RUC, we lost an awful lot of our own lives, and we blew up London, we blew up Belfast, we wrecked the place. Now we're back to where we started.[7]

By this he meant that all that was on offer was 'Sunningdale Mark II', republicans having contemptuously rejected the first version in 1974. Although the north-south body envisaged in the Frameworks Documents was a significant improvement on the Council of Ireland proposals of 1974, this critique omitted the radically different context of any settlement along these lines produced by Sinn Féin's subsequent emergence as a significant political force.

In 1980, six years after the UWC strike destroyed Sunningdale Mark I, Seán Cronin quite accurately noted that, 'The Provisionals have no political organisation worthy of the name in the North.'[8] By 1989, however, a knowledgeable commentator on the republican movmement observed that,

It is no secret that since 1982 Sinn Féin has attracted most of the best that the Provisional movement has had to offer – in terms of brains, ability, understanding of and commitment to the Armalite and ballot-box strategy. Sinn Féin has taken and continues to take talent away from the IRA.[9]

Danny Morrison, in the atmosphere of euphoric optimism that followed the Hunger Strike election victories, had made the famous declaration:

Who here really believes that we can win the war through the ballot-box? But will anyone here object if with a ballot paper in this hand and an Armalite in this hand we take power in Ireland?[10]

By the end of the 1980s Sinn Féin had consolidated its position as a political organisation representing about 11 per cent of the Northern Ireland electorate and a substantial minority of the Catholic population, but it had not shaken the grip of the SDLP on the majority of northern Catholics and, despite the removal of the ban on participation in the Dáil in 1986, there was little evidence of it being able to make a significant breakthrough in the Republic. The first edition of this book had noted of the latter failure that it had 'major implications for Adams's modernising project'.[11] This was true, although not for the reason assumed then – that the failure to develop a political base in the south would condemn republicanism to a significant but subordinate existence in Northern Ireland. It is now clear that the failure to develop a southern strategy with mass support, coupled with the evidence of the continued dominance of constitutional nationalism in the North, propelled Adams towards a political alliance with the greener elements in what, in their more radical moments, republicans had once described as the 'Free State Establishment'.

For the minority of republicans, like McIntyre, who had been politically educated and radicalised in prison, the TUAS strategy was a betrayal of the leftist vision of republicanism which they had developed in the 1980s. Thus Tommy Gorman, another ex-prisoner, who had participated in an ill-starred attempt by McIntyre to create a republican discussion group when he left prison, complained of pan-nationalist dilution of republican principles:

It's always been the case that we're not out to establish a 32
County nationalist, Catholic-ridden Ireland. We're out to establish a 32 County socialist republic. That's supposed to be in our
constitution. The one who cobbled together the thing with
Hume and Adams, Albert Reynolds, doesn't even allow trade
union representation in his factories. It's things like this here;
they're contradictions which can't be hidden for long.[12]

Yet although the goal of republican ideology remained that
stated in the TUAS document, 'a united 32 County democratic
socialist republic', republican leaders had made clear for some
considerable time that this was very much an 'ultimate' objective which was not to get in the way of the need to work politically with some of the most conservative forces in nationalist
Ireland. Indeed, Adams and other Sinn Féin leaders had been
downgrading the 'socialist content of the struggle' since the
mid-1980s.[13] Thus when, after the Canary Wharf bombing, a
Sinn Féin Ard Chomhairle member told Ronan Bennett that
the goal of a 32 County socialist republic was 'on the back
burner for now', it was much less important as a sign of republican 'new realism' than Bennett implied in a piece geared to
placing total responsibility for the end of the ceasefire on those
in the British establishment whose imperialist myopia sacri-
ficed Adams and the other 'political men' to the republican
militarists.[14]
Much more significant was the same Ard Chomhairle member's admission that, 'Brits Out Now is the worst possible
scenario for republicans and for Ireland as a whole. It would leave
a million very angry Unionists in Ireland.'[15] Here was the core of
republican revisionism. The peace strategy had been developed
in large part to construct the political coalition that would pressure the British government to create the conditions in which this
obstacle would be removed. This was implicitly a recipe for a long
haul through the institutions of a reformed northern state which,
with the hoped-for addition of 'dynamic' north-south institutions, could be presented as 'transitional arrangements'. Its logic
was very clearly articulated in a letter to *An Phoblacht* written by
Ronan Brady, previously a journalist on the paper, in the aftermath of Canary Wharf. He attacked the IRA's action for 'shatter-
ing the credibility of the Sinn Féin leadership':

Until Canary Wharf the nationalists were actually winning. At
Gerry Adams's suggestion they had assembled a huge caucus

including Leinster House, Washington and moderate opinion throughout the world. There has not been such international support for northern nationalists since the civil rights movement. Time was on the side of anti-partitionists. You win political battles like this in years, not months.[16]

Another republican, Joe O'Connell, imprisoned for thirty years in 1977 for his part in the English bombing campaign which ended in the siege of Balcombe Street in London in 1974,[17] wrote from prison in England to denounce 'the most stupid, blinkered and ill-conceived decision ever made by a revolutionary body'.[18] He took particular exception to the rationale for the bombing given in the IRA's statement ending the ceasefire. This had implicitly held out the possibility of a restored ceasefire by referring to 'the failure thus far of the Irish peace process' and making its main demand an inclusive negotiated settlement.[19] Anticipating the common republican belief that the two governments' joint communiqué of 28 February 1996, which provided a firm date for all-party talks on 10 June, was a direct product of the leverage of renewed violence,[20] he pointed out that this would have come anyway 'under the now binned peace process'.[21]

Ruairí Ó Bradaigh, president of Republican Sinn Féin and a consistent critic of the peace process as leading to a partitionist compromise, still detected the domination of a reformist agenda:

> If the Provisionals' renewal of conflict was unequivocally directed towards a British withdrawal form Ireland ... with the objective of creating a totally new Ireland, then it would be consistent with Irish republican philosophy. But if, as appears to be the case, it is being pursued merely towards gaining a place at 'all-party talks' confined to the Six Counties which the Unionists will dominate, then such action is clearly not justified.[22]

A moral queasiness over the purpose of renewed violence was also powerfully articulated by Bernadette McAliskey, who had emerged as an embarrassing critic of the peace process – when the ceasefire was declared she commented that, 'The good guys lost.' Just before the end of the ceasefire she had a meeting with Adams in which she had urged him to 'come clean' with the rank and file of the movement and openly admit that 'the war is over':

My main disillusionment at that point was that I had that terrible feeling, but I think that it has been born out, that whereas
we had fought long and hard politically and militarily, and men
and women had given their lives for freedom and justice and
independence, that the political leadership was prepared to see
a degree of sacrifice simply for a better seat at the table. You do
not die to move yourself up, that's not a commensurate sacrifice. If all you want to do is move two rows up from the back you
do not take your people to war for a seat near the front of the
cinema.[23]

Like McIntyre and Ó Bradaigh, McAliskey was convinced that
Adams was leading the republican movement into a 'partitionist fudge' and demanded that he be honest about it:

If you believe that all you can do is to accept partition for the
forseeable future and maximise the nationalist position within
the partitionist state, you can't do that effectively while you are
still pretending that's not what your are doing. Because the
effective way to do that is to join forces with the SDLP, whose
central policy has been that for years, and get on with it.[24]

However her pre-Canary Wharf proposal to Adams was that he
both declare that the war was over and reject participation in
the all-party talks process. Instead she proposed the convening
of a 'republican congress' to regroup republican and left-wing
forces in Ireland.[25] Sinn Féin was unlikely to take seriously such
a left republican critique. It echoed those of the IRSP/INLA,
which had been marginalised by the politicisation of the
Provisionals after 1977 and was subsequently wracked by
increasingly murderous internal feuds. Although the INLA
declared a 'tactical' ceasefire during the IRA cessation, the
IRSP was bitterly critical of the leadership of the republican
movement. Thus Kevin McQuillan, the most prominent IRSP
spokesman, declared that Gerry Adams 'is crassly stupid or he's
deviously cynical'.[26] McAliskey's proposals, coming from some-
one who had declared that Dominic McGlinchey, perhaps the
INLA's most formidable killer, was 'the finest republican the
struggle has ever produced',[27] were treated with predictable
contempt by the republican leadership which, whatever other
illusions it may have had, harboured none about the viability of
an all-Ireland, socialist and 'anti-imperialist' strategy involving
loose cannons like McAliskey and ultra-leftists like McQuillan.

Despite the political naïvety of the 'republican congress' idea, McAliskey's criticisms did raise a central issue. She claimed that the ceasefire was ended to prevent a split:

> The ceasefire was broken to maintain army unity, it had no other purpose. They went ahead and did it themselves before somebody went and did it unofficially, before the discipline, which had been very, very good, finally broke with frustration.[28]

That there was intense frustration amongst many IRA activists with the results of the TUAS strategy was clear by the end of 1995. Suzanne Breen claimed in the *Irish Times* that Canary Wharf was greeted with universal approval by grassroots republicans, quoting one as saying,

> They wouldn't talk to Sinn Féin, they wouldn't release the prisoners. They were just intent on humiliating us. We finally got our pride back. The bomb was long overdue. I hope there are more.[29]

In clear contrast was a leadership position expressed by 'Hilda MacThomas' describing her reaction to the news of Canary Wharf:

> My heart sank. Then I burst into tears. Later I found out without surprise that such scenes of shock, disbelief, despair and sadness had taken place in republican homes across Ireland.[30]

It is, of course, extremely difficult for an outsider to grasp fully the dynamics of very recent internal republican debates, but it is possible that Breen's story gave an exaggerated impression of the 'back to war' sentiment amongst republican activists. That there was an intense frustration with what was seen as lack of movement by the British had been obvious for some time. It was fuelled not simply by the issue of decommissioning arms but also by a niggardly approach to the key question of prisoners. While the Irish government introduced a programme of phased releases, British policy, heavily influenced by Michael Howard, the right-wing Home Secretary, was minimalist – the reintroduction of 50 per cent remission, a privilege prisoners in the North had enjoyed until 1989, when remission was reduced to one-third, while there was also a marked reluctance to move on the republican demand for the transfer of prison-

ers in British jails to Northern Ireland.[31] When this was combined with the decision in July 1995 to release a British soldier,
Private Lee Clegg, after four years in custody for the killing of
a joy-rider in West Belfast, the widespread rioting in nationalist
areas reflected a popular 'anti-Brit' feeling which was exacerbated by the Orange Order's march down Garvaghy Road and
which sharpened internal republican questioning of the TUAS
strategy.

Martin Mansergh has suggested that the republican leadership bore some responsiblity for the breakdown of the cessation because,

> There was no obvious sign either before or after the ceasefire of
> political educaiton or persuasive advocacy of the merits of
> peaceful democratic strategy by the republican leadership, and
> a war readiness continued to be maintained.[32]

A somewhat similar point has been made by Anthony McIntyre
from within Sinn Féin:

> While the 1995 Internal Conference at the RDS may have
> demonstrated that a high level of political debate does take
> place within the Sinn Féin cumainn [branches], it also demon-
> strated that many on the ground in Sinn Féin felt that they did
> not really know what was happening in the 'high-wire' act being
> performed by the leadership in the management and direction
> of the peace process. Many of the complaints made at that con-
> ference were precisely that the peace process was such a high-
> wire act which went over the heads of the rank and file.[33]

The TUAS document had made clear that this phase of the
peace process was driven from the top: 'The leadership has
now decided that there is enough agreement to proceed with
the TUAS option.' While conceding that it was a risky strategy,
the document placed a high degree of responsiblity for success
or failure on the republican base:

> Its success will depend greatly on workload. All activists must be
> pro-active. Those who continue their present work need to dou-
> ble effort. If you find yourself idle help in another field.[34]

But as McIntyre noted, there were real problems if so much
weight was to be placed on the non-military structures and tasks
of the movement:

One of the early reservations expressed about the post-ceasefire situation in which republicans found themselves was that republicans were moving into an unarmed struggle without any unarmed organisation capable of conducting and carrying through such a struggle.[35]

Could electoral activity, advice-centre work, community activism and street protests provide adequate compensation for armed struggle in the absence of relatively swift movement on the major political and constitutional questions? That question implicitly dogged the ceasefire. The TUAS strategy was *not* sold within the movement as a commitment to an 'unarmed' way forward. Rather, it was said to be the opening up of 'another front' which implicitly portrayed it as an initiative, which, if it were successful, would bring about radical political and constitutional changes, but left open the possiblity of a return to armed struggle if the high-risk strategy failed to deliver. It was one thing to admit that the armed struggle was stalemated, quite another to set about excising it from the republican movement's tactical repertoire. This was not simply because of the continuing weight of 'militarists' in the movement but reflected the fact that even those 'politicos' like Adams had, until the early 1990s, still seen a use for a refined and more carefully directed violence as a way of influencing debates on Irish policy in Whitehall. The very way in which the TUAS document emphasised the uniqueness of the conjuncture – 'These combined circumstances are unlikely to gel again in the foreseeable future'[36] – raised the question of what happened if the circumstances changed.

Activists were assured from the start of the cessation that there would be a return to armed struggle if the TUAS strategy failed to deliver. To prevent the ceasefire having the degenerative effects on IRA structures of the 1975 cessation, a programme of training, intelligence-gathering and targeting was maintained along with the IRA's 'policing' functions in nationalist areas. More pointedly, preparations were made from early in the ceasefire for a renewed bombing campaign in England.[37] It appears probable that, some months before President Clinton's peace mission to Belfast, the Army Council had decided to end the ceasefire, although Adams and other Sinn Féin leaders had been able to delay the inevitable for a while.[38]

None of this should lead us to adopt too quickly the view of most Ulster Unionists and some serious commentators, whom Garret FitzGerald labelled 'the Conor Cruise O'Brien/ Eoghan Harris/*Sunday Independent* school', that the cessation was a purely tactical device.[39] There was clearly a tendency in Sinn Féin that was interested in a purely political way forward, though this was never as strong as some peace process optimists in the Irish Department of Foreign Affairs believed. Also, for the core leadership group around Adams, there was a strong desire to break out of the situation of stalemate and a willingness to think flexibly about the steps necessary to build the pan-nationalist alliance to do this. At the same time this group knew it was part of a movement with a solidly rooted military structure, some at least of whose leading elements would only contemplate continued passivity if there was to be fairly rapid political movement.

Working in favour of the proponents of TUAS was the long-term shift in the balance of power in the movement produced by the adoption of the 'long war' strategy in the late 1970s. Given the smaller manpower needs of the armed struggle in a 'long war', there was much less chance of a new generation of military activists – the Martin McGuinnesses of the 1990s – reaching the critical mass necessary to challenge the strategic domination of the movement by people like Adams, Hartley, Gibney and McLaughlin. Ironically, Adams had begun to achieve what the incipient 'Stickies' had set out to do in the mid-1960s with their proposals to relegate the IRA to the role of the appendage of a movement whose main dynamic was a political one.[40]

Adams's problem was – what was the exciting alternative vista to armed struggle? For Goulding, it had been the 'Socialist Republic' and, in the short to medium term, the real possiblity of electoral progress in the Republic as a leftist alternative to the Irish Labour Party. For Adams, there was an electoral prospect with real opportunities, but it came up against the maximalist internal culture of the republican movement. The continuation of the ceasefire opened up real possibilities for Sinn Féin of breaking out from its substantial but secondary position in nationalist electoral politics in the North. Together with the eventual entry to all-party talks conceded by Major's electoral process, it could have produced a serious destabilisation of the relationship between Unionists and

London. Arguably, such a destabilisation, leading to an imposed set of structures along the lines of those envisaged in the Joint Frameworks Documents, was what the medium-term objective of the peace process entailed from the republican leadership's point of view.

It is here that the critique of the leadership's strategy from internal and external dissidents like McIntyre and McAliskey missed the point. For while it was true in the abstract that all-party talks would be bound by the consent principle in the Downing Street Declaration and the Frameworks Documents, thus apparently justifying the notion of 'Sunningdale Mark II', the shift in the political and ideological balance in the nationalist community brought about through TUAS made for less predictable and much less stable possibilities. A talks process involving a 'peaceful', electorally growing Sinn Féin would tend to push the Unionist political parties in a defensive and reactionary direction. Whilst this would probably spell disaster for the talks process and any possibility of an internally agreed settlement, it could increase the chances of the structures of the Anglo-Irish Agreement being developed in the direction of joint sovereignty while in the interim making a confrontation between loyalists and the British state over Garvaghy Road-type issues a strong probability. The TUAS strategy was not a recipe for the negotiated surrender of republicanism but, rather, a relatively rational wager on the inflexibility and lack of imagination of the Unionist political leadership – something which over two decades of IRA violence had done much to encourage.

Blaming 'the Brits': Sinn Féin and Nationalist Ireland

The peace process, as one supporter put it, 'represented the movement emerging from its historical isolation, and all nationalist traditions began to see each other's point of view'.[41] This was shown to be the case with regard to a strong consensus throughout nationalist Ireland that laid the fundamental blame for the breakdown of the ceasefire on the British government and saw the Unionists as having wasted an historic opportunity. Although the increasing emphasis placed by Adams and other Sinn Féin leaders on the party's separate identity and electoral mandate, as distinct from the IRA, was treated with scepticism by many in Whitehall and with derision by Unionists, it had increasing effect on what can be termed 'soft' SDLP support.

The complexity of northern nationalists' attitudes to the republican movement was only ever very imperfectly reflected in the division between constitutional nationalism and the Provisionals. In a series of interviews with northern nationalists, the journalist Fionnuala O'Connor provided illuminating material on what one Ballymurphy woman defined as the 'shifting, complex and ambiguous' nature of political allegiance in Catholic West Belfast.[42] A community worker from North Belfast revealed the possibilities that TUAS opened up for Sinn Féin:

> I vote for the SDLP although I'm very sceptical about them – I think I'm probably one of the many, many people from whom the SDLP gets votes but who are half-hearted about them ... I don't support the continuation of armed struggle. Nevertheless in my case it would be wrong to read my vote, that I have no sympathy for the political attitudes of republicanism.[43]

Since the Hunger Strikes and the subsequent expansion in the size and role of Sinn Féin as an electoral and propaganda machine, the republican movement had established an increasing ideological influence in the Catholic community, even amongst those who did not vote for Sinn Féin. The SDLP, with its structure focused on its MPs' constituency organisations, its lack of any significant signs of internal life or debate and its domination by the ideas and personality of John Hume, was a standing incitement to republicans with a modicum of political sense to go down the TUAS road.

Ironically, the first fruits were harvested after Canary Wharf. For despite further attacks in England, the IRA's restriction of its activities to targets outside Northern Ireland with no deaths, apart from that of an IRA member killed when the bomb he was carrying exploded prematurely on a London bus,[44] enabled Sinn Féin to obtain its highest ever vote in the elections for the Northern Ireland Forum on 30 May 1995. Sinn Féin obtained 15.5 per cent of the vote to the SDLP's 21.4 per cent.[45]

In the immediate aftermath of Canary Wharf the prospects for the republican movement had appeared bleak to many commentators. The response of grassroots republicans to the two governments' joint communiqué of 28 February 1996, which included proposals for elections and a definite date for all-party talks to begin – 10 June – was suspicious if not straightforwardly hostile. Particularly problematic was the stipulation that all participants would have to make clear at the beginning of the discussions 'their total and absolute commitment to the principles of democracy and non-violence set out in the report of the International Body'.[46] Ed Moloney, who had argued that John Major's perceived 'binning' of the Mitchell Report had saved the republican movement from the severe embarrassment of having to reject it, now argued that the communiqué placed the republican movement 'between a rock and a hard place. If they accept the communiqué there is no going back; if they reject it they face isolation, repression and possible defeat.'[47]

In fact, the republican movement, as in its response to the Downing Street Declaration, neither accepted nor rejected the communiqué. As one journalist who attended the Sinn Féin Árd Fheis noted, 'If it was left to the floor of the Árd Fheis, the elections, the Forum and the talks would be boycotted as a partitionist internal solution.' However he pointed out that the Ard Chomhairle had left the leadership's options open.[48] That the disposition of Adams and his closest supporters would have been to go for another ceasefire to maximise support in the elections and to allow Sinn Féin into talks on 10 June is a distinct possiblity, and Adams was under strong US pressure for a restoration of the ceasefire.[49] John Bruton declared at the end of April that prior decommissioning should not be a precondition for the progress of talks, and John Major subsequently appeared to soften the British position by saying that the issue would have to be 'addressed' at the beginning of the talks.[50]

However some indication of internal stresses in republican ranks was revealed in the speech given by Brian Keenan to a commemoration ceremony in West Belfast on 12 May. Keenan, who had been imprisoned in 1979 for his role in co-ordinating the IRA's English bombing campaign from 1973, was released from prison in 1994.[51] With a history of IRA involvement going back to 1970 and, according to Bishop and Mallie, with a reputation at the time as 'the best organisational brain in the IRA',[52] Keenan seemed to have emerged from a distinctly 1970s time-warp of fundamentalist militarism. Apart from denouncing John Bruton's government as 'those bastards in power in Dublin', he articulated a message on the arms issue and the British presence which would have been more appropriate at a Republican Sinn Féin gathering:

Do not be confused about the politics of situation and about decommissioning. The only thing the republican movement will accept is the decommissioning of the British state in this country.[53]

In contrast, Adams proclaimed on 20 May that Sinn Féin would agree to the Mitchell principles.[54] Intentionally or not, one suggested reading of these contrasting messages was that Sinn Féin's core leadership was intent, despite the urgings of recidivist militarists, to lead the movement into democratic politics. This reading, which continued to be encouraged by John Hume and the White House, was clearly that of an increasing proportion of northern nationalists and contributed powerfully to the striking Sinn Féin result in the elections.

Even after the *de facto* cessation of IRA activities in Ireland and Britain, which had lasted throughout May and the electioneering period, ended with the murder of a Garda during a mail-van robbery in County Limerick and the subsequent devastation of part of the centre of Manchester by a van-bomb on 15 June, Sinn Féin's alliance strategy was not fundamentally damaged. When Adams rang Tony Lake, Clinton's National Security Adviser, to tell him that he had no prior knowledge of the IRA mortar attack on a British army barracks in Germany on 28 June, his claim was accepted:

White House officials accepted what they were told in private, that Adams had 85 per cent of republicans behind him but that he needed the movement fully united to bring it voluntarily to the point where it would give up a tradition of armed struggle dating back to Fenian times while the national question remained unresolved.[55]

'Soft' nationalist support for Sinn Féin, which may have been hoping for a ceasefire before or soon after the elections, was maintained, not so much by evidence of continuing prestigious international support for Adams's peace-making credentials, but by the sharp deterioration in community relations brought about by the events surrounding the annual Orange Order parade to Drumcree church in Portadown on 6 July. The RUC's decision first to reroute the march away from the Catholic Garvaghy Road, and then, after a three-day stand-off between police, army and Orangemen which was accompanied by a province-wide campaign of loyalist disruption and rioting, to reverse the original decision and allow the march down Garvaghy Road, pushed large sectors of moderate Catholic opinion towards acceptance of the republican analysis of the 'irreformability' of the northern state.

At the same time, many Protestants who detected the influence of Sinn Féin in the Garvaghy Road and other residents' associations which challenged the Orange Order's right to march through predominantly nationalist districts feared that the original Drumcree decision reflected an underlying British desire to placate Sinn Féin and obtain another ceasefire, whatever the cost in alienating Unionists. There was a palpable increase in sectarian animosities with the boycotting of Protestant businesses and attacks on churches. Although the main loyalist ceasefire had been maintained after Canary Wharf, there were growing signs of restiveness, with attacks on Dublin airport and the murder of a Catholic taxi-driver during the Drumcree confrontation.[56]

Sinn Féin had to be extremely careful in exploiting this situation. With both Westminster and local government elections due within a year, there was clearly a crop of bitterness towards Britain and the Unionists to be harvested. Little was now expected from a Major administration increasingly pre-occupied with the forthcoming general election, and republican sights were on the possiblity of a Labour government with a secure majority, and thus free of dependence on Ulster Unionist support, together with a possible return of Fianna Fáil to power in Dublin. Yet the gains of the Forum elections would be threatened by IRA actions that precipitated an end to the loyalist ceasefire, thereby putting at risk the lives of innocent Catholics. Thus the return to violence in Northern Ireland with the bombing of Thiepval Barracks in Lisburn on 7 October, which caused the death of one soldier, did not, as one commentator claimed, represent the failure of the 'politicos': 'The Lisburn bombing would suggest that the current consensus within the IRA is that the electoral strategy . . . has served its purpose and is now expendable.'[57] Rather, it appears to have represented the effect of the temporary disruption of the campaign in England by the British security services, thus increasing pressure from more militarist elements for a return to action in Northern Ireland.[58] Journalists were briefed by security sources that the Thiepval bombing was not the beginning of an unrestricted campaign in the North and that IRA units were operating on a 'defence and retaliation' basis.[59]

October saw another attempt by Hume and Adams to persuade Major to ease Sinn Féin's entry into talks in the event of a renewed ceasefire by removing any 'preconditions' and setting out a definite time-period in which the talks process would be expected to make substantive progess. The Prime Minister's response, at the end of November, was to emphasise that any new ceasefire would have to be declared in terms that were 'convincingly unequivocal' and would then need to be tested for a period to assure him that paramilitary activity like surveillance, targeting and weapons preparation had ended.[60]

The rebuff certainly increased the problems facing those in the republican leadership who wanted to sit out the period before the British general election without an intensification of republican violence in Northern Ireland precipitating the end of the loyalist ceasefire and hurting Sinn Féin at the polls.[61] Their dilemma was intensified by the slow progress of the interparty talks at Stormont, where hopes of a deal on decommissioning between the SDLP, the Ulster Unionists and the Alliance Party came to an end in mid-December as a result of an apparent hardening of the Unionist position.[62]

On 23 December, at a time when Sinn Féin negotiators were discussing the conditions for a renewed IRA cessation with senior Irish officials, IRA members fired on RUC men guarding a DUP politician visiting his critically ill son in a Belfast hospital.[63] This was soon followed by a series of failed attempts to kill RUC members in landmine and mortar attacks. Though some speculated that these were part of a 'phoney war' to keep militants happy whilst not destabilising the loyalist ceasefire and damaging Sinn Féin's electoral prospects, it seems more likely that the botched operations reflected the debilitating effects of more than two years of military inactivity in Northern Ireland.[64]

The failure of IRA attacks in Northern Ireland allowed the Adams group to reassert its dominance in the movement as the British general election appoached. Whilst unable to restore a ceasefire and establish an electoral pact with the SDLP to maximise the number of nationalist seats at Westminster, Adams and other prominent Sinn Féiners began to talk up the prospects of 'real progress' with a new Labour administration.[65] Attacked by the SDLP leader for the continuation of IRA activities in England – a campaign focusing on the disruption of rail and motorway networks but including a bizarre disruption of the Grand National horse-race – leading Sinn Féiners hinted at a new 'positive abstentionist' approach if they were elected to Westminster, while IRA men in balaclavas brandished automatic weapons at an Easter commemoration ceremony in the Ardoyne.[66]

What amounted to a ceasefire in Northern Ireland during the election period, following the attempted murder of a policewoman in Derry, allowed both John Hume and John Bruton to accuse Sinn Féin of hypocrisy and claim that a vote for Sinn Féin was a vote for violence. But Hume's election rhetoric could not repress the obvious fact that he continued to see in men like Adams and McGuinness a 'peace party' in Sinn Féin. The long-term effects of the peace process on nationalist attitudes to Sinn Féin, coupled with the bitter legacy of Drumcree, ensured Sinn Féin success. In the general election on 1 May Adams won back West Belfast from Joe Hendron, and Martin McGuinness captured Mid-Ulster from the Reverend William McCrea, the DUP MP loathed by many nationalists. When compared to the 1992 results, the success of the peace strategy from Sinn Féin's point of view was obvious: in that election Sinn Féin had won the support of 29.8 per cent of the nationalist electorate to the SDLP's 72 per cent, while in 1997 the respective figures were 39.57 per cent to 60.43 per cent.[67] In the local government elections on 22 May, in which Sinn Féin's much more effective party machine was not counterbalanced by the strength that the SDLP derived from its sitting MPs, the result was even better for the republicans: their highest ever percentage of the vote – nearly 17 per cent and a 45 per cent share of the nationalist vote.[68]

At the Sinn Féin Árd Fheis in April Martin McGuinness had conjured up bright vistas of significant change if Sinn Féin did well in the coming elections: 'A strong mandate for Sinn Féin will reverberate throughout the corridors of power in Dublin, London and Washington.' In particular it would bring 'untold pressure on the incoming British government to engage in a credible process of inclusive peace negotiations'.[69] Republicans may well have been encouraged by Labour's shadow Northern Ireland Secretary of State, Mo Mowlam, who had stated that, 'The status quo is not an option,' and in her John Smith Memorial Lecture of June 1996 had declared that an IRA ceasefire should lead to Sinn Féin being welcomed into talks: 'Any procrastination, calls for further preconditions . . . should be rejected.'[70]

But such optimism had a tinge of desperation to it. After all, Tony Blair had replaced Kevin Macnamara, the 'green' shadow Secretary of State for Northern Ireland, and there had, in effect, been a shift from the 'unification by consent' formulation towards an emphasis on a settlement based on the reconciliation of the 'two traditions', with the emphasis clearly on the principle of consent. The shadow Cabinet's support for the government's handling of the peace process, including the Mitchell Report, had produced much disquiet in the 'green' fringes of the party. Ronan Bennett, a skilful proponent of republican 'new realism', had written a bitter critique of Blair and Mowlam in *New Left Review*, in part provoked by the warm reception given to David Trimble at the 1996 Labour Party conference.[71]

Post-election reality was both better and worse than republican expectations. The very size of the Labour majority removed any Westminster leverage which the Unionists may have possessed under Major. Yet as Adams himself noted, the problems republicans had with the Major government

> arose from that government's position towards Ireland and its support for the Union. It is this which has consistently underpinned London's Irish policy, not the government's majority or lack of a majority.[72]

From this perspective Blair was a profound disappointment. In a speech in Belfast on 16 May he moved beyond notions of a settlement that 'balanced' two traditions, the sort of ambiguity about British policy which infuriated Unionists, to a statement of outright support for the Union combined with an explicit dampener on nationalist aspirations:

> Northern Ireland is part of the United Kingdom, alongside England, Scotland and Wales . . . I beleive in the United Kingdom, I value the Union . . . none of us in this hall, even the youngest, is likely to see Northern Ireland as anything but a part of the United Kingdom.[73]

The speech served dramatically to underline the Sinn Féin leadership's dilemma. A significant sector of its new electoral strength clearly came from nationalists who blamed the British and the Unionists rather than the continued existence of the IRA for the breakdown of the ceasefire. Yet such support was premissed upon the fact that Adams had delivered one cease-fire and was perceived to be in the business of securing another. Blair's announcement in his speech that he would allow meetings between his officials and Sinn Féin intensfied pressure for an IRA ceasefire. However there was evidence that the Sinn Féin leadership's capacity to respond to such pressure was severely constrained by its own ambiguous presentation of its peace strategy to its internal constituency.

In his response to Blair's speech, Adams set out republican demands for the creation of a new peace process. None of these 'confidence-building measures', like the early release of political prisoners, removal of preconditions, i.e. a softening of the position on decommissioning, a specified time-frame for negotiations, a guarantee of Sinn Féin's entry into talks as soon as there was an unequivocal restoration of the IRA cessation, was necessarily impossible for the British. He also said, and this followed from his earlier commitment to accept the Mitchell principles, that Sinn Féin would accept the agreed outcome of the negotiations.

He added the demand that Britain join the ranks of the 'persuaders':

> The British government's failure to commit themselves to a pos-itive policy of working towards Irish reunification inevitably increases suspicions among Irish nationalists about Britain's real intentions.[74]

Although he claimed that Blair's speech was drafted by civil ser-vants from the old administration, this was a particularly lame attempt to shore up any residual optimism in republican ranks.[75]

For Adams and his supporters in the leadership of the move-ment, the way ahead was through Sunningdale Mark II which, they calculated, would, if driven by a rhetorically militant and expanding Sinn Féin and without the need for IRA violence, destabilise relations between Unionists and the British state and through a long 'transition period' lead eventually to a 'Brit-less Ireland'. This was a relatively subtle and risky strategy which might end up with exactly the sort of 'partitionist fudge' warned of by its critics. It was certainly too risky to win a long-term IRA ceasefire without the maintenance of at least some of the 'politics of illusion'. For while Adams and his core allies had done much to rid themselves of such politics, the top-down propagation of illusions for others remained necessary. Thus a 'senior Sinn Féin figure' informed the Irish Times after Blair's speech that an interim settlement leading eventually to a united Ireland was acceptable, 'But Irish unity would have to come in ten or fifteen years.'[76] How admittance to all-party talks held on the basis of the consent principle would contribute to this goal was not elaborated but, as Ed Moloney noted, the Blair speech had cut to the core of leadership cant: '[Blair] strongly challenged a key element of the current republican leadership's case to their grassroots for the peace strategy, that it could achieve Irish unity within their lifetime.'[77]

Republican discomfort over the Blair speech was soon reflected in an end to the *de facto* ceasefire in Northern Ireland with a failed landmine attack on the RUC in West Belfast and a 'punishment' shooting whose victim had to have a leg amputated – republican 'punishment' attacks had also ceased during the election period.[78] Mo Mowlam did not break off contacts with Sinn Féin as a result of these activities, despite demands from Unionists to do so, and pressure on the IRA to declare another ceasefire increased with the results of the Republic's general election on 6 June. Gerry Adams had made clear Sinn Féin's hope that John Bruton's coalition would be defeated and a government led by Bertie Ahern of Fianna Fáil returned. Ahern had criticised Bruton for what he saw as a failure to defend the Irish nationalist position adequately during the ceasefire, and had indicated that he might give Albert Reynolds a special role in northern policy if Fianna Fáil won. The return of a Fianna Fáil-Progressive Democrat coalition, with the latter party, suspect to Sinn Féin for its revisionist views on Northern Ireland, in a much reduced state of four seats to Fianna Fáil's 77, and the coalition's need to rely on a number of independents whose views on the North were traditionally nationalist, buoyed up republican champions of the TUAS strategy.

The original ceasefire had allowed Sinn Féin unprecedented exposure in the Republic and produced a very broad nationalist consensus that placed the blame for the breakdown of the cessation on the British and the Unionists. Building on its areas of traditional support in the border counties and Kerry and on work on the drugs issue in working-class areas of Dublin, Sinn Féin had its best ever election result in the Republic. It gained one TD, who topped the poll in Cavan-Monagahan, and a massive increase of support for its candidate in North Kerry, who had been released in 1994 after a long sentence for attempting to smuggle arms into the Republic. A number of Sinn Féin candidates received significant increases in support in Dublin – ironically, challenging the Democratic Left, which, as a result of the 1992 split and its subsequent participation in government, had lost the hard-left rhetoric and radical image developed by the Workers' Party.[79]

Yet this limited breakthrough, whilst holding out the possibility of Sinn Féin at last carving out a significant role for itself as a party of protest in the Republic, pointed more towards constitutionalism than an end to partition. Politically stronger than ever before, republicans looked towards the end of the millennium, with real, if limited, possiblities of power and influence in the shaping of any agreed settlement in Northern Ireland. Unionist inflexiblity could perhaps deliver them even more significant political and constitutional change. Adams and his co-strategists had achieved considerably more than appeared possible when the first edition of this book was published. Yet the continuing existence of a significant constituency for fundamentalism and militarism in the movement was reflected in a public discourse that still interwove illusion and reality.

IRA activities appeared to demonstrate the continuing influence of a mentality which believed that violence could achieve negotiating advantages for Sinn Féin. The shooting dead of two policemen in Lurgan on 17 June – the first killing of members of the RUC since the ceasefire of 1994 – came four days after the British government had sent Sinn Féin an *aide-mémoire* setting out a very accommodating response to republican demands for clarification of the likely response to a new ceasefire. Sinn Féin was promised entry to talks six weeks after an unequivocal ceasefire; the talks were to be given a strictly limited time-frame (until May 1998) thus dealing with republicans' fear of Unionist delaying tactics; and there was a commitment to so-called 'confidence-building measures' in areas like reform of the RUC and the strengthening of fair employment laws.[80] However the section on arms decommissioning, although it clearly put aside any idea of prior decommissioning, did propose to deal with the issue by implementing all aspects of the Mitchell Report, and this included the idea of decommissioning in parallel with the progress of political negotiations.

The Lurgan killings were a clear message that the IRA would not tolerate any idea of parallel decommissioning and raised a question-mark over Adams's strategic hegemony in a republican movement which was itself increasingly incoherent. For as long as the TUAS document was not repudiated, the leadership of the movement appeared to accept that armed struggle was incapable of realising republican objectives. Yet the significant political success that the peace process had brought to Sinn Féin, despite the ending of the ceasefire, appeared to have strengthened the hand of those who believed that it was possible to have it both ways. More depressingly, the Lurgan killings – so near to the sectarian cockpit of Garvaghy Road – indicated that for at least some in the organisation a future for the movement could be guaranteed simply by exploiting and deepening communal divisions. The problem for the republican movement was that the undoubted tendency towards following in the steps of de Valera and Goulding that can be detected in Gerry Adams's political trajectory requires more from the British state than can be realistically or democratically expected: the imposition of a 'transitional' settlement against the wishes of Ulster Unionists. Thus although the Blair government's decision to accept an Anglo-Irish decommissioning paper, which made it clear that Sinn Féin would have to do little more than discuss the arms issue during talks, produced a new IRA ceasefire on 21 July, the lack of euphoria in republican ranks reflected an increasing awareness of the partitionist implications of the leadership's strategy. Adams could now openly write about 'renegotiating the Union' rather than ending it.[81] Whether, on such an explicitly revisionist project, he could hold the movement together without a return to violence was the key question for the resurrected peace process.

Notes

1. Suzanne Breen, 'Punch Drunk', *Fortnight*, March 1996.
2. Speech to Sinn Féin Internal Conference, Dublin, 30 August 1995, copy in Linen Hall Library, Belfast.
3. In a letter from Belfast Lily Ryan wrote, 'Even if the British did decide to become fully engaged in the negotiations, would this provide a real chance for republicans? All the signs point in the opposite direction. If the republican delegation to the Forum for Peace and Reconciliation could not gain support for an end to the Unionist veto, what chance have they of persuading the British government of the same? As Emily O'Reilly [an Irish

journalist] pointed out last week, the bones of the eventual settlement are already known-an internal assembly plus some sort of institutional north-south links.' *An Phoblacht/Republican News* *(AP/RN)*, 14 March 1996.

4. In a conversation with the author.

5. 'Susini' (Anthony McIntyre), 'Armed Struggle A Strategic Imperative', manuscript dated summer 1991, copy available in the Linen Hall Library, Belfast.

6. Eamonn Mallie and David McKittrick, *The Fight For Peace: The Secret Story Behind The Irish Peace Process*, London 1996, p.381.

7. Anthony McIntyre quoted in Jonathan Stevenson, *'We Wrecked The Place': Contemplating An End To The Northern Ireland Troubles*, New York 1996, p.1. McIntyre was released from prison in 1993 after serving seventeen years for murder. He secured a first class degree in social sciences through the Open University when in jail and is at present completing a doctorate on the republican movement at Queen's University, Belfast.

8. Seán Cronin, *Irish Nationalism: A History of its Roots and Ideology*, London 1988, p.218.

9. Ed Moloney, 'Mistaken Strategy', *Fortnight*, May 1989.

10. Quoted in Bishop and Mallie, op.cit., p.301.

11. Henry Patterson, *The Politics of Illusion: Republicanism and Socialism in Modern Ireland*, London and New York 1989, p.195.

12. Quoted in Stephenson, op.cit., pp.118-9.

13. 'What's On the Agenda Now Is An End To Partition', interview with Gerry Adams by Fergus Pyle, *Irish Times*, 19 July 1988.

14. Ronan Bennett, 'The Party and the Army', *London Review of Books*, 21 March 1996.

15. Ibid.

16. *AP/RN*, 29 February 1996.

17. Bishop and Mallie, op.cit., pp.256-7.

18. *AP/RN*, 29 February 1996.

19. Paul Bew and Gordon Gillespie, *The Northern Ireland Peace Process 1993-1996: A Chronology*, London 1996, p.160.

20. See, for example the letters page of *AP/RN*. A typical response, on 14 March 1996, was from Tipp Guilfoyle of Nenagh, County Tipperary: 'Surely anybody with an ounce of political education knows that the bomb at Canary Wharf brought the British government to their senses. All-party talks are fixed.'

21. *AP/RN*, 29 February 1996.

22. Ruairí Ó Bradaigh, 'Stepping Around The Legacy Of 1921', *Northern Ireland Brief: A Parliamentary Brief Commentary On Northern Ireland*, March 1996.

23. Interview with Bernadette McAliskey by Rogelio Alonso on 12 April 1997. Transcript kindly provided by Rogelio Alonso.

24. Ibid.

25. Tommy McKearney, 'The Rising Star of Ireland's Pasionara – Bernadette McAliskey', *Northern Ireland Brief*, March 1996.

26. Quoted in Stephenson, op.cit., p.228.

27. Ibid., p.120.

28. McAliskey interview with Rogelio Alonso.

29. See the piece by Suzanne Breen in the *Irish Times*, 15 February 1996.

30. *AP/RN*, 29 February 1996.
31. The issue is dealt with at length in Bennett's *London Review of Books* article, 'The Party and the Army', in which he argues that British action on the prisoners' issue could have prolonged the cessation.
32. Martin Mansergh, 'Finding The Strength Of Sisyphus', *Northern Ireland Brief*, March 1996.
33. Anthony McIntyre, 'A Structural Analysis of Modern Irish Republicanism', unpublished manusript.
34. Mallie and McKittrick, op.cit., p.383.
35. McIntyre, 'A Structural Analysis of Modern Irish Republicanism'.
36. Mallie and McKittrick, op.cit., p.383.
37. Brendan O'Brien, *A Pocket History of the IRA*, Dublin 1997, p.141.
38. Ed Moloney claimed that the Army Council decision to end the ceasefire was made, in principle, some time before Clinton's Belfast visit, perhaps as early as June 1995, but that the attack was postponed on the initiative of Adams who 'wanted to explore every avenue before closing down the peace process'. 'Adams, At Arm's Length From Britain', *Sunday Tribune*, 18 February 1996.
39. Garret FitzGerald, 'The Only Clear Thing About IRA Strategy Is Uncertainty', *Irish Times*, 4 January 1997.
40. See IRA document printed in the appendix to the Inquiry of Lord Scarman, 'Violence and Civil Disturbances in Northern Ireland in 1969', *Report of a Tribunal of Inquiry*, Cmnd 556, Vol.2, Belfast 1972, p.47.
41. See letter from Owen Bennet: 'Republicans who say that the ceasefire brought nothing were looking in the wrong direction. Public attitudes to republicanism were transformed overnight.' *AP/RN*, 14 March 1996.
42. Fionnuala O'Connor, *In Search Of A State: Catholics In Northern Ireland*, Belfast 1993, p.59.
43. Ibid., pp.59-60.
44. On 18 February 1996 Edward O'Brien from County Wexford was killed when the bomb he was transporting exploded prematurely on a London bus. Bew and Gillespie, op.cit,, p.172.
45. Ibid., p.177.
46. *Irish Times*, 29 February 1996.
47. Ed Moloney, 'Republican Unity At The Crossroads', *Sunday Tribune*, 3 March 1996.
48. John O'Farrell, 'The Janus Option', *Fortnight*, April 1996.
49. O'Clery, op.cit., pp.242-3.
50. Bew and Gillespie, op.cit., p.176.
51. Liam Clarke, 'Deal With Hardliners Expected To Result In Tactical Ceasefire', *Sunday Times*, 29 December 1996, Irish edition.
52. Bishop and Mallie, op.cit., p.421.
53. Bew and Gillespie, op.cit., p.176.
54. Ibid., p.177.
55. O'Clery, op.cit., pp.243-4.
56. Bew and Gillespie, op.cit., pp.178-9.
57. Feargal Cochrane, 'Back to War?', *Fortnight*, November 1996.
58. Brendan O'Brien claimed that the discovery by Gardai, in June 1996, of a bomb-making factory in County Laois led to further arrests in London which undermined almost the entire planned British campaign, and that some of the IRA's most senior engineers and 'sleepers' were arrested.

O'Brien, op.cit., p.149.

59. Jim Cusack, 'Hardliners May Be In Control Of The IRA', *Irish Times*, 11 February 1997.

60. The text of Major's response to the Hume-Adams proposals was published in ibid., 29 November 1996.

61. Mary Holland, 'Progress Unthinkable This Side of British Election', ibid., 28 November 1996.

62. Gerry Moriarty, 'UUP Denies Return to Original Arms Stand', ibid., 17 December 1996.

63. Jim Cusack, 'IRA Attack Closely Followed Ceasefire Talks', ibid., 23 December 1996.

64. In an interview an IRA spokesman denied there was a 'phoney war'. He admitted that IRA members may have become 'more relaxed' during the ceasefire. Maol Muire Tynan, 'IRA Not Engaged in a Phoney War', ibid., 8 February 1996.

65. See interview with Adams by Deaglán de Bréadún in ibid., 23 April 1997.

66. Ed Moloney, 'Gun Display Is Part Of IRA's Double-Edged Strategy For Election', *Sunday Tribune*, 6 April 1997.

67. Ed Moloney, 'Sinn Féin Must Bite The Bullet', ibid., 4 May 1997.

68. Results are from the *Irish Times*, 24 May 1997.

69. Ibid., 21 April 1997.

70. Paul Bew, 'After The Mayhem', *Guardian*, 22 April 1997.

71. 'New Labour And The Unionists', *New Left Review*, No.220, November/December 1996.

72. 'A Talks Process Must Address All The Issues', article by Gerry Adams in the *Irish Times*, 21 May 1997.

73. An edited version of the text of Blair's speech at the Royal Ulster Agricultural Show in Belfast was published in ibid., 21 May 1997.

74. 'A Talks Process Must Address All The Issues'.

75. A confidant of Blair's wrote that the speech was 'a deeply considered and precisely judged text which reflects Blair's own purposes in Northern Ireland'. John Lloyd, *New Statesman*, 23 May 1997.

76. Deaglán de Bréadún, 'Blair Speech Dismays Republicans Who Want Unity Within 15 Years', *Irish Times*, 20 May 1997.

77. Ed Moloney, 'Long Way To Go Before IRA Ceasefire', *Sunday Tribune*, 25 May 1997.

78. Gerry Moriarty, ' "Provo Ayatollahs" Blamed After "Punishment" Victim Loses Leg', *Irish Times*, 9 June 1996.

79. The Sinn Féin national vote was 2.55 per cent, an improvement of 0.94 per cent on 1992, obtained with half the number of candidates. In Cavan-Monaghan its successful candidate received 19.37 per cent of the vote; in North Kerry, Martin Ferris, until his release in 1994 leader of the IRA prisoners in Portlaoise jail, got 15.9 per cent; in some Dublin constituencies with large working-class estates suffering from problems of poverty and drugs, its candidates saw major increases in support. 'Election 97 Results', ibid., 9 June 1997.

80. 'British Spell Out Position On Talks In Response to Sinn Féin', ibid., 26 June 1997.

81. See a frontal attack on the ceasefire and the Sinn Féin leadership by Anthony McIntyre, 'Sinn Féin Stance Hinders Republican Cause', *Sunday Tribune*, 20 July 1997.

Chronology

1791 Publication of Wolfe Tone's *Argument on Behalf of the Catholics of Ireland*.
Foundation of the United Irishmen in Belfast.
1795 'Battle of the Diamond' at Loughgall, Co. Armagh, leads to the form-ation of the Orange Order.
1798 May: United Irishmen's rebellion begins.
November: Wolfe Tone arrested after arriving in Lough Swilly, Co. Donegal, with a French force; commits suicide in prison.
1800 Act of Union.
1845 Potato blight marks the beginning of the Great Famine of 1845-49 in which at least 775,000 people died.
1858 James Stephens founds the Irish Republican Brotherhood in Dublin.
1867 Fenian rising.
1879 Foundation of Irish National Land League.
1893 Second Home Rule Bill passed by House of Commons but defeated in the House of Lords.
1894 Foundation of the Irish Trades Union Congress.
1896 James Connolly arrives in Dublin and forms the Irish Socialist Republican Party.
1903 The Wyndham Land Act, which provides for the buying out of the Irish landlord class by their tenants, becomes law. The process is to be financed by Treasury loans – the origins of the land annuities issue.
1905 The foundation of the Ulster Unionist Council – the first institutional embodiment of the Ulster Unionist movement.
1907 Formation of Sinn Féin League – from 1908 called Sinn Féin.
1909 Foundation of Fianna Éireann.
1912 Third Home Rule Bill introduced in House of Commons.
Formation of Irish Labour Party and Trades Union Congress.
1913 Foundation of Ulster Volunteer Force to resist Home Rule.
Formation of the Irish Citizen Army and of the Irish Volunteers.
1916 Easter Rising and subsequent execution of leaders including Connolly.
1917 Eamon de Valera elected President of Sinn Féin.

1918 General election: Sinn Féin, 73 seats; Irish Parliamentary Party, 6; Unionists, 26.

1919 First meeting of Dáil Eireann. The same day the Irish Volunteers kill 2 policemen at Soloheadbeg, Co. Tipperary.
September: Dáil Eireann declared illegal.

1920 Expulsions of Catholics and socialists from the Belfast shipyards in July mark the beginning of two years of intense violence in which over 450 are killed in the city.
November: the Ulster Special Constabulary is established.
The Government of Ireland Act provides for a Northern Ireland parliament and government.

1921 July: truce between the British forces and the IRA.
December: signing of the Anglo-Irish Treaty.

1922 January: Treaty approved by Dáil Éireann by 64 to 57.
April: Anti-Treatyites seize the Four Courts in Dublin.
June: the pro-Treaty forces – now Cumann na nGaedheal – are easily victorious in a general election in the Free State.
Attack on the Four Courts marks the beginning of the Civil War.
August: Liam Mellows sends out the first of his *Jail Notes*.
December: Mellows and three other leading republicans executed.

1923 May: Frank Aiken orders anti-Treatyites to dump arms.

1926 May: Inaugural meeting of Fianna Fáil in La Scala Theatre, Dublin.
Peadar O'Donnell launches campaign against land annuities in Donegal.

1931 September: Saor Éire has its first congress.
October: Irish bishops issue a joint pastoral letter denouncing Saor Éire as a 'frankly communistic organisation'.
The Free State government introduces Public Safety legislation banning twelve organisations including Saor Éire and the IRA. Military tribunals are introduced.

1932 February: formation of the Army Comrades' Association.
Fianna Fáil wins a general election and forms its first government.
Withholding of payment of land annuities to Britain and the beginning of the Economic War.
October: widespread disturbances in Belfast during strike of workers on Outdoor Relief.

1933 Army Comrades' Association becomes the National Guard and adopts the wearing of a blue shirt.
September: Cumann na nGaedheal, the Centre Party and the National Guard fuse to form Fine Gael.

1934 Peadar O'Donnell and his supporters leave the IRA to create a Republican Congress. It splits at its first conference in September.

1935 Severe rioting for three weeks in Belfast sparked off by an Orange parade in July.

1936 De Valera's government declares the IRA an illegal organisation.

1937 De Valera's new constitution approved by a referendum.

1939 January: the IRA declares war on Britain and initiates a bombing campaign which culminates in August with the murder of 5 people in an explosion in Coventry.

February: first contact between the Abwehr and the IRA.

1940 January: the Dáil passes Emergency Powers Act to deal with the IRA.

August: Sean Russell dies on a German U-boat en route to Ireland.

1944 Irish Labour Party splits – reunited in 1950.

1945 Irish TUC splits – not reunited until 1959.

1946 Formation of Clann na Poblachta.

1948 Fianna Fáil loses power for first time since 1932.

New inter-party government takes Ireland out of the Commonwealth and establishes a Republic.

1949 Westminster passes the Ireland Act guaranteeing that Northern Ireland will remain within the UK until its parliament decides otherwise.

1953 July: Cathal Goulding and John Stephenson arrested and sentenced to eight years' imprisonment for an arms raid in Felstead, Essex.

1954 June: successful IRA arms raid on Gough Barracks, Armagh.

October: raid on army barracks in Omagh, Co. Tyrone, leads to the capture of 8 IRA men.

1955 May: in Westminster elections Sinn Féin candidates receive 152,310 votes and 2 are elected.

1956 December: 'Operation Harvest' launched by the IRA.

1957 January: deaths of Feargal O'Hanlon and Sean South in IRA attack on RUC station at Brookeborough, Co. Fermanagh.

March: general election in Republic returns Fianna Fáil to power; 4 Sinn Féin TDs elected.

July: de Valera introduces internment in the Republic – it had been in existence in Northern Ireland since December 1956.

1959 The Fianna Fáil government launches the First Programme for Economic Expansion. Lemass replaces de Valera as party leader.

1962 February: the IRA publicly announces the end of its campaign.

1963 Terence O'Neill becomes Prime Minister in Northern Ireland.

1964 January: foundation of the Campaign for Social Justice in Northern Ireland.

July: publication of the Second Programme for Economic Expansion.

October: Divis Street riots in Belfast.

1965 January: O'Neill-Lemass meeting in Belfast.

December: signing of Anglo-Irish Free Trade Agreement.

1966 March: the IRA blows up Nelson's Pillar in Dublin's O'Connell Street.

1967 January: foundation of Northern Ireland Civil Rights Association.

1968 August: first civil rights march from Coalisland to Dungannon.

October: the RUC attacks civil rights marchers in Duke Street, Derry.

Formation of People's Democracy organisation by students at Queen's University, Belfast.

1969 January: 'Long March' from Belfast to Derry organised by People's

Democracy attacked by militant Protestants; rioting in Derry.

April: Rioting in Derry; the RUC invades the Bogside, seriously injuring a man who subsequently dies.

O'Neill resigns and is replaced by his cousin, James Chichester Clark.

August: Protestant Apprentice Boys' parade in Derry leads to violence and the 'Battle of the Bogside'.

Jack Lynch makes TV broadcast attacking the Stormont government and calling for the UN to intervene.

Serious violence in Belfast; British troops sent to Derry and Belfast.

December: special IRA Convention votes in favour of ending abstentionism and for a National Liberation Front; in response a Provisional Army Council is formed.

1970 January: Sinn Féin Árd Fheis votes on abstention and NLF – walkout by group which forms Provisional Sinn Féin.

April: Ian Paisley wins a seat in Stormont parliament.

May: Charles Haughey and Neil Blaney are sacked by Jack Lynch, and Kevin Boland resigns from government. Blaney and Haughey are arrested and tried on charges of conspiracy to import arms; both are acquitted.

June: Paisley elected to Westminster; Conservatives form government.

July: British army search for arms in Lower Falls leads to riot, 36-hour curfew of the district and the 'Battle of Lower Falls' with Official IRA.

August: formation of the Social Democratic and Labour Party.

1971 January: serious anti-army riots in Ballymurphy for five days.

February: the Provisionals kill first British soldier.

March: Brian Faulkner replaces Chichester Clark as Unionist Prime Minister.

April: Provisionals launch a major bombing campaign against commercial targets which intensifies through the spring and summer.

August: internment introduced – 342 picked up.

1972 January: British paratroopers kill 13 civil rights marchers in Derry.

February: Official IRA bombing of Parachute Regiment officers' mess at Aldershot kills an army chaplain and 5 women cleaners.

March: resignation of the Unionist government and introduction of Direct Rule; William Whitelaw becomes the first Secretary of State for Northern Ireland.

April: Official IRA leader, Joe McCann, shot dead by British troops while walking unarmed through the Markets area of Belfast.

May: referendum in Republic gives a massive majority for membership of the EEC.

The Official IRA in Derry kills William Best, a 19-year-old home on leave from the British army.

The Official IRA declares a ceasefire.

June: Whitelaw concedes to the Provisional's demand for political status for prisoners.

The Provisionals declare a ceasefire.

July: 6 leading Provisionals, including Gerry Adams, are flown to London for a secret meeting with Whitelaw; the meeting is fruitless.

Provisionals' ceasefire ends.

'Bloody Friday': the Provisionals detonate 22 car-bombs in Belfast, killing 9 civilians and 2 soldiers.

1973 February: Fianna Fáil loses power, for the first time since 1957, to a coalition of Fine Gael and Labour.

June: elections for a Northern Ireland Assembly – the SDLP receives 22 per cent of vote; Sinn Féin campaign for a boycott ignored.

December: Sunningdale Conference leads to formation of a power-sharing government in Belfast.

1974 May: Ulster Workers' Council strike destroys the power-sharing government.

November: a Provisional campaign in Britain culminates in the bombing of two pubs in Birmingham, killing 21 people.

December: formation of the Irish Republican Socialist Party (IRSP).

1975 January: Provisionals and the Northern Ireland Office negotiate a ceasefire.

February: armed conflict between the Official IRA and IRSP/INLA in Belfast leads to the death of Billy McMillen.

October: Provisionals launch attack on the Officials.

November: end of Provisionals' ceasefire.

1976 March: Britain announces decision to abolish special category status.

September: Provisional prisoner Ciaran Nugent refuses to wear prison uniform – the beginning of the 'blanket protest'.

1977 February: Official Sinn Féin becomes Sinn Féin – The Workers' Party.

June: Fianna Fáil wins general election.

1978 February: Provisional fire-bombs incinerate 11 people in La Mon restaurant, near Belfast.

1979 August: Provisionals blow up Lord Mountbatten's yacht off Mullaghmore, Co. Sligo, killing him and 3 others. The same day a Provisional ambush at Narrow Water, Co. Down, kills 18 soldiers.

December: Haughey becomes leader of Fianna Fáil and Prime Minister.

1980 October: start of Hunger Strike by Provisional prisoners in the Maze; called off on 18 December.

1981 March: beginning of the second Hunger Strike.

March: Bobby Sands elected MP for Fermanagh-South Tyrone.

May: Sands is the first of 10 hunger-strikers to die.

June: general election in Irish Republic – Fianna Fáil loses power to a coalition of Fine Gael and Labour. 2 hunger-strikers elected as TDs in border constituencies; SFWP has its first TD elected.

October: the Hunger Strike is called off.

1982 February: general election in Irish Republic returns Fianna Fáil to power; SFWP wins 3 seats.

April: Sinn Féin – The Workers' Party becomes The Workers' Party.

October: elections to Northern Ireland Assembly – Sinn Féin wins 10.1 per cent of the vote, the SDLP 18.8 per cent.

1983 March: announcement of New Ireland Forum.

June: Westminster election – Sinn Féin wins 13.4 per cent of vote to the SDLP's 17.9 per cent and Gerry Adams becomes MP for West Belfast.

December: Provisionals car-bomb Harrods, killing 8 people.

1984 May: publication of Report of New Ireland Forum.

October: Provisionals bomb the Grand Hotel, Brighton in attempt to kill Margaret Thatcher; Thatcher survives but 5 others are killed.

1985 May: local elections in Northern Ireland; Sinn Féin wins 11.4 per cent of the vote and 59 seats.

October: Thatcher and FitzGerald sign Anglo-Irish Agreement at Hillsborough, Co. Down.

1986 October: Sinn Féin Árd Fheis votes to remove abstention from Leinster House from its constitution; Ruairí Ó Bradaigh leads a walk-out and establishes Republican Sinn Féin.

1987 February: general election in the Irish Republic – Fianna Fáil returned to power as a minority government; the Workers' Party wins 4 seats and 3.8 per cent of the vote – with 7.5 per cent in Dublin it outpolls the Labour Party; Sinn Féin gets 1.9 per cent of the vote and no seats.

June: British general election – Sinn Féin gets 11.4 per cent of the vote and Adams keeps his seat.

November: Provisional IRA bomb at the Remembrance ceremony in Enniskillen, Co. Fermanagh, kills 11 people.

1988 March: 3 IRA members shot dead by security forces in Gilbraltar.

John Hume and senior SDLP members enter into discussions with Gerry Adams and leading Sinn Féiners; the discussions last until September.

October: Home Secretary, Douglas Hurd introduces ban on TV and radio interviews with Sinn Féin members except during elections.

1989 January: at the Sinn Féin Árd Fheis Adams criticises the IRA for an increasing number of 'mistakes' in which civilians have been killed.

May: in Northern Ireland local elections Sinn Féin wins 11.3 per cent of the poll.

June: general election in Irish Republic sees a significant swing to the left – the Workers' Party wins 5 per cent of national vote and 7 seats. The Irish Labour Party wins 9.5 per cent of the national vote and 15 seats. In Dublin the WP increases its lead over the Labour Party – 11.4 per cent and 6 seats to 9.5 per cent and 3 seats. Sinn Féin's vote declines to 1.2 per cent and it wins no seats.

European election in Irish Republic – the Workers' Party wins 7.5

per cent of the national vote. In Dublin its president de Rossa wins 15.8 per cent of the vote and wins a seat. The Labour Party wins 9.5 per cent of the national vote and 12.2 per cent of the vote in Dublin where it wins a seat. Sinn Féin wins 2.3 per cent of the national vote – a decline from 2.9 per cent on its performance in the previous European election.

European election in Northern Ireland; Sinn Féin vote slumps to 9.2 per cent of the total – in 1984 it got 13.4 per cent of the total vote.

September: an IRA bomb kills 10 Royal Marines bandsmen in Kent.

1990 July: the IRA bombs the London Stock Exchange.

July: 3 policemen and a nun are killed by an IRA bomb near Armagh.

Ian Gow, Conservative MP for Eastbourne, is killed by an IRA car-bomb.

October: 6 soldiers and a civilian are killed when the IRA forces 3 Catholic men who they claim work for the security forces to drive cars loaded with explosives to army check-points near Derry, Newry and Omagh while their families are held hostage.

November: Mary Robinson, a 46-year-old lawyer with liberal and feminist opinions, is elected President of Ireland.

November: John Major becomes leader of the Conservative Party and Prime Minister.

December: the IRA announces a three-day ceasefire over Christmas for the first time in 15 years.

1991 February: an IRA mortar lands in the garden of 10 Downing Street while John Major is chairing a Gulf War Cabinet meeting.

June: inter-party talks begin at Stormont; they end in July.

December: after an upsurge in violence throughout the year, Secretary of State Peter Brooke, announces a freeze on public spending in several areas to meet the increased cost of IRA bomb damage.

1992 January: 8 Protestant building workers at a security base in Co. Tyrone are killed when the IRA bombs their minibus at Teebane Cross.

February: 5 Catholics are murdered by loyalist gunmen at a bookmaker's shop on the Ormeau Road, Belfast.

Albert Reynolds is elected leader of Fianna Fáil in succession to Charles Haughey.

Workers' Party leader Proinsias de Rossa and 5 other TDs walk out of a party meeting in Dublin and announce the formation of a new organisation, later called Democratic Left.

March: an IRA bomb destroys the commercial centre of Lurgan and another causes extensive damage in Belfast city centre.

April: in the Westminster general election the Sinn Féin vote declines slightly to 10 per cent from 11.4 per cent in 1987 and Gerry Adams loses West Befast to Joe Hendron of the SDLP.

An IRA bomb at Baltic Exchange in the City of London kills 3 people and causes £800 million of damage.

All-party talks reconvene at Stormont.

July: after 'Strand One' talks at Stormont the two main Unionist parties agree to 'Strand Two' talks involving the Irish government.

October: an IRA bomb destroys the main street in Bangor, Co. Down.

November: after two years, the inter-party talks collapse.

In a general election in the Irish Republic, the Irish Labour Party wins an unprecedented 19.3 per cent of the vote; the Democratic Left, 2.8 per cent and Sinn Féin, 1.6 per cent.

1993 February: 3 IRA bombs planted at a gasworks at Warrington in Cheshire cause a massive explosion. The IRA threatens to attack other industrial and commercial centres in Britain.

March: a 3-year-old boy is killed and 56 people injured when two IRA bombs explode in a shopping centre in Warrington; a 12-year-old boy dies later from injuries received in the explosions.

April: the continuing talks between John Hume and Gerry Adams become public knowledge.

An IRA bomb at the NatWest Tower in London kills 1 person and causes over £1 billion of damage.

July: a 1,500 lb IRA car-bomb explodes in Newtownards, Co. Down.

September: the centre of Armagh is severely damaged by a 1,000 lb IRA car-bomb.

October: an IRA bomb in a Shankhill Road fish shop kills 10 people.

October: UFF gunmen kill 7 people in attack on the Rising Sun Bar in Greysteel, Co. Londonderry.

November: the *Observer* reveals that the British government has had secret communications with Sinn Féin and the IRA for three years.

December: in London John Major and Albert Reynolds issue a Joint Declaration on Northern Ireland.

1994 January: the Irish government announces that the ban on Sinn Féin members appearing on radio and television will be removed.

Gerry Adams is granted a visa to enter the United States.

March: the IRA declares a three-day ceasefire.

June: in the European elections in Northern Ireland, Sinn Féin obtains 9.9 per cent of the first preference vote.

July: at a special Sinn Féin Ard Fheis the rank and file give a hostile response to the Downing Street Declaration.

August: the IRA announces a 'complete cessation of military operations'.

September: in an *Observer* interview Albert Reynolds declares the unification of Ireland will not come about 'in this generation'.

October: the Combined Loyalist Military Command declares a ceasefire whose permanence will depend on 'the continued cessation of all nationalist/republican violence'.

Reynolds opens the Forum for Peace and Reconciliation in Dublin.

November: a man is murdered in an IRA robbery of a postal sorting office in Newry, Co. Down.

Albert Reynolds resigns as Taoiseach following controversy over the appointment of the President of the Irish Supreme Court.

December: first formal meeting between Sinn Féin and British civil servants at Stormont.

Formation of new coalition government led by John Bruton in Dublin.

1995 February: the Joint Frameworks Documents are issued by John Major and John Bruton in Belfast.

March: speaking in Washington, Sir Patrick Mayhew outlines a three-point plan for the decommissioning of IRA weapons.

Routine army patrols are suspended throughout greater Belfast.

April: in an *Observer* interview Albert Reynolds criticises 'British intransigence' over decommissioning and adds, 'If they [the IRA] went back to the armed conflict people won't blame them because they have shown good faith.'

July: the release of Private Lee Clegg, after four years in custody for killing a joy-rider, leads to widespread rioting in nationalist areas.

The RUC and Orange marchers are involved in a stand-off after police prevent Orangemen marching along the nationalist Garvaghy Road in Portadown. The 'Siege of Drumcree' ends after a confrontation between 1,000 policemen and 10,000 Orangemen and trouble in loyalist areas. 500 Orangemen march along Garvaghy Road, unaccompanied by bands.

August: James Molyneaux resigns as leader of the Ulster Unionist Party.

September: the Irish government calls off a summit meeting between Major and Bruton after officials fail to reach agreement on the notion of a body to oversee arms decommissioning.

David Trimble is elected as leader of the Ulster Unionist Party.

November: the two governments launch a 'twin-track' strategy: a commitment to achieve all-party talks by the end of February 1996 and the creation of an international body to provide an independent assessment of the decommissioning issue.

Bill Clinton becomes the first serving US President to visit Northern Ireland.

December: the international body headed by former US Senator George Mitchell begins to hear submissions on the arms issue.

1996 January: the Chief Constable of the RUC says the IRA operating under the *nom de guerre* 'Direct Action Against Drugs', has killed 6 alleged drug-dealers since the ceasefire.

The publication of the Mitchell Commission Report suggests 'parallel decommissioning' and six principles of 'democracy and non-violence' to which participants in any talks process should committ themselves.

John Major accepts the report but says that if paramilitaries will not begin to decommission before talks then an elective process will provide an alternative means of entry.

February: in Dublin the Forum for Peace and Reconciliation publishes its report. Sinn Féin refuses to subscribe to the clauses in the report which say that any new agreement in the North must have the consent of a majority.

The IRA ends its ceasfire with the bombing of Canary Wharf in London, killing 2 people and causing £85 million of damage.

Edward O'Brien, an IRA member, is killed when the bomb he is carrying explodes prematurely on a London bus.

The two governments launch a package to restart the peace process through elections and a firm date for all-party talks.

March: the British government announces that elections to the Northern Ireland Forum will be on 30 May.

May: Gerry Adams declares that Sinn Féin agrees to the six Mitchell principles.

In the Forum elections Sinn Féin's vote is its best ever, 116,377 votes or 15.5 per cent of the poll; the SDLP share of the vote is 21.4 per cent.

June: the IRA murders Garda Gerry McCabe during a mail-van robbery in Co. Limerick.

The IRA explodes a van-bomb in centre of Manchester, injuring 200 people and causing damage estimated at £100 million.

July: the RUC announces the rerouting of the Orange parade to Drumcree church in Portadown away from Garvaghy Road. After three days of loyalist protests and rioting across Northern Ireland, the original RUC decision is reversed and the Orangemen walk along Garvaghy Road, provoking days of rioting in nationalist areas.

October: the IRA returns to violence in Northern Ireland with the bombing of the Thiepval barracks in Lisburn, killing a soldier.

1997 March: Mo Mowlam, Labour's shadow Secretary of State for Northern Ireland, says that there is a strong possiblity that Sinn Féin could join the multi-party talks in June if the IRA immediately restored its ceasefire.

April: a female RUC officer is shot in the back by the IRA in Derry.

May: the Westminster general election returns Labour with a massive majority; Sinn Féin wins 2 seats, West Belfast and Mid-Ulster, and 39.6 per cent of the nationalist vote to the SDLP's 60.4 per cent.

The new Prime Minister, Tony Blair, makes a speech at the Royal Ulster Agricultural Show in which he says he values the Union and that he does not expect to see Northern Ireland leaving the United Kingdom in the lifetime of the youngest person in the hall.

In the Northern Ireland local elections Sinn Féin receives its highest ever vote, almost 17 per cent or 45 per cent of the nationalist vote.

June: in the Republic's general election John Bruton's coalition is defeated and a minority coalition of Fianna Fáil and the Progressive Democrats dependent on independents is elected.

Sinn Féin's candidate in Cavan-Monaghan tops the poll and its candidates in Dublin significantly increase their support.

The IRA kills two neighbourhood policemen in Lurgan, Co. Armagh.

July: the IRA declares a ceasefire.

Index

Abwehr II, 84

Adams, Gerry: and Anglo-Irish Agreement, 198, 202-3, 232; and armed struggle, 210, 212, 215-7, 239; and British Labour Party, 199, 235, 294-5; and British neutrality, 218, 228, 232-3, 242, 248, 250, 255, 295; 'Brownie' articles, 182, 184-5, 191; on Downing Street Declaration, 250-1, 253, 264; and *Eire Nua* policy, 187; and elections: Westminster: 1983, 194; 1987, 200; 1992, 237; 1997, 293; local: 1989, 214; European: 1984, 195-6; 1989 (Irish Republic), 213, (Northern Ireland), 215; Dáil: 1987, 206; 1989, 212, 214; on Enniskillen bomb, 211; and Fianna Fáil, 202, 208, 226-7, 236, 249, 279; and formation of Provisionals, 125-6, 183; and Hunger Strikes, 193-4; and John Hume, 235-6, 241, 47-50, 261, 292; and IRA, 196, 212; and Irish nationalist consensus, 202, 205, 207-8, 215, 226-7, 256; on joint sovereignty, 248; and Michael Collins, 247-8; and loyalism, 202-3; and Mitchell principles, 267-8; and New Ireland Forum, 195; and Cardinal Tomás Ó Fiaich, 227; and Official IRA, 152, 205; *Pathway to Peace*, 213; *The Politics of Irish Freedom*, 198; and SDLP, 195, 198-9, 208, 292; and

social republicanism, 12, 205-6; and 'TUAS' strategy, 255-6, 264, 266, 268-9, 285-6, 292; and ultra-leftism, 198-9, 204-5, 280; and Unionist veto, 249; on Workers' Party, 206, 213, 286; and William Whitelaw, 181

Agnew, Kevin, 110

Ahern, Bertie, 296

Aiken, Frank, 33, 35

Atkins, Humphrey, 196

Alliance Party, 292

Ancient Order of Hibernians, 71, 122

Ancram, Michael, 263

Anglo-Irish Agreement, 196, 198, 200, 201-3, 209, 213, 217, 227-30, 232, 234, 240, 247-48, 253, 258, 287

Anglo-Irish Financial Agreement (1923), 38

Anglo-Irish Free Trade Agreement (1966), 102-3

Anti-Partition Campaign, 85

Anti-Tribute League, 46, 55

Army Comrades' Association, 61, 63

Armstrong, Lord, 30

B Specials, 90, 92-3

Ballygawley landmine, 210

Baltic Exchange bomb, 240, 243

Barnhill, Senator, 153

Barrett, Frank, 46

Barry, Tom, 83

Bean, Kevin, 260-1

Behan, Brendan, 87

Bell, Bowyer, J., 53, 83

Bell, Ivor, 210